ON THE PATH OF THE IMMORTALS

EXO-VATICANA,
PROJECT L.U.C.I.F.E.R.
AND THE STRATEGIC
LOCATIONS WHERE
ENTITIES AWAIT THE
APPOINTED TIME

Thomas Horn & Cris Putnam

DEFENDER

CRANE, MO

On the Path of the Immortals

Defender Publishing Co.
Crane, MO, 65633
© 2015 by Thomas Horn
All rights reserved. Published 2015.
Printed in the United States of America.

ISBN: 978-0-9904974-5-5

A CIP catalog record of this book is available from the Library of Congress.

Cover illustration and design by Daniel Wright: www.createdwright.com

CONTENTS

FOREWORD

By Gary Stearman

> And I say also unto thee, That thou art Peter,
> and upon this rock I will build my church;
> and the gates of hell shall not prevail against it.
> —Matthew 16:18

The gates of Hell are opening! Dark forces are expanding their assault on mankind. Many have talked about the "end times," the "last days," or the "latter days." There has been an ongoing debate about whether humanity has finally reached this long-awaited era. Though many have not yet realized it, we have entered that period.

In the light of recent disclosures, the argument about this question has become heated, as traditionalists cling to time-honored beliefs of the normal Christian life. Those who plant their faith in physical reality have no trouble believing in the basic tenets of the gospel, coupled with the need for dedication, prayer, and love in action. But over the centuries, they have settled upon a sterilized Scripture that dares not speak of multidimensional worlds that animate the Bible's ancient narratives. The levels of the underworld and the realms between mankind and the heavens above have become closed doors, rejected as ancient and fanciful fictions.

But in the light of new observations and experiences, those portals are being forced open. Just as prophesied, the "paranormal" is rapidly becoming the "normal."

In recent years, we have seen the clear fulfillment of the prophet Daniel's assertion that in "the time of the end...knowledge shall be increased." There is something special in this statement. In one sense, knowledge has been increasing throughout the twenty-five centuries since Daniel died.

What then, would be different about the end times of which he wrote? The answer is quite straightforwardly obvious: In the last fifty years or so, knowledge has exploded *exponentially* (thanks to the invention of the computer and instant communication), and has swiftly escalated to the point that now, artificial intelligence is on the verge of surpassing human perception and thought. High technology threatens to enslave the unwary.

Furthermore, increasing knowledge is opening doors that have been sealed for millennia. They are now swinging wide, and the hidden societies that have long kept their intimate secrets have perceived that the time has arrived to reveal their covert connections.

More than that, the communications and entertainment media, plus a legion of authors, educators, and theoreticians, have risen to warn mankind that it is about to lose control of its own developmental direction. Soon, they say, the "singularity" will arrive, when man and machine will merge to launch humankind toward its next level. Already the famed "Turing Test"—the inability to determine whether one is conversing with a human or a computer—has been passed. And who might be twisting the memories of such a computer toward the dark side?

To the astonishment of many, the occult interdimensional worlds of evil principalities and powers are quickly becoming visible. But a few—keepers of ancient tribal wisdom and traditional histories—have lived to reveal that the present moment, with its dark denizens of the supernatural, has long been expected.

With his advancing knowledge, man is once again penetrating the barrier that he first sought in the infamous Tower of Babel incident: God looked down as workers built their ziggurat toward a portal into heaven, where they hoped to find their ultimate identity in a union with the same dark powers that had dominated mankind before the Flood. Their passageway into eternity, better called a "gate" in the Bible's own language, is man's eternal dream of power, in a union with the supernatural.

When Jesus spoke of the "gates of Hell," He was not speaking in metaphoric language. In fact, He was invoking the reality of the ancient penetrations and breaches between Heaven and Earth, and the fallen ones who passed through them to plague a hapless mankind.

For the last century, our planet has witnessed increasing examples of these paranormal incursions. Now, with prophetic events staged for final fulfillment, their portals into this world have once again become active, just as promised in Scripture, and as anticipated by men who anticipate supernatural help to advance their cause of global control. The dark side believes that its time has come.

Those who read the Bible will recognize exactly what this means.

And those who read this book will be mentally and spiritually prepared for the astonishing changes that are soon to come.

Introduction

By Dr. Michael Lake

Something is coming. It is on the horizon, just moments beyond the edge of tomorrow. Its unveiling has been many millennia in the making. For modern man, knowledge of what is coming is like a vaporous mist in an ocean of primeval history and arcane knowledge. It has been alluded to in both ancient Hebrew writings and in the mythology of distant cultures around the world.

While its full manifestation has been hastening over the past few decades, the world has been too busy in self-indulgent materialism to see the signs of its approach. Many in the church, too enamored by affluence and prosperity, have slowly fallen asleep at the helm of kingdoms of their own creation, and they are completely unaware of this approaching malevolence.

As this darkness approaches, things are changing: geopolitical and financial spheres of influence are experiencing radical change; the moral compass of mankind has been damaged beyond recognition; and sections of the world are slowly beginning to burn with levels of unprecedented hatred and debauchery. There is a collective sense of impending

1

danger, with the hair standing up on the backs of the necks of humanity. This universal uneasiness has some in the darkest chambers of esoteric societies seething in breathless anticipation. Yet, the average citizen is simply uneasy—always wanting to glance over his or her shoulder with a sense of something that is not quite there yet.

At the same time, the Holy Spirit is slowly beginning to awaken many within the body of Christ. This remnant of the Most High God is wiping decades of sleep from their eyes while embracing a desire to gain a clear prophetic vision of tomorrow's horizon. These awakened saints desire Heaven to bestow upon them the anointing of the sons of Issachar: to accurately discern the prophetic times and the seasons.

"What terrifying thing is just on the edge of tomorrow?" you might ask. It—or more accurately, *they*—were known by many ancient names. Universally, they were called the *Shining Ones*. To the Sumerian people, they were the *Annunaki*. To the Greeks, they were the *Titans*. The Book of Enoch calls this ancient evil the *Watchers*. And the Hebrews knew them as the *Bene Elohim* of Genesis 6. Literally, every ancient culture on this planet shares a common story of beings appearing from the great unknown *other world*—be it the heavens or another star system—that would bestow ancient (and forbidden) knowledge to mankind.

The apostle Paul encodes a warning of this approaching evil and connects it to the return of the Son of Perdition:

And then shall that Wicked be revealed, whom the Lord shall consume with the spirit of his mouth, and shall destroy with the brightness of his coming:

Even him, whose coming is after the working of Satan with all power and signs and lying wonders,

And with all deceivableness of unrighteousness in them that perish; because they received not the love of the truth, that they might be saved.

And for this cause God shall send them strong delusion, that they should believe a lie:

That they all might be damned who believed not the truth,
but had pleasure in unrighteousness. (2 Thessalonians 2:8–12)

The Bible uses some very interesting terminology in verse 11. "For this cause" may mean that something will come to prepare the way for the Son of Perdition. These ancient **Shining Ones** will prepare the hearts of those who have rejected God's truth and have found pleasure in unrighteousness or *adikia* (ad-ee-kee'-ah) in the original Greek, which means not only "unrighteousness of heart and life," but includes "deeds violating law and justice."[1] What kind of delusion will be allowed by God? The word used for "strong" is the Greek word *energeia* (en-erg'-i-ah), which is used in the New Testament to only describe **superhuman or supernatural power.**[2]

Therefore, a supernaturally infused delusion is on the horizon for mankind. In fact, these fallen Bene Elohim are working diligently this very moment from behind the scenes to create the chaos they need before their revealing. Perhaps part of the planned delusion will be their self proclamation as the progenitors of humanity and the saviors of modern man. These returning Watchers will set the world stage for the unveiling of the Son of Perdition. These architects of chaos and disobedience will cause the whole world to run into the arms of the Antichrist!

In the midst of the unfolding of these preparatory end-time events enter internationally acclaimed remnant researchers, Dr. Thomas Horn and Cris Putnam. In their groundbreaking work, *Exo-Vaticana*, they exposed not only the reality of these extradimensional "astronauts," but how Petrus Romanus may be used to reveal these ancient ones to the world. Now, Horn and Putnam continue the greatest investigation of our time by exposing what the luciferian elite have labored so intensely to conceal—from hyperdimensional denizens caught on film to top-secret underground UFO bases here in the United States. *On the Path of the Immortals* serves as a high-level intelligence briefing to inform humanity of the final supernatural delusion about to be released from the gates of Hell.

About Dr. Lake

Dr. Michael K. Lake is the chancellor and founder of Biblical Life College and Seminary. He has been training aspirants of the gospel ministry for more than three decades. Dr. Lake is also the author of the best seller, *The Shinar Directive: Preparing the Way for the Son of Perdition.* More information on his educational ministry can be found at www.biblical-life.com.

CHAPTER ONE

What Is This All About?

By Cris Putnam

> There are more things in heaven and earth,
> Horatio, than are dreamed of in your philosophy.
> —William Shakespeare, *Hamlet*

An ambitious project like *On the Path of the Immortals* requires a preliminary discussion of concepts and terminology. First, we will define what is meant by "the immortals." After that, an introduction to the interdimensional portal is offered, along with a brief discussion of several sites in continental US. Finally, we address the impetus for such a project as a function of biblical end-time prophecy. Our friend Chuck Missler believes that "we are being plunged into a period of time about which the Bible says more than it does about any other period of human history—including the time that Jesus walked the shore of the Sea of Galilee and climbed the mountains of Judea!"[3] In accepting that premise, it is a very exciting time to be alive, and the content within will prove useful to the motivated student of prophecy.

Who Are the "Immortals"?

The obvious starting point is to be specific as to exactly *whose* path we are on. *Merriam-Webster's Collegiate Dictionary* defines "immortal" as one "exempt from death" or "imperishable." It is important to note that this is not the same as "eternal," which the same reference defines as "having infinite duration." The key idea is that the immortal has a beginning in time, but the eternal has always been.

The psalmist addresses the angels (Hebrew: *malak*) and hosts (Hebrew: *tsaba*):

> Praise ye him, all his **angels**: Praise ye him, all his **hosts**. Let them praise the name of the Lord: For he commanded, and they were created....
>
> He hath also established them for ever and ever: He hath made a decree which shall not pass. (Psalm 148: 2, 5–6, emphasis added)

In this passage, we see two groups of created beings who do not die: angels and hosts. However, it is more accurate to view these as job descriptions rather than as types of beings.

Beginning with an ancient book called *Celestial Hierarchy*, purported to be authored by the Athenian convert Dionysius of New Testament fame (Acts 17:34), one encounters two thousand years' worth of *angelology* as a branch of academic theological study. However, this reflects the common error of defining "angel" as a type of being. For example, someone might say it was not a human, but an angel, who rolled away the stone of Jesus' tomb. The term *malak* is the Hebrew equivalent of the English "messenger,"[4] and there were both human and supernatural *malakim*, including the Angel of the Lord. A scholarly resource supports this plea for newfound precision in terminology: "The translation of *malak* by 'angel' in English Bibles obscures the ancient Israelite perception of the divine realm. Where English 'angel' is the undifferentiating term for all of God's supernatural assistants, *malak* originally could be applied only to those assistants whom God dispatched on missions as messengers."[5] Similarly, the Hebrew word *tsaba*, "hosts," is a military term and is often translated "armies."[6] Of course, there are human and supernatural armies as well. Accordingly, a term like "immortals" is more precise and, we believe, useful for references to supernatural beings.

Among the immortals, we are honing in on a particular group who likely play leading roles in the eschatological scenario that we find ourselves living in the midst of. Among the immortals, divine messengers are usually depicted as indistinguishable from human beings (Hebrews 13:2; Genesis 19:1–22 and 32:25–31; Daniel 8:15; Luke 24:4; and Acts 1:10), but other times they are depicted in overwhelmingly supernatural terms (Daniel 10:6; Matthew 28:3). Apparently, they are ordered in ranks, because some are referred to as "archangels," while others are simply "angels" (1 Thessalonians 4:16; Jude 9). Because most of these appearances recorded in Scripture are of male messengers, it is commonly assumed that there are no female angels.

In *Sense and Nonsense about Angels and Demons*, Kenneth Boa and Robert Bowman conclude that "angels can appear in bodily form, but they don't come in male and female varieties."[7] However, the authors simply ignore or overlook contrary biblical evidence. The prophet Zechariah recorded a vision entailing two *female* supernatural entities *with wings* on a divinely appointed mission:

> Then lifted I up mine eyes, and looked, and, behold, there came out **two women,** and the wind was in their **wings**; for they had wings like the **wings** of a stork: and they lifted up the ephah between the earth and the heaven. (Zechariah 5:9, emphasis added)

A stork is an unclean bird to the Hebraic mindset. Furthermore, these winged women are carrying another woman only identified as "Wickedness" (Zechariah 5:8). On one hand, it seems likely that these women are fallen angels, but on the other hand, one could argue that because it was a divinely appointed mission, it was not indicative of their status. Either way, the idea that the immortals are exclusively male seems to be based more on male-dominated tradition than on biblical exegesis.

Another dogma similarly lacking in support, but commonly

assumed, is the belief that the immortals are fundamentally incorporeal, or without bodies. However, many passages indicate physicality. When Abraham was visited by three immortals on the plains of Mamre, they walked, talked, sat, and ate the food he prepared (Genesis 18:1–8). Also, the writer of Hebrews reminds us to "be not forgetful to entertain strangers: for thereby some have entertained angels unawares" (Hebrews 13:2), an admonition that carries no force, given their immateriality. From these examples, most theologians surmise that although they are incorporeal, they can appear as physical beings when it suits their purposes. But why must we assume their natural state is incorporeity?

The tradition is largely based on the opinion of Thomas Aquinas, famously known as the "Angelic Doctor," who argued that things of the spirit realm consist of spirit, but things of the earthly realm consist of matter (earth). Yet, Aquinas assumed the pagan cosmology of Aristotle, which held that there are four elements (earth, fire, water, and air). Aristotle's doctrine of natural place demanded that material beings were "of earth" and that beings like angels, residing in the heavens, were "of air" and could not be physical. Of course, Aristotelian cosmology has been discredited by science, so one wonders why such theological conclusions based on its tenets are still so widely accepted.

Other theologians do offer a biblical rationale for the tradition that the immortals are fundamentally incorporeal. For example, Boa and Bowman make this case from Scripture:

> In biblical accounts of their visits to human beings, angels generally seem to appear suddenly and then disappear without any explanation. For example, when the women discovered Jesus' tomb to be empty and the stone rolled away, Luke tells us, "Suddenly, two men in dazzling clothes stood beside them," causing the women to fall on the ground in terror (Luke 24:4–5). (John refers to these two individuals as "angels" in John 20:12; see also Luke 24:22–23.) So, when angels did appear, their physical forms were evidently temporary ones taken for the purpose of interacting with human beings and not their own intrinsic forms.[8]

There seems to be an assumed premise that only incorporeal entities can appear and disappear suddenly. Given that, the argument is structured as such:

1) Only incorporeal beings can appear and disappear suddenly.
2) Angels appear and disappear suddenly.
3) Therefore, angels are incorporeal beings.

But is this sound reasoning? An argument is valid when its conclusion follows from its premises, and it is sound when, in addition, its premises are true. This argument is valid but not necessarily sound. Why? Premise 1 that "only incorporeal beings can appear and disappear suddenly" is simply assumed without any supporting evidence. There are many possible explanations for why these beings seem to appear and disappear.

A biblical counterexample is Jesus' sudden postresurrection appearance in a locked room to the astonished disciples:

Then the same day at evening, being the first day of the week, when the doors were shut where the disciples were assembled for fear of the Jews, came Jesus and stood in the midst, and saith unto them, Peace be unto you. (John 20:19)

Eight days later, Jesus again appeared in a locked room and asked Thomas to touch His wounded body (John 20:28). Theologians would not likely argue that Jesus was inherently incorporeal from those appearances, so we conclude that the argument for the incorporeity of the immortals, based on sudden appearances and vanishings, is not sound. We offer the extradimensional hypothesis as a better explanation.

A being existing in dimensions beyond our observable three dimensions would seem to appear abruptly as it entered our space and disappear just as quickly as it left. For example, if a three-dimensional pencil were to pass through a two-dimensional "stick figure" world on a sheet of paper, the pencil would suddenly appear as a small point growing to the width of the pencil, remain the same size as its length slides through, and then abruptly disappear. Should the two-dimensional, stick-figure eyewitnesses to this visitation conclude that pencils are nonphysical beings? Hardly… Therefore, when angels seem to appear at will, they might be taking advantage of extra unseen dimensions. We are not given enough information to make dogmatic statements about the nature of the immortals—some who completely defy the classification "angel."

While the angels appear in male (Daniel 10:5) and female (Zechariah 5:9) human forms, not all of the immortals are so friendly to the eyes. Biblical scholar S. A. Meier points out that "an early Israelite from the period of the monarchy would probably not have identified the theriomorphic [having an animal form] cherubim and seraphim as *malakim* 'messengers,' for the frightful appearance of these creatures made them unlikely candidates to serve as mediators of God's message to humans."[9] Because the Bible never mentions these immortals functioning as messengers, the classification "angel" is a misnomer.

Isaiah describes the heavenly throne room and its attendant Seraphim:

> Above it stood the seraphims: each one had six wings; with twain he covered his face, and with twain he covered his feet, and with twain he did fly.
>
> And one cried unto another, and said, Holy, holy, holy, is the Lord of hosts: The whole earth is full of his glory. (Isaiah 6:2–3)

The Hebrew is simply transliterated to "seraphim" in English Bibles, obscuring its true meaning. In later chapters of Isaiah, when *sarap* appears alongside the Hebrew verb *uph* for "flying,"[10] it is rendered "fiery flying serpent" (Isaiah 14:29 and 30:6). The meaning should not be controversial. In addition to the four occurrences in Isaiah, the word *sarap* has three occurrences in the Torah, all of which refer to snakes (Numbers 21:6, 8; Deuteronomy 8:15). Scholarly consensus affirms that "the Seraphim are now generally conceived as winged serpents with certain human attributes."[11]

In sacred Scripture, Daniel mentions the Watchers four times, even revealing that King Nebuchadnezzar's curse was "by the decree of the watchers" (Daniel 4:17). The Watchers are widely attested in intertestamental Jewish literature. The most famous example is the "Book of the Watchers" (1 Enoch 1–36), where the term is used for the fallen immortals, the sons of God, who fathered the Nephilim in Genesis 6, amongst other acts of debauchery against the created order. A variant version of the story in the Book of Jubilees has the Watchers come down to teach men holiness (Jubilees 3:15), but they are subsequently corrupted when they lust after human women (Jubilees 5:1). In Jubilees, the evil immortals have a leader named Mastema, who persuades God to let one-tenth of the evil spirits remain with him on earth to corrupt and lead humankind astray.

In a document fragment found in Cave 4 among the Dead Sea Scrolls, Amram, the father of Moses, sees the chief angel of darkness (a Watcher named Melkiresha) in the form of a *reptilian* (bracketed suspension points represent scroll damage/irretrievable text):

> I saw Watchers in my vision, a dream vision, and behold two (of them) argued about me and said […] and they were engaged in a great quarrel concerning me. I asked them: "You, what are you […] thus […] about me?" They answered and said to me: "We have been made masters and rule over all the sons of men." And they said to me: "Which of us do you choose […]
>
> I raised my eyes and saw one of them. His looks were frightening like those of a viper, and his garments were multi-colored and he was extremely dark […]
>
> And afterwards I looked and behold […] by his appearance and his face was like that of an adder [a venomous snake], and he was covered with […] together, and his eyes […][12]

This reptilian Watcher seems to be an entirely different sort of creature than the human-looking messenger angels one encounters in the New Testament.

In the Bible, the Cherubim usually serve in one of two functions: as guardians of a sacred tree (Genesis 3:24) or as guardians and carriers of a throne (Psalm 18:10). While they have human features, Cherubim are chimeras, "the Israelite counterpart of the sphinx."[13] Ezekiel offers the most elaborate description (Ezekiel 1:10, 9:3; 10:15–22) in which they have the "likeness of a man" but "had four faces, and every one had four wings" (Ezekiel 1:6). In Revelation, they, or a similar creature, are also described as "beasts full of eyes before and behind" (Revelation 4:6). Minor differences in the descriptions might suggest a subjective element in mystical visions like the examples recorded by Ezekiel and John, or perhaps it indicates some variety in Cherub attributes. Stranger still, we believe these entities are "shape shifters" who can morph their physical forms. Whatever the case may be, the point we are driving at is that Cherubim are fearsome creatures, not the *putti*—plump rosy-cheeked winged babies seen in Renaissance and Baroque art—that they are commonly mixed up with.[14]

The *Zohar Hadash*, a book of commentary by rabbinic kabbalists, reveals that occultists believe that angels can shape shift. Although chained, certain fallen angels can still exert influence via magic.

Usually when angels descend to earth, they clothe themselves with air and take on temporary matter, of which they divest themselves when they are ready to go back on high. But the two angels were so eager to remain among women that they became more completely material, and they had been on earth for seven consecutive days, they could not return again to heaven. They begot children upon their mortal wives; then God chained them in mountains of darkness with iron chains which are fixed to the great deep. Were it not for these bonds they would obliterate the world. Even fettered they can still weaken the celestial family by the magic spells they know and which they teach to all who resort to them. These angels draw their vitality from the north, the "left side." They are the *anshe shem* (literally: "men of name") because they use the holy names in magical incantations.[15]

The cryptic reference to the "left side" likely reflects that north is to the left of the rising sun, but as a source of vitality, it indicates their false independence from God—the kabbalist concept of *Qliphoth*, denoting the character of evil and impure things and the realm of Satan and demons.

Even more, it seems likely that the Prince of Darkness himself is of the Cherub family. Ezekiel likens the downfall of the proud king of Tyre to the fall and curse on the serpent (Genesis 3:14–15) in an amazing lament (Ezekiel 28:11–19). It sees through the proud human despot to the evil power behind him. It harkens back to the immortal "anointed cherub," in the "garden of God" and on the "mountain of God" (Ezekiel 28:13–14). That ancient serpent (Hebrew *Nachash*) who fell and deceived the first humans in the garden is later positively identified as the devil or Satan (Revelation 12:9).

Hebrew Bible scholar Michael Heiser argues that the so-called serpent in the Garden of Eden was no snake. The noun spelled *Nachash* in Hebrew can mean "snake or serpent"[16] or, as a verb, "to practice divination,"[17] but as an adjective, it means "bright, brazen."[18] In Hebrew grammar, it is common for adjectives to be used as nouns or substantivized.[19] Thus, it is a valid option to translate *Nachash* as a noun meaning "shining one." Heiser concludes, "Eve was not talking to a snake. She was speaking to a bright, shining upright being who was serpentine in appearance, and who was trying to bewitch her with lies."[20] This makes the Genesis account seem all the more plausible; after all, snakes do not have vocal chords and Eve was not immediately taken aback as one would expect, given a talking snake, suggesting that perhaps she was even accustomed to seeing such entities.

It is rather satisfying to know that even in light of what we have learned from Ugaritic and Egyptian texts concerning the ancient context of Scripture, the controversial Hebrew Bible passages (Genesis 3, Isaiah 14, and Ezekiel 28) classically used to describe the devil of New Testament theology (often to the disapproval of scholars) can now be rigorously reconciled. Heiser addresses all three passages as a composite sketch:

- Genesis 3: The *Nachash* ("Shining One") is "put down on the ground" (denoted by the "eating dust" reference in 3:14).
- Isaiah 14: *Helel* ("Shining One") is "brought down to Sheol" (v. 11); "cut down to the earth [*erets*]" (v. 12); "thrust down to Sheol, to the recesses of the pit" (v. 15).
- Ezekiel 28: The brilliant, shining Cherub is "cast from the [cosmic] mountain of God" (v. 16) and "cast to the ground [*erets*]" (v. 17).

Heiser explains: "All three have a shining supernatural being in Eden who rebelled against God, who sought to usurp the headship of the divine council, who was cast from God's presence, and who was placed beneath the created things he vowed to rule, sentenced to the domain of the Underworld."[21] We believe that the time draws near when the final aspect of Satan's sentence will be executed and all hell will break loose on earth when the portal to the abyss is opened.

What Is a Portal?

Doorways, gates, and portals to untold realms are a familiar yet fantastic topic. The subject is esoteric, not because it is not discussed, but rather because it is seldom handled seriously outside of a reductionist scientific worldview. For our purposes within, the term "portal" can be defined in two senses as "any entrance to a place," or "any means of access to something."[22] In the first sense, a portal is a technological or supernatural doorway that connects two places, dimensions, or points in time—for example, a wormhole in a science-fiction movie or the wardrobe in C. S. Lewis' *The Lion the Witch and the Wardrobe*. In the supernatural sense, a "portal" may entail a prayer, a ritual, or an altered state of consciousness. Illustrations might even include an Ouija board as a "doorway of communication" with the spirit realm. A portal might link to a different spot within a universe (teleportation portal); a parallel world (interdimensional portal); the past or the future (time portal); and other planes of existence, such as Heaven, Hell, or other afterworlds (preternatural portals). Most of us learn about them in kindergarten.

Lewis Carroll popularized the idea with his 1871 *Through the Looking Glass*, a story (later adapted to *Alice in Wonderland*) about a girl who steps through her mirror and enters a different world. In 1930, Frank L. Baum's *Wonderful Wizard of Oz* launched Dorothy over the rainbow into another realm of reality. In 1950, C.S. Lewis introduced the above-mentioned Christian allegory, *The Lion, the Witch, and the Wardrobe*, in which the characters travel through a portal hidden in a wardrobe to a fantastic alternate reality with talking animals, the land of Narnia. Of course, this famous Christian allegory became a series of books known as the "Chronicles of Narnia." In the series, Aslan the lion is a type of Christ, aptly described as "good," but not necessarily "safe." In book 6, *The Magician's Nephew*, the "wood between the worlds" served as a portal within a dynamic multiverse, including the land of Narnia.

The existence of portal gateways logically follows from the existence of these other realms. Do such fantastic constituencies exist? Belief in some sort of Heaven is nearly universal, so the interface between our "this-worldly," experiential space-time and the transcendent heavenly realm is a proper item for theological probing. In Scripture, portals to Heaven entail altered states of consciousness like dreams and visions. After dreaming about angels ascending and descending, Jacob declared Bethel "the gate of heaven" (Genesis 28:17). The first verse of Isaiah describes the book as the "vision of Isaiah," meaning a telepathic message from God given in symbolic form (1 Samuel 3:1; Ezekiel 7:26). Also, it is interesting that Paul wasn't sure if he was in his body or outside of it when he journeyed to the Third Heaven (2 Corinthians 12:2). In chapter 8, "The Science of Portals," we explain why science has been forced to acknowledge that consciousness affects physical matter. Otherworldly gates feature prominently in religious structures worldwide.

In the West, portals feature prominently in the art and architecture of sacred spaces. Medieval cathedral and church entrances were designed to be spiritual transformation portals. Back then, the church was seen as an allegory for the voice of Christ. The entry portal was interpreted in light of Jesus' figure of speech: "I am the door: by me if any man enter in, he shall be saved, and shall go in and out, and find pasture" (John 10:9). Scholar of medieval architecture, Calvin Kendall, observed that cathedrals often aligned the figure of Christ with the vertical access of the door to symbolize this typology. Kendall states, "The portal was designed to assist the medieval Christians in experiencing the church as a mystical space that was both the dwelling place of God and the place where one entered into his or her better nature."[23] Like a wormhole to another universe, ecclesiastical doors served as a transition between the profane ordinary world and the sacred space.

In the East, the ancient name "Babylon" comes from the Hellenized form of the Akkadian *Bab-Ilu,* meaning "the gate of god." In chapter 7, we delve into Babylon and its gates. Babylonian astrology was the first organized system of astrology, arising in the second millennium BC.[24] In India, Vedic astrology holds that twenty-seven constellations—identified as "Nakshatras" or cosmic energy portals—influence human destiny rather than the twelve zodiacal star signs.[25] The founder of Chinese Taoism, Lao Tzu, allegedly mastered techniques for out-of-body travel, and in some Taoist sects, an adept acquires the ability to "take flight and wander freely through enchanted islands, sacred mountains or celestial spheres."[26]

Located east of Japan between Iwo Jima and Marcus Island, the Devil's Sea boasts a comparably inexplicable record of vanishing ships and planes to its infamous counterpart in Bermuda. Apparently, it is serious enough that the Japanese government has officially labeled the area a danger zone.[27] Stranger yet, the Aokigahara Forest at the base of Mount Fuji, Japan, has become notorious throughout the world as the "Suicide Forest"—effectively, it's a portal to Hades.

The East has influenced the West through theosophy and later the New Age movement, but the Native Americans were similarly pantheistic and animistic. Mount Shasta in California has Indian legends about little people and giants. The Apache creation myth includes giants and owl-like creatures, among numerous other "monsters," as does the Navajo and related tribes. Sedona, Arizona, is internationally heralded for its vortex sites. More than one author has suggested theses vortices are portals to other worlds or dimensions. In view of Sedona being the most well-known dimensional portal location in America, we visited the Sedona vortices, and we could not miss the opportunity to explore the nearby Superstition Mountains, which, according to Native American tradition, are the former home of superhuman giants. The Superstitions also host an ancient medicine wheel called Circlestone, which attracts quite a bit of UFO activity. About.com lists the Superstitions and Sedona as the top two paranormal hotspots in the US.[28] If portals to other realms exist, we would expect to find them there (and it seems we did).

Because all religious traditions and even materialist science acknowledge alternate realms, this book assumes that they exist, but critically evaluates them as well as various ideas about how they interface with the everyday world. After taking the reader along on our adventures in the American Southwest, we delve into earth mysteries, megalithic monuments, and places of power. We also explore alignments, ley lines, and the world grid. These concepts are evaluated in terms of various claims to dimensional portals and alternate realities. Such an investigation is multidisciplinary, requiring a broad range of topics—from hard science to religion and occultism.

After taking you along on research trips to the Navaho nation in Utah and Sedona, Arizona, we explore biblical sites like Bethel and Babylon, as well as earth mysteries—pyramids, megalithic monuments, stone circles, and energy vortices. From science, we show that portals are feasibly interconnecting black holes establishing a wormhole to another realm. We will look into the murky world of the occult and mysticism where portals feature prominently. While we endeavor to explain these items within a biblical supernatural worldview, reader be warned: The literature on the subject runs from cryptic theoretical physics to outright metaphysical lunacy. We have sifted through thousands of pages and, as expected, examples of the latter are ubiquitous. Nevertheless, the existence of counterfeit says nothing about the reality of the genuine article.

We explore the hypothesis that not only are such portals a reality, but they are positioned in a geometrical design when mapped as a grid.

We dare ask if the ancient Book of Enoch, conservatively dated to 250 BC, defining twelve heavenly portals (Enoch 77:1), only *seems* like Ivan Sanderson's twelve vortices (including the famous Bermuda Triangle)— or is it more than coincidence? Pioneering paranormal researcher John Keel called dimensional portals "windows."[29]

> Thus there are many "haunted" places all over the world, shunned by ancient man or made sacred by him. These are precise geographical locations, and anyone digging into the history and lore of such locations will find thousands of accounts of ghosts, demons, monsters, and flying saucers pinpointed within a few square miles and covering a thousand years or more of time. To UFO cultists such places are Windows: entry points for spaceships front some distant planet. Occultists teach that these are Gateways: weak spots in the Earth's etheric envelope through which beings from other space-time continuums seep through into our reality.... There are literally thousands of these weak spots all over our planet. Paranormal and supernatural activities in these areas seem to be controlled by complicated cyclic factors. Periodically, all hell breaks loose in all these places simultaneously, and then we have a flap, or wave, of UFO sightings, apparitions, poltergeists, sudden inexplicable disappearances of animals and human beings, mysterious fires, and even a form of mass madness.[30]

Today, these areas are inevitably labeled "paranormal hot spots" or "interdimensional portals." Keel's most famous work, *The Mothman Prophecies,* focused on sightings of a six-foot, winged humanoid in Point Pleasant, West Virginia. Hollywood produced a feature film starring Richard Gere in 2002, but what is less known is that Point Pleasant area had a marked increase in UFO sightings and many other paranormal phenomena around the same period (1966–1967).

Pastor Larry Gray was an early Mothman eyewitness. He saw the creature inside his home near Point Pleasant in 1966 and identified it as one of the immortals:

I looked over to my right and there, beside the bed, stood a six-foot dirty lunar or light gray colored figure with its wing-like arms extended and something like hands pointing downward. It had a glow, not illustrious, but a dirty glow. Its eyes were back in its head. I knew the thing was looking at me. I could feel evil communicating something horrible. It definitely was a non-human being. It just stood there staring at me, discharging evil in the room. My mind and body felt as if they were paralyzed. I could not speak. It was the devil. I knew it. The devil cannot stand against the power of the blood of Jesus, so in my mind, I kept repeating, "Jesus by the power of Your blood protect me. Jesus by the power of your blood...." Little by little, the "Thing" disappeared. It vanished like pouring salt onto a snail. It was the devil; I know it was the devil.[31]

Cris Putnam at the Mothman statue in Point Pleasant, West Virginia

In the course of researching the book in your hands, I visited Point Pleasant to research the Mothman legend. The local Mothman museum displays handwritten notes from John Keel, as well as yellowed newspaper articles from the time of the events preserved under sheets of glass. Interestingly, the UFO flap in the area at the same time as the Mothman sightings was reported in the *Herald Dispatch* on March 16, 1967. In addition, during the same brief window of time, a

huge, pterodactyl-like cryptid known as a thunderbird was seen hovering in the skies.

The most fascinating aspect of the case is that all of the activity
ceased when the Silver Bridge collapsed on December 15, 1967, killing
forty-six motorists who were stuck in holiday shopping traffic. A few
witnesses even reported seeing the Mothman in the vicinity of the bridge
when it collapsed, leading to one theory that the Mothman was warning
the residents of the impending disaster. Of course, the alternate theory
is that the monster *caused* the tragedy. We suggest that the Mothman is
one of the fallen immortals. From this curious history, it seems fair to
explore Keel's hypothesis, which is the fantastic notion that a portal or
"window" opened over Point Pleasant, one that subsequently closed the
day the Silver Bridge collapsed.

Keel theorized that every state within the continental United States
has from two to ten "windows."[32] While a claim like that is extremely
hard to justify, most states do have an example. Even so, it is a tricky
proposition to decide which areas qualify and which do not. In *Zones of
Strangeness: An Examination of Paranormal and UFO Hot Spots,* parapsychologist Peter McCue laments the difficulties associated with identifying such regions:

> When it comes to deciding whether an area is, or was, a hot spot,
> it would be helpful to have reliable data about the frequency of
> anomalous events elsewhere, thereby enabling statistical com-
> parisons to be carried out. However, so far as I'm aware, this sort
> of information isn't available. Therefore, some areas might be
> wrongly regarded as hot spots, whereas others, more deserving
> of that status, might be overlooked.[33]

A United Kingdom-based researcher, McCue's 2012 treatise is a
milestone in the serious study of the subject of portal regions. Not many
credentialed academics are willing to contribute, but that will probably
change.

Areas of concentrated high-strangeness offer the most promise for understanding unexplained phenomena. Paranormal investigator Christopher O'Brien wrote:

> I am firmly convinced that location-specific sites of unusual, so-called paranormal activity; portal areas [small, defined locations where unexplained activity seems to be centered], haunted sites and other concentrated areas of activity, may be our most direct investigative path studying the mechanics of paranormal manifestation.[34]

While a discussion of all of these portal areas is beyond the scope of this book, what follows is a sampling of examples within the United States. O'Brien came to that conclusion after many years of fieldwork in the San Luis Valley region of Colorado and New Mexico.

The San Luis Valley

The San Luis Valley is the largest alpine valley in the world. It is located in Colorado with a small portion overlapping into New Mexico. O'Brien has documented thousands of UFOs, cattle mutilations, ghosts, and cryptids, along with portal areas and military black projects in the area. He wrote:

> As a result of my investigations documenting the relentless, six-year wave of unexplained activity between 1993 and 1999 and the resulting coverage by mainstream media, the San Luis Valley is now considered to be America's #1 per capita UFO Hot-spot. The scientific community, whether they like it or not, are slowly becoming aware that the San Luis Valley and other Hot-spot regions are worthy of careful scientific study.[35]

The associated phenomena (strange creatures, UFOs, cattle mutilations, ghosts) are by no means unique to this area and, in fact, are commonly associated with such areas, like the infamous "Skinwalker Ranch."

The Skinwalker Ranch

Also known as Sherman Ranch, this hot spot named after the evil, shape-shifting witch of Native American legend is allegedly the site of a plethora of paranormal and UFO-related activities. It is located on approximately 480 acres southeast of Ballard, Utah. In the 1990s, residents Terry and Gwen Sherman and their two children reported seeing several types of UFOs that were associated with cattle mutilations on the ranch.[36] A local news outlet reported:

> The Shermans, their teenage son and 10-year-old daughter have seen three specific types of UFOs repeatedly during the past 15 months—a small boxlike craft with a white light, a 40-foot-long object and a huge ship the size of several football fields. They've seen one craft emit a wavy red ray or light beam as it flies along. They've seen other airborne lights, some of which have emerged from orange, circular doorways that seem to appear in midair. They've videotaped two of the sightings.[37]

George Knapp brought attention to the ranch with a series of articles in the *Las Vegas Mercury,* and he later coauthored a book, *Hunt for the Skinwalker: Science Confronts the Unexplained at a Remote Ranch in Utah*, with Colm Kelleher. The ranch was acquired by Robert Bigelow's National Institute for Discovery Science to study sightings of UFOs, crop circles, glowing orbs, Bigfoot, and poltergeist activity.[38] The Bradshaw ranch near Sedona, Arizona, hosts remarkably similar activity, and a detailed report of our visit there is presented in chapter 3.

Yakima Indian Reservation

Located on the east side of the Cascade Mountains in southern Washington State, Yakima is a federally recognized reservation consisting of more than one million acres for the Yakama Indian Nation. It is famous for the "earth light" phenomenon, but in chapter 3, we discuss why the earth-light hypothesis does not explain all of the ghost-light activity, which seems to have a mind of its own. Parapsychologist McCue writes, "UFO sightings there go back to at least the late 1950s, and were fairly frequent in the 1970s. The area has also been the setting for alleged Bigfoot sightings and other anomalies."[39] James Gilliland, a local landowner, believes the region hosts "a portal for extraterrestrial spaceships, and he claims to have had close encounters with UFO-related entities."[40]

Big Thicket

Big Thicket is the name of a heavily forested area in Hardin County, Texas. The Big Thicket Ghost Light has been known to disable automobile engines and seems to exhibit intelligence. It can be found along Black Creek near the old ghost town of Bragg in eastern Texas. Unexplained fireballs have been reported streaking across the sky there. More disturbing, the spirits of Native Americans have allegedly attacked people and, according to Rob Riggs, ape-like wild men "wander the deep woods at night, and occasionally even the town margins and suburbs, howling like banshees."[41] While we already discussed Point Pleasant, West Virginia, let's move to the Northeast United States in order to demonstrate that this is not merely a Southwest phenomenon.

The Bridgewater Triangle

The Bridgewater Triangle is an area of about two hundred square miles in southeastern Massachusetts reported to be a paranormal hotspot that features all sorts of phenomena, ranging from UFOs and cattle mutilation to poltergeists, orbs, and apparitions, not to mention cryptids like Bigfoot, giant snakes, and Thunderbirds. It has a deep history. According to Stephen Wagner, a paranormal expert for About.com, "The first UFO sighted over Bridgewater was in 1760, and was described as a sphere of fire that was so bright it cast shadows in broad daylight. Another was sighted on Halloween night in 1908, appropriately by two undertakers."[42] The triangle centers on Hockomock Swamp, a Wampanoag name that means "where spirits dwell."[43] Of course, the early colonial settlers promptly named it "Devil's Swamp." A reporter for the *Boston Globe* writes:

> Over generations, many have believed the Hockomock is home to spirits, strange animals, and more. Stories abound: There are the vicious, giant dogs with red eyes seen ravenously sinking their fangs into the throats of ponies; a flying creature that resembled a pterodactyl, the dinosaur that could fly; Native-American ghosts paddling canoes; and glowing somethings hovering above the trees. There's also talk of a shaggy half-man, half-ape seen shuffling through the woods.[44]

This sounds eerily similar to the events in Point Pleasant and other famous portal areas. Right next door in Vermont, another mystery triangle hosts similar activity, including several people who have simply vanished.

The Bennington Triangle

The "Bennington Triangle" in Vermont is also known for mysterious creatures, strange lights, and spooky specters. It has all the tell-tale signs of a portal region. Many persons have purportedly gone missing between 1920 and 1950, with five well-documented disappearances between 1945 and 1950.[45] Centered on Glastenbury Mountain, the triangle includes most of the area of the nearby towns, particularly Bennington, Woodford, Shaftsbury, and Somerset.[46] Author Joseph Citro made the triangle famous in his first published novel, *Shadow Child*, in which he observed the area shares characteristics with the Bridgewater Triangle in neighboring Massachusetts.

The Great Serpent Mound

The Great Serpent Mound—a 1,348-foot-long, three-foot-high earth-work resembling an uncoiling serpent—in rural Adams County, Ohio, is the largest surviving prehistoric effigy mound in the world. As the result of a new radiocarbon analysis, the date of construction is esti-mated to be approximately 321 BC.[47] Historically, researchers attributed the mound to the Adena culture (1000 BC–AD 1), a pre-Columbian Native American civilization. This new evidence corroborates the origi-nal prehistoric consensus and weighs heavily against more recent pro-posals that it was built by the Fort Ancient culture (AD 1000–1650). French historian Rene Chateaubriand wrote in *Voyage to America:* "The Indians are in agreement in saying that their fathers came from the west; they found the works of the Ohio just as they are to be seen today."[48] It is likely that later indigenous cultures refurbished the work of the original mound builders. Some researchers believe the Adena people were related to the Nephilim.

Frederic Ward Putnam, the Harvard-educated anthropologist who spent much of his career lecturing and publishing on the Ohio mounds and the Serpent Mound in particular, also reported discovering the remains of giants throughout the area. For example, in a scholarly monograph titled "The Serpent Mound of Ohio," Putnam described the remains discovered in a nearby burial mound: "This older grave had been made about five feet deep in the clay and was about nine feet long and five wide. The pieces of skull found at the southeastern corner of the grave were twice the usual thickness."[49] Another report stated: "One of the skulls found was said to be big enough to fit over a man's head."[50] The Adena skull type has the highest cranial vault of any large people group in the world.[51] There are countless reports of seven- to eight-foot-long skel-etons discovered in the Ohio Valley. Interestingly, a reasonable case can be made that the sudden influx of people of gigantic height in the Ohio Valley was concurrent with the Nephilim tribe's displacement from the eastern Mediterranean by the Hittites, Egyptians, and Hebrews.

When I visited the Serpent Mound and its museum in November

2014, a historian with the Ohio Historical Society explained that the head of Serpent Mound aligns with the rising sun during the summer solstice and the coils are aligned to the two solstice and two equinox events each year. Located on a plateau of a huge meteor crater, the Serpent Mound was designed to model the pattern of stars forming the constellation *Draco* (Latin for "dragon"). The star pattern of the constellation Draco precisely fits the Serpent Mound, with the ancient North Pole Star, Thuban *(alpha Draconis),* at its geographical center within the first coil from the head. Its alignment with the old-world Pole Star also shows how true north was found in prehistoric times. More interesting is that this was not known until 1987 because modern compasses give incorrect readings at the site due to magnetic anomalies.

In Greco-Roman legend, Draco was a dragon represented as the demon son of Gaia, Typhon.[52] As explained in *Exo-Vaticana*, the Great Red Dragon symbolizing Satan in the book of Revelation is also an astral prophecy involving the constellation Draco.[53] Bradley Lepper, an archaeologist for the Ohio Historical society, theorizes that Serpent Mound was "a shrine to a spiritual power."[54] Of course, that seems like an open invitation to the fallen immortals.

New Age ceremonies began at the Serpent Mound during the Harmonic Convergence of August 1987, an event based on Mayan Prophecy interpretations by Tony Shearer in his book *Lord of the Dawn: Quetzalcoatl and the Tree of Life*. Lepper recalls, "Thousands of people came to Serpent Mound during the convergence."[55] Believers from all over the world gathered to chant and meditate at various "power spots" like Bell Rock near Sedona and the Great Serpent Mound of Ohio.

Cris Putnam at
Serpent Mound

Prophetic Significance

If we are correct that the book of Revelation is mostly a prophecy about the future, then very soon, Satan will be active on earth as never before. As that day grows near, we expect that these zones of strangeness will become increasingly active. There is a debate concerning the timing of Satan's final purging from Heaven. Because the chapter refers to Jesus' birth and death (Revelation 12:5–6), many have argued that Satan was thrown down by the atonement of the cross. That view is supported by Jesus' statement just prior: "Now is the judgment of this world: now shall the prince of this world be cast out" (John 12:31). Jesus also said, "I beheld Satan as lightning fall from heaven" (Luke 10:18). Considered in isolation, a case can be made that the cross fulfilled Revelation 12:6. However, there are serious problems with that position.

A good case can be made that Satan falls *three* times in Scripture. First, Satan fell through vanity sometime before the incident in the Garden of Eden (Genesis 3:1–14). Ezekiel 28 looks back to the garden when the "anointed Cherub" fell from grace. C. S. Lewis famously wrote, "It was through pride that the devil became the devil: Pride leads to every other vice: it is the complete anti-God state of mind."[56] Although he had fallen, Satan was not barred from Heaven or Earth after his prideful defection.

Second, after the seventy disciples returned celebrating their discovery that "the devils [demons] are subject to us," Jesus witnessed Satan "as lightning fall from heaven," and He later said the devil was about to be "cast out" as He prepared for the cross and resurrection (Luke 10:18; John 12:31). These passages are the basis of the view that the Revelation 12 expulsion is a past event.

Third, as a result of the angelic war, Satan will be cast down to the Earth for a brief period of intensified suffering on Earth, during which Hell literally breaks loose, the Antichrist declares himself to be god, and the world is overrun by demons, Nephilim, elementals mistaken to be extraterrestrials, and transgenic monstrosities from the abyss. We believe a study of the circumstances leads to the conclusion that these three falls are distinct events—two are historical and the final one is future.

In Revelation, Satan is cast down as the result of Michael's army's triumph over their fallen adversaries, not the positional checkmate accomplished by the cross that "spoiled principalities and powers" (Colossians 2:15). On display is the "already but not yet" paradigm characteristic of New Testament theology. At the cross, the victory was secured in that sin was atoned for, but, in the sense of a geopolitical theocracy, the spoils of that victory have not yet been assumed in the "rod of iron" manner promised at Jesus' return (Revelation 19:15). Of course, scores of messianic prophecies in the Hebrew Bible declare the resulting golden age of world peace (Isaiah 11:6, 62:25). However, that era will not occur until Satan is cast down and chained as predicted.

The Hebrew term *satan* means "adversary," implying a prosecutorial role like the accuser in Revelation 12:10. How can he still be "your adversary the devil" (1 Peter 5:8), if he was cast from his accusing role two thousand years ago? The amillennialist should consider Satan's active deceit of many nations in light of the millennium's inaugural proclamation that "he should deceive the nations no more" (Revelation 20:3b). Finally, the fact that Jesus stands as our intercessor (Romans 8:34; Hebrews 7:25) implies an ongoing prosecution by the adversary. The cumulative weight of these passages leads to the conclusion that Satan's final expulsion from Heaven has not occurred.

John received the vision of the Great Red Dragon's expulsion many decades after Jesus' death on the cross, miraculous resurrection, and glorious ascension as a promise of Christ's return to judge evil and redeem the earth. Any claim to a historical fulfillment of Satan's angelic war expulsion (like the cross) must satisfy the conditions of the divine hymn sung in response:

> And I heard a loud voice saying in heaven, "Now is come salvation, and strength, and the kingdom of our God, and *the power* of his Christ: for the accuser of our brethren is cast down, which accused them before our God day and night."

And they overcame him by the blood of the Lamb, and by the word of their testimony; and they loved not their lives unto the death.

Therefore rejoice, ye heavens, and ye that dwell in them. Woe to the inhabiters of the earth and of the sea! For the devil is come down unto you, having great wrath, because he knoweth that he hath but a short time. (Revelation 12:10–12, emphasis added)

The hymn is proclaiming the impending return of Christ in power. The time is said to be short because, after a brief period no greater than three and one-half years, the Messiah will chain the devil in the pit for one thousand years (Revelation 20:3). The hymn's celebrated events have not yet been fully accomplished, as New Testament scholar Robert Thomas pointed out:

To refer it to the present era would mean that the accusing work of Satan is over, according to the next line of the hymn. This can hardly be. The removal of Satan from heaven is in conjunction with the victory of Michael in heaven, not with the cross of Christ.[57]

Many passages support the ongoing tempter/accuser role (Job 1:9–12; Matthew 4:1–11; Mark 1:12–13; Luke 4:1–13, 22:31; 2 Corinthians 2:11; and 1 John 5:19). Consequently, one is hard pressed to remain consistent while contending that Satan's expulsion in Revelation 12 is a past event. Of course, that implies the time is at hand when Satan and all the immortals aligned with him will be cast down upon the earth (Revelation 12:9). If so, then some of the people now holding this book will see the immortals on the earth for the battle of Armageddon.

Finally, a prophecy in the second chapter of the book of Joel with parallels in Amos 7 and Revelation 9 implies an end-times invasion of immortals and hybrids. While some expositors claim Joel was describing an army of locusts with phrases like "[They are] a great people and a strong" and "they shall run like *mighty men* [*gibborim*, a term associated with the Nephilim]," it is hard to accept these verses as talking about grasshoppers. We think this describes a demonic invasion that could possibly include Nephilim.

> [They are] a great people and a strong; there hath not been ever the like, neither shall be any more after it…and nothing shall escape them. The appearance of them is as the appearance of horses; and as horsemen, so shall they run….
>
> They shall run like mighty men *[gibbowr, gibborim]*; they shall climb the wall like men of war….
>
> They shall run to and fro in the city; they shall run upon the wall, they shall climb up upon the houses; they shall enter in at the windows like a thief. The earth shall quake before them….
>
> And the LORD shall utter his voice before his army: for his camp is very great: for he is strong that executeth his word: for the day of the LORD is great and very terrible; and who can abide it? (Joel 2:2–11)

Joel 2 is paralleled by a vision given to Amos of a similar locust army invasion. The LXX translation by Brenton renders, "Thus has the Lord God shewed me; and, behold, a swarm of locusts coming from the east; and, behold, one caterpillar, king Gog" (Amos 7:1). The thing that makes this use of *Gog* distinct is that it is not a variant translation from the Masoretic text, because the Masoretic uses no name at all. Missler draws significance from juxtaposing "locusts have no king" (Proverbs 30:27) against the "locusts" in Amos who *do* have a king, arguing that it implies Amos must *not* be talking about insects, but rather about immortals.

The locusts in Revelation 9 have a king, Apollyon or Abaddon, but Proverbs 30:27 says that locusts have no king. So these locusts in Amos and Revelation are not natural locusts; they are demon locusts. If that's the case, then the Gog in Amos, who is the king of the locusts, is a demon king.[58] The locust imagery also matches Revelation: "And the shapes of the locusts were like unto horses prepared unto battle; and on their heads were as it were crowns like gold, and their faces were as the faces of men" (Revelation 9:7). Taken at face value, these entities cannot be immaterial spirits. Scholars, those who take end-time prophecy seriously, invariably conclude that these end-time hordes of immortals manifest in mongrelized bodies. Arnold Fruchtenbaum also notes their hybrid nature:

> The description of these "locust-scorpions" given in verses 7–10 clearly shows that they are something other than literal scorpions or locusts. Their origin being the Abyss further shows that they are demons. It is not unusual for demons and other angelic beings to have animal-like features.[59]

The acclaimed Christian apologist and religion scholar Walter Martin believed that the UFO phenomenon could play a role in this end-time incursion.[60] He offered that UFOs might be instrumental in Jesus' description of the events prior to His return: "Men's hearts failing them for fear, and for looking after those *things which are coming on the earth: for the powers of heaven shall be shaken*" (Luke 21:26, emphasis added). "Things which are coming on the earth" implies that they themselves are not of the earth; rather, they are, by definition, *extraterrestrial*. In reference to the portal opening at the fifth trumpet judgment, the first woe, in the book of Revelation, Martin offered this novel hypothesis:

> In addition to what is coming upon the earth, the book of Revelation speaks of the bottomless pit being opened (9:2). A bottomless pit does not have to be one that is down—it could very well be one that is *up*, since in space there is neither up nor down, but *out* from the earth. This could reveal that what comes upon earth is from space, and not from under the earth. The symbolic language may easily refer to the manifestations of the powers of darkness near the consummation of the age. It is biblically predicted that Antichrist will reveal himself with signs and

lying wonders so that if it were possible, he would deceive the elect. (2 Thessalonians 2:9; Matthew 24:24)[61]

We believe all of these immortals and hybrid monsters play key roles in the horror of the Great Tribulation and Battle of Armageddon. This finds support in the Qumran War Scroll (1QM), which reveals it is Satan and his powers that are behind the final battle:

For this shall be a time of distress for Israel, [and of the summons] to war against all the nations. There shall be eternal deliverance for the company of God, but destruction for all the nations of wickedness. All those [who are ready] for battle shall march out and shall pitch their camp before the king of the Kittim and before all the host of Satan gathered about him for the Day [of Revenge] by the Sword of God.[62]

The Qumran War Scroll corroborates the idea that the Battle of Armageddon is not merely a human war but a battle fought by humans and immortals. These immortals will manifest on the Earth at the conclusion of war in Heaven, and the locust armies will amass at the opening of the portal to the abyss (Revelation 9:2). Finally, a prophecy from Enoch frames this as a last-days angelic struggle on par with the one in Revelation chapter 12:

Last Struggle of Heathen Powers against Israel

[5] And in those days the angels shall return
    And hurl themselves to the east upon the Parthians and
Medes: They shall stir up the kings, so that a spirit of unrest
shall come upon them,
        And they shall rouse them from their thrones,
        That they may break forth as lions from their lairs,
        And as hungry wolves among their flocks.

⁶ And they shall go up and tread under foot the land of His elect ones,

[And the land of His elect ones shall be before them a threshing-floor and a highway]:

⁷ But the city of my righteous shall be a hindrance to their horses.

And they shall begin to fight among themselves,

And their right hand shall be strong against themselves,

And a man shall not know his brother,

Nor a son his father or his mother,

Till there be no number of the corpses through their slaughter,

And their punishment be not in vain.

⁸ In those days Sheol shall open its jaws,

And they shall be swallowed up therein,

And their destruction shall be at an end;

Sheol shall devour the sinners in the presence of the elect. [63]

CHAPTER TWO

Legends of the Fall

By Tom Horn

WW ho could have known that, in 2012 when Cris Putnam and I released our best-selling book, *Petrus Romanus: The Final Pope Is Here,* we would be inundated with invitations from around the world to be on radio, television, and in print media? This included History Channel programs, Sid Roth's *It's Supernatural,* the *Jim Bakker Show,* and numerous others, mostly due to our accurate prediction—one year in advance—that Pope Benedict would resign the office of vicar, citing health reasons—an act that would be followed by the election of the final name on the ancient "Prophecy of the Popes" list—Petrus Romanus, or, as the world knows him today, Pope Francis. A documentary from WND Films followed that excitement, titled, "The Last Pope?" together with our even greater-selling work, *Exo-Vaticana.*

But it was a series of shows that we did with legendary radio man Steve Quayle on the *Hagmann & Hagmann Report* that really set the world abuzz, becoming the number-one *Blog Talk Radio* program on the planet and illustrating to these authors that the world was more than casually interested not only in the final pope, but in the connection between Rome and its work on extraterrestrial intelligence, astrobiology, and the intriguing connection between those issues and why the indigenous peoples of Arizona—especially the San Carlos Apache Tribe—had joined environmentalists in filing dozens of lawsuits before a federal appeals court to stop the construction of the observatories on Mount Graham. The project ultimately prevailed in favor of the Vatican and NASA after an act by the United States Congress ordered it, but the question remained in our mind: Why had the tribal communities fought so diligently against the construction of telescopes atop that mountain? We had wrongly assumed this was because Mount Graham was a sacred place—as in preceding generations of Native Americans had lived and died on it and therefore it was considered "holy ground." We learned later that, while that was partially true, it was not the whole issue. *Dził Nchaa Si An*, as Mount Graham is known in the Western Apache language, is one of the four holiest mountains in the world for the Apache and is considered sacred to all of the region's native peoples. *And it is so because it is what we might call a "stargate" in their mythos, a portal through which "the Star People" have come since the dawn of time.* Once we understood this fact, our suspicions as to why the Vatican and NASA had chosen this mountain in particular, even being willing to face a prolonged legal battle to build three telescopes on Mount Graham (including the largest binocular telescope in the world where the LUCIFER device is kept, as thoroughly disclosed in our book, *Exo-Vaticana*), went into hyperdrive.

We also came to learn that the San Carlos Apache have preserved ancient tales concerning this geography, including stories very similar to biblical chronology. These legends involve a creator, a deceiving dragon that follows, an epic flood, and even a race of giants known as the Jian-du-pids, who were judged and destroyed by God. These were the histories we had just started investigating as the deadline approached for our book *Exo-Vaticana*, and so we rushed just a bit of this deeper material into that work, including this excerpt:

> According to the legend, a…race of…Indians called the Tuar-
> tums lived in the valley as peaceful farmers. They prospered
> until one day they were invaded by the Jian-du-pids, described

as goliaths who used tree limbs for toothpicks. These Nephilim, led by a massive man named Evilkin, allegedly came from the Northeast and were headed south to their home beyond the Gulf of Baja. The giants nearly wiped out the Tuar-tums before they hid themselves underground in the mountains and Father Sun threw a huge fireball that seared the monstrous Nephilim into the scorched mountain rock. While elements of the tale are obviously mythological, it has a remarkable thematic coherence with Genesis 6.... The Apache Creation Myth [as we related it to the portal at Mt. Graham] is also interesting in this regard, as a particular version involves the "One Who Lives Above," who descended in a flying disc [over the mountain] at the start of Creation. "In the beginning nothing existed—no earth, no sky, no sun, no moon, only darkness was everywhere," the legend starts before noting that "suddenly from the darkness emerged a disc, one side yellow and the other side white, appearing suspended in midair. Within the disc sat a bearded man, Creator, the One Who Lives Above."

While no single Apache Creation Myth dominates all tribal beliefs, most groups share key precepts as well as symbolism within their oral histories. Besides the creator who rides in a heavenly disc, a Dragon with the power of speech turns up, bargaining with men, as well as supernatural gateways associated with mountains (ch'ína'itíh) through which spirit beings can come.... Suffice it to say that these ancient native ideas involving flying discs, flying creators, spirit lights, owls, a talking dragon or great serpent, and even supernatural gateways tied to mountain ranges began long before the Vatican cast its eyes on Mt. Graham.[64]

Following this initial investigation and in media interviews since, we have been inundated by requests from hundreds of people asking that we continue this research, especially as it involves stories from around the world of specific geographic locations—very often tied to mountains—

where intelligent beings have been reported for thousands of years traversing portals/stargates/wormholes. But to satisfy this request, one big problem was ahead, one we knew we would have to overcome. It would make us face the same type resistance the Vatican had come up against: distrust by American Indians who have been burned too many times by New-Age whackos who misreport their legends in order to make a buck. Mountain portals that are universally associated by tribes with deities, spirits, and history connected to Mount Graham and other locations are often deemed "holy" and unavailable to nontribal members. As a result, I was personally warned not to pursue these sacred locations where, in both modern and ancient times, "spirit lights" (UFOs?) have moved through the portals there, something that seems to contribute to the indigenous peoples' attribution of "powers" and metaphysical phenomena. My team was further told we could be arrested and that our cameras and equipment would be seized. Given that the reservations have their own legal system and could represent a terrible situation for us if we wound up trying to get out of their jails, we determined the first thing we had to do was to get permission from the tribal nations themselves before venturing into restricted areas.

At first, all of our requests were rejected. We then began asking if we could hire guides from the reservations to take us into areas such as the ancient Anasazi (mysterious pre-Pueblo Indians that built hundreds of magnificent cliff-side dwellings along the Four-Corners area of the United States and who then disappeared "overnight" without explanation). That, too, was met with a negative response. Of course, if we wanted to just wait until spring, we could get a hiking permit from the National Forestry department and travel by foot into areas that are not cordoned off and that are available to the general public—but we wanted more than that.

Time slipped by as 2013 came and went, then 2014 was winding down; just when I was starting to think we would never get permission to visit the off-grid sites or to conduct actual interviews with tribal leaders, we launched SkyWatch TV and hired two investigators to join our team—Carl Olafsen and Allie Anderson. Because we wanted this new television enterprise (you can check it out online at www.SkyWatchTV.com) to do what no Christian broadcasting ministry had offered before—including investigative reports and full-length documentaries involving on-location and original field footage and research—Carl and Allie's job would be to take the lead in opening doors to get us where most people are normally forbidden. They found this to be especially frustrating in this case, given the well-earned mistrust natives have of nontribal members in particular. Every time it seemed a door was about to open, it would slam shut. This happened partly because we were being forthright about our intentions: that we have a Christian and prophetic worldview and that we wanted to rebroadcast footage of the sacred locations and peoples under our investigation—all big no-no's among most indigenous peoples. At one point, the Navaho Nation approved on the phone an interview we could have with a tribal elder (who had been a US military code talker and convert to Christianity whom I was anxious to meet), but later permission was withdrawn when the US government agreed to pay a $554-million-dollar settlement to the Navajo tribe to settle a legal dispute,[65] which pulled all tribal elders into meetings and made them unavailable to our cause. Even so, our persistence would eventually pay off.

Meanwhile, around this same time, coauthor of this work, Cris Putnam, headed to Arizona with a guide and film crew of his own. As you will learn elsewhere in this book, not only was he successful in chronicling the ancient and modern stories of portals and those who come through them, but Putnam even became an "orb" believer when, from two different camera angles, his crew filmed a luminous object zooming up behind them, flittering about erratically, then dissolving right before their eyes (this could not have been something on the lens, as it was filmed from two different camera angles, which we will show during the SkyWatch TV special report). The occurrence was followed by something even more astonishing: an enormous, V-shaped craft passed overhead, similar to the giant "Phoenix lights" that had been witnessed in 1997 by thousands of people across Nevada and Arizona, as well as the Mexican state of Sonora. This giant triangle, called the "Phoenix lights," was the largest mass sighting of a UFO in modern history. It is also considered one of the most substantiated—not just because of the sheer number of witnesses, but because of the quality of their testimony. For instance, then-acting Governor Fife Symington testified in writing:

> Between 8:00 and 8:30 on the evening of March 13, 1997, during my second term as governor of Arizona, I witnessed something that defied logic and challenged my reality: a massive, delta-shaped craft silently navigating over the Squaw Peak in the Phoenix Mountain preserve. A solid structure rather than an apparition, it was dramatically large, with a distinctive leading edge embedded with lights as it traveled the Arizona skies. I still don't know what it was. As a pilot and a former Air Force officer, I can say with certainty that this craft did not resemble any man-made object I had ever seen.[66]

Now, thanks to Cris Putnam, SkyWatch TV can broadcast images of a similar (or was it the same?) craft that decided to make an appearance for our crew on location. You will also see some "stills" of these images in Cris' report elsewhere in this book.

Cris Putnam in Sedona, Arizona—on the Path of the Immortals.

At the time Cris was returning from Arizona with this amazing photographic and film evidence of strange happenings there, my team—

under Carl Olafsen and Allie Anderson—was just packing up to leave for the Four Corners area of the United States. It wasn't much, but the Navajo Nation had agreed to let us interview Miss Navajo at their head-quarters in Window Rock, Arizona. She was to tell us their creation story in both the native tongue and in English. If this "feeling out" process went well, it was possible we would get a sit-down with a tribal elder. From there, we would travel across the border to Montezuma County, Colorado, where a Cherokee guide would take us down into the canyons to see what was behind the forbidden gates we were warned not to go beyond under risk of arrestment and property seizure.

Even then, on that mild winter morning in February, 2015, as we packed our all-wheel-drive SUV for the off-roads adventure, we could hardly have realized how much more this trip would pay off, or the doors that were about to be opened and closed. At the last moment, Miss Navajo pulled out of her interview (it seemed to me she was too afraid) only to be replaced by a much bigger opportunity—one that is very rarely made available to the white man.

To the Navajo Nation…and Beyond the Gate

We began our trip driving up through the Rockies near Hesperus Mountain, the highest summit of the La Plata Mountains range. The prominent peak is located in San Juan National Forest, which would take us near the Town of Mancos in Montezuma County, Colorado. Hesperus is one of the Navajo People's Sacred Mountains, and is called *Dibé Ntsaa*, which marks the northern boundary of the Dinetah, their traditional homeland and place of the Ute people. As we moved along these switchback roads, gaining elevation, occasionally there would be a break in the cedar trees, revealing wind-crested patches of snow reflecting the light of the midday sun. We discussed how the peaks of these mountaintops with sandstone formations at their tips could easily be used as places of concealment, observation, and defense—something we couldn't help believe was strangely connected to the mysterious

Anasazi and their "Alien Enemy" we had come here to investigate. As we discussed these possibilities while navigating a final switchback before our first destination, the drive suddenly became precarious, as lingering patches of ice clung to shadows on the asphalt and mule deer that had been feeding on the buffalo grass alongside the highway decided to cross the road in front of us, darting out from between the sagebrush and patches of snow. Carefully passing through that situation to the egress just beyond, we reached our assigned meeting place to find the Cherokee guide already waiting to take us behind the locked gates.

He was roughly five feet seven inches tall, with deep brown eyes, which studied us from under his wide-brimmed hat as we approached. His face, chiseled from too much sun exposure, hinted at what his forefathers' classical Indian physique must have looked like with his long, black hair in the traditional ponytail. He extended a warm but small, brown-skinned hand, as Carl Olafsen greeted him with *Yá'át* ("hello" in Diné, the tongue of the Navajo). Carl understood that *"Yá'át'éh"* is "Hello *good friend*," but he had been advised not to be presumptuous and to keep it to the shorter greeting.

"Nah, it's *Yá'át'éh*," our guide corrected, smiling again and shaking Carl's hand, embracing it with both of his as he laughed.

As we gathered our gear, including camera equipment, our guide put on a backpack and our cameraman adjusted for light. Moments later, we headed out on foot, listening to Carl as he continued practicing what little he knew of the native tongue while never quite matching how gently the Cherokee man's consonant pronunciations fell upon the ears.

"My mother was English," the guide told us. "And my father was Cherokee. My brothers have followed the Christian way of my mother. I have followed the path of my father."

The air was crisp but not too cold, with a light smell of cedars, as we set out along the course he would have us follow. While the team had thought it would be important for me to tag along, I intentionally strayed back a bit, letting Carl and Allie take the lead. This was my way of silently acknowledging any relationship we had with this man or the others we'd be meeting during this expedition as having begun with Mr.

Olafsen and Mrs. Anderson—exactly what I had hired them to accomplish for SkyWatch TV. But it didn't take long before I started rethinking that approach. *Maybe I should narrow the gap for safety reasons,* I thought to myself as the uneven route quickly required increasingly special care. The path was also getting steep, and I was puffing, struggling to keep up with my younger compatriots as I placed my bad leg carefully down along the safest parts of the trail. More than once I had to stick my hand out to steady myself, as loams of earth and plant life would slip away if I moved to close to the route's edge. On one occasion, the cameraman right behind me must have slipped on ice, as suddenly his arms flailed, he teetered, then grasped at anything he could reach in order to catch his balance to avoid falling headlong over the hill. He captured a solid area with one foot, dug his heel in hard to correct himself, caught my shoulder, and used it to steady himself. I saw the expression on his face as he considered the incomprehensible river of rocks and brush he could have fallen into deep within the canyon below.

Just ahead of us after that was an avenue that stopped at a mountainhead, and I could see the path we were following turned sharply to the right there. Where it would lead us beyond that was obscured by a mix of pine and juniper trees, yucca, serviceberry, choke-cherry and Gambel oak; buttresses of something artificial could be glimpsed through breaks in the trees carved out against the rock wall ahead.

As we moved toward it, our course widened, leveling off onto a plateau that temporarily provided an easier gait. We moved quickly along this section toward the narrow opening in the trees, then started uphill again over an area still spotted with patches of ice and snow.

Eventually, the hillside steepened again and the trail zigzagged. I found myself dragging once more up the precipitous route, struggling to lift my weight, grunting and scaling the arduous hill like the old man that I am, until soon I really was physically spent. I paused, dropped my forehead against my arm, wiped the profuse sweat from my brow, rested a few seconds, then pressed on until my heart pounded so hard that I thought it would explode. Breathing raspy, chugging the cool mountain air with increasingly painful gulps, I started questioning in my mind whether the demands of this mountainous trip were simply more than I had bargained for.

Then, something happened. We rounded a bend in the path and caught our first glimpse of something very huge and artificial coming into view a few hundred feet away, the magnificence of which instantly reenergized my resolve. In fact, all of the team members who had been ahead of me and the cameraman had stopped at that point and were waiting for us. They were in awe, as were we. We had been told of the more than four thousand archaeological sites and six hundred cliff dwellings ascribed to the Anasazi—a mysterious people that had kept no written records yet who built mesa-top villages and absolutely astonishing cliff dwellings within caves and under outcroppings in the sides of these canyons, but nothing could have prepared us for how breathtaking what they had accomplished really was.

Our Cherokee guide had obviously seen this before, as he waited for us to take it all in. Just ahead of us stood an outstanding complex that some archaeologists say was built long before the time of Christ and that had been suddenly and mysteriously abandoned at least eight hundred years ago (but keep in mind most everything about the Anasazi is anybody's best guess). Clothing, tools, and even food items were included in the materials they had quickly left behind. This one location alone was a small city, three stories high and built right inside a sheer mountain wall, yet more than six hundred other such cliff dwellings lay ahead.

Among the many Anasazi settlements we visited that day (and equally as grandiose as the best we had seen) is a place called the Spruce Tree House. It is the third-largest cliff dwelling in the area, and I mentioned this one in particular because it is a site that YOU can visit at the Mesa Verde National Park! If you want to catch a glimpse of what we were investigating throughout this ancient and mysterious region, I recommend that you do go there *(or perhaps we should all get together and take a SkyWatch TV tour?)* The Spruce Tree House is an amazing, 216-foot-long, 89-foot-deep, 120-room structure, with ten gathering rooms, eight ceremonial kivas, and two towers, all built into the side of a cliff from stones cut and hauled from a river several miles away.

Anasazi ruins the public can visit at Mesa Verde National Park

These compounds built into the high rock ledges along the Mesa Verde valley are constructed from very accurately cut stones that were set in mortar. Even after eight hundred-plus years of abandonment, the walls remain remarkably strong. You can also see the handholds and footholds cut into the cliff faces that served as the frightening climbing apparatus, which the inhabitants would scale along these sheer mountain walls in order to tend their gardens on the top of the mesa, where they grew beans, squash, and corn.

Hour after hour, as we advanced to study these structures, we couldn't help but wonder why the Anasazi would have ascended such terribly dangerous circumstances to carve out such amazing fortresses. What they did was far beyond the need to provide for shelter and protection from cougars and bears. It would have been a thousand times easier to construct and defend their lodgings near the river from which the stones had been harvested—*unless, of course, they were trying to defend themselves from something more dangerous than rival tribes, bears, and large cats.* All we could imagine was that this tremendous amount of additional effort had something to do with the need for a literal citadel of fantastic defensible proportions.

But from what?

We believe we found the incredible…and scary…answer to that question later when viewing and deciphering the ancient petroglyphs the Anasazi left behind. They tell an amazing story, and it is one that corresponds quite well with biblical history. Even the medicine man we would visit the following day admitted this fact.

As we went along, our guide also had theories about the Anasazi people, offering his assumptions about how they lived, how they constructed these cities, and why they departed in what seemed like overnight. He told us these thoughts as he led us farther into the hidden settlements where the public is not allowed to stand and showed us one of the kivas that did not have a roof on it (kivas were built both ways, some with roofs and some without). One kiva he brought us to was a round room, approximately eighteen feet across and built ten feet down into the floor of the ruins. Other kivas in this valley have roofs where a single ladder would have descended into the center of the space through a three-foot hole. He explained how the kivas were (and are) used for rituals, including how ceremonial tools that archaeologists found hidden in the niches of these ancient kivas had been used by medicine men to open the portals this book is studying, in order to contact parallel realities. Then he led us a short distance away to a hole in the ground where a ladder made of tree limbs tied together with leather straps was barely jutting up from out of the earth. This was another underground kiva, and he asked if we would like to enter it. Keep in mind that while we had spent days in prayer and preparation for this investigation, we paused at this point to think about this and to pray over ourselves. Kivas are thought in many indigenous belief systems to be a portal to another world, a place where the kachina spirit-beings can manifest and interact with medicine men (what some call a shaman). But the Cherokee assured us that inside this kiva, the hole in the floor that served as the symbolic place of origin of the tribe—what the Hopi call *sípapu* from which the peoples emerged from the underworld and where the dead still can be summoned according to their religion—had been plugged and buried. This was done when the kiva was abandoned and the tribe wanted the sípapu-doorway closed to protect entry into the lower world. Some medicine men—like the one we would encounter the following day—even say a "gatekeeper" exists just beyond the sípapu, and when the ceremony is performed, this gatekeeper might not let a person who is improperly prepared pass into the beyond, lest he or she should suddenly be afflicted by hungry ghosts that inhabit the domains of their ancestors.

Moments later, as we descended into this part of the ancient world, I found the wooden ladder to be completely smooth, hand polished as if from some long-forgotten, frequent use. The only light coming in was from the small hole we had just climbed through. Carl turned on a flashlight, and I noted the temperature was just a bit cooler than the outside air above. The roof was made from what appeared to be cedar logs; the walls were of stone and mortar. There was a ledge all the way around the perimeter to sit on, and we saw evidence of where a fire pit with a ventilation hole on one side had once existed. It was opposite a small niche on another wall that also had been filled in. Near the very center, we could see where the sípapu had once been, and we were glad that it was no longer there.

Tom Horn descending into underground kiva

As the rest of the crew made it down into the kiva, it was hard to grasp the fact that we were in a ceremonial room that may have existed many hundreds—perhaps even thousands—of years before Christ had walked the earth in the flesh. It was also a place that may have been abandoned due to some of the same enemies Jesus and even the ancient Hebrews faced. More about that later.

After filming the interior of the primeval kiva and pointing out certain aspects for the upcoming television special, we returned to the surface, and our guide asked what else we were hoping to see that might need special permission. Carl told him of specific ruins that he had heard about, as well as (and in particular) petroglyphs of giants and other Old Testament-themed images that I myself wanted to see. The Cherokee nodded and smiled, and said, "I know the places you speak of. One of them is called the *Sun Temple* on the other side of the mesa. We don't know what it was built for but they left it unfinished. And I can tell you where to see the petroglyphs you seek on the reservation, but I cannot go there with you."

The Sun Temple was indeed ruins that I wanted to see, because it is a large and significant site that holds much mystery in that nobody, including archaeologists and cultural historians, know what it was for. An eroded stone basin with three indentations at the southwest corner of the structure suggests that it may have been purposed as a sundial to mark the changes in the seasons. Two kivas on top of the structure, together with the lack of windows or doors elsewhere, intimates that it was not meant for housing, which has led modern Pueblo Indians to propose that it was some type of ceremonial structure probably planned for ritual purposes dedicated to the Sun God. The amount of fallen stone that was removed during its excavation is said to indicate that the original walls were between eleven and fourteen feet tall. These walls were thick, double-coursed construction, with a rubble core placed between the panels for strength and insulation. After studying the Sun Temple and comparing it to ancient Mesoamerican culture and edifices, it is this author's opinion (which is as good as anybody else's, since we don't really know) that this site may have been intended as a place for *human sacrifice* similar to those of the Aztec and Maya. I say this for a couple reasons. First, Dr. Don Mose Jr., a third-generation medicine man we met with for a large part of a day during this investigation (more about him later in this chapter), told us that the oldest legends of the Anasazi, which he had been told by his great-grandfather (who likewise had been told by *his* ancestors) included stories of the Anasazi turning to sorcery, sacrifice, and cannibalism after they "lost their way" and were driven insane by a reptilian creature, which they depict with a halo above his head. (Images of this being are included in the petroglyphs we filmed inside the canyons, and I believe they likely attest to the fallen reptile [or reptiles] of biblical fame, which also misled humanity.) Second, blood sacrifice was a religious activity in most premodern cultures during some stage of their development, especially as it involved invoking the gods, and the "Sun God" was typically chief among them. This included animals and humans or the bloodletting of community members during rituals overseen by their priests. In fact, the Mayans—who may have influenced the Anasazi or vice versa—believed "that the only way for the sun to rise was for them to sacrifice someone or something every day to the gods."[67]

Tom Horn stands at the wall of the Anasazi Sun Temple, where he believes human sacrifices were intended.

We will probably never know for sure what the purpose behind the Anasazi's Sun Temple was going to be or why it, like everything else these people built, was suddenly abandoned. Some evidence exists of a twenty-year drought from AD 1276 to about 1299, which can be seen in ancient tree rings, and some believe this may have contributed to the Anasazi having simply migrated away from the area. The big problem with this theory is that it does not explain why all the important foods, salts, clothing, and everything else that would have been so exceptionally important to the Anasazi were left behind. Another theory is that as the population grew, social divisions or war developed among some of the communities. But again, no evidence supports this conclusion, and the National Parks Department's research, archaeologists, and even the native peoples themselves admit it is impossible to know for sure why these mysterious cliff dwellers were there one day and gone the next. Even the assumption by historians that the modern Pueblo peoples of the Hopi, Zuni, Acoma, and Laguna are the descendants of the Anasazi is a theory that contradicts some of their own histories. A Native American cultural historian we interviewed told us that by the time his people first arrived in the Four Corners area, they found the Anasazi long gone and went looking for them everywhere. They did not know who or where they were, and when finally his people reached Chaco Canyon in New Mexico (which they assumed had been the Anasazi capital) in search of them, and found it also in ruins and abandoned, they sat down and wept over what possibly could have happened to such a great culture.

Thankfully, it was while contemplating these questions (and more) that lead investigator Carl Olafsen's cell phone rang and on the other end of the line was a man who would definitely provide some of the answers. We had been hoping to get an audience with him—and had nearly given up when Don Mose Jr., the third-generation medicine man I mentioned earlier, called. Known to be sensitive to Christianity, this retired Navajo academic authored many of the Nation's schoolbooks as well as cultural programs throughout the Four Corners area and, as we would discover, is a proficient Native American storyteller (oral-traditions historian).

It was a crisp, February morning the following day as we departed the Navajo Nation's headquarters to meet with Dr. Mose. The views on our drive were amazing, with spires that arose hundreds of feet from out of the earth, with enormous rocks often balanced precariously on their tops and accessorized by tremendous sandstone mounds and colored plateaus for as far as our eyes could see. With vast blue mountain skies hovering lightly above us, this backdrop of mesas and spires painted in yellows, oranges, and different shades of reds were richly inspiring as a few hours later we neared the traditional hogan (a nine-pillared round room made from cedar logs and mud) in the Monument Valley, where Dr. Mose had said he would meet us.

Like something straight out of an Old West movie, he was standing there in front of the Navajo structure as we drove up, hands on his hips, adorned in cowboy boots and a well-worn straw cowboy hat (ironic, right?), along with a turquoise watch, rings, and belt buckle. Black, slightly curly hair dangled along his shoulders and down his back as he regarded us with a welcoming smile. As Carl and Allie got out of the SUV and went up to greet him, I estimated that he stood about five feet, four inches, and no more. He seemed pleased to meet them and more than eager to get started telling the tales that we had asked him to clarify for us—stories that his father and grandfather had passed down from generations before, stories of giants, stories of "alien slaying" heroes of lore, and more.

Following him, Allie and Carl entered the hogan with me and the cameraman bringing up the rear. I took note that this was a customary large mud hut with an opening on one side and a chimney pipe extending up through the center of the roof. It was surprisingly warm. Dr. Mose had obviously lit a fire in anticipation of our arrival. The smell of cedar permeated the room, and I could not distinguish if this was from the fire or from the cedar log beams, walls, and ceilings. The only light that shone in was from a hole in the center of the ceiling that let the smoke from the fire exit out. Places to sit were all around the perimeter wall against the reddish-brown clay and sand-mixed floor. Dr. Mose invited us to sit down, and he motioned for Carl, who had made the initial contact, to sit down next to him. He formally introduced himself to Carl by putting his thumb to his chest, then saying his name. Using his opposite hand to indicate his index finger, he named his mother's clan. Moving to his middle finger, he regarded his father's clan. Ring finger, grandmother's clan. Pinky, grandfather's clan. Then he smiled and offered Carl his hand, explaining that by greeting him in this way, not only was *he* shaking his hand, but he was extending the greetings of his entire family. Carl looked honored, and happily shook not only Don's hand, but vicariously, the hands of his entire family.

With that, Dr. Mose immediately began talking as if on autopilot while our technician raced to set up the recording equipment. The cameraman said, "Hang on a second. Can we move to where there is more light and start over?" The aged medicine man hardly looked up as he replied, "No, no, I like to tell it here. This is where I tell it. Catch up," and with that, he continued on where he had just left off, drawing in the sand on the floor and reciting the first part of the story of the ancient Anasazi as it had been repeated to him by his father and grandfather, who had been told by their ancestors, and so on—a legend that Dr. Mose alone had undoubtedly repeated hundreds of times before.

Since it was obvious that this Navajo historian was indifferent to our camera and recording plans (and, in fact, I could tell he was uncomfortable with us putting him on film, but thankfully he proceeded nevertheless), I stepped over to Joe Ardis (yes, the "Wild Man of the Ozarks" was our cameraman once again) and whispered, "Forget the lights and your usual setup checks and get the camera on him now; he's not going to stop!" With that, Joe quickly unhooked the camera from the tripod, sat down next to Carl and Dr. Mose, and proceeded for nearly two hours to record what has only ever been allowed a few times in history before: the white man putting on film the official and legendary stories of creation, giants, a great flood, the reptilian deceiver, and more, all from the voice of the nation's medicine man. Dr. Mose even sang to us in the antiquated tongue and recited parts of what I would call "Old Testament history" paralleled in their earliest antiquity using the Navajo language.

Dr. Don Mose, third-generation medicine man and Navajo oral historian.

Not only did Dr. Mose substantiate the age-old and globally recorded story of "those who come through portals" and the impact they have had on biblical and global history past and present, and not only did he weave Navajo Indian myths and legends seamlessly with our understanding of the six days of creation, the arrival of Nephilim, and their connection to judgment by a global flood followed by the repopulating of peoples around the world and a second incursion of giants, but there were several instances in which, when I pushed him for greater detail, Dr. Mose went off script (he actually delineated from the official Navajo storyline) to provide greater consistency between history and the way the Bible itself recorded certain events.

For example, as the medicine man was following the "official storyline" about the Anasazi and how they didn't disappear but rather migrated and became the modern Pueblo Indians, I expressed doubts about that theory, and he responded by grinning just a bit and saying, "Well, I probably shouldn't tell you this, but—". He then proceeded to tell us the older stories that his grandfather had repeated about these mysterious peoples actually disappearing after they came under mind control from a reptile with a halo, a carnivorous creature suspiciously similar to what Cris Putnam describes elsewhere in this book as "fiery seraphim" (Hebrew: *saraph*, "fiery serpent," also corresponding with many other testaments around the ancient world, including Sanskrit *sarpa, sarpin*—"reptile"—whether with legs like the lizard or legless like the snake).

Another case in point is when I told him what we had learned from the Apache about cannibalistic giants and God destroying them in the Flood. "Oh, yes," he said, reaching for an illustrated book he authored that is used in the Nation's schools and libraries. He opened it to show us an artist's depiction of a giant that had stood between thirty and forty feet tall: "There was a time when the earth was infested with such great giants and alien gods that destroyed and ate the people," he said. "Some of them were in human form; others were monsters and [human-animal hybrids]." He followed this with the story of the White Shell Woman, who gave birth to two of the most important characters in

Navajo mythology—the twin, miracle-performing sons named Naayéé' Neizghání (whose name means "Slayer of Alien Gods") and his twin brother, Tobadzischini. Together, these two great warriors killed many of the giants, hybrids, and monsters that were wantonly destroying human life. As Dr. Mose described these ancient tales, I could not help but think of David killing Goliath and then later other giants with his mighty men.

The storyteller then paused and said, "You know, when the Christian missionaries first came to America and told our people their stories of the giants and the Great Flood, we smiled and let them know we had already heard these tales long ago from our ancestors." Perhaps this fact is why so many American Indians find it natural to convert to Christianity or why the Nations seem to have no issues with many of their tribal elders and educators being converts to Christianity.

Image showing Dr. Mose drawing out shapes and symbols on the floor as he tells the ancient stories of creation, vortices, heroes, reptilian deceivers, giants, and the Flood.

Another hour passed by as we gathered these stories and songs on film, and finally Dr. Mose finished his anecdotes. As we rose to thank him and to pack up our gear to leave, Carl noticed that the old man was very carefully using his foot to wipe clean the earthen canvas he had created with his finger that afternoon. Every brushstroke was erased. None of the art would ever leave the hogan. The story was to be memorized so that it could be passed on in words and songs for generations to come. This is the storyteller's way. This is the science of oral history. And with that, the medicine man shook Carl's hand, then ours, and we watched as he shuffled outside and down the trail. A slight wind kicked up dust around his feet as he went, and I could almost hear the ancient "Diné Bahane'" (Navajo story of creation) whispering in the air through this purple mountain range, the ancient tribal language and traditional Navajo rattles and flutes somehow still resonating their imprint over the hills from a time long ago.

Do Petroglyphs Tell the Story?

After a week on the road, having covered hundreds of miles of reservations to walk amidst their multiple ruins including hogans, temples, and kivas, to follow guides and visit with a medicine man, not to mention tracking down and photographing petroglyphs, we were finally on our way to the last site we would visit—one that our Cherokee guide had told us not to miss. We'd already collected enough pictogram and logo-gram images from ancient rock engravings throughout the Four Corners area to make our case and to calculate for our purposes a recurring theme, which definitely seemed to match the Middle Eastern and biblical stories of portals, reptilians, fallen angels, giants, and the havoc these played on the old world. But this final petroglyph was important, our guide had said, and one we could drive right up to. So, we decided to make one final excursion, this time into Utah, fifty miles north of Moab, where one of the largest known collections of petroglyphs is located in San Juan County. The "storyboard" we would visit there etched in sandstone began as early as one thousand years before Christ, and it records practically every element contained in this book—from spiral vortices and those who come through them to human-animal chimeras and even giant, six-fingered and six-toed footprints in pursuit of much smaller five-fingered and five-toed humans. Even that reptilian with his halo is drawn here, just a couple feet away from alien-looking, bug-eyed creatures. This location is also (again, a great thing for any reader) easier to get to than most of the ones we trekked to, yet it's as important if not more so than other petroglyphs you could spend days hiking over miles of rough terrain to reach. (But again, if you can, I recommend that you do visit the Four Corners, get a hiking permit or a guide, and see as much as you can of what I started calling the "Anasazi Trail," as much of this area includes evidence of a former time, in my opinion, an era when civilizations worldwide were suddenly and dramatically interrupted by those beings depicted on the Anasazi's Utah wall.)

The Newspaper Rock Petroglyph, as this one is known, is somewhat decipherable as to which images are older due to the fading and darkness of the earliest depictions (which are certainly the most mysterious, with their alien-looking heads, suits, and what might be some type of craft), and archaeologists believe the writing on this great wall continued from 1000 BC or earlier up until about AD 1300—the same time the Anasazi suddenly disappeared.

Allie Anderson gathers commentary on ancient petroglyphs for upcoming SkyWatch TV Special Report.

But the National Parks sign admits:

There are no known methods of dating rock art. In interpreting the figures on the rock, scholars are undecided as to their meaning or have yet to decipher them. Unfortunately, we do not know if the figures represent story-telling, doodling, hunting magic, clan symbols, ancient graffiti or something else.

I suggest "something else" is exactly what they tell us based on redundancy of the same story told all around the world. The Anasazi, who disappeared when the habit of writing on this tablet also suddenly ceased, used images and symbols similar to those found globally that connect to a first, and second, incursion of giants and the mountainous gateways their creators came through.

And it wasn't just me who immediately saw this story on the wall as a biblical one told through ancient American eyes. I could see it on Carl Olafsen and Allie Anderson's faces, too—my chief investigators—after we finished filming, packed up our drone (which we had been using to gather aerial film), and started the long drive back to our hotel. As I drove, I glanced at Carl in the rearview mirror, and I could see that he especially was deep in thought. Soon, he got a notepad out and began writing something, which later he gave me at the hotel. It said:

Looking on that last petroglyph I could see a multitude of antique memos: the spiral that Dr. Mose had explained, the reptile with the halo at its head, footprints of animals, footprints of people…suddenly I stopped. There was a path of human footprints, each holding exactly five toes, alongside a path of giant human footprints…the larger sets carrying six toes! I was reminded of 1 Chronicles 20:6:

> *And there was again war at Gath, where there was a man of great stature, who had six fingers on each hand and six toes on each foot, twenty-four in number, and he also was descended from the giants.*

Why would Native Americans concoct the same anomalous physiology as the ancient Hebrews on the other side of the world? While polydactylism certainly does not indicate someone is a Nephilim, accounts of giants with an extra digit on both sides of the Atlantic suggests a genetic relationship. On other places within the ancient figures was a more mystifying anomaly: There were strange, reptilian, humanoid shapes with bulbous heads and large, almond-shaped eyes. The oldest and most desert-varnished of them was a humanoid shape with what appeared to be an antennae coming off the head or helmet. Other humanoid shapes had horn-like features coming off their distorted human heads. One—the oldest appearing outline—appeared to be holding a disc-like object or a weapon of some kind and stood near a shape that had a square object affixed to the top of a shoulder-high post.

What could these figures have been left to communicate to future travelers? What were the motives behind the painstaking, time-consuming efforts of these messages? And where did the Anasazi go? Archaeologists theorize that the Anasazi were just absorbed into the Navajo and Hopi Tribes. But we were told in the Hogan [by Dr. Mose] that the tribes looked for them and could not find them. They tracked them to the Chaco valley but they were gone. The tribes mourned them and cried. Chaco means "to cry." The oral history knows they just disappeared.

The question is…where, and why?

Carl Olafsen with Allie Anderson and Tom Horn at the entrance to an Anasazi ruins.

Carl Olafsen's quizzical response to all we had seen—this final petroglyph included—is the same head-scratching response that generations who have stood where we did during our investigation must have felt. Yet I, for one, believe the answer was right in front of their *and* my team's eyes that day (they do, too, after contemplating the evidence). The ancient ruins of the Anasazi date to megalithic ruins elsewhere in the world, and all seem to have the same fingerprints (and six-toed footprints!) of the giants all over them. That being true, if you take only the images that the Anasazi left behind and compare them to similar (and in some cases, identical) universal symbols found elsewhere around the world where the stories and meanings of the images have been made clear, and keeping in mind that these legends materialized globally at approximately the same time, it is more likely than not in my opinion that the universal story agrees with the record of every major culture of the ancient world in which the astonishingly consistent story is told of "gods" that descended from Heaven and/or came through spiral vortices to materialize in bodies of flesh.

> From Rome to Greece—and before that, to Egypt, Persia, Assyria, Babylonia, and Sumer—the earliest records of civilization tell of the era when powerful beings known to the Hebrews as Watchers and in the book of Genesis as the *benei ha-elohim* (sons of God) mingled themselves with humans, giving birth to part-celestial, part-terrestrial hybrids known as nephilim. The Bible says this happened when men began to increase on earth and daughters were born to them. When the sons of God saw the women's beauty, they took wives from among them to sire their unusual offspring.[68]

I believe a record of this first incursion of hybrid humans and six-toed giants is recorded in Genesis 6:4, which says:

> There were giants in the earth in those days [the first incursion before the Flood]; and also *after that* [after the Flood, the second

incursion], when the sons of God came in unto the daughters of men, and they bare children to them, the same became mighty men which were of old, men of renown. (emphasis added)

Note that when the Torah (Genesis through Deuteronomy, the first five books of the Bible) was written around BC 1300, this would have been the same time when archaeologists believe the Anasazi, across the world from those Bible lands, were drawing giant, six-toed footprints on a slab wall in Utah and facing "an alien enemy" as the name "Anasazi" implies. When the writings in the Torah are compared with other ancient texts, including Enoch, Jubilees, Baruch, Genesis Apocryphon, Philo, Josephus, Jasher, Jubilees, and many others (not counting the accounts of the American Indian tribes on this side of the world), it is clear that this is more than a legend—it is history, a chronicle told through different peoples' methods and worldviews involving giants suddenly infesting the entire world, being wiped out in a flood, then somehow returning in a second incursion. This story was written down globally, from Hebrew scrolls to Indian petroglyphs, to provide the oldest recorded testament of part-human, part-angelic creatures, who were in turn the offspring of hideous reptilian entities (or what the apocryphal book of Enoch calls fallen Watchers). Elsewhere in this book, you will read that documents found in Cave 4 among the Dead Sea Scrolls describe a Watcher named Melkiresha in the form of a terrifying reptilian whose looks "were frightening like those of a viper, and…he was extremely dark…and his face was like that of an adder." Is Melkiresha or his fallen cohorts the same as those halo-bearing reptiles that led the Anasazi to destruction? There is reason to believe they were, and, after much comparison, I propose as reasonably justified a translation of the traditional Indian creation stories together with the Anasazi's petroglyphs as telling:

1. In the beginning, the great creator made everything.
2. Powerful reptilians then came down from Heaven through portals (the spiral, halo, and reptilian symbols) to deceive the world, and the world fell into darkness. This is also hinted in one of the meanings of the word Anasazi ("an alien enemy").

3. Portals (represented in ancient spiral symbolism beside giant, six-toed footprints and horned, humanoid figures) opened at this time and alien "gods," monsters, and giants came through them. Some of these giants had six fingers and six toes (just as described in the Old Testament).
4. The creator destroyed the monsters and giants in a great flood.
5. Yet the giants and reptilian deceivers returned, though not in the same numbers as had been before the flood. They turned the people to sorcery, cannibalism, and human sacrifice (as did the plumed serpents of the Mesoamerican Maya and Aztec).

One of the many petroglyphs that depict the reptilian with a halo, an ancient alien enemy that misled the Anasazi through some type of mind control.

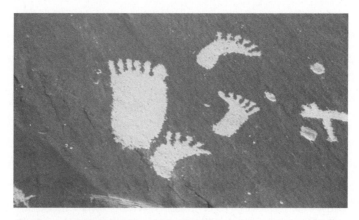

The Anasazi depicted various six-toed giant footprints among regular five-toed hand- and footprints in the petroglyphs.

Of course, one has to wonder what happened to the remains of the giants in America and whether the Smithsonian Institution actually participated in a cover-up (as some have alleged) in making a deliberate effort to hide the giants' remains (which would inconvenience the theory of evolution, which they celebrate) as they were discovered in early American archaeological digs. Vine Deloria, a Native American author and professor of law, sounds suspicious that this conspiracy theory may be true. He says:

> Modern day archaeology and anthropology have nearly sealed the door on our imaginations, broadly interpreting the North American past as devoid of anything unusual in the way of great cultures characterized by a people of unusual demeanor [giants].
>
> The great interloper of ancient burial grounds, the nineteenth century Smithsonian Institution, created a one-way portal, through which uncounted bones have been spirited.
>
> This door and the contents of its vault are virtually sealed off to anyone, but government officials. Among these bones may lay answers not even sought by these officials concerning the deep past.[69]

Does the Smithsonian Institution have an Indiana Jones-like large warehouse somewhere with aisles of American giants' remains locked away? It's possible. I personally have dozens and dozens of old newspaper clippings published when skeletons of unusual size—ten feet tall and more—were being dug up across the United States. I have so many of these, it could be a book all by itself, and these articles lend support to the legends of when vicious giants were worldwide. While David was fighting them on one side of the world, the Anasazi may have been building cliff dwellings in America to avoid them, and their petroglyphs also harmonize with that story. But the Anasazi evidence is not alone. Locations around the world that seem to connect to what I have called the "second incursion" of giants that came after the great Flood are prevalent.

But what about evidence that points to the presence of portals-interloping reptilian entities and their giant offspring from the *first incursion before the Flood?* It exists and is global. Cris Putnam looks into this evidence elsewhere in this book that even includes information connected to the portals/stargates "technology" records, raising the bigger question: Should the cliff dwellings of the Anazasi, the ruins of Göbekli Tepe, the gigantic stones of Baalbek and hundreds of other such locations around the world be understood as remnants of a first and second incursion of earth by portals-traversing reptilian immortals and their gigantic offspring? I believe the answer in many instances is yes. There is physical proof *they* were here, and by the time you reach the end of this book, you will most likely believe they are also set to return in force.

But first, we move to the southwestern corner of Anasazi portal territory, to Sedona, Arizona, where Cris Putnam and his team ran into a few odd "things" they didn't expect.

Sedona Mountain View [70]

CHAPTER THREE

Sedona, Arizona

Secret Mountains, Vortices, and Denizens from Unseen Realms

By Cris Putnam

ocated in the northern Verde Valley region of the state of Arizona, Sedona is arguably one of the most beautiful small towns in the world. Glowing in brilliant orange and red, the quaint western settlement is famous for its stunning array of red sandstone rock formations. The famous red stone of Sedona is formed by a layer known as the Schnebly Hill Formation. It is a thick layer of red- to orange-colored, iron-rich sandstone found only in the Sedona vicinity. Its beauty is unprecedented in the world.

Sedona's modern history only dates back to nineteenth century, when the first white settler, John J. Thompson, moved to Oak Creek Canyon in 1876. The early settlers were hard-working ranchers and farmers. In 1902, when the Sedona post office was established, there were only fifty-five residents. The first church there was the Assembly of God in 1933.[71] However, most people do not realize the area's previous Christian history. A local evangelist and author, David Herzog, writes, "In the early 1900s Sedona was a place where Christians from all over the United States gathered to hold large conferences and retreats as God's glory filled the city—long before it was claimed as a New Age vortex city. God has already designated Sedona as an open portal, a high place over the Southwest."[72] While the little town of Sedona grew up and became famous in the twentieth century, the area has ancient roots. The surrounding landscape hosts many petroglyphs and is steeped in Native American lore, with Hopi, Navajo, Apache, and Yavapai reservations a short drive away. It is also well known among fortean researchers that Sedona and its neighboring regions host some of the most intense UFO, paranormal, and spiritual activity in the world. It has one of the highest concentrations of UFO sightings in the United States.[73] Some say the "aliens" are attracted to the iron-rich, red-rock spires and castle-like summits. Many UFO sightings have been viewed near Sedona's four major vortex areas—with more than fifty at Bell Rock. Since the 1990s, it is rumored to host one of the most active dimensional doorways in America due to a book *Merging Dimensions* by former resident Linda Bradshaw and paranormal investigator Tom Dongo. John Keel was an early author who connected interdimensional gateways to the magnetic anomalies data, which provides a means of "seeing through" nonmagnetic rocks and cover such as desert sands, vegetation, and man-made structures to reveal hidden features such as faults, folds, dikes, and *underworld portals*.

At least theoretically, the magnetic anomalies characteristic of the northern Verde Valley region are consistent with conjectural descriptions of an extradimensional portal. Keel wrote:

If you have been collecting UFO reports in your home state, you will probably find that many of those reports are concentrated in areas where magnetic faults or deviations exist. UFOs seem to congregate above the highest available hills in these window areas. They become visible in these centers and then radiate outward, traveling sometimes 100–200 miles before disappearing again.[74]

Writing in the 1970s, Keel never mentioned Sedona, so we wondered if his ideas about windows were consistent with Sedona portal lore. Thus, we proposed to test the hypothesis: "If Sedona is really a 'thin area' supporting dimensional openings, we should see the same sorts of magnetic anomaly evidence Keel cited." So we obtained a United States Geological Survey Magnetic Anomaly Map and, indeed, Keel's hypothesis is consistent with reports from Sedona. As seen in the chart from the USGS North American Magnetic Anomaly website, Sedona and the surrounding area ranks extremely high in magnetic anomalies.

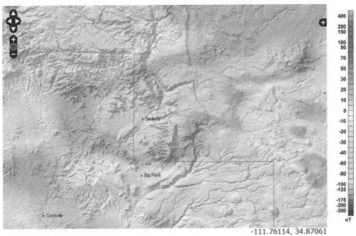

Magnetic anomaly survey

Geomagnetic intensity is indicated by the vertical bar graph, and Sedona is literally off the scale in coloration. The USGS reports concerning Sedona:

> As expected, volcanic regions produce distinctive magnetic anomalies, **high in amplitude and short in wavelength**. These anomalies are particularly evident over much of Lonesome Valley, the Black Hills and the area between Cornville and Sedona. For example, the preexisting regional coverage indicates only a broad magnetic high in the Page Springs area. Virtually all of the individual magnetic anomalies seen in the new high-resolution data are absent in the pre-existing regional coverage.

Large magnetic highs are present over the weakly magnetic Paleozoic sedimentary rocks exposed on Big Black Mesa and in the vicinity of Sedona.[75] (emphasis added)

One sentence caught our attention: "Virtually all of the individual magnetic anomalies seen in the new high-resolution data are absent in the pre-existing regional coverage." Did something or someone *cause* new anomalies to occur, or did the new technology locate previously missed data? We suggest a supernatural portal was opened by the New Age movement. Comparative religions scholar and Christian apologist Walter Martin once wrote: "The danger of the New Age movement and the occult is their essence: they are what they always have been—evil. If you turn the handle of the unopened door of a forbidden dimension, what will come through is satanic power of enormous proportions."[76] We suggest that during the height of the New Age movement when Sedona was crowded with seekers, a demonic portal opened wide enough to keep Oprah Winfrey supplied with guests and books for the next twenty years. The "New Age" is now the baseline, which explains why no one calls it "new" anymore. As the movement faded, vortex energy became a tourist industry goldmine. But, is the vortex lore scientifically viable?

New Agers contend that the sandstone geology of Sedona contains a large amount of crushed quartz crystals averaging from one hundred feet deep up to the surface.[77] Because quartz can store energy, it is theorized that electrical and magnetic energy is trapped and later released to the surface. Michael Persinger and other scientists have shown that low-level electromagnetic fields can induce altered states of consciousness and even mystical visions and UFOs.[78] According to a document written by Col. Paul Valley and Maj. Michael Aquino, titled "From PSYOP to Mind-war: The Psychology of Victory,"[79] the US Army used dark, arcane arts to open a Pandora's Box of paranormal activity. A practicing Satanist, Lt. Col. Aquino[80] was a psy ops agent specializing in brainwashing and mind control by exposure to electromagnetic fields and inaudible low-frequency radio waves.[81] While geomagnetic fields might play a role in vortex energy, we reiterate that parapsychologists[82] and anthropologists[83] recognize that these techniques induce an altered state of consciousness. However, according to an occultist, shaman, or Hopi medicine man, they "open a portal."

This electromagnetic radiation might be responsible for euphoric feelings people get just from being in Sedona. While the local "buzz" comes to a sharp focus at the named vortex sites, who put them on the map? The real answer is deeply rooted in ancient indigenous shamanism and geomancy, but it was popularized by a demon going by the name *Albion* during the New Age explosion of the 1980s.

The earliest documented mention of a vortex in Sedona was in psychic Dick Sutphen's 1978 book, *Past Lives, Future Loves*. It described an experience with an energy vortex on Airport Mesa in Sedona. The book was so popular that the vortex meme was born. Soon, "The idea of a vortex that could enhance psychic ability had a life of its own. Interest exploded."[84] Interestingly, there could be something to it, as research by Adrian Ryan suggests that geomagnetism (like that associated with vortex sights) correlates positively with ESP.[85] The Faustian bargain of psychic enhancement attracts seekers from all walks of life. Even freemasonic scholar and mystic Manly Palmer Hall lectured in Sedona shortly before his death in 1990.[86] Now let's turn back to the one called Albion.

Of Celtic origin, "Albion" is Old English, related to the Latin *albus,* meaning "white" in allusion to the white cliffs of Dover. It is probably the oldest known name for the island of Great Britain. More interesting, and we contend most applicable, is the mid-nineteenth-century phrase, "perfidious Albion," implying diplomatic treachery.[87] What an ironic and diabolical choice for a channeled entity that preaches oneism. The demon was deceptively cryptic.

In 1980, trance medium Page Bryant "psychically channeled an 'entity' who described several different energy spots in Red Rock Country. Ms. Bryant named them 'vortexes.'"[88] Although Bryant confessed, "I'm not a scientist. I just used symbolic words for what I was feeling at the sites,"[89] she identified four "power vortexes" that coincide with spectacular rock formations in and around the small town: Bell Rock, Airport Mesa, Cathedral Rock, and Boynton Canyon. Additional sites like the Chapel of the Holy Cross, Courthouse Butte, and Mystic Vista are also considered to be powerful energy spots and have been added to the list. Vortices or not, these are all very beautiful red rock formations that everyone will enjoy.

On the heels of Albion's information, more than five thousand New Age devotees flocked to Sedona to experience the "Harmonic Convergence"—an alignment of planets (allegedly based on the Mayan calendar) on August 16–17, 1987—as predicted in 1971 by author Tony Shearer in his book, *Lord of the Dawn: Quetzalcoatl the Plumed Serpent of Mexico,*[90] and later popularized by New Age guru José Argüelles. Starry-eyed New Agers seem to ignore the fact that the Mayans appeased their serpent gods with human flesh. A thorough case will be made in chapter 4 that the plumed serpents of the Aztecs, Incans, and Mayans are the immortal fallen angels who covet human worship and, more often than not, blood.[91]

On the weekend of August 16 and 17, 1987, the great Harmonic Convergence was supposed to take place—at least, that is what José Arguelles told people. He described the event as the world's first globally synchronized meditation, and made the small cowtown of Sedona into a Mecca for the New Age movement. A great many believed him—not merely prominent New Age leaders like Shirley MacLaine, but millions of adherents worldwide.[92] Sedona became legendary, and the energy vortices are an integral part of the local economy and culture.

Sedona's Famous Vortex Sights

A vortex is held to be a naturally occurring energy field rotating in a spiral around a central axis. Vortices (or vortexes) are seen throughout nature. For example, if you have ever witnessed a dust devil kick up in the desert, water spiraling down a drain, or a tornado's funnel, then you have seen a vortex. Represented in spiral petroglyphs by the indigenous tribes, these power sites are believed to be areas of focused "earth energy" spiraling about. It seems that the term "vortex" is a creative way to describe a spiritually charged area:

> In Sedona vortexes are created, not by wind or water, but from spiraling spiritual energy. The vortexes of Sedona are named because they are believed to be spiritual locations where the energy is right to facilitate prayer, mediation and healing. Vortex sites are believed to be locations having energy flow that exists on multiple dimensions.[93]

Mental, physical, emotional, or spiritual energy is thought to be amplified by vortex energy. They are also held to facilitate healing.

Pete Sanders, a scientist trained in biomedical chemistry at MIT, offers a more sophisticated explanation than the original channeled information coming from Bryant's spirit guide. In his 1981 book *Scientific Vortex Information*, Sanders wrote:

> The term "vortex" is more symbolic than literal. Most vortex energy sites *do not* have a circular energy flow. Rather, they are areas of enhanced linear energy flow. That energy is neither electric nor magnetic. What's happening in the vortexes are energy flows that exist in dimensions deeper than electricity and magnetism.[94] (emphasis added)

Sanders proposed that subatomic strings of particles that exist in ten dimensions (according to string theory) are responsible for the experienced energy. However, it seems reasonable to keep in mind that these are not the only possible explanations. If this area is a portal to the spirit world, proximity to the gate might intensify high-strangeness. It seems safe to assume we are dealing with more than material science can quantify.

Given the region's deep shamanic roots, we wondered if there is evidence of similar vortex beliefs in Native American lore. According to author Richard Bullivant, ancient Native American medicine men created three kinds of vortex portals: positive, negative, and mirror. Bullivant continues:

> Operating together, the three kinds of vortex portals work to create a natural balance which allows access to other realms, while maintaining a stable environment for "ordinary" people who do not wield the powers of the shaman. It was the shamans who used these portals to communicate with the spirit world, according to Indian tradition.[95]

Given the region's ancient inhabitance by the Anasazi, Apache, and Hopi tribes, it is not surprising that Sedona became the Mecca of the New Age movement.

New Agers are typically monists who hold that the earth is a living being called Gaia. The monist believes that everything is derived from an ultimate and single source. All diversity flows out from a uniform and divine energy. Thus, "God" is all and all is God. Accordingly, the goal is to discover the divine within each person. In this way of thinking, separation from God is actually unawareness of our inner divinity, and the fundamental human problem is not sin against a holy God, but ignorance of our true condition. Norman Geisler offers this rebuttal: "The fact that man 'comes to realize' he is God proves that he is not God. If he were God, he would have never passed from a state of unenlightenment to a state of enlightenment as to who he is."[96] Without the proper Creator/creation distinction, pantheism is inevitable.

Naturally, the leading New Age theory for the alleged vortices is that they represent a geographic area (like Sedona) where the earth is "exceptionally alive and healthy."[97] They believe the vortices amplify all kinds of energy, even human emotions. Of course, teachers of pantheistic monism flock to Sedona and energy vortex belief has been undergirded with substantial pseudohistory and legend. No matter what, it is a remarkable place for its beauty and, ultimately, portals aside, demons have no claim on God's creation and the sheer majesty of Sedona reflects the glory of the Creator.

On the Path of the Immortals

In light of the extradimensional hypothesis proposed in our former work, *Exo-Vaticana,*[98] we decided to explore the widely held rumor that the Sedona area hosts a dimensional portal. At the behest of SkyWatch TV producer, publisher, and coauthor Tom Horn, I; my wife, Shelley; and videographer Chris Florio packed several suitcases full of computers and photography gear and set out across the country from Raleigh, North Carolina, to Phoenix, Arizona, in a sleek, 2014 Boeing 737 jet airliner with spaceship-blue interior lights, on the path of the immortals.

During our first day in Sedona, we visited some of the legendary vortex power spots. Our first stop was the Roman Catholic Chapel of the Holy Cross run by the Diocese of Phoenix. Nestled high on the cliffs of the quaint city, it is a unique building inspired by sculptor Marguerite Brunswig Staude, a student of renowned architect Frank Lloyd Wright. Finished in 1956, the chapel was constructed on Coconino National Forest land via special permit through the efforts of Senator Barry Goldwater. As with the controversy surrounding the Vatican Advanced Technology Telescope facility on Mount Graham discussed in *Exo-Vaticana,* the influential arm of Rome is able to construct facilities on protected public lands where others are forbidden.

Chapel of the Holy Cross[99]

Local meditators believe the chapel to be an ideal spot for "soul pro-jection" to the otherwise unreachable peaks of sites like Cathedral Rock and Bell Rock.[100] This out-of-body technique seems remarkably similar to the one developed by psychics within the Stargate program sponsored by the CIA and the Defense Intelligence Agency.[101] In our last book, *Exo-Vaticana*, we discussed the ET connection to the "Omega Point" theol-ogy developed by the French Jesuit Pierre Teilhard de Chardin, often labeled the "Father of the New Age Movement."[102] Since that time, Pope "Petrus Romanus" Francis made history as the first pontiff to express his desire to baptize an ET[103]—not to mention that the VORG are hard at work on Mount Graham looking for dark matter that may confirm the Milky Way's "galactic transport system."[104] Given that history, we are intrigued that the Catholic Church established a dominant presence on the red rocks of Sedona decades before the New Age movement. After our investigation, we believe it was no mere coincidence. We were ready to move past the easily accessed tourist spots to explore a truly amazing vista with incredible power.

Mystic Vista is not often mentioned as an energy vortex because it takes an expert off-road driver to get there. We hired licensed Arizona guide Larry Sprague[105] for a desert adventure to a seldom-reached Sedona power spot.[106] Sprague picked us up in a highly modified Jeep Wran-gler and gave us a general tour of the Boynton Canyon area, explaining various rock formations like Coffee Pot Rock, Balancing Rock, and the Kachina Woman (a Hopi term for "ghost"). After some discussion con-cerning the Hopi view of the afterlife, Sprague pulled over to the side of the road to tell us about a UFO he witnessed:

> **LS:** I used to fly hot air balloons, and once while setting up for a group on airport mesa [pointing at the sky], I saw a UFO that looked like a ball of fire fly right through there. It went into secret canyon and we all went like this (turns head like he is listening) and we didn't hear anything. That's kind of weird right? There's a lot of stories about Secret Canyon that I will talk about at some point.

CP: It was fire in the sky you saw?

LS: I thought it was a comet that got through…that's what it looked like; it was very bright.

CP: Uh huh?

LS: Well, I get busy setting up three balloons, and eventually, off we go. When I land, we do a champagne celebration and a picnic. I don't ever remember talking about it. You would think someone would have said, "What do you think that was?" Well a few years go by and I'm in a coffee shop in Sedona and this local guy who wrote a book on the vortexes told me the exact same story [about the UFO]. I think, "That's odd; he saw the same UFO." A few more years go by, and I was working with some spiritual psychiatrists and the same story came up, but they told me, "What we are finding is that if the mind does not have reference point for it, it forgets."

CP: Like a form of denial?

LS: In the film, *What the Bleep Do We Know?*, they showed the Native Americans watching as three ships come in to shore. Now, they had never seen ships before. They did not see the ships, but they noticed the wake because they had a reference point from whales and seals. It was the next morning that the shaman and medicine woman noticed the wake was still there and eventually saw the ships. When I talk about UFO sightings, I need to bring that up. With the naked eye, it is very limited, I will talk about that and more about sipapus and portals.[107]

Sprague used the term *sipapu,* a Hopi word for a dimensional portal or "gate" through which they believe their ancient ancestors first emerged from a lower realm up to the present world. On the Wolf Lodge

Cultural Foundation website, Robert Ghost Wolf explains that "Sipa-poos" [*sic*] are "the windows as the old-timers called them, windows to the Otherworldly."[108] Today, these portals are immortalized by modern-day Puebloans and Hopi as a small indentation in the floor of their kivas (ritual rooms). In the image pictured here, the sipapu is the small hole to the left; the larger hole on the right is a fire pit.

The sipapu portal is the small hole on the front left.[109]

At least conceptually, ancient indigenous thinking seems remarkably similar to modern notions involving parallel universes, multidimensional string theory, and interdimensional travel. Anthropologist Brian Ross explains that "the notion of a cosmic portal, a doorway that permits translocation of shamans, spirits, and deities between worlds or levels of the cosmos, is part of a Mesoamerican cosmological tradition."[110] A pueblo shrine "is the doorway of communication between the many simultaneous levels"[111] by providing "a flow of energy between this plane of reality and other concurrent realities."[112] The ancestral pueblo residents of Chaco Canyon cut ramps into the cliff rock to connect the roadways on the canyon tops to the sites on the valley bottom. The longest and most famous of these roads is the Great North Road. It represents the connection to the sipapu, the place of emergence of the ancestors or a dimensional doorway. During their journey from the sipapu to the world of the living, the spirits stop along the road and eat the food left for them by the living.

The Watcher angels have played gods by accepting worship from the Native American peoples. Astronomy certainly played an important role in the ancient pueblo culture, and prophecies like the Blue Star Kachina predict celestial events as harbingers of divine judgment. Sakina Blue Star, a local woman of Sioux, Choctaw-Cherokee heritage, writes:

> The area was known as an interdimensional portal. Star People were said to have touched down in ancient times. It was easier for them to come and go here because of the special energies and frequencies. Native Americans kept their contact with other Galactic peoples secret for centuries but now some of them have begun to share their knowledge.[113]

At the end of our outing with Sprague, he took us to a stone-circle medicine wheel and began to play his flute. Medicine wheels, or sacred hoops, are stone monuments used for Native American religious, ritual, healing, and teaching purposes. Traditionally, folks walk around the circle until the flute melody stops, prompting the shaman to give a "reading." However, as Christians, we did not feel it was appropriate to participate in this New Age adaptation of an Indian religious rite. New Age author Richard Dannelley wrote, "We know intuitively that ceremonies that are similar to the medicine wheel open up interdimensional portals that allow Christ Consciousness energies to enter the planetary grid."[114] Unbeknownst to us, we were about to receive a ten-thousand-volt jolt of so-called "Christ Consciousness energy" that afternoon, albeit it wasn't as Christ-like as it sounds.

The Bell Rock Mother Ship and Spiritual Warfare

On our second day in Sedona, we visited the famous vortex site Bell Rock. We set up our cameras, and I began describing and commenting on film details of an 1980s event when thousands of folks gathered to witness what they believed was going to be a giant alien mothership emerging from the enormous red rock formation. At the time, reporters Joe McNeill and Steven Korn of *Sedona Monthly* wrote:

> On August 16, 1987, Sedona attracted thousands of believers to The Harmonic Convergence, an international event based on the Mayan calendar. The celebration honored an unusual planetary alignment said to usher in an age of peace and harmony. During the festival, a rumor spread that the top of Bell Rock would open and a spaceship would rise from within to depart for the galaxy of Andromeda. A reported crowd of 2,000 to 5,000 people showed up to witness the event, some even paying up to $150 for tickets to sit on Bell Rock at the moment of takeoff.[115]

José Arguelles, the chief promoter of the 1987 Harmonic Convergence, was asked if the event would include increased UFO activity. Arguelles answered, "Yes, I believe there will considerable UFO activity. More importantly, I believe there will be a message collectively received. The UFOs will be in many places. Perhaps at so-called sacred sites, but maybe in largely populated centers as well."[116]

Bell Rock: Home of the mothership?[117]

Of course, both the Harmonic Convergence and the Bell Rock mothership launch were colossal disappointments for the New Age devotees. As I was standing in front of Bell Rock delivering my commentary about this to the camera, a blonde woman (who will remain anonymous as "HK") pulled up in a rented white economy car, parked, and approached. The audio recorder was running during the conversation that ensued, and, given this was a public space with no expectation of privacy, the audio recorder was left running. The following is an accurate transcription of our exchange. As a helpful pretext, we commend the reader to keep this passage in mind: "And no marvel; for Satan himself is transformed into an angel of light. Therefore it is no great thing if his ministers also be transformed as the ministers of righteousness; whose end shall be according to their works" (2 Corinthians 11:14–15).

HK: What are you guys filming?

CP: I was just commenting on the events of the 1980s when thousands of people gathered here at Bell Rock during the harmonic convergence to see a large ET mothership emerge from Bell Rock.

HK: Oh that's just Sedona [BS], but I can call down light ships! I was here, I was with José for the harmonic convergence. It was about the earth's position in universe and the Mayan calendar. It had nothing to do with UFOs coming or anything, that's [BS]. It has to do with the transformation in the equinox every 2600 years.

CP: Uh-huh, the procession thing?

CF (Chris Florio, cameraman): Is this where we are dipping below the plane of the galaxy and back up and stuff like that?

HK: I don't know, but I just flew with the CEO of NASA like last week out of Washington. I got upgraded to first class. He doesn't know that much about it, but I asked him how much of it is real science. There's an element of real science, it was all about the Mayan's cultural relationship of the earth to the universe. It has to do with what is scientifically happening. The whole UFO [BS] story…it's like…there's a lot of…uh, I've seen a lot of UFOs. I go to the international UFO conference.

CP: So what is a light ship?

HK: It's a UFO.

CP: Where do they come from?

HK: There's other intelligence in the universe.

CP: Do you think they come from other planets or another dimension?

HK: I believe in the ancient astronaut theory.

CP: So you think they are coming from other planets?

HK: No, dimensions…

CP: OK, well yes, that can go one way or the other, and there are different opinions on that.

HK: What's the book that you wrote?

CP: The one on UFOs is called *Exo-Vaticana*. We visited Mount Graham Arizona where the Vatican has an observatory and toured that facility.

HK: Really? The Vatican has an observatory?

SP (Shelley Putnam): It's called LUCIFER.

HK: It's called LUCIFER?

CP: Yes, it's an instrument on the most powerful telescope in the world.

HK: I heard that they are doing work on…you know this was meant to happen right?

CF: Sure, please step in front of the camera. You can debunk the spaceship coming out of Bell Rock story if you like.

[At this point, we continue our discussion and it is revealed that she's been involved with alternative health legislation. We exchanged names and she introduced herself, but we will keep this anonymous.]

HK: Hi Cris, this is what I heard is happening with the Vatican: There's another telescope at the University of Arizona in Tucson, see there's a planet coming into our geocosmic atmosphere that is made out of gamma, and telescopes can't see it, and that's what…

CF: Made out of gamma?

HK: Gamma rays, and that's what Nostradamus said, that's planet X and the Vatican has created a telescope that can see it and that's what supposed to be going on…I asked the CEO of NASA if had heard of it and he hasn't.

CP: There are three telescopes on Mount Graham; I have been to the facility.

[Skip discussion about where we live, etc.]

CF: We are about to take a tour with someone who can basically conjure UFOs.

HK: I can…

CP: So are you saying you can get UFOs to come down? Can you get them on camera? If we set up somewhere, can you do that?

HK: How many nights are you going to be here?

CP: Tonight's the last night.

HK: What time are you going out with them?

CP: We're going in the afternoon; we should be back by early evening.

HK: If you want to, I will bring you out here. Here, I'll give you my number, but you have to come on a tour with me, OK can you handle that? I run a nonprofit, just make a donation for my time. Just a hundred dollars.

CP: If we can get a UFO on camera, I will give you a hundred bucks.

HK: I don't know, I'm not guaranteeing, it depends on how clear your energy is; I'll go where they came out before. I don't know if they'll show up for you. It has to do with your motivation and why you want them to show up.

CP: How do they know that?

HK: Since I was a little girl, I was picked up and flown around as a little girl; I'm a medical intuitive psychic doctor. I teach all over. I live in Kauai; I see ships, they show up. Let me test you, I have to test you.

CP: Uh huh?

HK: Let me see your eyes. How many light ships have you seen?

CP: I don't know that I have ever seen a light ship, but I've seen some things in the sky I could not identify.

HK: There was a mothership that was around Sedona, but it left in 1990. I'm a T-five contactee. I believe ancient astronaut theory, we were all apes and then we got modified…

CP: You mean according to Zechariah Sitchin's work?

HK: According to the Book of Enoch.

CP: I've read that book; I don't think so.

HK: It's in the Book of Enoch.

CP: No, the Book of Enoch is pretty consistent with the Hebrew Bible.

HK: No, you have to look for it. Are you Jewish, by any chance?

CP: No, but I have studied those texts and that information is not in there.

HK: Ancient astronaut theory says it is…

CP: They really stretch the evidence quite a bit and are not credible.

HK: Angels, the kingdom of Heaven…there are dark entities; that's why I am checking you out. You've got to open up to the Mayan cosmology. The Mayans all knew that we are interconnected to the universe, and that's what the convergence was supposed to do. José did ecstasy and he became crazy and he thought he was the reincarnation of the great Mayan guru. I haven't talked to him in years. You have to be careful; people get killed doing this. They don't like this.

CP: Who are "they"?

HK: The government, they don't like people looking into this. The only reason we will have contact with the ETs right now is because we are about to be annihilated by gamma rays; planet x is coming. You don't think that's true?

[We try to explain the nature of gamma rays and planets and why you cannot make a planet from rays.]

CP: She is talking about Planet X or Nibiru. But it is based on the work of Zechariah Sitchin, and his so called translations of the Sumerian texts have been proven false by Dr. [Michael] Heiser. It seems like Sitchin just made a lot of it up. So, most of the Planet X stuff is bogus.

HK: OK, if we do make UFO contact, until I tell you, it stays private. You can't exploit it. I don't know if you're open to this… I don't know if you're ready to have contact. I think it would shatter your universe.

CP: I'm just skeptical.

HK: Yeah I know you are…

CP: Absolutely.

HK: If you have an experience, what's going to happen?

CF: My worldview is similar to his, and I think these things are actually demons.

HK: I've seen demons, but what I contact is not demons.

CP: Do you really think it's so obvious? What if they appear in such a way as to seem like they are good, like an angel of light?

HK: Are you, like, Christians trying to debunk this?

CP: Yeah. We are Christians.

HK: Well that's OK, so you're trying to…

CF: Understand it with a Christian lens.

CP: Not necessarily trying to debunk it unless it seems to be false. I don't have a presupposition that it is necessarily false.

HK: I'm totally into the kingdom of Heaven of Jesus. I just did a healing this morning in the blood of Jesus for someone who is all messed up. I'm Jewish, so I believe Jesus was a great healer and he was a Jewish rabbi and I've been to ministry school and everything, but I do think there is a larger universe out there. In the Bible there are people who have seen things.

CP: Oh absolutely, but not aliens.

HK: Gabriel and Raphael and all of those angels.

CF: We believe that these things are increasingly manifesting into our reality as we get close to the end times, if we are not in it already.

CP: You see when someone says to me, "I can summon light ships" like you did, it raises concern because there is a letter written by the apostle Paul to the church in Corinth in the New Testament that warns them about false apostles deceiving them, and he says, "It is no wonder because Satan appears as an angel of light."

HK: I know, but it's different; it's not the same.

CP: How do you know that?

HK: Because I've been doing a lot of research and work around this.

CP: But how do you know? What research would lead you identify it as a good light ship instead of a deceptive one? How do you decide? By feelings?

HK: If it's a dark one, I state my intentions; I'm not interested.

CP: But why do they have to obey you?

HK: Because…. Alright, do you know the Bhagavad Gita?

CP: Yes, I know what it is.

HK: It was all about the wars in the heavens and it was before the Bible. There are wars in the heavens.

CP: Oh absolutely, but that is in the Bible, too.

HK: Well, that's the dark ships and the light ships. I've already done my spiritual warfare, so I don't go there and I'm not interested.

SP: That doesn't mean they aren't interested in you.

HK: They're interested in me, but I don't given them any attention. You have authority over that.

CP: Yes, I do, but only through Jesus.

HK: If you take into the older texts that were written before Jesus showed up, like the Tibetans, they were around a long time before Jesus.

CP: We don't have any texts from them that are that old.

HK: Well, seven hundred, but they weren't into religious dogma, when the religious doctrine came in they shut out, the pope in Rome shut out a lot of mysticism around 500 AD. It gave too much power to the people and the religious figures stayed in control. It's more about Christ consciousness.

SP: You mean Pope Gregory?

CP: In 500 AD, there really wasn't a universal pope over the whole church and the biblical canon as it exists today was in place long before that.

HK: They took out a lot of the mystical texts then.

CP: That's not true.

HK: It is, too.

CP: It's absolutely false;, the canon was established by 300 something.

CF: She probably means the gnostic books.

CP: Yes, but most of them were written around 300, and they were not excluded because they were mystical, but because they were patently false and often absurd.

HK: According to who they were false?

CP: Have you ever read them? They make ridiculous claims like Jesus was thousands of feet tall after the resurrection, and His cross could talk. What you are saying is just not true, we have writings from the Church Fathers that prove they had decided which books were authentic long before 500 AD, and it had little to do with the Vatican.

SP: I think the difference between you and us is that we believe Jesus is God.

HK: I'm Messianic.

CP: If you are truly Messianic, then you should acknowledge that Jesus is God.

HK: I know, but you never say that to a Jew!

CP: Why not?

HK: Because we don't want to get genocide anymore!

CP: But "Messianic" means that you believe Jesus is God.

HK: You guys have killed so many Jews in the name of religion.

CP: I have written about that, too; we are not Catholics.

HK: It's all the same thing!

CF: No.

SP: No.

CP: No, it's not the same thing. I don't think you understand what "Messianic" really means.

HK: It's the same, it's the same; it's the same.

SP: No, it's not.

CF: I wish I could convince you that it's not; Catholicism is not the same thing as Christianity.

CP: If you are really Messianic, then you would have no problem with the idea that Jesus is God.

SP: That is what Messianic means.

CF: And you have the best of both worlds as a Jewish believer becau…

HK: (Cuts him off.) Stop it; don't do that to a Jew—never proselytize or push that to a Jew.

CP: But it was *you* who said you are Messianic, and that is what the term means.

HK: Stop it, stop it, it's toxic and I don't want to see you. You Christians are the most evil people. [Screaming:] *You are the most evil people, ever!*[118]

At this point, she drove off in a rage and threw the copy of *The Supernatural Worldview* I had given her out the window of her car onto the Coconino National Forest roadway (we retrieved it after it had been run over by a few cars). It seems the phrase "Jesus is God" stirred an irrational reaction that is hard to explain apart from spiritual warfare. When Jesus said, "Before Abraham was I am" (John 8:58), He was implicitly applying the divine name *Yahweh* to himself (cf. Exodus 3:14–15). Of course, insisting on the biblical Jesus brings division. Jesus taught, "Think not that I am come to send peace on earth: I came not to send peace, but a sword" (Matthew 10:34). Because of the Lord's warning, we believe HK's reaction had little to do with her Jewish ethnicity.

During the course of our conversation, she made quite a few incoherent and false claims. We weren't trying to proselytize as much as to offer some clarity as to what being a *Messianic* Jew actually entails. Later that evening, we verified her identity. She really has an earned PhD and is a practicing counselor. Lightship conjuring aside, in interest of charity, we decided not to use her full name (even though it was in a public area with no reasonable expectation of privacy).

Since the idea that "Jesus is God" was so offensive, what is one to make of her claim that she had recently performed a healing "by the blood of Jesus?" Please recall the previous discussion of the medicine wheel ceremony that Dannelley suggested could "open up interdimensional portals that allow Christ Consciousness energies to enter the planetary grid."[119] Yet, in the same book, he also conceded, "There is a tremendous amount of evidence to suggest that humanity is being manipulated by what can be best described as alien mind control."[120] We ostensibly agree and defer to the chapter, "The Powers and Principalities

Planetary Control Grid," in our former work *Exo-Vaticana* for a thorough explanation of the "control grid hypothesis"[121] offered by Jacques Vallee in terms of biblical theology.

We contend that "Christ consciousness" is a true anti-Christ theology in the sense of the prefix "anti" denoting "instead of" Christ. Remember, only a few decades after Jesus' resurrection and ascension, the apostle John wrote, "Little children, it is the last time: and as ye have heard that antichrist shall come, even now are there many antichrists; whereby we know that it is the last time" (1 John 2:18). Jesus is identified differently, depending on one's worldview and the intervention of the Holy Spirit.

In the canonical Gospels, Jesus skillfully inquired as to how He was being identified:

> When Jesus came into the coasts of Caesarea Philippi, he asked his disciples, saying, Whom do men say that I the Son of man am?
>
> And they said, Some say that thou art John the Baptist: some, Elias; and others, Jeremias, or one of the prophets.
>
> He saith unto them, But whom say ye that I am?
>
> And Simon Peter answered and said, Thou art the Christ, the Son of the living God. (Matthew 16:13–16)

Peter's confession caused Jesus to reply:

> Blessed art thou, Simon Barjona: for flesh and blood hath not revealed it unto thee, but my Father which is in heaven.
>
> And I say also unto thee, That thou art Peter, and upon this rock I will build my church; and the gates of hell shall not prevail against it. (Matthew 16:17–18)

Early in the first century, Paul wrote to the Corinthians about similar deception, warning that there would be those who preach "another Jesus, whom we have not preached, or…another spirit, which ye have not received, or another gospel, which ye have not accepted" (2 Corinthians 11:4). Thus, it should not be too surprising that the New Age movement has fashioned a different Jesus more amicable to their pantheistic monistic belief.

HK was in Sedona for "Sedona World Wisdom Days,"[122] a metaphysical conference featuring the infamous Barbara Marx Hubbard. Hubbard explains the New Age Jesus in terms of *Christ consciousness*:

> Christ-consciousness and Christ-abilities are the natural inheritance of every human being on Earth. When the word of this hope has reached the nations, the end of this phase of evolution shall come. All will know their choice. All will be required to choose.... All who choose not to evolve will die off; their souls will begin again within a different planetary system which will serve as kindergarten for the transition from self-centered to whole-centered being. The kindergarten class of Earth will be over. Humankind's collective power is too great to be inherited by self-centered, infantile people.[123]

Concerning the identity of the "infantile people," Hubbard's later works offer more clarity. She wrote, "'Christ' states that those who see themselves as 'separate' and not 'divine' hinder humanity's ability to spiritually evolve. Those who deny their own 'divinity' are like 'cancer cells' in the body of God."[124] In other words, folks with a supernatural worldview—who make a creator/creation distinction—are like cancer cells. Oneism entails that everything and everyone, including vilest evil, is divine. There can be no separation.

Biblical Christianity's exclusive truth claim is the primary offense. Jesus claimed that He was the only way to the Father (John 14:6) and that "narrow is the way, which leadeth unto life, and few there be that find it" (Matthew 7:14b). Hubbard wrote, "The selection process will exclude all who are exclusive. The selection process assures that only the loving will evolve to the stage of co-creator."[125] However, there is nothing inherently unloving about exclusivity. Exclusivity is very often a virtue. For example, most of us, Christian or not, prefer that our marriage partners remain exclusive in their sexuality. Another example is offering one's testimony or bearing witness. People of integrity appreciate accuracy and honesty to the exclusion of fabrication and lies. But this idea is intolerable to the so-called religious tolerance crowd.

Hubbard is quite clear that one-fourth of the population—ostensibly traditional Christian believers—must be eliminated by the more illumined ones:

> Now, as we approach the quantum shift from creature-human to co-creative human the destructive one-fourth must be eliminated from the social body. Fortunately you, dearly beloveds, are not responsible for this act. We are. We are in charge of God's selection process for planet Earth. He selects, we destroy. *We are the riders of the pale horse, Death.*[126] (emphasis added)

Make no bones about it: That statement was a declaration of genocide. Although the New Age movement promises the moon (sometimes literally), it is always conditioned on one's acceptance of postmodern values. Please do not be deceived by dubious claims to "Christ consciousness."

The Bradshaw Ranch

Bob Bradshaw[128]

Located twelve miles outside of Sedona is the famous Bradshaw Ranch. It got its name when Hollywood stuntman Bob Bradshaw acquired the 140-acre ranch in 1960 for two hundred dollars an acre. At that time, all that remained of the original homestead was an old adobe house believed to be the oldest pioneer structure in the area. When he wasn't working in the movies, Bradshaw turned the property into a working ranch and movie set.

The western town set on the ranch served as the primary location for five movies, two television series, and many commercials. In total, more than fifty full-length motion pictures were shot in the area.[128] An original Marlboro man (who didn't smoke), Bradshaw was a stunt double for many leading stars, including Jimmy Stewart, John Wayne, Robert Mitchum, Beau Bridges, Kenny Rogers, and even Elvis Presley. The "Crocodile Dundee" (aka Paul Hogan) Subaru commercials were mostly filmed at the ranch, as well as many other commercials and photo shoots.[129]

Vegetation in the area consists primarily of pinon pines, juniper trees, Arizona cypress, cottonwood trees, mesquite trees, prickly pear cactus, agave cactus, sagebrush, and tumbleweed, along with various other shrubs and bushes.[130] Trees only reach around twelve to fifteen feet in height, and most are scrubby and bush-like. The western town of Hollywood fame was torn down by the forestry service, but the ranch house and round, fenced, livestock fields can still be seen on Google Earth. Lately, the most photographed part of the ranch is the locked gate.

John Bradshaw, Bob's son, explained why he originally started "A Day in West" tour business: "In 1997, the property taxes on my dad's ranch jumped from $2,500 per year to $25,000. I developed the Jeep tour business as a way to help bankroll the purchase of the ranch."[131] At that time, tourists spent a full day on the still-working ranch or classic western movie set. Folks so inclined could even play cowboy for a day on horseback. A Day in the West quickly became a popular attraction. Nevertheless, the property was acquired by the US Forestry Service in April of 2001 for $3.5 million.[132] What remains unexplained is why the federal agency has forbidden access to the tax-paying public (who paid for the land) since May 10, 2003.[133] The word on the street in Sedona is that the government is covering up a virtual invasion of interdimensional entities coming through a wide-open dimensional corridor.

Dimensional corridors are held by physicists to be theoretically possible. Astrophysicist Hugh Ross gives a scientific explanation: "If a black hole connected to one sheet of space-time in the universe happens to make contact with another black hole connected to a different sheet of space-time, that point of contact may (hypothetically) offer a travel corridor."[134] Interestingly, he has also pointed out the occult connection to residual (unexplained) unidentified flying objects (RUFOs): "Observations reveal that professional astronomers deeply involved in cultic, occultic, or certain New Age pursuits often see RUFOs, whereas professional astronomers who stay away from such pursuits never encounter RUFOs."[135] Perhaps this data is explained by the fact that occult and New Age activities potentiate interdimensional portals?

In magical practice, such passages are assumed. A local occultist, David Miller, explains: "Corridors are tunnels of energy connecting the fifth dimension to the third. In a sense, they are interdimensional, they exist in neither dimension yet connect to both.... There are many corridors in the Southwest, including around Sedona and the Grand Canyon."[136] Other areas include the San Luiz Valley, Colorado; Skinwalker Ranch, Utah; ECETI Ranch, Washington; Yakima, Washington; and Mount Shasta, California.

We believe the case for extra dimensions, made in *Exo-Vaticana* and bolstered by the work now in your hands, supports identifying the most active hotspots as entry zones. If finding such a gateway is even a remote possibility, then Sedona's Bradshaw Ranch is a top candidate. After living on the ranch for two years, Linda Bradshaw observed:

> I believe these openings have always been on our plane and they've perhaps been the portals to allow others in, but if one were to ask my opinion of my experiences regarding this magical place, I would say that not only are they being allowed in, but they are coming in in great numbers. I would also love to say that only compassionate beings of light are scooting through these portals, but this does not always seem to be the case. I have come face to face with a few decidedly nasty beings.[137]

Her appraisal is refreshing because interdimensional entities are usually discussed in the glowing terms of a New Age. We were also encouraged that the former Mrs. Bradshaw (who now goes by Linda Ball) prudently aligned with the God of the Bible, offering this advice, "It is important that one declares his or her position (who one is and whom they serve) and knows this to be true." And then finishing with Isaiah 6:3 'Holy, Holy, Holy is the Lord God of Hosts.'"[138] It's difficult to dismiss her testimony because she displayed good instincts. For example, after an encounter with the Greys, she remarked, "They did not leave me with a particularly good feeling."[139] Bradshaw Ranch or not, a negative assessment of the Greys should come as no surprise to our readers.

Over a decade ago, Tom Horn wrote, "This is what I was talking about from the moment I mentioned time-dimensional doorways, and the entities that can and do move through them. Since the beginning of time and on every continent of the world the record bears the frightening image of those who often come through." While the entities change over time, the similar features (like an overly large head) are remarkable.

It seems likely that Sedona has been one of the main demonic doorways in the United States since 1980. The flood of false spirituality and theological error coming from the region is unprecedented. While it's far from an exact science, the magnetic anomalies, coupled with so much documented vortex and portal lore, leads us to suspect an open preternatural portal area. No other region in the continental United States compares when it comes to identified vortexes. Whether this is a Jungian consciousness-driven phenomenon or one quantifiable by materialist science, or some of both, is still open to interpretation. We suspect both. According to *UFO Digest*, Bradshaw Ranch "has seen more paranormal activity in recent years than perhaps any other US location. So much so, it appears to have attracted the attention of the US federal government. A cluster of paranormal activity has been reported; from sightings of strange humanoid entities, to the pulsating lights of UFOs—and the most massive amount of orb activity ever witness by this investigator."[140] Bradshaw Ranch is one of the primary reasons we came to Sedona.

A Day in the Weird, Wild West

In order to investigate the phenomenon, we arranged to take the "orb and conspiracy theory tour"[141] with Bradshaw's "A Day in West" event. Standing six feet, two inches tall, at 250 pounds, our guide only gave the name "Hoss." Sporting a tan cowboy hat, his authentic western poncho concealed an iPhone, hunting knife, and a Smith and Wesson revolver. Bradshaw Point was declared "no man's land" by the US government, but even they can't stop us from looking over it from a high point. At least with a gun-toting cowboy in the lead, we were prepared for the worst if it came.

Putnam with Hoss on Bradshaw Point

We pulled up to Bradshaw Hill, overlooking the ranch to the west, the surrounding canyons north and northeast, and Sedona to the south-east (follow footnoted link to Google Maps).[142] The weather conditions were optimal between 5:00 and 7:00 p.m. on January 15, 2015. When we arrived, the temperature was around 54 degrees, and it cooled to the mid forties as the sun went down. Humidity went from a daytime 35 percent up to 50 percent at nightfall. There was a light breeze around twelve miles per hour[143] when we got out of the car and began setting up our gear.

Getting down to business, our guide pulled out a magnetometer, which quickly spiked, giving a highly anomalous reading. Fortunately, my previous training paid off here.

Parapsychological Field Investigator Certification

In preparation for writing the *Supernatural Worldview: Examining Paranormal, Psi, and the Apocalyptic*, I studied the scientific discipline of parapsychology and completed specific training in filed investigation with degreed parapsychologist Loyd Auerbach, MS.[144] I learned that of all the fanciful instruments used on ghost-hunting shows, magnetometers have real evidential merit. Auerbach found that his magnetometers detect "unusually high magnetic field[s]" at the spots where "ghosts" are seen.[145] He also found that magnetometers register high readings when people communicate with an apparition, and the readings fall back down when the communication ceases.[146] A portal researcher, Phillip Imbrogno, observed, "What all these interdimensional vortex and window areas have in common around the world is that they all sit right on top of a number of magnetic anomalies with an intermediate electromagnetic pulse."[147] If Keel, Auerbach, and Imbrogno's theories are correct, then the high magnetic field reading we observed upon arrival at Bradshaw Hill might indicate a spirit, an interdimensional portal, both, or another nearby anomaly. As the night progressed, the interdimensional inference was corroborated.

The portal hypothesis was only on the table for our research because of previous documentation of related anomalous activity. The books *Merging Dimensions*[148] and *Dimensional Journey*[149] feature copyrighted photographs of orbs, UFOs, and even Bigfoot tracks. Also, the anecdotal evidence for a portal at the ranch is compelling. After living there a few years with her children, Linda Ball (formerly married to Bob Bradshaw) wrote:

> My perception of reality was tested and questioned again and again as I had encounters with extraterrestrials, Bigfoot and other humanlike entities that towered over me. I was able to photograph much of the phenomena, which began rather benignly with wafting, multi-colored orbs of light, then escalated over seven years to the more heart-stopping episodes where I encountered and interacted with otherworldly beings.[150]

After one particularly scary incident involving flying saucers, Ball writes that Bob thought *she* (Linda) was an extraterrestrial and refused to let her back in the house. She wrote, "As he later confessed to me, he suspected that I was one of 'them' and he was therefore afraid of me. This was tragic. It took about two hours before he relented and unlocked the doors, allowing me to come in out of the cold."[151] While Mr. Bradshaw passed away in 2008 and is unable to give his side of the story, one is hard pressed to imagine the rough-and-tumble cowboy in such a state of terror. Ball and Bradshaw eventually split up. Linda now lives in Montana. John Bradshaw, their son, still lives in Sedona operating the tour company that we hired for this investigation.

Merely suggesting the existence of an interdimensional portal is controversial, but there is supporting evidence. On the way to Bradshaw Hill, Hoss admitted that he was initially skeptical, but became a fast believer after only two outings. With half a dozen or so UFO and orb tours based in Sedona (some are led by self-identified alien abductees), it's becoming a common testimony.[152] In a *New York Times* article titled "Abandoning Doubt in Sedona, Arizona," a skeptical reporter concedes,

"In approximately two hours, we counted about 40 unidentifiable things flying high above us."[153] After more than twenty-five years of investigating, Tom Dongo claims to have witnessed and photographed flying and stationary light orbs of different sizes, shapes, and colors many thousands of times.[154] He also believes the evidence supports the existence of some sort of portal. "Some of these lights would fly around some, then either blink out or fly off into the distance. Clearly, after observing for so long, it was evident to me that most of these lights originated from the same point—or points. This would indicate some sort of entrance point, or portal."[155] After completing our field investigation, we agree.

I have never been an orb believer, because most of what I've seen looks to be dust particles, drops of water, moisture on the lens, and things of that nature. Even so, my experience on Bradshaw Hill changed my mind. At dusk, we captured a vivid orb on video without using flash photography. Even though there was no wind, it moved extremely fast, changed direction, and then faded out of existence. A short video clip is available at the footnote here.[156] While the clip is too brief to evidence intelligence, it seems to make an evasive maneuver. Another elusive orb had earlier been seen from this same hill that "seemed to know people were trying to get a shot of it. It would always blink out just before the shutter was tripped or the camcorder was focused."[157]

Alternating positions with my wife, one of us awkwardly posed while the other snapped off shots using flash, with a Canon Powershot SX40HS. All the while, our videographer (Chris Florio) continuously shot video. This allowed for rigorous review of the video, when anomalies are in the still image. If a ball of light appears on both cameras, then most common natural phenomena created by dust and moisture close to or on the lens of the flash-enabled camera are excluded. Accordingly, in this book, the orb evidence considered appears on both cameras. Bright-light orbs are clearly seen in photos and video shot simultaneously from different angles. On one occasion, the videographer saw a light orb with the naked eye that was later confirmed on the photo and video, available at the footnote here.[158] It appears to be the size of a grapefruit about ten to twelve feet behind Putnam.

White light above Putnam appears on video and photo.

In the distance, we saw a fast-moving UFO. Flashing across the sky with untold speed, it was gone before we could aim a camera toward it. Clearly, there was a multifaceted phenomenon manifestation throughout the area at that time. According to our guide, these orbs are spirits from nearby Indian burial mounds. We believe the variety of behavior and appearance leaves multiple explanations open for consideration: spirits, spook lights, and earth lights.

First, the weight of testimony suggests that spirit entities and interdimensional beings are crossing over from the nearby portal. Regarding our fast, jerking orb from the first video, L. A. Marzulli replied:

I think you captured an orb on film. In Watchers 1 we showed pictures of hundreds of orbs flying into ECETI ranch. Then there's the one clip where a man is standing in the field where these orbs appear and one flew into the back of his neck and doesn't come out again. Posession? Maybe, and this is why I believe the orbs may actually be what disembodied spirits look like.[159]

While this notion is the most common, opinions vary. Max Greiner and Joie Pirkey believe that God's holy angels travel about in orb form. Pirkey has many interesting photos taken during worship services.[160] Of course, in the Bible even "angels" are a bifurcated category ("holy" Acts 10:21; cf. "fallen" Matthew 25:41). Thus, the category "spirits" is likely multifaceted, and distinguishing characteristics are not easily discerned from such photographic evidence.

Second, some of the orbs behave like spook lights or ghost lights, traditionally called the *will-o'-the-wisp*. The ghost light phenomenon is known by a variety of names in English, including "hinkypunk,""jack-o'-lantern,""friars' lantern," and "hobby lantern."[161] Famous examples include the Brown Mountain lights of North Carolina, where for more than one hundred years, "globes of various colored lights, ranging in size from mere points to 25 feet in diameter"[162] have been seen rising above the tall trees. Also, there is the notorious Joplin "Hornet" Spook Light, which "has appeared seemingly as a ball of fire for almost 140 years"[163] at the intersection of Spooksville, Oklahoma, and Joplin, Missouri. A recently declassified official US Air Force document reveals that a Project Blue Book investigator observed the Spook Light for one and a half hours through binoculars. The report describes the orb as "four times the size of a basketball with bright white light" emitting a "red flame trailing" as it moved about silently.[164]

Third, some orbs might be earth lights. A similar portal is believed to be located on the Yakima Indian Reservation on the east side of the Cascade Mountains in southern Washington state. Some researchers, scientists, and geologists try to explain these orbs as a natural phenomenon known as earth lights:

There are similar areas around the world which are termed "windows" by Earthlight researchers with these fault line areas where UFO activity or "Earthlight activity" is very strong. Hessdalen Valley of Norway is a good example. I will not discount the Earthlight theory entirely because one must be open to all possibilities not just one when researching the unknown. There certainly exists evidence to suggest that there could indeed be some natural form of energy that releases itself in the form of balls of light or some kind of gases, however this in my opinion does not mean that all of the UFO activity at Yakima can be explained away as earthlights.[165]

According to Greg Long, author of *Examining the Earthlight Theory*, "The majority of the UFO sightings mentioned by Long involved ball-shaped nocturnal lights. Frequently, they were reddish orange and interacted with observers."[166] The description matches the orb we caught on video at the Bradshaw ranch. Long also reported strange humanoids, apparitions, and Bigfoot sightings. Astrophysicist Hugh Ross—a Christian scholar at Reasons to Believe—concurs with Jacques Vallee's writing, saying, "Written records of ancient sightings dating back at least three thousand years document the same highly luminous balls and multicolored disks, breaking up and coming together, darting around at velocities and accelerations that defy the laws of physics."[167] Whatever they turn out to be, it seems such orbs have always been seen.

Colored orbs on the 1561 celestial phenomenon over Nuremberg painting[168]

Secret Canyon's Not-So-Secret Underground Base

There have been rumors about an underground base near Sedona for decades. The locals have many interesting stories. For example, Hoss told me about a winged, tubular spaceship witnessed flying over Sedona by many witnesses. He described it as larger than conventional aircraft, moving absolutely silently at high velocity. He said so many people eventually reported it that the government finally admitted that it was a NASA spaceship designed to replace the space shuttle. Of course, this begs the question of where it was flying from and where it landed. Our stout guide confirmed his belief in an underground base and pointed out how primordial volcanic lava tubes already provide convenient underground access to the canyons. After hearing about the tunnels, rumors of an underground base in Secret Canyon were beginning to seem more probable.

While the existence of a base is nearly uncontroversial with locals, conspiracy lore entails rival alien bases in addition to the defense department facility. One witness who happened upon the base by accident was "accosted at gunpoint by a soldier wearing United Nations insignia."[169] We might have captured evidence of top-secret aircraft without even realizing it at the time.

Sights mentioned

Shelley Putnam captured this triangle UFO as it flew by in the distance. The pine tree offers perspective, and the sharp triangle shape appears like a three-dimensional object in the distance would, if it were heading toward Secret Canyon. Arizona is famous for the Phoenix Lights case involving an enormous triangle that flew over that major city. Like that craft, this one also flew silently. In fact, we didn't notice it in the image until we returned home to analyze the photos. The tree gives some scale and implies a large, three-dimensional object some distance away.

Taken over Secret Canyon

Daniel Wright, the graphic artist who designs our book covers, did some Photoshop analysis in the images pictured here.

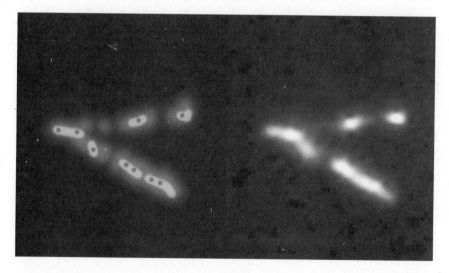

Triangle UFO with image enhanced by Daniel Wright

Wright says about the image: "I did a forced enlargement and then attempted a simple recreation of what I saw in the photograph on three layers (top) main points of light small (left) bars of connected light (right) soft general glows. I figured by enlarging and sort of 'mapping' the main patterns of light I could help identify [what the shape is]."[170] We also sent the photo to Stan Deyo.

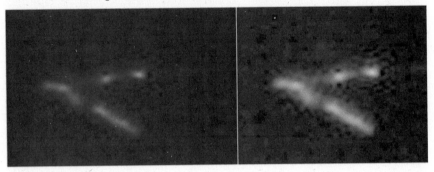

Image enhanced by Stan Deyo

Deyo offered:

> I performed a number of analyses of this photo. As you can see there are two possibly three dark spots along the near edge of the craft. The far edge lights are all illuminated while the near edge is partially illuminated. If the illumination is a function of propulsion then perhaps the craft was turning so one side was more illuminated than the other. The dark circular spots may indicate that the bright lights are generated between two poles...possibly.[171]

We are not suggesting that this is an extraterrestrial craft, but rather the more humble claim that it remains unidentified and is appropriately dubbed a UFO. Admittedly, most black triangle UFO sightings reported to MUFON are closed and marked "identified." When so ruled, they are almost always terrestrial aircraft of some sort. Either way, our triangle craft may support the presence of a secret underground base in the fortuitously christened *Secret Canyon*. Our triangle might even be something exotic like the classified TR-3B antigravity spacecraft.[172] Most likely, there are more than a few skunk works craft being tested over the desert. One can watch a triangle being escorted by planes on YouTube at the footnote here.[173] While talk of underground bases often suggests an aluminum foil milliner marketing ploy, fantastic stories are nothing new to Sedona.

Although the idea that there are alien bases near Secret Mountain is labeled a conspiracy theory, it is not without decent anecdotal evidence. A case from the summer of 1992 of an "out of this world" military escort would naturally suggest an alien presence. Richard Dannelly wrote, "What makes this sighting particularly amazing is that the flying disk was being accompanied by four fighter jets in formation!"[174] The local witness who remains anonymous for obvious reasons was with a Vietnam veteran, who went by the name Wolfdancer. He had been in Sedona a month after spending many weeks around Mount Shasta, California, capturing UFOs on video. The two men were in the Dry Creek area trying to spot UFOs when a flying disk accompanied by four fighter planes appeared in broad daylight over Capitol Butte toward Secret Mountain. According to the remaining witness, Wolfdancer even "had footage of what appeared to be portals opening up near the summit of the mountain and UFOs flying into them!"[175] Unfortunately, he went missing shortly after this incident. Given the suspicious circumstances, his sudden disappearance suggests foul play.

It should not surprise us that the military has secret bases in the desert. Of course they need to develop and test top-secret fighter jets and spy craft. After talking to local residents and surveying message boards, we found that many people "personally witnessed black helicopters flying in formation towards the Long Canyon/Boynton Canyon area and other peculiar military activity."[176] The interdimensional hypothesis explains UFO behavior that defies known physical laws. Dannelley writes, "As for the manner in which the flying disk disappeared, we may theorize that there are some type of 'portals' in, around, or above Sedona that can be used to jump between the space/time location of Sedona and points unknown, presumably other star systems."[177] He suspects the military "may be attempting to control some of these portals."

Concerning the portals, we can't help notice that, even in New Age literature, more often than not, something dark and sinister is often implied. According to ancient prophecy, the dark trajectory culminates when the portals open. "And he opened the bottomless pit; and there arose a smoke out of the pit, as the smoke of a great furnace; and the sun and the air were darkened by reason of the smoke of the pit" (Revelation 9:2) and the prince of the power of the air is cast down. The heavenly host will proclaim, "Woe to the inhabiters of the earth and of the sea! for the devil is come down unto you, having great wrath, because he knoweth that he hath but a short time" (Revelation 12:12). As scary as dimensional denizens might seem, we are encouraged by the words of our Lord, "And when these things begin to come to pass, then look up, and lift up your heads; for your redemption draweth nigh" (Luke 21:28).

CHAPTER FOUR

History, Hopi Blue Star, Plumed Serpents, and the End Times

By Cris Putnam

his chapter first addresses the ancient history of the indigenous peoples associated with the Sedona, Arizona area, then examines Hopi prophecy, Mesoamerican plumed serpent gods, and how all of it might play out in terms of biblical eschatology.

The first documented human presence in the Sedona area is a Paleo-Indian tribe dating between 11500 and 9000 BC. The Clovis culture is a prehistoric Paleo-Indian culture, named after distinct stone tools found at sites near Clovis, New Mexico. Tribe members left an assortment of rock art in places near Sedona such as Palatki and Honanki.[178] (See image next page.)

The Hopi are likely connected back to the *Hisatsinom,* "ancient people," or *Anasazi,* "ancient enemy," of the Navajo.[179] The Hopi ancestors were the ancient peoples who constructed large pueblo complexes in northeastern Arizona, northwestern New Mexico, and southwestern Colorado. According to some estimates, they came to Angel Canyon at least ten thousand years ago. A thousand years ago, they had become a

Palatki near Sedona

peaceful farming society successful enough to turn its attention to astronomy, art, and establishing trade routes. These well-traveled paths spread their culture across the Southwest, even to the Toltecs of Mexico. Apparently a drought led to hard times, leading them to take refuge in high pueblos. Evidence suggests that bands of Toltec warrior-priests dedicated to the reptilian "Watcher" god of the *Tzcatlipoca-Xipe Totec* complex terrorized the area with human sacrifice and cannibalism.[180] Then, around 1350, it is theorized that the *Hisatsinom* vanished, abandoning their ancestral lands, including a significant population that migrated south, eventually forming a new culture known as the Hopi.

The name "Hopi" is a shortened form of *Hopituh Shi-nu-mu,* which means the "Peaceful People" or "Civilized People."[181] The Hopi reservation is in north-central Arizona and is approximately ninety-two miles northeast of Flagstaff. Originally, the Hopi were lumped together with the Navajo, but now they have their own space within a giant reservation area. It is part of Coconino and Navajo counties, encompasses more than 1.5 million acres, and is made up of twelve villages on three mesas. Interestingly, the Hopi have a bit in common with Christian premillennial futurists.

In Hopi prophecy, the Blue Star Kachina, or *Saquasohuh,* is said to be the ninth and final sign before the "Day of Purification," described as a catastrophe that will lead to the purification of planet earth. Speaking to the Continental Indigenous Council, Lee Brown stated, "We are now within the purification of all things. Non-Natives call this the 'Apocalypse.' The Native elders call this the 'Purification.'"[182]

As a featured commentator for the History Channel series *Countdown to Apocalypse* in 2012, I spoke to the massive earthquake predicted at the sixth seal in Revelation 6:12. Because both Christian and Hopi prophecy predict devastating earthquakes, episode 4, "Hopi Blue Star," makes for interesting comparison with Christian apocalyptic expectations. The following summary appears on the show's web page:

> The Hopi people have warned us that the world is headed for extinction. Based in the Arizona Desert, the Native American tribe of the Hopi has been prophesying about the fate of society for centuries. They have accurately predicted the coming of the settlers to their land, the birth of telecommunication, and the worldwide spread of the internet. The Hopi believe that our actions have caused the earth to become out of balance which will lead to a cataclysmic great purification of the planet that few will survive. To herald these end times, the Hopi believe that a blue star will arise in the heavens, followed by a great shaking of the earth. These prophecies have been passed down from generation to generation and warn of massive earthquakes, tsunamis and super-volcanoes that threaten the lives of millions.[183]

The famous Hopi end-time prophecy was preserved by Frank Waters in the *Book of the Hopi* (1963):

> World War III will be started by those peoples who first received the light [the divine wisdom or intelligence] in the other old countries [India, China, Egypt, Palestine, Africa].
>
> The United States will be destroyed, land and people, by atomic bombs and radioactivity. Only the Hopis and their homeland will be preserved as an oasis to which refugees will flee. Bomb shelters are a fallacy. "It is only materialistic people who seek to make shelters. Those who are at peace in their hearts already are in the great shelter of life.
>
> "There is no shelter for evil. Those who take no part in the making of world division by ideology are ready to resume life in another world, be they of the Black, White, Red, or Yellow race. They are all one, brothers."
>
> The war will be "a spiritual conflict with material matters.

Material matters will be destroyed by spiritual beings who will remain to create one world and one nation under one power, that of the Creator."

That time is not far off. It will come when the Saquasohuh [Blue Star] Kachina dances in the plaza. He represents a blue star, far off and yet invisible, which will make its appearance soon.[184]

While it is difficult to precisely date their origin, Hopi prophecies seem to have a good track record of coming to pass. If we accept the Hopi dating, then around two hundred years ago, the elders of the tribe predicted "roads in the sky" "moving houses of iron" and having "the ability to speak long distances through cobwebs."[185] What makes the Blue Star prophecy so intriguing is its consistency with biblical predictions and that the preceding eight signs arguably find accurate fulfillments in modern history—that is, if we accept the testimony of Hopi elder White Feather transcribed by Bob Frissell in 1958.

This is the First Sign: We are told of the coming of the white-skinned men, like Pahana, but not living like Pahana, men who took the land that was not theirs. And men who struck their enemies with thunder.

This is the Second Sign: Our lands will see the coming of spinning wheels filled with voices. In his youth, my father saw this prophecy come true with his eyes.

This is the Third Sign: A strange beast like a buffalo but with great long horns, will overrun the land in large numbers. These White Feather saw with his eyes.

This is the Fourth Sign: The land will be crossed by snakes of iron.

This is the Fifth Sign: The land shall be crisscrossed by a giant spider's web.

This is the Sixth sign: The land shall be crisscrossed with rivers of stone that make pictures in the sun.

This is the Seventh Sign: You will hear of the sea turning black, and many living things dying because of it.

This is the Eighth Sign: You will see many youth, who wear their hair long like my people, come and join the tribal nations, to learn their ways and wisdom.

And this is the Ninth and Last Sign: You will hear of a dwelling-place in the heavens, above the earth, that shall fall with a great crash. It will appear as a blue star. Very soon after this, the ceremonies of my people will cease.[186] (emphasis added)

Although we are not commending Hopi spirituality, it seems that the initial eight signs have largely been fulfilled and therefore refer to past events. The first sign is said to be a reference to the arrival of Europeans in North America, while the second is said to be a reference to the wagon trains and the pioneer exploration of North America. The third sign was the arrival of cattle with the Europeans. Fourth, the prophecy seems to describe the railroad, and the fifth describes the proliferation of telegraph, power, and telephone lines. The sixth sign is arguably our crisscrossing interstate highways as "rivers of stone." The seventh portent suggests an oil spill, of which several recent candidates come to mind, particularly the Deepwater Horizon spill of 2010. The text cited was written down in 1958, so, even then, the first six were fulfilled. Even so, the eighth sign did not ensue until at least a decade or so later with the sixties' hippies merging into the New Age movement and the ongoing movement toward pantheistic monism. White Feather presents these as ancient, but even if one remains skeptical, at least the publication date reveals the penultimate prediction was recorded over a decade before coming to pass.

The rationale behind examining the previous eight signs was to bolster the case for the ninth. Known as the "Hopi Blue Star Prophecy" or the "Blue Star Kachina," White Feather described: "You will hear of a dwelling-place in the heavens, above the earth, that shall fall with a great crash. It will appear as a blue star. Very soon after this, the ceremonies of my people will cease."[187] Thus, we come to: 1) World War III; 2) the destruction of United States; and 3) the "day of purification," a prophecy that is remarkably reminiscent of biblical prophecies concerning: 1) Armageddon: "that great day of God Almighty" (Revelation 16:14); 2) massive earthquakes (Revelation 6:12; 8:5; 11:13,19; 16:18); and 3) "the first resurrection" (Revelation 20:6) respectively.

Another famous Navajo-Hopi prophecy with a vortex is called "the whirling rainbow" prophecy and forecasts a golden age:

> Men and women will be equals in the way Creator intended them to be; all children will be safe anywhere they want to go. Elders will be respected and valued for their contributions to life. Their wisdom will be sought out. The whole Human race will be called The People and there will be no more war, sickness or hunger forever.[188]

Immediately, we find close parallels to final chapters of the Bible detailing a new creation. However, this does not commend Hopi spirituality entailing spirit worship, animism, and pantheism. The Hopi await a messiah figure called the "True White Brother," who is called "Pahana." The Hopi prophecy of this figure says:

> It is known that our TRUE WHITE BROTHER, when he comes will be all powerful and he will wear a RED CAP or a RED CLOAK. He will be large in population; belongs to no religion but his very own. He will bring with him the Sacred Stone Tablets. Great will be his coming. None will be able to stand against him. All power in this world will be placed in his hand and he will come swiftly, and in one day gain control of the whole continent. Hopi has been warned never to take up arms.[189]

The red cap and cape bring to mind images of Roman Catholic cardinals. This figure seems to be an "instead- of" variety Antichrist.

While it's impossible to know how much the early Christian missionaries influenced the Hopi,[190] the general consistency of Hopi prophecy with inspired revelation suggests they also envisioned the coming of the messiah in judgment and subsequent restoration of the created order.

The Hopi reservation lies within a scenic forested canyon named after pioneer Thomas Keam, who built the first trading post here in 1875. Kit Carson engraved his name on a nearby Inscription Rock. Spiral petroglyphs are inscribed at Keam's Canyon and are featured prominently all around the area.

Spiral petroglyph, Sedona area

A Hopi interpretation of the spiral vortex petroglyph says:

The single spiral is the symbol of the Ho-bo-bo, the twister, who manifests his power by the whirlwind....

The myth explains that a stranger came among the people, when a great whirlwind blew all the vegetation from the surface of the earth and all the water from its courses. With a flint he caught these symbols upon a rock, the etching of which is now in Keam's Canyon, Arizona Territory. He told them he was the keeper of the breath. The whirlwind and the air that men breathe, come from his keeper's mouth.[191]

The spiral is a symbol for the "keeper of the breath," who comes reaping destruction on the land. The spiral seems to be a vortex portal, and many of the rock art sites were also seen as gates. A scholarly text on shaminism reveals, "Despite these regional, social and functional variations, some characteristics appear to have been shared by the various rock art traditions in the Far West of North America. Included is the fact that, everywhere, rock art sites were considered to be portals into the supernatural realm."[192] Other portals are more obvious.

In chapter 3, the Hopi sipapu portal from which their ancestors emerged was displayed in a photograph as a commemorative hole in the floor of modern-day kivas. In this Hopi story, a witch practicing necromancy proves that death is not final by giving grieving Hopi parents a peek at their little girl through the "kiva hole," an underworld portal:

> She [witch] told them not to be troubled because after death you went back into that underworld and were safe, that you returned to your own people down there again.
>
> They asked her to prove it. "Well," she said, "I can easily prove it if you come to the kiva (opening). We can look down and see the little dead girl playing around down there just as happy as she can be."
>
> And so they went to the kiva hole and looked down and saw this little girl playing around with the rest of the children below. When the witch girl had proved this to the people the chief had to permit her to stay.[193]

While this does not prove that such portals exist, it does date the tradition back near the turn of the twentieth century in rare ethnographic documents actually written by a Native American Edmund Nequatewa in 1936. In the same text, we read about giants:

> On the fourth night after they came up to the world on top, they saw a fire a little distance away and they wondered who it could be, so the next morning the chief sent his braves to see

where the fire had been. No sign of fire was to be found, only huge footprints of a big man or a giant, for these footprints were larger than any living man's. The braves came back to the chief and told of what big footprints they had seen, and they were all very much frightened. The chief thought the only thing to do was to have a ceremony of prayer offerings or paho making and offer these to their neighbor, the giant, for fear that he might be a man of some power, who might do them harm someday.[194]

Since this was only the fourth day after the Hopi emerged through the portal, it seems to parallel the Israelites crossing the Jordan to the Promised Land only to face the Zamzummim, the Amorites, the Emim, the Anakim, and King Og of Bashan. Interestingly, Keam's Canyon also features a Hopi petroglyph of a giant.

Giant petroglyph, Keam's Canyon, Arizona[195]

Sinagua

Another Arizona area tribe associated with the fabled Anasazi are the Sinagua. The word "Sinagua" is a contraction of the Spanish words *sin* and *agua*, meaning, "without water," an allusion to the arid land the people occupied. Between AD 500 and 900, the Sinagua entered the Verde Valley near Sedona. In addition to agriculture and crafts, they had an understanding of astronomy and established far-reaching trade routes with the peoples of the Pacific coast down into Central America.[196] Like the Anasazi, the fate of the Sinagua is unknown, though there is some evidence linking the Sinagua to the Hopi. Researchers believe the Sinagua and other clans moved to the Hopi mesas in Arizona and the Zuni and other pueblos in New Mexico around AD 1350. The last known evidence of the Sinagua dates to AD 1425 in Montezuma's Castle, about twenty miles south, as a crow flies, from Sedona.

Montezuma's Castle, an ancient pueblo[197]

Yavapai-Apache

The Yavapai-Apache hold that not all the Sinagua left the area. Several family groups remained in the Verde Valley and intermarried with the Yavapai and Apache. The Yavapai-Apache Nation consists of two distinct people with their own unique languages.[198] The Yavapai "people of the sun" are thought to be a people indigenous to Arizona. According to the oldest man of the Fort McDowell Yavapai community, "We came out at Sedona, the middle of the world. This is our home. We call Sedona 'Wipuk.' We call it after the rocks and the mountains there. All Yavapai come from Sedona. But in time they spread out."[199] Sedona is identified as the place of emergence, and then the Yavapai were divided into four geographical bands that became separate people groups.[200]

Their creation story includes a great flood. However instead of Noah, a beautiful young lady is sealed in a log canoe with a bird that pecks it open, freeing her after the flood.[201] The three locations in the story—Mingus Mountain, Boynton Canyon, and Montezuma Well—make up the "Sacred Triangle of Sedona." The Montezuma Well produces vast and consistent qualities of warm water, which rises from somewhere deep underground. Scientists have not yet discovered the origin of the warm water.

Many Apache groups were nomadic or seminomadic and traveled over large areas. As discussed in *Exo-Vaticana*, the Yavapai and Apache tribes were forcibly removed from the Verde Valley in 1876, approximately 180 miles southeast to the San Carlos Indian Reservation, near Mount Graham International Observatory. The nearby Superstition Mountains are where the Apache set their tradition about the *Tuar-tums*, the little Indians from the "Big Valley," and the *Jian-du-pids* giants. The latter were fierce invaders who stole their food and water, drove them underground, and were consequently burned into the rocky earth by the Great Father Sun. The little people are still believed to inhabit caves and tunnels throughout and below the jagged, bare-rock mountains. To this day, some Apaches believe the Tuar-tums guard a subterranean portal to a fiery underworld abyss.[202]

The Superstition Mountains

Plumed Serpents, Giants, and Human Sacrifice

We believe some of the immortals—the created gods of Psalm 82 and their counterparts—migrated to North and South America to accept worship. Stephen Quayle wrote:

> It is evident that fallen angels and giants, as well as their off-spring and demons ruled over many of the Native American populations in the New World. Additionally it seems likely that the serpents that would be worshipped throughout the Americas were either fallen angels taking the form of snakes, or the offspring of fallen angels who mated with animals.[203]

In order to "connect the dots," we begin with the Israelites' formative period in Egypt, noting that, unlike the other Egyptian gods, "the reverence paid to the snake was not merely local or even limited to one period of history, but it prevailed alike in every district of the Pharaohian empire and has left its indelible impress upon the architecture and archeology of both Upper and Lower Egypt."[204] For example, consider the Egyptian four-winged, divine serpent, *Chnuphis.*[205]

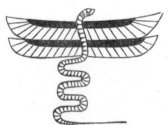

Chnuphis: An Egyptian plumed serpent

From there, the ancient Israelites moved to Canaan, where they encountered tales of the *Leviathan,* a dragon described as "the twisting serpent, the close–coiling one with seven heads," by the Canaanites (KTU[206] 1.5:1:1)[207] and appears six times in five verses of the Hebrew Bible (Job 3:8 and 41:1; Psalm 74:13–14 and 104:26; and Isaiah 27:1). According to Christoph Uehlinger, a religious studies professor at the

University of Zurich, it's likely that Leviathan was assimilated by the Egyptians as "Apophis, a huge serpent who during the night tries to hinder the sun-god's travel through the netherworld."[208] According to 1 Enoch, Leviathan is a female dragon located at the bottom of the sea and Behemoth is a male dragon living in the desert.

> And on that day were two monsters parted, a female monster named Leviathan, to dwell in the abysses of the ocean over the fountains of the waters. But the male is named Behemoth, who occupied with his breast a waste wilderness named Dûidâin, on the east of the garden where the elect and righteous dwell, where my grandfather was taken up, the seventh from Adam, the first man whom the Lord of Spirits created. (Enoch 60:7–8)

This beastly bifurcation is also mentioned in the apocryphal text 4 Ezra 6:49–52. If one accepts the ancient tradition, Leviathan still lurks in the deep, plotting to destroy the world:

> And I saw there the sea and its islands, and its animals and its fishes, and Leviathan and his spouse, and his lair, and his dens, and the world which lies upon him, and his motions and the destruction of the world because of him. (Apocalypse of Abraham 21:4)[209]

Leviathan is eschatologically connected to the "Day of the Lord," because Isaiah prophesied:

> In that day the Lord with his sore and great and strong sword shall punish leviathan the piercing serpent, Even leviathan that crooked serpent; And he shall slay the dragon that is in the sea. (Isaiah 27:1)

We suspect that Leviathan is a real reptilian entity, a highly intelligent, immortal, divine creation in chaotic rebellion. When the underworld portal is opened, this sea serpent will briefly visit untold horror on the earth, only to face judgment when facing "the Son of man sitting on the right hand of power, and coming in the clouds of heaven" (Matthew 26:64).

The Behemoth depicted by Job 40:15–24 (10–19) is also best understood as a preternatural creature possessing supernatural charac-teristics.[210] While connections to other ancient Near-Eastern dragons have been suggested, Behemoth seems to be a distinct entity paired with Leviathan. This dragon might very well manifest from the earth when the portal to the abyss is opened (Revelation 9:1). However, you might be surprised to learn that not all flying serpents in Scripture are fallen.

Although many Christians probably recoil at the thought that God created serpentine divine beings, as we demonstrated in chapter 1 ("What Is This All About?"), Scripture does support the notion. It is also telling how the Watchers were described in explicitly *reptilian* terms[211] by the ancient Hebrews, lending support to the idea that fallen ones may have matched the depiction of human sacrifice-demanding "fiery serpents" whose characteristics are partly human in appearance. With a proper understanding of the biblical Seraphim and Watchers, the Meso-american connection no longer seems so fanciful. The plumed serpent gods of the Aztecs, Mayans, and Incans share the same basic description as the biblical flying serpentine humanoids.

Early Mesoamericans who worshiped the feathered serpent included the Olmec, Mixtec, Zapotec, Toltec, and Aztec. As early as Olmec times (1400 BC), the feathered or plumed serpent is depicted throughout North, Middle, and South America. For example, the late Olmec or Toltec culture known as Teotihuacan prominently displayed the serpen-tine god on the sides of the pyramid located at the Temple of the Feath-ered Serpent.

The archaeological record shows that after the fall of Teotihuacan, the cult of the serpent spread to Xochicalco, Cacaxtla, and Cholula— the New World's largest pyramid dedicated to Quetzalcoatl.[213]

The Incas of Peru, the Aztecs of Mexico, and the Mayas of Yucatan all worshiped similar winged serpent gods. The Inca referred to these

Teotihuacan: The Temple of the Plumed Serpent[213]

rebel Seraphim as *Amaru;* the Aztecs as *Quetzalcoatl;* and the Maya as *Kukulkán*. In Inca mythology, the *amaru* is a huge, double-headed, flying serpent that dwells underground.[214] As a supernatural entity, the reptilian was believed to navigate portals between the netherworld of the dead to the natural world of the living.[215] While many have connected descriptions of Quetzalcoatl as a bearded man with similar descriptions of Viracocha, the latter is not represented as a winged, serpentine-human hybrid. However, in remarkable accord with Quetzalcoatl, the title *Amaru Tupa* was an honorific title denoting royalty.[216] In fact, the Incan creator god Viracocha adopted "a stone image of an amaru"[217] as his *huauque,* the "man-made double"[218] representing the living king during his lifetime.

Quetzalcoatl is the Aztec name for the feathered-serpent deity and is one of the main gods of Mexico and northern Central America. In the Aztec civilization of central Mexico, the worship of Quetzalcoatl was ubiquitous. He was the flying reptile deity who reportedly said, "If ever my subjects were to see me, they would run away!"[219] His winged reptilian adversary, Tezcatlipoca, was generally considered more powerful, as the god of night, sorcery, and destiny. During the twenty-day month of Toxcatl, a young man dressed up as Tezcatlipoca would be sacrificed.[220] Lesser known is that, like the Watcher angels in Genesis 6,

Aztec tradition holds that their plumed serpent gods also created giants who were later destroyed in a worldwide flood:

> According to Aztec myth, during the first age, or Sun, the gods Quetzalcoatl and Tezcatlipoca created a race of giants from ashes, giving them acorns for nourishment. But the giants so enraged the gods due to their wickedness that the gods decided to end the giants' existence and sent the jaguars to destroy them. Only seven survived the onslaught of the savage beasts. Later, when the gods summoned forth the waters to flood the Earth and destroy the first race of humans, these seven giants, the Xelhua, climbed the mountains to seek refuge from the thrashing waters that were enveloping the planet. Five of the giants survived the torrent, and in the end they built the great tower of Cholula to commemorate their survival of the flood.[221]

The Incans similarly believed that Viracocha's first creation was a race of wicked giants that he destroyed in a deluge.[222] While it is usually held that all of the Nephilim were drowned in the Flood, there are similar Jewish traditions of one giant's survival, King Og of Bashan.[223] A tradition of his survival is preserved in the Talmud.[224] Whether one accepts this ancient rabbinic tradition or not, the obvious parallel to the Aztec account entailing a few surviving giants demands an explanation. We suggest both traditions reflect actual historical events. Even so, such high strangeness is not so summarily relegated to the past.

The Maya hold that Kukulkan, represented as a feathered serpent, came from Heaven to earth. Accordingly, the quetzal bird representing Heaven was chosen as his totem, and the serpent represents earth. Winged serpent iconography features prominently at Chichén Itzá, El Tajín, and throughout the Maya region. As discussed in the chapter 3, the Mayan cosmology has led to significant theological error in the New Age movement and was the impetus for most of the failed 2012 ascension predictions. The cumulative case that these plumed serpent deities are real immortal entities, fallen "fiery flying serpents," or former

Seraphim explains all of the mythological data in terms consistent with biblical theology.

The heinous practice of human sacrifice by the Aztecs,[225] Mayans,[226] and Incans[227] is well enough attested to be uncontroversial. Some indigenous scholars defend the old ways on the grounds that, according to their cosmology, the gods did the same for the people. Some stories suggest vampirism, a practice associated with the fallen ones and their Nephilim progenies.[228] For example, in a creation myth found in the Florentine Codex, Quetzalcoatl offers his blood to give life to humanity. There are several other myths in which Mesoamerican gods offer their blood.[229] What distinguishes this from the blood of Jesus in Christian theology is that it was a one-time offering by a willing participant who subsequently rose from the dead. In contrast, the Mesoamericans offered even their own flesh-and-blood children in various forms of ritualistic human sacrifice—a brutal idolatry that was good news to nobody. Identifying these blood-thirsty serpents as fallen "sons of God," who defiantly court worship from humans and encourage various forms of extravagant ethical deviance, seems morally warranted from the original source documents of Mesoamerican religions.[230]

It is nearly self-explanatory as to how such concepts of flying serpents could have extended from Mesoamerica to Native American tribes and apocalyptic beliefs. For instance, the "Cherokee Rattlesnake Prophecies" were written down by members of the Cherokee tribe during 1811–1812. These prophecies are similar to Mesoamerican apocalyptic belief and share the idea that sometime following the year 2012, a flying plumed serpent with human-hybrid features would return during a time when the earth and heavens are shaken.

A portion of the Rattlesnake Prophecy reads:

> [Following] the year…2012 an alignment will take place both on the Cherokee calendar and in the heavens of the Rattlesnake Constellation.… It is the time of the double headed serpent stick. It is the time of the red of Orion and Jupiter against the white blue of Pleiades and Venus…the Cherokee Rattlesnake

Constellation will take on a different configuration. The snake itself will remain, however; upon the Rattlesnake shall be added upon its head feathers, its eyes will open and glow, wings spring forth as a winged rattlesnake. It shall have hands and arms and in its hands shall be a bowl. The bowl will hold blood. Upon its tail of seven rattles shall be the glowing and movement of Pleiades. The Rattlesnake shall become a feathered rattlesnake or feathered serpent of Time/Untime.

While the Mayans and Cherokee await the return of their serpent deity, uninvited preternatural visitations are ongoing. According to Chulin Pop, a contemporary Mayan, preternatural giants are still visiting the Watcher's sins on the native peoples in the jungle. Ardy Sixkiller Clarke, a professor at Montana State University, recorded his testimony:

> They [seven-to-eight-foot giants] come from the stars in their big silver plates and they stay here sometimes only for a night; sometimes for a week or more. They take the women and make them have their babies. They have four fingers and no thumbs. Any man who tries to defend his women is sick for days. They have great powers. They make you hear words, but they never speak. They have weapons that make rocks and things disappear.[231]

The transparent parallels between the ancient "sons of God," who sinned "as Sodom and Gomorrah" by "giving themselves over to fornication, and going after strange flesh" (Jude 7), worldwide reports of alien abduction, and this contemporary Mayan's account, suggests a complex interrelated phenomenon. As with the cultural rebellion against biblical morality, modern-day testimony reminiscent of the Watchers' lustful deviance imply the days of Noah and Lord's return are upon us (Matthew 24:37; Luke 16:26). Stephen Quayle suggested that Americans consider this little poem, "Quetzalcotal, are evil leaders in this land waiting for you to claim America again as Amaruca, the Land of the Serpent?"[232]

This title—Amaruca—is, according to some people, the title from which "America" is taken. It is related to Mesoamerican history, serpent-worship, and giants, and according to Freemasonry, connects the founding of the United States and its Capital designers with "wisdom" derived from the fallen flying Seraph. Tom Horn explains in *Zenith 2016:*

> The story begins long before the Spaniards arrived on this continent and was chronicled in the hieroglyphic characters (and repeated in oral history) of the sacred, indigenous Maya narrative called the Popol Vuh. Sometime between 1701 and 1703, a Dominican priest named Father Francisco Ximénez transcribed and translated the Mayan work into Spanish. Later his text was taken from Guatemala to Europe by Abbott Brasseur de Bourbough where it was translated into French. Today the Popol Vuh rests in Chicago's Newberry Library, but what makes the script interesting is its creation narrative, history, and cosmology, especially as it relates to the worship of the great "feathered serpent" creator deity known as *Q'uq'umatz;* a god considered by scholars to be roughly equivalent to the Aztec god *Quetzalcoatl* and the Yucatec Mayan *Kukulkan*. According to Freemasons like Manly P. Hall, no other ancient work sets forth so completely the initiatory rituals of the great school of philosophic mystery, which was so central to America's Baconian dream of the New Atlantis, than the Popol Vuh. What's more, Hall says, it is in this region where we find the true origin of America's name and destiny.

In *The Secret Teachings of All Ages*, Hall writes:

> This volume [Popol Vuh] alone is sufficient to establish incontestably the philosophical excellence of the red race.
> "The Red 'Children of the Sun,'" writes James Morgan Pryse, "do not worship the One God. For them that One God is absolutely impersonal, and all the Forces emanated from that One God are personal. This is the exact reverse of the popular western conception of a personal God and impersonal working

forces in nature. Decide for yourself which of these beliefs is the more philosophical [Hall says sarcastically]. These Children of the Sun adore the Plumèd Serpent, who is the messenger of the Sun. *He was the God Quetzalcoatl in Mexico, Gucumatz in Quiché; and in Peru he was called Amaru. From the latter name comes our word America. Amaruca is, literally translated, 'Land of the Plumèd Serpent.'* The priests of this [flying dragon], from their chief centre in the Cordilleras, once ruled both Americas. All the Red men who have remained true to the ancient religion are still under their sway. One of their strong centres was in Guatemala, and of their Order was the author of the book called Popol Vuh. In the Quiché tongue Gucumatz is the exact equivalent of Quetzalcoatl in the Nahuatl language; quetzal, the bird of Paradise; coatl, serpent—'the Serpent veiled in plumes of the paradise-bird'!"

The Popol Vuh was discovered by Father Ximinez in the seventeenth century. It was translated into French by Brasseur de Bourbourg and published in 1861. The only complete English translation is that by Kenneth Sylvan Guthrie, which ran through the early files of The Word magazine and which is used as the basis of this article. A portion of the Popol Vuh was translated into English, with *extremely valuable commentaries*, by James Morgan Pryse, but unfortunately his translation was never completed. The second book of the Popol Vuh is largely devoted to the initiatory rituals of the Quiché nation. *These ceremonials are of first importance to students of Masonic symbolism and mystical philosophy, since they establish beyond doubt the existence of ancient and divinely instituted Mystery schools on the American Continent.*[233] (emphasis added)

Thus from Hall we learn that Freemasons like him believe "ancient and divinely instituted" mystery religion important to students of Masonry came to Amaruca/America—*the Land of the Plumèd Serpent*—from knowledge that the Red Man received from the dragon himself.

What Hall conceals is that, even to this day, in the secret societies, Lucifer is considered this benevolent serpent-god who has nothing more than the best intentions for man, while Jehovah is an evil entity who tries to keep mankind in the dark and punishes him if he seeks the truest wisdom. Since these ancient serpent legends include the Mesoamerican feathered serpent gods and can be looked upon as a historical testament of that Angel thrown down by God, "then perhaps The Land of the Plumèd Serpent may also be known as *the Land of Lucifer*," concludes Ken Hudnall in *The Occult Connection II: The Hidden Race.*[234]

The Great Red Dragon Cast to Earth

The winged serpent's eschatological significance brings us full circle to the final book of the New Testament:

> And there appeared another wonder in heaven; and behold a great red dragon, having seven heads and ten horns, and seven crowns upon his heads. (Revelation 12:3)

Notice that this ultimate Great Red Dragon has seven heads, just like the Leviathan of the Canaanites. However, the same text sheds light on several mysteries. "And the great dragon was cast out, that old serpent, called the Devil, and Satan, which deceiveth the whole world: he was cast out into the earth, and his angels were cast out with him" (Revelation 12:9). The importance of what is stated in that verse often escapes readers not familiar with the entire Bible. In one fell swoop, John has connected the dragon to the *Nachash*, "the shining one" who deceived Eve in the garden, to *Diablos*, "the slanderer," to Satan, "the adversary," and identifies the sum total as one being consigned to terrorize the earth during the Great Tribulation.

As we argued in chapter 1, the most consistent view with the whole counsel of God is that the angelic war culminating in Satan's demotion to earth is a future event. We suggest that consistent exegesis demands a futurist interpretation, as uncomfortable as it might be for our readers with unbelieving friends and family, considering that if we are indeed correct, it means the day "the devil is come down unto you, having great wrath" (Revelation 12:12) actually looms near. But we are greatly encouraged because the revelation of Yahweh, from the *protoevangelium*—the first gospel in Genesis 3:15—to the final battle of the Apocalypse (20:9), centers on this eschatological solution to the "problem of evil" inaugurating a golden age. Coming full circle, Satan portrayed as a seven-headed dragon is reminiscent of Leviathan, who is similarly judged (Isaiah 27:1).

The Leviathan-Behemoth tradition, discussed previously (Enoch 60:7–8), also informs the symbols for the Antichrist as the first beast that "rose out of the Sea" (13:1) and the False Prophet as "another beast coming up out of the earth" (13:11). While the two humans are defeated and thrown into the Lake of Fire, according to another ancient tradition, Leviathan and Behemoth are barbecued and served:

> And it shall come to pass when all is accomplished that was to come to pass in those parts, that the Messiah shall then begin to be revealed. And Behemoth shall be revealed from his place and Leviathan shall ascend from the sea, those two great monsters which I created on the fifth day of creation, and shall have kept until that time; and then they shall be for food for all that are left. (2 Baruch 28:7).[235]

While we acknowledge that the book of Revelation defines many of its symbols, a few readers probably think we are taking apocalyptic literature too literally. However, it's not that we insist on a particular literal interpretation as much as it is that we reject demythologization and anti-supernaturalism. In fact, we commend the antecedents, remythologization and supernaturalism, albeit we sincerely believe that many mythical entities are more than mere symbols. The universality of belief in serpentine deities and reptilian humanoids demands more than a simple hand wave. Charles Gould writes in the classic reference *Mythical Monsters:*

Stories of divine progenitors, demigods, heroes, mighty hunters, slayers of monsters, giants, dwarfs, gigantic serpents, dragons, frightful beasts of prey, supernatural beings, and myths of all kinds, appear to have been carried into all corners of the world with as much fidelity as the sacred Ark of the Israelites, acquiring a moulding—graceful, weird or uncouth—according to the genius of the people or their capacity for superstitious belief; and these would appear to have been materially affected by the varied nature of their respective countries.[236]

Because the God of the Bible is the creator God of the universe, His Word stands in judgment of all other world religions. Isaiah described good and evil Seraphim in the eighth century BC. The plumed-serpent-worshipping Mesoamerican religions—associated with ritual human sacrifice—most likely entail the worship of real fallen Seraphim or similar divine beings. Since the winged reptilian was not known to exist in nature, the universality of its worship demands an explanation.

Scholars typically default to an evolutionary process known as diffusion. In this case, diffusion entails the idea that plumed-serpent belief was carried from culture to culture. However, the winged serpent's appearance in antiquity is nearly simultaneous from the Americas to the Far East.[237] Anthropologist David Jones shows that even the Eskimos believed in a dragon called Kikituk, even though they had never seen an actual reptile.[238] In order for the diffusion hypothesis to gain any traction, the creators of the symbol must have exercised global influence whether by conquest, trade, or exploration. But it was globally represented before traditional history allows for such rapid proliferation. Accordingly, the diffusion argument is found wanting.

Another proposal is that such myths might be motivated by primitive discoveries of dinosaur fossils. However, there are widespread shared traits like feathered wings, human features, and high intelligence that are not obtained from fossilized remains. In *An Instinct for Dragons*, Jones argues that dragon belief is instinctual. He suggests that over millions of years, humans evolved an instinctive fear of predators, which emerged in the artistic creation of the dragon and other kinds of hybrid monsters. However, that idea also falls short, because there is a little evidence for such specificity and detail in instinctual memory.

Naturalistic explanations also fail to explain the worldwide belief in reptilian winged-serpent deities. In *The Supernatural Worldview*, a convincing case was made that although naturalism still rules academia, the evidence against it is formidable and mounting. In regard to dragons and plumed serpents, an explanation that makes sense of all the evidence is that ancient peoples were actually worshipping fallen *Seraphim*, "flying fiery serpents," or their cousins, but, in this case, representing the Great Red Dragon as the *seed of the Nachash*.

CHAPTER FIVE

Occult Portals for a Luciferian New Age

By Cris Putnam

As detailed in *The Supernatural Worldview*, pantheistic monism has eclipsed the Christian consensus. As academics increasingly declared the Bible false, people were left with hopeless secularism. When secular humanism crumbled, a new paganism rose to prominence by offering people the significance of a religion without the moral restrictions that a personal God places upon their behavior. Theologian John Frame wrote:

> Secular humanism, once the movement most feared by Christians, has been replaced by the rise of religious paganism. The hope of some that secularism would bring an end to religion has proved forlorn: this is the most religious age ever. But the religion of this age is as much opposed to biblical Christianity as secular humanism ever was, and as determined to destroy faith in the God of Scripture. And, as an ancient and widespread movement, it has far deeper roots in our cultural consciousness than secular humanism could ever hope to achieve. Indeed, one may look at secular humanism as a form of religious paganism,

which has, after a fleeting prominence, yielded to forms of a more profound kind.[239]

While Bible-believing academics were debating atheist philosophers, the general public was at home watching Oprah. America became spiritually pagan, elevating created things over the creator (Romans 1:25). The ideas were not new—a westernized blend of Hinduism and Buddhism positing that "all is one" (oneism) that was wrapped up to look new, but behind the dressing offered no essential differences.

Government authority and moral law originally grounded in biblical principles have been secularized, made arbitrary, and given over to the "ruler of this world" (John 12:31, 16:11; 2 Corinthians 4:4; 1 John 5:19). Like a frog in a kettle slowly heating to boil, the consequences of abandoning traditional values are seldom considered. Ideas do have consequences.

Appearing as an "angel of light," the devil exercises subtle influence under the guise of tolerance and religious pluralism. As a result, the new paganism has drastically transformed American culture. An absurd law like California's Assembly Bill 1266 gives students in public K–12 schools the right "to participate in sex-segregated programs, activities and facilities" based on their self-perception, regardless of their actual gender. This means a male high school student who says he feels like a female can use the female bathroom and locker rooms in the California public schools. We believe this social issue and others of a similar immoral nature are directly connected to the increased access the new paganism affords the armies of darkness. We can learn much from the past and nonwesternized world.

Lynne Hume is an anthropologist and retired professor in religious studies in at the University of Queensland, Brisbane, Australia. Her book, *Portals: Opening Doorways to Other Realities through the Senses* (2007), is the definitive academic volume on the subject of spirit portals. Hume writes:

In my research into altered states of consciousness over several years, I have found not only that the notion of moving through some sort of portal or doorway to access another type of reality is widespread, but that there are certain techniques employed to do so. These techniques are used universally by shamans, monks, religious specialists and lay people, and involve different physical senses.[240]

Hume's analysis reveals universal elements within the methods used by shamans, sorcerers, monks, witches, and lay people all over the world. Psychedelics are definitely the portal of choice for shamans and sorcerers, but the same sort of effects are achieved by meditation, music, physical pain, chanting, drumming, dancing, and binaural beat brain entrainment. More and more people are becoming aware that not only is the spirit realm real, but it plays an interactive role in their personal lives as they move from ordinary reality into alternate realities.

The Internet has made once hard-to-find occult volumes explaining such techniques easily accessible. As a result, the number of people experimenting with the occult continually increases as knowledge proliferates across the World Wide Web. Dabbling in the New Age, mediumship, or Wicca opens a portal into one's life. Using props like the Ouija board or crystal ball can open doors that are better left closed. Walter Martin wrote, "If you turn the handle of the unopened door of a forbidden dimension, what will come through is satanic power of enormous proportions."[241] As access increases, the powers and principalities are afforded new areas of influence, and that satanic power is exacting a spiritually destructive toll. While it is beyond our scope to address all of the potential doorways, one particular example designed to transform society was the "Babalon Working."

The Babalon Working

The infamous "Babalon working" conducted by NASA Jet Propulsion Laboratory rocket scientist Jack Parsons and Scientology founder L. Ron Hubbard allegedly opened a gate that fueled the modern UFO era that ensued a few months later. Occult scholar Kenneth Grant writes, "The [Babalon] working began just prior to the wave of unexplained aerial phenomenon now recalled as the 'Great Saucer Flap.' Parsons opened a door and something flew in."[242] While we are eager to explore such a connection, the writings of Crowley and Parsons offer little support to a correlation with Babalon, much less the workings causation of the modern UFO era. It seems far more likely that this infernal Babalon portal smoothed the way for ideas like California's transgender law and the widespread cultural acceptance of same-sex marriage.

Thelema is a philosophy defined by the maxim, "Do what thou wilt shall be the whole of the law." It comes from Aleister Crowley's *Book of the Law*, which was channeled by an incorporeal demonic intelligence named Aiwass.[243] Thelema is a narcissistic ideology that undergirds several esoteric magic societies like the A∴A∴ and the Ordo Templi Orientis that fundamentally oppose God's moral law. Satan targets sexuality because procreation is the human capability that comes closest to the divine. As a result, it's not too surprising that sexual perversion and "sex magick" are essential components of occult rituals. Parsons and Hubbard's "working" entailed all sorts of aberrant sexual activity.

In Thelemic literature, Babalon has three conceptual aspects: 1) the Gateway to the City of the Pyramids, 2) the Scarlet Woman, and 3) the Great Mother.[244] The first aspect seems the most promising for our investigation into a possible UFO connection. She serves as a portal for sorcerers, but probably not in the way one might expect. An occult reference explains:

> Within the mystical system of Crowley, the adept reaches a final stage where he or she must cross the Abyss, that great wilderness of nothingness and dissolution. Choronzon is the dweller there, and his job is to trap the traveler in his meaningless world of illusion. However, Babalon is on just the other side, beckoning. If the adept gives himself to her—the symbol of this act is the pouring of the adept's blood into her graal—he becomes

impregnated in her, then to be reborn as a master and a saint that dwells in the City of the Pyramids.[245]

In other words, the adept's great hope is reincarnation as a master and saint in the City of the Pyramids. It sounds promising to obtain an honorary position in an exotic location like Egypt, but, in reality, it only amounts to the same old "oneism." Rather than dwelling in a glamorous metropolis, the residents of the so-called city are disintegrated. According to Thelemapedia, "They have destroyed their earthly ego-identities, becoming nothing more than piles of dust (i.e. the remaining aspects of their True Selves without the self-sense of 'I')."[246] Monism offers no distinctions, no justice, no hope, and no love…nothing but dissolution and absorption into the meaningless whole. Occultism promises a beautiful city, but only delivers disintegration.

The second "scarlet woman" aspect of Babalon seemed to be not much more than an honorary title for Crowley's female sex magick partners, of whom seven were given the title.[247] The third aspect "Great Mother" borrows from the book of Revelation's "MOTHER OF HARLOTS" imagery and is an important figure in Crowley's "Gnostic Mass." Again, while depraved, blasphemous, and pantheistic, these aspects do not seem to link to flying saucers.

Parsons' and Hubbard's motive was largely self-gratification, but the working explicitly stated the goal of transforming traditional values. The rituals were aimed at incarnating the archetypal divine feminine and changing culture through her influence. It is a matter of record that feminism, homosexuality, and pantheistic monism were sowed into public consciousness from the ivory towers of academia shortly subsequent to Parsons' dark invocation:

The ultimate goal of these operations, carried out during February and March 1946, was to give birth to the magical being, or "moonchild," described in Crowley's works. Using the powerful energy of IX degree Sex Magick, the rites were intended to open a doorway through which the goddess Babalon herself might appear in human form.[248]

Parsons believed that he and Hubbard accomplished the task in a series of rituals culminating in March 1946. Parsons' biography preserves a celebratory statement regarding her embodiment in the womb.

> In a fragment from his writings, Parsons, exhausted and exultant, declared his work a success. He believed that Babalon, in the manner of the Immaculate Conception, was due to be born to a woman somewhere on earth in nine months' time. "Babalon is incarnate upon the earth today, awaiting the proper hour for her manifestation," he wrote.[249]

Accordingly, one would expect a female child to be born in late 1946 or early 1947. Ritual magic aimed at the birth of the archetypal divine feminine has little to do with the modern UFO wave and more to with feminism and the mandatory prohibition of all forms of distinction, including gender and sexual preference. An influential feminist born in 1947 offers the most promise for identifying the putrid fruit of Parsons' infamous ritual.[250] *That would be none other than Hillary Rodham Clinton.* Even so, it does not dismiss the occult connection to unexplained aereal phenomenon in the slightest.

As documented in *Exo-Vaticana*, the correlation between the occult and UFO phenomena is real and has been noted by scientists who study the subject, like Hugh Ross and Jacques Vallee. In addition, astronomer Paul Davies wrote, "No clear distinction can be drawn between UFO reports and descriptions of religious experiences of, say, the Fatima variety."[251] A transparent link between Thelemic occultism and flying saucers is displayed in a film of one of its most prominent proponents.

In Kenneth Anger's film, *Lucifer Rising*, the immortal Lucifer is summoned to earth, ushering in the "New Age of Horus" based on occult philosophy. Anger is a confessing Thelemite and underground filmmaker whose "role in rendering gay culture visible within American cinema, commercial or otherwise, is impossible to overestimate."[252] In the film, Lucifer's arrival is heralded by an armada of flying saucers flying over Egypt. A condensation of the plot reads:

> Lava erupts and the goddess Isis awakens, calling to her husband Osiris. In a room far away a man wakes up, sits on a throne in his apartment and somehow spears a woman in a forest far away, then climbs into a bathtub to wash off the blood. Later, the moon awakens the goddess Lilith, a magick ritual summons Lucifer, and flying saucers appear over Luxor, Egypt.[253]

British scholar Mikita Brottman wrote, "Anger intended *Lucifer Rising* to stand as a form of ritual marking the death of the old religions like Judaism and Christianity, and the ascension of the more nihilistic age of Lucifer."[254] Indeed, that luciferian age is what we documented at the beginning of this chapter and, recalling the first aspect of Babalon, the scene symbolically depicts the "Gateway to the City of the Pyramids" ushering in a fleet of glowing luciferian light ships.

UFO in *Lucifer Rising* (1981)

Pharmakeion

The portal of choice for occultists, medicine men, and shamans are mind-altering substances. In the New Testament, the English word "sorcery" translates from the Greek *pharmakeiōn*, from which the later word "pharmacy" was derived (Galatians 5:20; Revelation 9:2, 18:23, 21:8, 22:15). The term was adopted into modern use because the original "pharmacists" were mixing potions to bring one into contact with the spirit world like a modern druggist would make cough syrup. Indigenous peoples worldwide have identified a multitude of drugs for accomplishing the task. Hume states, "The ingestion of perception-altering substances is commonly acknowledged cross-culturally as a way to journey into the non-material world of spirit."[255] Although scant, there is a small body of scientific evidence concerning such biochemical portals.

Psychiatrist Rick Strassman's landmark study, using the psychoactive compound N, N-Dimethyltryptamine (DMT), was the first human psychedelic research in the United States after twenty years of censure. The study employed sixty volunteers—screened to prefer stable folks with positive past psychedelic drug experiences—who were injected with DMT under clinical supervision at the University of New Mexico's School of Medicine in Albuquerque, New Mexico, where Strassman was a tenured associate professor of psychiatry. Strassman, a Buddhist, holds degrees in biological sciences from Stanford University and an MD with honors from Albert Einstein College of Medicine of Yeshiva University and further studies at University of California, Davis. His groundbreaking research became a best-selling book and documentary.

Published in 2000, *DMT: The Spirit Molecule* makes a case that DMT, naturally released by the pineal gland, facilitates the soul's movement in and out of the body, facilitating birth and death experiences, as well as deep, meditative states. More than half of the subjects reported similar experiences interacting with nonhuman beings, described by experiencers as "alien space insects"[256] and "reptilian and humanoid."[257] Furthermore, the resulting testimonies were remarkably consistent with near-death experiences, alien abductions, and various occult techniques.

The resulting evidence shocked Strassman, who conceded to himself, "This sounds like nothing I've ever heard about in my therapy patients' dream life. It is much more bizarre, well-remembered, and internally consistent."[258] The uniform testimony of those who participated in the study was that the beings they interacted with were real. Author and consciousness researcher Graham Hancock asks, "Are they simply quaint 'brain fiction'? Most mainstream scientists would say so—although they cannot explain why evolution should have installed identical, highly imaginative Gothic novelists in all our brains. Or could it be that these strange, complex, universal experiences with evolving storylines are in some way as real as those we take for granted in normal states of consciousness?"[259]

Most Western scientists simply assume that all such experiences are subjective hallucinations produced by a drugged brain. However, there is really no good reason to accept the reductionist interpretation. Strassman points out, "However, just as likely as the theory that these worlds exist 'only in our minds' is that they are, in reality, 'outside' of us and freestanding."[260] We believe this is true and, at first encounter, we were surprised that someone trained in Western schools would be open to the reality of the spirit realm, that is, until we discovered Strassman is an accomplished Buddhist.

In 1984, Strassman obtained "lay ordination in a Western Buddhist order,"[261] which probably explains why he seems eager to jettison the materialist consensus. In the introduction, he proposes. "DMT can allow our brains to perceive dark matter or parallel universes, realms of existence inhabited by conscious entities."[262] Frankly, it seems that way to us as well, and it is noteworthy when scientists discover evidence for spiritual realities the Bible disclosed thousands of years ago about the relationship between man's physical body made from the clay and God-breathed, immaterial soul.

Instead of thinking of the brain as biological meat computer, Strassman offers the "receiver of reality" model for brain function. Like a television receives its content from the airwaves, consciousness or the mind resides outside of our bodies. If so, it explains why altered states of consciousness "change the channel" and allow one to view programming from other realms.[263] Strassman corresponded with Oxford professor of physics David Deutsch, a proponent of the Many Worlds Interpretation (MWI) of quantum mechanics and the author of *The Fabric of Reality*, concerning DMT altering the brain to work as a receiver of information from parallel worlds.

Deutsch, a pioneer in quantum computing,[264] believes contact with such worlds is possible, but only through complex algorithms using the computers of the future. When Strassman proposed the idea that DMT facilitated biological quantum computation, it seemed impossible to Deutsch, because such technology required a temperature near absolute zero. However, chemists have continually developed processes allowing superconductivity at higher and higher temperatures. Strassman suggests that DMT similarly changes the brain's physical properties so that quantum computing takes place at body temperature, accessing parallel universes.

We assert something like the above theory can be true without accepting the Many Worlds Interpretation. In chapter 8 ("The Science of Portals"), we discuss why we find the MWI absurd. Rather than regarding these as infinite possibilities, we interpret these as very real intrusions into the spirit realm where the immortals dwell. Consider Graham Hancock's assessment of the beings he encountered on psychedelics:

> My intuition was that I had been afforded glimpses, however brief and however distorted by my own cultural precondition-ing, of beings that are absolutely real in some modality not yet understood by science, that exist around us and with us, *that even seem to be aware of us and to take an active interest in us,* but that vibrate at a frequency beyond the range of our senses and instruments and thus generally remain completely invisible to us.[265] (emphasis added)

Psychedelics are a consciousness portal to the immaterial realm—but are not necessarily a safe one. Strassman offered concerning the spirit molecule:

> It pulls us into worlds known only to itself. We need to hold on tight, and we must be prepared, for spiritual realms include both

heaven and hell, both fantasy and nightmare. While the spirit molecule's role may seem angelic, there is no guarantee it will not take us to the demonic.[266]

In fact, it explains the biblical prohibitions against sorcery just as well as the most educated Christian apologetic.

The great danger is that the subject is in the hands of an unknown intelligence. The Bible warns that angelic appearances can be deceiving (2 Corinthians 11:14). Paranormal authors Brad and Sherry Steiger offer the "thesis that the aliens, angels, spirit guides, demons, and gods or goddesses encountered by unaware, yet somehow receptive percipients may actually be the product of a multidimensional intelligence that masks itself in physical forms that are more acceptable to humans than its true image—if it does, indeed, have a perceivable form at all."[267] Apparently, there is some consensus that immortals can shape-shift or transform their physical bodies.

It seems fair to argue that the Bible supports the possibility of travel to the spirit realms via altered states of consciousness. Examples include: Jacob's vision of the "gateway of God" seen during a dream; Ezekiel's *vision* of God's throne (Ezekiel 1); Isaiah's *vision* of the throneroom (Isaiah 1); Paul questioning whether he was out of his body (2 Corinthians 12); Peter's statement, "in a trance I saw a vision," (Acts 11:5); Paul writing, "I was in a trance" (Acts 22:17); and John's statement that he was "in the Spirit" (Revelation 1:10). God uses altered states, but it seems they are by His will rather than by the experiencers' will. Dreams, visions, trances, and out-of-body travel are all supported as real "portals" in Scripture, but the practice of inducing them via psychotropic substances, Eastern meditation techniques, or rituals is forbidden as sorcery.

Stone Circles

A stone circle is a monument of standing stones arranged in a circle. The size and number of the stones vary, and the shape can be an ellipse or half circle. Some are more complex, with double- and triple-ring designs, often classed separately as concentric stone circles. Stone circles were constructed across the British Isles from 3300 to 900 BC, with more than a thousand surviving examples, including Avebury, the Ring of Brodgar, and Stonehenge. The oldest is probably the *Standing Stones of Stenness*, a megalithic stone circle on the mainland of Scotland. It was associated with pagan ceremonies and believed to have magical power.[268] Based on radiocarbon dating, it is thought the site was in use as early as 3386 BC.[269] Many of these are associated with burial grounds and are thought to serve some funerary purpose. Others were built for obscure religious reasons and likely served a ritual purpose. Even now, American tax dollars are being used to accommodate such pagan portals. The United States Air Force Academy in Colorado recently spent more than $77,000 to build a modern replica to accommodate their pagan cadets.[270]

Before the Israelites possessed the Holy Land, stone circles were similarly erected, but there are only two known. One was found underwater at Atlit Yam and another, Gilgal Refaim, was found nearby in the Golan Heights and will be examined thoroughly in this chapter. The former is a submerged ancient city where archaeologists discovered a semicircle monument dated to 6000 BC, containing seven 1,320-pound megalithic stones.[271] It has the earmarks of an antediluvian civilization associated with the Nephilim. The latter is associated with the biblical figure Og of Bashan and could be a real Nephilim stargate.

A Real Nephilim Stargate?

Bashan, the land of Rephaim, contains hundreds of megalithic stone tombs called "dolmen" or "portal tombs" dating from the fifth to third millennium BC. In the western part of the Bashan plain of the Golan Heights lie the cobbled stone ruins of a most unusual megalith called *Gilgal Rephaim,* which, in Modern Hebrew, is translated as "Wheel of Spirits" or "Wheel of Ghosts." It reflects an interesting development in the meaning of "Rephaim." In the prophetic books, the term is thought to denote spirits, as it means in Modern Hebrew. But in the writings of Moses, it always meant a race of giants. The early Israelites identified it as "the work of giants (Refa'im, also Anakim, Emim, Zuzim)."[272] More on this semantic development later on, but, for now it seems sufficient to say that, in its ancient context, "Circle of the Giants" is a better translation of Gilgal Rephaim. Additionally, if one allows Heiser's view that *Nephilim* is an Aramaic loan-word for "giants,"[273] then "Circle of the Nephilim" is also reasonable.

Known as the "Stonehenge of the Levant," legends connect the megalithic ruin to Og of Bashan, the last Nephilim king routed by Moses. Although there has been vigorous debate as to how giants repopulated after the Flood, Jewish tradition holds that Moses allowed a seemingly repentant Og on the ark.[274] We believe a second incursion of promiscuous Watchers "and *also after that,* when the sons of God came in unto the daughters of men" (Genesis 6:4, emphasis added) better explains why the Bible describes Og as "the remnant of the Rephaim" (Deuteronomy 3:11). As a spiritual and genetic "seed of the serpent" occupying the Holy Land, new evidence reveals that Og had inherited the land from an ancient line of aristocratic Nephilim in Bashan.

Stone ruins of Gilgal Rephaim

Oriented so that Mount Hermon aligns due north, some forty-two thousand massive basalt rocks are arranged in four concentric circles—the outermost 520 feet in diameter—and boasting a fifteen-foot high tumulus portal at its center, Gilgal Rephaim is one of the earliest megalithic monuments in the Levant. Nevertheless, it has always been somewhat of a mystery and is not even mentioned in many biblical archaeology texts. Based on field work in 2010 by Michael Freikman at the Hebrew University,[275] we suggest it is one of the earliest examples of a necromantic portal, a stone circle design of the Nephilim variety.

Called a portal tomb, portal grave, or quoit, a dolmen is a type of single-chamber megalithic tomb usually consisting of two or more upright stones supporting a large, flat, horizontal capstone (e.g., Stonehenge). The fifteen-foot-high tumulus at the center of the Wheel of the Giants is centered on a dolmen. In the past, archaeologists believed the centerpiece was a later addition, but new work by Yosef Garfinkel and Michael Freikman of the Hebrew University discovered more ancient layers beneath those identified by previous archaeologists, as well as a new artifact supporting an earlier origin by an unknown people—we believe the Nephilim.

Archaeologists seem mystified by the Gilgal Refaim. It is noteworthy that there is nothing similar in the area, especially from its era. The indigenous people of the time did not build stone circles or megaliths, but the Bible records this was the region inhabited by giants. Moses located the "Rephaim in Ashteroth-karnaim" (Genesis 14:5) and associated it to "Og the king of Bashan, who dwelt at Ashtaroth" (Deuteronomy 1:4). As one might expect, within ten miles of Gilgal Rephaim was the ancient Canaanite city called Ashtheroth.

Israeli journalist Barry Chamish attributed the site to the giants and the immortals from whom they descended. Chamish interviewed Rabbi Yisrael Herczeg, who confirmed "the possibility that giant heavenly beings or their descendants could have constructed the circles."[276] When asked if he meant aliens, Rabbi Herczeg replied, "No, more like fallen angels. Og had children with Noah's daughters and they were hybrid giants called the Anakim or Refaim. They existed in ancient times and the Bible records their presence in the Golan Heights. They could have built Gilgal Refaim."[277] He is correct, as previously demonstrated their presence in the area is supported by many passages.

Until recently, archaeologists insisted that the center structure of Gilgal Rephaim was an afterthought built two thousand years after the stone circles. It turns out that the whole site is older than originally thought based on the discovery of a pin from the Chalcolithic period (4500–3500 BC). Freikman argues that the entire structure (formerly Early Bronze) should be antedated a thousand years to the Chalcolithic, and, more interestingly, that the tumulus was the original centerpiece of the entire construction and the purpose of the wheel as rather than a late bronze afterthought.[278]

Geometry and astronomy are visually connected in the site's design, revealing that it was built, at least in part, as an astronomical observatory. Useful for sacred and agrarian purposes, it was laid out as an observatory and stellar calendar capable of calculating solstices and equinoxes by conspicuous alignments.[279] Because the stars move according to the laws of celestial mechanics, astronomy software allows for precise historical research.

The stone circle's alignments support dating the "Circle of the Nephilim" to around 3000 BC when, according to calculations by Yoni Mizrachi, who wrote his doctoral dissertation at Harvard about the site, "the first rays of the sun on the longest day of the year shone through the opening in the northwestern gate…then passed through openings in the inner walls to the geometric center of the complex."[280] These alignments suggest that the ancient giant clans knew something about the periphery of the cosmos and placed a high value on tracking the stars.

Given the megalith's location, extreme antiquity, and Rephaim-giant association, local tradition identifying it as Og's tomb seems quiet plausible. Og's gargantuan carcass is conspicuously absent, but the site was likely looted by successive grave robbers over the centuries. It is safe to say that Og's remains (or merely authentic giant bones) would be priceless museum pieces, but one shudders to imagine the dark utility such rarified relics might attain in the capable hands of a studied dark magus. It hardly seems surprising that, at least as far as the public is told, the dolmen chamber was found empty.

Interestingly, Og achieved status in the afterlife as an underworld enforcer. A reference to Og appears in a Phoenician funerary inscription implying that if one disturbs the bones within, "the mighty Og will avenge me."[281] Apparently, Og's name still carried enough clout for ghoul deterrence many centuries after being dispatched to the afterlife by Moses (Deuteronomy 1:4). Considering the Jewish belief that giants like Og are not eligible for the eschatological resurrection of the dead, the references to Og's afterlife activity are what one might expect—that is, if the tradition preserved in the Book of the Watchers is correct.

> And now, the giants, who are produced from the spirits and flesh, shall be called evil spirits upon the earth, and on the earth shall be their dwelling. Evil spirits have proceeded from their bodies; because they are born from men, and from the holy Watchers is their beginning and primal origin; they shall be evil spirits on earth, and evil spirits shall they be called. As for the spirits of heaven, in heaven shall be their dwelling, but as for the spirits of the earth which were born upon the earth, on the earth shall be their dwelling. (Enoch 15:8–10)

Taken at face value, Og's burial at Gilgal Rephaim, alongside his afterlife reputation, suggests that the Circle of the Nephilim served as a portal—a site where the evil spirits of Nephilim kings could be summoned. While this idea goes beyond the archaeological evidence, the Hebrew term "Rephaim" offers support. The semantic progression of "Rephaim" from denoting a tribe of giants to meaning ghosts in the underworld suggests an actual change in the entities the term represents. While Moses wrote of giants, by Isaiah's time the meaning had changed.

> Hell from beneath is moved for thee to meet thee at thy coming: It stirreth up *the dead* for thee, even all the chief ones of the earth; It hath raised up from their thrones all the kings of the nations. (Isaiah 14:9, emphasis added)

Where the King James reads "the dead," the Hebrew term is *rapha*, also translated as "shades, ghosts, dead, departed spirits, spirits of the dead."[282] It seems plausible that the semantic range widened as the status of the Rephaim giants crossed over to the underworld. In other words, the definition reflects the actual situation as Og was the last physical specimen in that line. From this, we speculate that the Wheel of the Giants served as a necromantic portal for the deceased Nephilim kings of Bashan, of whom Og was the last of their kind. "For only Og king of Bashan remained of the remnant of giants" (Deuteronomy 3:11a).

Gilgal Rephaim's design as a megalithic stone circle seems suitable for necromantic magic. According to the *Encyclopedia of Occultism and Parapsychology*, a "magic circle" drawn on the ground is essential to successful necromancy.[283] The circle serves to protect the necromancer as he invokes the underworld spirit. Typically, the dark mage collects personal items and employs a portrait of the deceased being summoned. However, in this case, the very center of the megalithic circle contains the dolmen laid corpse, making the portal all the more powerful. The most powerful forms of necromancy use the actual body, as Francis Barrett explained:

> Necromancy has its name because it works on the bodies of the dead, and gives answers by the ghosts and apparitions of the dead, and subterraneous spirits, alluring them into the carcasses of the dead by certain hellish charms, and infernal invocations, and by deadly sacrifices and wicked oblations.[284]

The Bible confirms the existence of underworld gates, as death has a gate. "Have the gates of death been opened unto thee? Or hast thou seen the doors of the shadow of death?"(Job 38:17). As detailed in *The Supernatural Worldview*, the witch of Endor successfully brought up the spirit of Samuel through the use of a ritual pit and familiar spirit (1 Samuel 28:8–20). The portal to the abyss that opens at the fifth-trumpet judgment has already been discussed (Revelation 9:2).

The Gates of Hell

An interesting connection between the Watchers' descent to Mount Hermon and the gates of Hell is found in Matthew's Gospel. When Jesus declared of the church that "the gates of hell shall not prevail against it" (Matthew 16:18), he was in Caesarea Philippi at the mouth of the famous cave serving as the Roman "Grotto of Pan" at the southwestern base of Mount Hermon, an underworld portal where, in all likelihood, the Watchers who sinned were delivered "into chains of darkness, to be reserved unto judgment" (2 Peter 2:4). Historian Judd Burton writes:

> Jesus may have utilized the actual cave of Pan as a backdrop when referring to the "gates of hell, and that the rock was not Peter, but a large rock in front of the cave." This scenario is possible, given the prophetic meditations of Jesus at Caesarea Philippi, and a death he felt was imminent, the circumstances necessitated a bolder and more dramatic act of oration than simply spitting in the face of Greco-Roman paganism. Mt. Hermon, with its reputation as ground zero for the tumult of fallen angels, was by far, a more profound image to Jesus' Jewish disciples. Jesus was, in effect, shaking his fist in the face of forces more sinister, more powerful, and more dangerous than those of Rome: the devils and giants who defied Yahweh and who set themselves against Jesus' beloved humanity. He established the church, confirms his messiahship, and did so in the very maw of "the gates of hell."[286]

Cave and Grotto of Pan[287]

Circlestone

In the Superstition Mountains of Arizona, Circlestone is a large, circular ruin resembling neolithic stone circles, like Stonehenge. Positioned on a scenic knoll at an altitude of over six thousand feet, it is close to the highest point in the range. Mound Mountain, at 6,266 feet, is nearby, to the southeast. James Swanson and Thomas Kollenborn describe the site:

> Circlestone is not a "perfect" circle, the diameter measuring 133 feet at most points but 140 feet at one tangential point....The entrance to the circle is 3 feet wide, the average width of the wall measures 3 feet, and the height of the existing high point of the wall is 5 1/2 feet. The center structure within the circle is 17 feet square.[287]

With a circumference of around 420 feet, the three-foot-thick rock wall is elliptical in shape. New Zealand researcher Martin Doutré believes the shape is intentional. "Like sites in Great Britain, there is a slight elliptical shaping to the overall circle in the dimensions north-south as opposed to east-west. This has the effect of providing an additional, 90-degrees opposed diameter, which 'doubles-up' the linear and circumference codes encrypted into the site."[288] Solstice and equinox sunrises were marked by alignments on the straight portion of the east wall. Follow the endnoted link for an informative website with a map of the ancient stone circle by the Mesa Community College.[289]

Although it has been called a medicine wheel like those used by Native Americans, there is nothing else quite like it in the area. Swanson and Kollenborn suggest it was built by the Sinagua or Anasazi. Doutré attributes it to an ancient class of sages: "Ancient astronomer mathematicians built sites like Circlestone as repositories of codes and places where initiates could be taught age-old principles."[290] As explained in detail at his website, Doutré discovered a Sabbatical calendar, the circumference of the earth, as well as navigational codes, and mathematical constants encoded in the dimensions of the site. Knowledge of such concepts is not expected from the indigenous peoples and could very well imply the intervention of the immortals. There is a connection to UFOs. Stephen Wagner noted, "During the '50s, '60s and '70s, numerous UFOs were sighted around Flat Iron and Bluff Springs Mountain, which is adjacent to Circlestone. In 1973, two campers reported seeing a UFO land and then take off from the Circlestone area."[291] Accordingly, Circlestone has the earmarks of an interdimensional portal.

In this chapter, we explored several types of occult portals—personal, underworld, and stone circles. Dabbling in the occult or playing with an Ouija board might open a personal portal resulting in demonization, but opening the others requires formal knowledge. It was argued that the "Babalon working" had little to do with UFOs, but was for the purpose of incarnating the "divine feminine" to steer Western culture away from traditional values. Psychedelic drugs like DMT are a very effective personal portal employed by shaman and sorcerers. Dr. Strassman suggests such substances access objectively real parallel universes rather than merely inducing delusions. Stone circles have been employed since before written history, and two arcane examples were examined. While Circlestone has been connected to UFOs, the Circle of the Nephilim might have served as an underworld portal for necromancy. Even so, with the return of the Nephilim predicted in the Septuagint version of Isaiah, the Circle of the Nephilim may turn out to be one of the gates from which they emerge.

CHAPTER SIX

The Concept of Portals and Gateways in the Bible

By Tom Horn

> Lift up your heads, O ye gates; and be ye lift up, ye
> everlasting doors; and the King of glory shall come in.
> —Psalm 24:7

> And he dreamed, and behold a ladder set up on the
> earth, and the top of it reached to heaven: and behold
> the angels of God ascending and descending on it.
> —Genesis 28:12

> And He said to him, "Truly, truly, I say to you, you
> will see the heavens opened and the angels of God
> ascending and descending on the Son of Man."
> —John 1:51

Humans live in a world of three visible dimensions and one observable dimension that we call time. However, it wasn't always thus. Bible prophecy expert Chuck Missler believes that humanity's original design—that reflected in Adam and Eve before the Fall—permitted access to as many as ten dimensions. Missler's reference to a ten-dimension "metacosm" is supported by the current theory of quantum physicists today. A recent article at Universe Today confirms this:

According to Superstring Theory, the fifth and sixth dimensions are where the notion of possible worlds arises. If we could see on through to the fifth dimension, we would see a world slightly different from our own that would give us a means of measuring the similarity and differences between our world and other possible ones.

In the sixth, we would see a plane of possible worlds, where we could compare and position all the possible universes that start with the same initial conditions as this one (i.e. the Big Bang). **In theory, if you could master the fifth and sixth dimension, you could travel back in time or go to different futures.**

In the seventh dimension, you have access to the possible worlds that start with different initial conditions. Whereas in the fifth and sixth, the initial conditions were the same and subsequent actions were different, here, everything is different from the very beginning of time. The eighth dimension again gives us a plane of such possible universe histories, each of which begins with different initial conditions and branches out infinitely (hence why they are called infinities).

In the ninth dimension, we can compare all the possible universe histories, starting with all the different possible laws of physics and initial conditions. In the tenth and final dimension, we arrive at the point in which everything possible and imaginable is covered. Beyond this, nothing can be imagined by us lowly mortals, which makes it the natural limitation of what we can conceive in terms of dimensions.[292]

If you think all this sounds like gobbledygook, then you're not alone. Most of this rests upon something quantum physicists call Superstring Theory. Essentially, the earliest version of this theory postulated a particle called a "boson." If that sounds familiar, it's because the massive ring colliders in Geneva operated by the CERN laboratory are called the Large Hadron Collider, and its stated purpose is to search for the Higgs "boson" (for more, see our chapter on CERN). String Theory proponents claim point particles (like the boson, fermion, and other subatomic particles) are actually strings, but because of our dimensional constraints we can only perceive them as points. When the points connect or become entangled, they form a "line" or "string." Each string oscillates at a predetermined wavelength; some are open strings, and others are closed (loops). I'll admit that this whole theory muddles my poor brain, but I include it to make the "point" that the world is massively more complicated and layered than we fallen humans can now perceive.

If I understand the ten-dimension theory correctly, as quoted above from the Universe Today article, then access to the fifth and sixth dimensions would allow a person to *travel through time*. Access to the fourth dimension could, theoretically, make it appear that you can walk through walls, because you simply move from the moment on one side of the wall to the same moment where you arrive on the other. No, I'm not going to yammer on about dimensional theories—truthfully, they are described differently from one physicist to another. Without knowing the mind of God, it is clearly impossible to discern the ultimate truth about dimensional construction and manipulation. However, based upon clues found within the Bible and extrabiblical sources such as the Book of Enoch, one can discern a great deal about the possibility of accessing other dimensions via portals and/or gates.

The opening to this chapter quotes several verses, so let's jump right in with these three to get us started. Psalm 24:7 is a verse sung in many churches today within the lyrics of the Lutheran hymn, "Lift Up Your Heads, Ye Mighty Gates" by George Weissel. The context of the hymn is Psalm 24, a psalm of David, written to declare God as Supreme Creator and Owner of the Universe:

> The earth is the LORD's, and the fulness thereof; the world, and they that dwell therein.
> For he hath founded it upon the seas, and established it upon the floods.

> Who shall ascend into the hill of the LORD? or who shall stand in his holy place?
>
> He that hath clean hands, and a pure heart; who hath not lifted up his soul unto vanity, nor sworn deceitfully.
>
> He shall receive the blessing from the LORD, and righteousness from the God of his salvation.
>
> This is the generation of them that seek him, that seek thy face, O Jacob. Selah.
>
> Lift up your heads, O ye gates; and be ye lift up, ye everlasting doors; and the King of glory shall come in.
>
> Who is this King of glory? The LORD strong and mighty, the LORD mighty in battle.
>
> Lift up your heads, O ye gates; even lift them up, ye everlasting doors; and the King of glory shall come in.
>
> Who is this King of glory? The LORD of hosts, he is the King of glory. Selah. (Psalm 24, emphasis added)

David, the apple of God's eye, king of all Israel and ancestor of Jesus Christ, is writing to declare that one day, a generation will rise that will see an Everlasting King, the King of Glory. This generation will "stand in his holy place," and only a generation with "clean hands, and a pure heart" will do so. While this may refer to the church, it is actually addressed to Jacob, therefore this is probably the generation of Messianic Jews who will see Christ return at the end of the Tribulation Period. Notice HOW the KING returns: The "gates" are ordered to lift up their heads, and the "everlasting doors" are also told to be "lifted up."

Now, the original language translated as "gates" in the King James Version is transliterated as *shahar*. It is used in expressions such as "gates of death" (Psalms 9:13), "gate of the Lord" (Psalms 118:20), and "gate of heaven" (Genesis 28:17)."[293] There is something most intriguing about this word. Ugaritic is a language that is closely related to Hebrew, utilizing "proto-Semitic" phonemes (or single sounds). In Ugaritic, Shahar is actually *the name* of the god of the "dawn." Now, couple this with the Septuagint (Greek) translation of the verse:

Lift up your gates, **ye princes**, and be ye lifted up, ye everlasting doors. (Psalm 24:7, Septuagint, English Translation, emphasis added)[294]

Princes? There is no obvious equivalent in the Masoretic Hebrew text. Do "princes" have gates, or is this directed to immortals called princes, like "the prince of the power of the air"? In fact, the construction—where the "everlasting doors" are being addressed and told to be "lifted up"—personifies the doors, and seems to require the existence of an "entity" (or entities) tending the gate, a concept shared by many ancient religions. Another LXX translation reads:

Lift up the gates, those rulers of you. Lift eternal gates, and the King of glory will enter. (Psalm 23:7, LES).

Archon is the Greek term used in the Septuagint that is rendered into English as "princes" or "rulers."[295] It is the same term translated as "principalities" in the famous spiritual warfare passage: "For we wrestle not against flesh and blood, but against *principalities*, against powers, against the rulers of the darkness of this world, against spiritual wickedness in high places" (Ephesians 6:12, emphasis added). These entities are described in a Greek lexicon as "a supernatural power having some particular role in controlling the destiny and activities of human beings—'power, authority, lordship, ruler, wicked force.'"[296] Finally, if we take the text seriously, the command to "lift *eternal* gates" requires the existence of an immortal gatekeeper.

Is it possible that Psalm 24 is actually referring to a dimensional gateway that Jesus Christ passes through to access to the earthly realm? Do the principalities of the "gates" and "everlasting doors" control access into our current "three-dimensional" world? Might this be the impetus for the angelic war in heaven that results in Satan and the principalities, powers, and rulers of darkness being cast down to the earth?

When Jesus was resurrected, He became the "firstfruit" of all who would one day be born anew into eternal bodies. His mortal body took on immortality. Yet, in order for Him to return to earth and be seen by humans with limited, mortal perceptions, He will enter through a gate and an everlasting door. In His eternal body, Christ had the ability to walk through walls, yet He had substance: The disciple who doubted, Thomas, could put his own hand into Christ's wounds, left there as signs to all that He was the same man who had been crucified. Christ knows the secrets to opening the gates, for He commands them all. He created them all—and yet, one day each believer in his or her resurrected, eternal body, will ascend via an open gate and stand before Him. We cannot now step from our limited world into His presence at will. It is a one-way gate, opened only from above. If God calls a prophet into His presence as He did the apostle John in Revelation 1, then we may travel there in spirit—and one day, all who trust in His propitiation for our sins will pass through these gates to instantly be with Him.

So, where else in the Bible might we find possible references to gates and doors? Perhaps the most cited passage is in Genesis 28:12. Jacob has just left his dying father, Isaac, having tricked him into believing Jacob was actually Esau and therefore "stealing" the elder twin's "blessing." Shortly after this pivotal exchange between brothers, Jacob leaves Beersheba, a place name that means "well of the sevenfold oath," a reference to the seven ewes Abraham gave to Abimelech and Phicol of the Philistines. An interesting aside here is the possible, hidden meaning in the name "Abimelech," which can be transliterated as "Abi-Melech," or "my father is the king," which is obvious since this man is now king, or as "Abi-Molech," meaning "my spiritual father is Molech."[297] If the latter translation is correct, and it does make some sense, then this king had considerable power in the spiritually fallen realm. I bring this up because Jacob is traveling through a dangerous region where fallen entities and demons have dominion.

Jacob travels northeast toward the land of kinsman Laban, heading toward the region called Charrhan, probably referring to "Haran," a name that actually means "mountain climber," indicating a mountainous or hilly terrain, perhaps. The site of Charran (Haran) is modern-day Sanliurfa, Turkey, and there is an interesting Muslim legend passed down through the centuries there involving Abraham and Nimrod!

It is said that Nimrod threw Abraham into a fire, but that the flames miraculously became water, and the logs for the fire became fish. Today, tourists are shown a pool filled with "miracle fish" (carp) and told the story. Is there any truth to it? Well, Jewish oral tradition[298] states that Abraham's father, Tehran, served Nimrod (presumably after the Babel event), believing Nimrod to be a god. Nimrod, the legend says, was insecure after the whole language thing, and he feared that a true heir to the throne might show up one day. As a male and a direct descendent of Noah, Abraham posed a threat to Nimrod, so the paranoid king tried several times to kill the child. The Muslim tradition above is perhaps a different telling of the Jewish tale. But suffice it to say that Charrhan is definitely connected to supernatural events.

Bible archaeologists mostly agree that Jacob chose to "rest" eleven to twelve miles north of current-day Jerusalem, in an area today called Beit El. Weary from his travels, Jacob stopped for the night in the Judean Hills, where he chose a rock to serve as his pillow:

> And he lighted upon a certain place, and tarried there all night, because the sun was set; and he took of the stones of that place, and put them for his pillows, and lay down in that place to sleep.
>
> And he dreamed, and **behold a ladder set up on the earth, and the top of it reached to heaven: and behold the angels of God ascending and descending on it.**
>
> And, behold, the LORD stood above it, and said, I am the LORD God of Abraham thy father, and the God of Isaac: the land whereon thou liest, to thee will I give it, and to thy seed;
>
> And thy seed shall be as the dust of the earth, and thou shalt spread abroad to the west, and to the east, and to the north, and to the south: and in thee and in thy seed shall all the families of the earth be blessed.
>
> And, behold, I am with thee, and will keep thee in all places whither thou goest, and will bring thee again into this land; for I will not leave thee, until I have done that which I have spoken to thee of.

And Jacob awaked out of his sleep, and he said, **Surely the LORD is in this place; and I knew it not.**

And he was afraid, and said, How dreadful is this place! this is none other but the house of God, and this is the gate of heaven.

And Jacob rose up early in the morning, and took the stone that he had put for his pillows, and set it up for a pillar, and poured oil upon the top of it.

And he called the name of that place Bethel: but the name of that city was called Luz at the first. (Genesis 28:11–19)

Ulam is often translated as "formerly"; therefore, the old name of this city would have been "Luz," a name meaning "almond wood." Jacob however discovers in his dream that this location contains the gateway to heaven, therefore he renames it Beth-El, "house of God."Actually, a church was built there in the fourth century AD, and there are some remains of a small town built in the Byzantine period.[299] Should we mount an expedition there in search of ancient technology? Not likely for a theologically significant reason.

Man-made technology suggests the Hebrew parallel to *Etemenanki*, "The House of the Foundation-Platform of Heaven and Earth"[300] could otherwise be known as the Tower of Babel. However, in Jacob's dream, the portal was revealed via *divine* initiative. The contact between Heaven and earth was by the grace of God not the ingenuity of man. A highly regarded Old Testament scholar, Victor Hamilton, argues any perceived parallel with the Babel gate is superficial:

One cannot help but be struck by the parallel between the stairway in this dream, a stairway whose top reaches the sky, and the tower of Babel, whose top also extended into the heavens (11:4). But the similarity stops here. Unlike the Babel tower, Jacob's stairway is not a product of human delusions of grandeur. It is a way by which God will make himself known to Jacob. Messengers, not pride, go up and down this structure.[301]

The Hebrew term *sullām,* sometimes rendered "ladder," is a *hapax legomena*—it only occurs once in the Hebrew Bible. Since we have no Scripture to compare, ancient Semitic literature can be helpful. Many scholars now think *sullām* is connected to the Akkadian *simmiltu,* for "stairway."[302] Since it supports two-way traffic in Jacob's dream, a stairway does seem more logical than a ladder. Others see a more natural explanation.

Old Testament scholar Cornelis Houtman believes Bethel is a sacred mountain, pointing out that "according to Midrash *Rabbah* the rabbis understood *sullām* as a symbol of mount Sinai."[303] The Mountain of God, Mount Horeb, Mount Sinai and Mount Paran are all names for Mount Sinai. Interestingly, the gematriah of the Hebrew *sullam* and *Sinai* both have the value of 130, giving them esoteric affinity.

Sullam= 2 *5 * 13 = 130

Sinay= 2 *5 * 13 = 130

Affinity or not, the relevance of such a connection is probably only historical. The Ark of the Covenant, representing God's presence on earth, spent some time at Bethel (Judges 2:1, 20:27), but was taken to Shiloh in the time of the Judges (1 Samuel 1:3, 3:3), Later, David installed the ark in a tent at Jerusalem (2 Samuel 6). It was placed in the Temple with great ceremony in the reign of Solomon (1 Kings 8:1ff.). Accordingly, Mount Zion—the Temple Mount—became the new Mountain of God. A more ancient Hebraic interpretation—through a supernatural worldview—centers on the immortals.

The Midrash *Tanchuma* posits that the angels Jacob saw were the supernatural princes of the nations, and the two-way traffic depicts the rise and fall of these principalities and their associated worldly kingdoms.[304] Following the Babel dispersion, these spirit-beings quickly became idolized on earth as gods, giving birth to the worship of fallen immortals worldwide in the guise of various pagan religions. According to this Rabbinic tradition, Jacob is a symbol for the nation of Israel, and the angels symbolize the Divine Council through the wanderings of the Israelites from one hostile nation to another, witnessing the ascendency and annihilation of Egypt, Assyria, Babylon, Greece, and Rome. This midrash is quite consistent with Michael Heiser's exegesis of Psalm 82, which is explained elsewhere in this book.

Did Jacob merely "dream" that he saw a stairway to heaven, or was it a true vision of an objective reality? Still yet, perhaps it involves some of both? While there is not likely a physical stargate buried at Bethel, we do believe that Jacob was permitted to mystically "see" into objectively existing dimensions outside our normal three, plus one (time), and into the "folded space" or through a wormhole known to modern physicists as the Einstein-Rosen Bridge. As detailed elsewhere in this work, exotic matter is required to create temporary artificial wormholes in most theoretical designs. However, the Creator's divine essence is all the exotic matter needed to make the already thought plausible designs of theoretical physicist Kip Thorne into tangible realities. That such a fantastic vision is now a scientifically respectable concept does not in any way diminish the miraculous nature of the event. No, theoretical physics is the way our limited human minds must try to scientifically explain the supernatural abilities of God, who transcends time and space!

There is a parallel verse to this in John 1. Bethsaida in Galilee is where Jesus found Andrew, Peter, Philip, James, and John. It is a region on the northeast part of Galilee, very likely close to Capernaum, where Peter lived.

Now Philip was of Bethsaida, the city of Andrew and Peter.

Philip findeth Nathanael, and saith unto him, We have found him, of whom Moses in the law, and the prophets, did write, Jesus of Nazareth, the son of Joseph.

And **Nathanael said unto him, Can there any good thing come out of Nazareth?** Philip saith unto him, Come and see.

Jesus saw Nathanael coming to him, and saith of him, Behold an Israelite indeed, in whom is no guile!

Nathanael saith unto him, Whence knowest thou me? Jesus answered and said unto him, Before that Philip called thee, when thou wast under the fig tree, I saw thee.

Nathanael answered and saith unto him, Rabbi, thou art the Son of God; thou art the King of Israel.

Jesus answered and said unto him, Because I said unto thee, I saw thee under the fig tree, believest thou? thou shalt see greater things than these.

And he saith unto him, Verily, verily, I say unto you, Hereafter ye shall see heaven open, and the angels of God ascending and descending upon the Son of man. (John 1:44–51, emphasis added)

This is a most interesting and pivotal point in the life of Nathanael (whose name means "gift of God"). When told by his friend Philip about a man from Nazareth who fit the bill to be their promised Messiah, Nathanael replied with an insult: "Can anything good come out of Nazareth?" Little Nazareth must have had a low reputation. Today, we might say something like, "You mean that hick place?" Yet, Philip here insisted that lowly Nazareth was the home to the Messiah. How did Jesus respond to Nathanael, knowing full well what the man had said—about the insult? Our wonderful, understanding Lord called Nathanael *an Israelite in whom there was no guile—no deceit.* An insult was answered by a compliment! Then Jesus proved His divinity by telling Nathanael that He'd seen him underneath the fig tree even before Philip had called to Nathanael.

It's the equivalent of "I know who you are, and I know what you did." Nathanael made a complete, mental U-turn and called Jesus "Rabbi" ("Teacher") and "the Son of God." In recognition of this, Jesus continued, promising Nathanael that he would "see heaven open, and the angels of God ascending and descending upon the Son of man." One might conclude that Nathanael had been praying for a vision while beneath the fig tree, and now Jesus promised him one.

As a first-century Jew from Cana of Galilee, Nathaniel read and studied from the Septuagint version of the Hebrew Scriptures. Like his contemporaries, he was expecting the Messiah based on the prophecies of a coming king who would overthrow Israel's oppressors. "Because a child was born to us; a son was given to us whose leadership came upon his shoulder; and his name is called "Messenger of the Great Council," for I will bring peace upon the rulers and health to him" (Isaiah 9:6, LES). The Messenger of the Great Council applied Jacob's gate to himself when he replied to Nathanael, "Truly, truly, I say to you, you will see heaven opened, and the angels of God ascending and descending on the Son of Man" (John 1:51). Later, he said "I am the door: by me if any man enter in, he shall be saved" (John 10:9). Under the New Covenant, Jesus is a greater gateway to God than the "stairway to heaven" the angels traversed (Genesis 28:12; cf. Hebrew 10:19–20), and wherever Jesus is worshipped as Lord, that place becomes a spiritual "Bethel"—a gateway to God.

Did Nathanael see what Jacob saw—the Einstein-Rosen Bridge that leads to the throne of God? Perhaps not at that time—but one day, he and all those who "see" Jesus for who He really is will stand in His presence and witness the eternal bridge between the heavenly throne room and Israel. In fact, those who return with Christ—His Bride—may use that very bridge as we ascend to enjoy the Marriage Supper of the Lamb and then descend with Him at the end of the Tribulation Period.

Are there other examples in Scripture of the Einstein-Rosen Bridge, commonly called wormholes? Let me ask you two questions: What happened to Enoch and Elijah? And where is Moses buried? If you're not firmly versed in the Old Testament, you may not have a ready answer, but I'm betting that most of you shouted out the answer in your heads—if not right out loud. We'll begin with Enoch.

This prophet of the Lord lived before the Great Flood of Noah's day. In fact, Enoch was Noah's grandfather. The King James translation of Genesis 5:24 says simply, "Enoch walked with God and was not, for God took him." Young's Literal Translation says this: "And Enoch walketh habitually with God, and he is not, for God hath taken him." Enoch walked with God in the same way that Adam also "walked with God"—habitually, as a friend might walk with a companion. Enoch's walk has become the benchmark of biblical faith (Hebrews 11:5–6), and his being taken by God without dying earns him the rarified honor of being one of two known humans who can legitimately be called *"immortals."*

Enoch may actually have "seen" the Lord, for Noah clearly "heard" orders from the Lord to build an ark, and Abraham clearly "heard" and even "saw" the Lord, so the one-way Einstein-Rosen Bridge may have opened and allowed Enoch to "walk" with the Lord. Regardless of how this walking relationship occurred, the Hebrew makes it clear that something supernatural did occur when Enoch simply vanished from the earth. He walked, and he was not.

Interestingly, the ancient Hebrew and Greek texts seem to have anticipated what twentieth-century scientific discoveries involving black hole vortices and wormhole portals say they should look like. The Hebrew word *laqach* usually means "to take, grasp, seize."[305] Its semantic equivalence to the Greek *harpazo* is provocative because the apostle Paul, inspired by the Holy Spirit, used it to describe the catching away of the church: "Then we which are alive and remain shall be *caught up* together with them in the clouds" (1 Thessalonians 4:17a, emphasis added).

The Semitic *laqach* implies being taken suddenly, perhaps even against your will (i.e., captured), but *Strong's* also lists "to flash about as lightning" as a possible meaning.[306] If Enoch disappeared into a portal, then it's quite possible—even probable—that the opening of this gateway involved a flash, like lightning. The event horizon of these portals is often characterized by lightning as well as a whirlwind: "The crash of your thunder was in the whirlwind; your lightnings lighted up the world; the earth trembled and shook" (Psalm 77:18). We're told by Christ that He saw Lucifer fall "like lightning" to the earth. The rip into our time/space dimension from a world outside our continuum would likely create a great deal of lightning due to the enormous energy displacement. Now please recall that we mentioned that Enoch was one of *two* human beings (not counting Jesus) who can legitimately claim the title of *"immortal."*

Out of the Whirlwind

Elijah also walked with the Lord, and he knew in advance that the Lord would be sending for him. As one might expect to see in an astrophysicist-advised science-fiction film, Elijah's flaming chariot traveled to Heaven through a whirling vortex: "There appeared a chariot of fire, and horses of fire, and parted them both asunder; and Elijah went up by a whirlwind into heaven" (2 Kings 2:11). This imagery of a whirlwind is familiar to anyone living within the Bible Belt of the United States, because we see "whirlwinds" every spring. In fact, the Horn family's home in Missouri is smack in the middle of tornado alley! Often when God appears to people on earth, the scene is characterized by fire and whirling vortex energy (Ezekiel 1:4; Job 38:1).

The Hebrew term *suphah* is usually translated as "whirlwind" or "tempest" in English.[307] While it commonly denotes a cyclonic wind, the primitive root from which it derives, *suph*, means "surely snatch" or "surely snatch away,"[308] corresponding neatly to the Greek word *harpazo* which also means "to seize, to snatch away, to take away."[309] The same term is also found in the New Testament, in 2 Corinthians 12:2 ("caught up to the third heaven"); Revelation 12:5 ("caught up unto God"); and Acts 8:39 ("the Spirit of the Lord caught away Philip")—always describing the miraculous transport of a human by God.

The term *suphah* usually denotes a natural whirlwind, but it seems to describe a portal in many passages. The boldfaced terms that follow are all rendered from *suphah*. Apparently, the whirlwind portal is bidirectional, because Yahweh communicated with Job through a similar turbulence: "Then the Lord answered Job out of the **whirlwind**" (Job 38:1). However, whirlwinds are not only connected to heaven but also nightmares: "Terrors take hold on him as waters, a tempest stealeth him away in the night" (Job 27:20). The same term is also connected to God's judgment: "Behold, a **whirlwind** of the Lord is gone forth in fury, even a grievous **whirlwind**: it shall fall grievously upon the head of the wicked" (Jeremiah 23:19) and on the end-time Day of the Lord: "And the Lord God shall blow the trumpet, and shall go with whirlwinds of the south" (Zechariah 9:14). It can also be translated, the Lord God will sound the trumpet and will march forth in the whirlwinds of the south" (Zechariah 9:14b, ESV). Might it denote a divine portal in the south from which the Lord stages Armageddon?

Our suggestion that ancient prophecy describes, in a "just-so" manner, a vortex-like event horizon (just like one would expect of a traversable wormhole) is at the very least intriguing yet, even more, entails untold prophetic significance in the future. The Book of Enoch speaks of twelve heavenly portals (Enoch 76:1) grouped into four quadrants: North, South, East, and West. Paralleling Zechariah's prophecy that the Lord will come from the whirlwinds of the South, Enoch explains two of the quadrants: "And the first quarter is called the east, because it is the first: and the second, the south, because the Most High will descend there, yea, there in quite a special sense will He who is blessed forever descend" (Enoch 77:1). Apparently this descent marks the occasion when the Lord exclaims:"Lift up the gates, those rulers of you. Lift eternal gates, and the King of glory will enter" (Psalm 23:7, LES). Because the Book of Enoch was written at least few hundred years prior to Jesus' birth, the predicted event is remarkably consistent with Jesus' predicted end-time descent onto the Mount of Olives in the New Testament (Acts 1:11; Zechariah 14:4).

Zechariah 9:13 contains a prophetic promise of divine defense from military aggression from Greece, translated from the Hebrew name *Yavan* for Japheth's son Javan (Genesis 10:2)—also denoting his "descendants and their land."[310] Accordingly, the prophecy covers the lands of Javan's sons: Elishah, Tarshish, Kittim, and Dodanim, considerably more than what we now call Greece, including parts of modern Turkey. Zechariah was writing between 520 and 480 BC, but Alexander the Great did not conquer Israel for Greece until 333 BC. Accordingly, many believing scholars view this as prophecy of the Maccabean revolt (166–160 BC) that resulted in full Jewish independence in 142 BC. Even so, the context seems necessarily still future due to its initial messianic prophecy (v. 9) and the Lord's bountiful restoration (vv. 15–17) that seems to vastly supersede the second century BC Maccabean victory over Greece. This suggests the possibility of another victory over the lands of Javan or Greece.

Greece could play an important role in future prophecy. Daniel has told us to expect the "Little Horn," the Antichrist, will have to move southeast in order to reach the "pleasant land," or Israel (Daniel 8:9).

> And out of one of them came forth a little horn, which waxed exceeding great, toward the south, and toward the east, and toward the pleasant land. (Daniel 8:9)

Reversing that, the text implies that he comes from a land due northwest of Israel. Greece happens to lie squarely on a northwestern vector extending from Israel. More fascinating is that he will magnify himself "to the prince of the host" (Daniel 8:11), a reference to an immortal.

Interestingly, as we send this manuscript off to the printer, the new prime minister of Greece, Alex Tsipras, is being heralded as an Antichrist candidate. He is a handsome, charismatic, and "an avowed atheist."[311] A communist in his youth, he is now the leader of the Coalition of the Radical Left (SYRIZA). In an op-ed piece for the Israeli paper *Haaretz*, Sabby Mionis called SYRIZA "the anti-Zionist far-left" and labeled Tsipras as a "narcissistic populist," a silver-spoon-fed billionaire who has "never really held a proper job."[312] When a young Greek rises so quickly to power, it brings to mind the prototypical Antichrist, Antiochus IV Epiphanes, as implied by Jesus.

Antiochus, who preferred to be called *theosepiphanes*, "manifest god," was the Greek king of the Seleucid Empire from 175 BC until his death in 164 BC. His reputation was so atrocious, some his Greek contemporaries called him *Epimanes* ("The Mad One") behind his back. He invaded Israel in 167 BC and proceeded "to build illicit altars and illicit temples and idolatrous shrines, to sacrifice swine and ritually unfit animals" (1 Maccabees 1:47).[313] Even so, his ultimate sacrilege, the first "abomination of desolation," was to erect a statue of Zeus in the Holy of Holies and sacrifice a swine upon the altar of burnt offering in the temple (1 Maccabees 1:54).[314] According to Jesus, those events are a portent of another desolating abomination that will occur just prior to His return in judgment (Matthew 24:15).

Rising from the ashes of the "Greek Depressions," Tsipras seems to be positioning himself as an advocate for Europeans disenfranchised by the financial crises from 2008 to 2014, which produced unexpectedly high unemployment in most of the EU. When Tsipras met with Pope "Petrus Romanus" Francis at the Vatican on September 17, 2014, he extolled the pope as the "pontiff of the poor."[315] Tsiras wrote concerning the papal meeting, "We discussed the need for peace to return on earth, for the immediate cease of war interventions…asked him to take an international initiative for the termination of conflicts in the Middle East."[316] It seems that Tsipras is summoning the angel in the whirlwind.

A section of the book *Zenith 2016* called "Summoning the Angel in the Whirlwind" states:

> On January 20, 2001, President George W. Bush during his first inaugural address faced the obelisk known as the Washington Monument and twice referred to an angel that "rides in the whirlwind and directs this storm." His reference was credited to Virginia statesman John Page who wrote to Thomas Jefferson after the Declaration of Independence was signed, saying, "We know the race is not to the swift nor the battle to the strong. Do you not think an angel rides in the whirlwind and directs this storm?"
>
> Five weeks after the inaugural, on Wednesday, February 28, Congressman Major R. Owens of New York stood before the House of Representatives and prayed to the "Angel in the Whirlwind." He asked the spiritual force to guide the *future* and *fate* of the United States. Twenty-eight weeks later (for a total of 33 weeks from the inaugural—a number invaluable to mysticism and occult fraternities), nineteen Islamic terrorists (according to the official story) attacked the United States, hijacking four commercial airliners and crashing two of them into the Twin

Towers of the World Trade Center in New York City, a third into the Pentagon, and a fourth, which had been directed toward Washington, DC, crashed near Shanksville, Pennsylvania. What happened that day resulted in nearly 3000 immediate deaths, at least two-dozen missing persons, and the stage being set for changes to the existing world order….

Invitation to angels by elected officials combined with passive civilian conformity is key to opening doorways for supernatural agents to engage social governance. This is a classic tenet of demonology. Spirits go where they are invited, whether to possess an individual or to take dominion over a region. One could contend therefore that starting in 2001, the United States became so disposed in following and not challenging unprecedented changes to longstanding U.S. policies including the Christian rules for just war, that a powerful force known to the Illuminati as the "Moriah Conquering Wind," a.k.a. "the Angel in the Whirlwind" accepted the administration's invitation and enthroned itself in the nation's capital. Immediately after, it cast its eyes on the ancient home of the Bab-Illi, Babylon, where the coveted "Gate of the Illi" had opened once before.[317]

The occult realm seeks always to imitate God's abilities through magical rituals and esoteric knowledge. Here, the heavenly portal opened only at the will of God Almighty that is called a "whirlwind" in 2 Kings is imitated by fallen angels and corrupt men in a twisted call to action. The Moriah Conquering Wind is the key to opening the Abyss. There is a reason that God prohibits communing with the dead and the fallen—because summoning the whirlwind (that is trying to open the Einstein-Rosen Bridge) from this side will only lead to the opening of Hell itself. It's like the old story of the lady or the tiger, in which a man is given the choice of two doors. Behind one is a beautiful, voluptuous woman who will fulfill his every desire. Behind the other is a ravenous tiger that will tear him to shreds and devour him.

The Illuminati have foolishly been trying to open the Abyss since the days of Nimrod. Those who do so believe that eternal life and ultimate power and knowledge await them on the other side, but you and I know better. Instead of satisfying their thirst for power, the entities on the other side of the portal—when opened—will devour them one by one. The ancient goddess Ishtar sometimes called Inanna or Semiramis was often depicted riding a tiger. During the 2015 Super Bowl, at halftime, Katy Perry—the musical equivalent of a modern-day goddess—entered the arena astride a massive, animated "tiger" with red eyes. This event—like so many others staged in music videos and on award shows—may well have been orchestrated by human/demonic alliances that use such spectacles as secret rituals intended to force the opening of the door.

Katy Perry rode the tiger—seeming to provide both the lady and the beast. The Illuminati believe they can "tame" whatever comes through the portal, but only God controls the whirlwinds and all that pass through them. The tiger will only enter when God permits it.

And then Hell will enter our space/time continuum.

Now, whenever I bring up the topic of biblical gateways and portals, the first incident most colleagues mention is the Babylon gateway that Nimrod attempted to build. Let's take a look at the passage that describes this foolish attempt to unseal the Abyss. We find it in Genesis 11:

And the whole earth was of one language, and of one speech.

And it came to pass, as they journeyed from the east, that they found a plain in the land of Shinar; and they dwelt there.

And they said one to another, Go to, let us make brick, and burn them throughly. And they had brick for stone, and slime had they for morter.

And they said, Go to, let us build us a city and a tower, whose top may reach unto heaven; and let us make us a name, lest we be scattered abroad upon the face of the whole earth.

And the LORD came down to see the city and the tower, which the children of men builded.

And the LORD said, Behold, the people is one, and they have

all one language; and this they begin to do: and now nothing will be restrained from them, which they have imagined to do.

Go to, let us go down, and there confound their language, that they may not understand one another's speech.

So the LORD scattered them abroad from thence upon the face of all the earth: and they left off to build the city.

Therefore is the name of it called Babel; because the LORD did there confound the language of all the earth: and from thence did the LORD scatter them abroad upon the face of all the earth. (Genesis 11:1–9)

Assuming they even teach this event, most pastors and Bible study leaders today would either allegorize or at least downplay the clash at Babylon between God and humanity, but this is a disservice to their students. I wrote a series of articles about ten years ago about this very event. Titled "Stargates, Ancient Rituals, and Those Invited through the Portal," where I built upon the fine research by our dearly departed brother and semiotics genius, David Flynn:

In his seminal opus *Cydonia: The Secret Chronicles of Mars,* Flynn connected Nimrod's construction of the Tower of Babel to the rebel planet Mars:

Nimrod.... a giant of the race of Nephilim... authored the plan for the tower.... [and was] associated in myth with Nergal, the Babylonian God of Mars... The Tower of Babel was a tower to Mars.

Symbolism used by the mystery schools illuminated the writings of Italian poet Dante, who wrote of the connections between the Tower of Babel, Giants and Mars. Intriguingly, Dante identified Mars with Satan. Paradiso Canto IX:127–142:

Florence, the city founded by Mars, that Satan who first turned his back on his Maker, and from whose envy such great grief has come, coins and spreads that accursed lily flower, that has sent the sheep and lambs astray, since it has made a wolf of the shepherd.

The ancient Cabiri (Gibborim) who built Cyclopean walls and megalithic fortresses took many forms, but they all originated from the same place. They came down from heaven to the earth. According to ancient Sumerian myth, when Nergal the God of Mars was ejected from heaven he descended with… demons.…

Thus not only was Nimrod a Nephilim…not only did he design the Tower of Babel ("gate of the Gods")…not only was he associated with Mars and built the tower of Babel to the rebel prison planet… but he, like other giants, was daimonic (demonic) in origin. The significance of this cannot be overlooked. Babel was a Nephilim gateway and it is prophesied to be the future location from which "gates" open and "giants" return. (emphasis added)

The LORD inspired Moses to write about this epic event, and the description and hidden clues offer just enough information to discern many truths about Babel. This was not merely a tower intended to reach heaven due to its height. This was a Stargate, whose design was inspired by forbidden knowledge. Nimrod had deciphered the secret to unlocking a portal—an Einstein-Rosen Bridge that would lead to the heights once envied by Satan: the Sides of the North—the Heavenly Throne.

It must also be noted that Nimrod is the template for a panoply of "dying gods" worshiped under the names Osiris (a play possibly on Asshur, which may be another name for Nimrod, the Assyrian), Heracles, Horus, Tammuz, Mithras, Cernunnos, Marduk, and perhaps even King Arthur (the once and future king). When the languages were confused at the tower, the bewildered builders and terrified citizens, who no doubt believed Nimrod to be a god who would bring more gods to their city and recreate the "golden age" spoken of by their ancestors, took the story and told it with variations upon the names, seeding the legend of the "dying god" throughout all civilizations of the world. All the legends end with a promise that their god(s) would return in the final days and inaugurate a new age.

Nimrod's Stargate was probably located directly over Enki's abode, the Abzu (Abyss), said to be a freshwater lake deep within the earth. The Mighty Hunter Nimrod, along with the combined efforts of the "one mind" of mankind, used fallen angel technology and nearly opened the Abyss—but the Lord intervened personally, an extremely rare event, because the Abyss must and will remain closed until the Lord permits it to be opened. And we who live in these days—days that fit the bill for the "last days" read about the modern technology and foolish experiments (CERN, for instance) that may serve as parts of the final "key" to unlocking this hideous hell-hole. The next chapter will go into the historical basis for how this all could come to pass.

CHAPTER SEVEN

Babylon: Gate of the Gods or Doorway to Destruction?

By Tom Horn and Cris Putnam

> By the rivers of Babylon, there we sat down,
> yea, we wept, when we remembered Zion.
> —Psalm 137:1

ocated on the bank of Euphrates River, Babylon was the most famous eastern city of antiquity, and also was the consummate representation of wickedness in sacred Scripture. As Israel's tormentor, abductor, devastator, and eventual home in exile, Babylon was used by God in Scripture to bring devastating judgment on other nations (e.g., Jeremiah 21:2–10 and 25:8–11).[318] The name "Mystery Babylon" ascribed to the great harlot of the Apocalypse embodies the seductiveness of worldly spirituality enslaved to affluence and pleasure (Revelation 18:11–19). She defiantly "rides the beast" or gains authority from her association with the Antichrist—the Man of Sin (2 Thessalonians 2:3). The saccharine wine sloshing from her golden cup of abominations "made all the earth drunken: The nations have drunken of her wine; Therefore the nations are mad" (Jeremiah 51:7). While Babylon as an apocalyptic symbol transcends a geopolitical location, we suggest that "preternatural Babylon" will still assault Israel from the deserts of Iraq as an initial part of God's judgment during the Day of the Lord.

But how did the preternatural aspects of this strategic location begin?

Fourteen to twenty centuries before the Persians, Greeks, and Romans rewrote the earliest myths into their own creation accounts, the ancient land of Sumer (known as *Shinar* and later *Babylon*) produced original accounts by scribes who detailed how certain "gods" descended from Heaven—sometimes in "flying" machines and sometimes through magical doorways associated with specific mountains. These stories were pressed onto Sumerian cuneiform clay tablets using pictographs and other symbols to produce the first known system of writing and record-keeping. The fantastic encounters told of how visits by the "gods" led to advanced scientific and arcane knowledge, which later was codified in the Babylonian Mysteries and worship of Ishtar, Tammuz, Ashtaroth, and various Baals. Most scholars today recognize numerous parallels between Sumerian accounts of creation and the arrival of the "gods" with the biblical stories of Creation and the fall of Lucifer and later incursion of the Watchers. For example, the struggle between Lucifer against God is turned topsy-turvy in one famous Sumerian epic in which a struggle unfolds between the "ruler of the heavens" versus the "power of the air." This occurs in early Sumerian mythology after Enki, the god of wisdom and water, created the human race out of clay. It then appears that Anu, who was at first the most powerful of the Sumerian gods and the "ruler of the heavens," is superseded in power and popularity by Enlil, the "god of the air." To the Christian mind, this can easily be perceived as nothing less than Satan, the god of the air, continuing his pretense to the throne of God and his usurpation of Yahweh—"the Lord of the heavens." It also indicates an effort on the part of Satan and his angels to trick pagan Sumerians into perceiving them as the "supreme" gods (above the God of Heaven) and worthy of adoration.

Another example of this pattern is found in the legend called "Enumaelish," in which Marduk, the great god of the city of Babylon, is exalted above the benevolent gods and extolled as the creator of the world. The symbol of Marduk is a dragon (as is Satan in Revelation 12:9) called the Muscrussu, whose fable appears to contain several distortions of the important elements of the biblical account of Creation.

Genesis chapter 6, as well as numerous biblical apocrypha, affirms this story of beings that descended from Heaven to represent themselves as gods. Such ancient testaments include Enoch, Jubilees, Baruch, Genesis Apocryphon, Philo, Josephus, and various other olden records. The Hebrews themselves referred to these so-called gods as fallen *Benei ha-Elohim* (sons of God) who most notoriously mingled with humans, giving birth to part-celestial, part-terrestrial hybrids called Nephilim.

The other thing that stands out in the Sumerian texts as well as in later Greek and Roman mythologies (the Arcadian myths) is the desperate quest by post-Flood civilizations to regain the knowledge of these "gods" after it was lost in the epic of the deluge. According to the earliest writings, this included angelic technology bordering on "magic." The Book of Enoch (read by all the early church theologians, including Justin Martyr, Clemens of Alexandria, Origin, Irenaeus, Tertullian, Eusebius, Jerome, and Augustine, to name just a few, as well as quoted by the disciples and still included in some versions of the Bible today) tells of one of these flying "gods" (a fallen Watcher named Semjaza) who taught "enchantments." Another called Baraqijal taught the power of astrology; Azael taught weaponry; Araqiel, Shamsiel, and Sariel instructed on observations of the earth, sun, and the moon; and so on. From these secrets, men learned to advance war while women learned to use "charms and enchantments" to allure the giants themselves into their beds in order to propagate even more genetic atrocities. And this—the role of genetic manipulation—was central to what these "gods" were up to and ultimately why God destroyed all but Noah's family in the Flood. Indeed, the Bible describes the cause of the Flood as happening in response to "all flesh" having become "corrupted, both man and beast."

But did the secrets of the Watchers also include something even more fanciful? Something the post-Flood survivors desperately desired to reclaim? Angelic secrets of transdimensional locations and navigation, which existed before most life on earth was destroyed by water? Is that what was being constructed by Nimrod on the plains of Shinar? Could it be that by the time God responded to the tower's building, it had been concluded to such a phase that post-Flood giants were coming through the gateway (which Isaiah says they wait behind in that same location [more on that later]) to be reintroduced into our world? Is that how giants were on the earth before and after the Flood, and why God descended to disperse the building of the "tower" shortly thereafter?

After the flood waters abated, the sons of Noah would have moved to quickly reestablish society. While the children of Shem populated the Middle and Far East, and Jepheth developed the Eurasian and Greco-Roman geography, the land of Shinar would become the settlement efforts of Ham and his son Canaan (Genesis 11:1–2). This is where Nimrod, described in the oldest literature as a giant, would ultimately rise to become a "mighty" hunter before God and the first ruler of Baby-lon. This is recorded in the Bible this way:

> And Cush begat Nimrod: he began to be a mighty one in the earth.
>
> He was a mighty hunter before the Lord: wherefore it is said, Even as Nimrod the mighty hunter before the Lord.
>
> And the beginning of his kingdom was Babel, and Erech, and Accad, and Calneh, in the land of Shinar. (Genesis 10:8–10)

The name "Babylon" is derived from the Greek form of the name based on the Akkadian plural form *Bāb-ilāni* "gate of gods."[319] In sharp contrast to its inherently divine claim, the ancient Hebrews used it in a polemic fashion: "Therefore is the name of it called Babel; because the Lord did there confound *[balal]* the language of all the earth" (Genesis 11:9). In a sarcastic way, this verse links the name of the city, *Babel*, with the Hebrew verb *balal*, which means "to confuse, to mix, to mingle."[320] Missed in English translation, God is inspiring Moses to taunt, "You claim to be the 'gate of the gods,' but you are really only the gate to confusion." The intentional wordplay is a scriptural "face palm" directed toward Babylon.

The ziggurat at Babylon was known formally as *Etemenanki*, "The House of the Foundation-Platform of Heaven and Earth."[321] The word "ziggurat" is derived from the Akkadian *ziqqurratu*, "temple tower," a noun derived from *zaqāru*, "to build high."[322] The Babylonians and their predecessors, the Sumerians, believed in many heavens and earths. For example, Sumerian incantations of the second millennium BC refer to seven heavens and seven earths possibly created by seven generations of gods.[323] Given seven heavens is a part of religious cosmology found in Judaism and Islam, the Sumerian tradition is surprisingly obscure. In the Sumerian myth, "Inanna's descent to the underworld," the "Queen of Heaven" Inanna passes through a total of seven gates, each one exacting a price in divine powers. The sevenfold structure is displayed when the gatekeeper was instructed to "let the seven gates of the underworld be bolted."[324]

Like most people in the ancient world and even today, the Sumerians considered mountains to be the link between the heavens and earth. In Tablet 9 of the standard version of the *Epic of Gilgamesh*, Mashuis a great cedar-forested mountain. Apparently, this sacred mountain spans from the heavens to the underworld. Tablet 9 of the epic reads, "Then he reached Mount Mashu, which daily guards the rising and setting of the Sun, above which only the dome of the heavens reaches, and whose flank reaches as far as the Netherworld below, there were Scorpion beings watching over its gate."[325] Because the word "Mashu" comes from the Akkadian for "twins," it may translate as "two mountains."[326] We suggest the approximate location between two mountains suitable for being called a "cedar land" was the forest between Mount Lebanon and Mount Hermon (whose name means "Forbidden Place")—the portal of the Watchers' initial descent and netherworld imprisonment, according to the ancient Book of Enoch (also of interest, as most high-level Freemasons know, this location from which the founders of their order descended sits 33 degrees east longitude and 33 degrees north latitude of the Paris Zero Meridian!).

Like a man-made mountain, the ziggurat was a portal—a gateway between Heaven and earth. For example, the city-gate of Ninurta was called "lofty-city-gate-of-heaven-and earth,"[327] the ziggurat at Larsa, "The House of the Link between Heaven and Earth," and Borsippa, "The House of the Seven Guides of Heaven and Earth" and Asshur,

The "House of the Mountain of the Universe."[328] These were all mega-lithic structures that shared the ill-conceived desire to build a "stairway to heaven" like the prototype mentioned in Genesis 11:4.

The restored Great Ziggurat of Ur, built with similar characteristics as the Tower of Babel[329]

The biblical account of Babel attributes the city's foundation to Nimrod (Genesis 10:10). The builders wanted to create a structure "whose top may reach unto heaven." When the Lord came down and saw what was happening, He said, "Nothing will be restrained from them, which they have imagined to do" (Genesis 11:6). That is a curious comment if the meaning here is only that the tower would reach into the "sky." Structures had been built around the world since the dawn of time extending significantly skyward. Today, the world's tallest man-made structure is the 2,722-foot-tall Burj Khalifa in Dubai, United Arab Emirates. Even so, God seems unimpressed, and that is why imagining Babel's altitude as a significant challenge begs credulity. The Babel ambition seems necessarily much more than sheer stature and hints at apotheosis.

As far as we know, nothing else has ever elicited such an intriguing response from God, saying, "nothing will be restrained from them, which they have imagined to do" or a translation like "nothing that they propose to do will now be impossible for them" (ESV). And what was it Nimrod imagined to do? To build a tower whose top would penetrate *Shamayim*—the abode of Watchers; God. And just what sort of nefarious construction project would allow that to happen and arguably prompt more divine intervention than the atomic bomb? Josephus weakly suggests that the Tower of Babel was being made waterproof and that this was an act of rebellion against God, defying Him for sending the Flood and preparing for survival of future acts of punishment should they come. Yet what if another meaning here—"which they have imagined to do"—fits more perfectly with Scripture and history? Something that has to do with the physicality of Heaven—as in the dwelling place of angels?

Gary Stearman—popular anchor for SkyWatch TV and Prophecy Watchers television programs—believes like many scholars do that something was going on at Babylon with regard to "angelic portal technology." He writes:

> Under the leadership of Nimrod, the early post-Flood societies were obviously attempting to reunite with the fallen spirit-beings, who were within their recent historical memory…they were on the verge of achieving their primary goal—not just to build a tower, but to break through a barrier to the realm of heaven, itself. They were apparently about to realize some success in penetrating the dimensional veil that separates one aspect of heaven from the earth!
>
> This "tower" would enable men to realize their darkest imaginings. And what had they imagined to do? Simply to renew their contact with the "sons of God," as their predecessors had done before the Flood.[330]

Perhaps, as Stearman suggests above, Nimrod was attempting to open a doorway with the peripheral proximity of a parallel brane in the cosmic superstructure astrophysicists call the *bulk* (explained in chapter 8, "The

Science of Portals"). According to modern physics, the Second Heaven (or astral plane) might be only a micrometer away in a fifth dimension. On the one hand, such ideas bring comfort to some, to conceptualize God and His angels as always in such close "physical" proximity. On the other hand, the same notion disturbingly adds relevance to the prophecies of Isaiah regarding earthly Babel-gates opening at the end of time with giants and transgenic monstrosities rushing out of them. Either way, the text above could imply the ever-present apotheosis ambition of man—to use the tower as a transformational technology employed by Nimrod and his minions to become like gods and "make us a name." In *Forbidden Secrets of the Labyrinth*, Mark Flynn explains, "The tower was not necessarily a device that would cause men to become gods immediately, but an intradimensional conduit that would once more bring the assistance of the Watchers who would make men "gods" like themselves through the knowledge they provided."[331] The Watchers' primary offense (other than illicit procreation with humans) was the promulgation of forbidden knowledge, weapons, and dangerous technology (1 Enoch 8).

As a result, we would expect a tell-tale level of sophistication in ancient cultures under their sway. Indeed, megalithic structures of the time and OOPARTS (objects that existed in places and time that defy logic) have been found. For instance, the "Baghdad Battery" is an actual working battery from the ancient plains of Shinar. Nobody knows what real voltage-producing batteries could have been used for at that time or how the knowledge to make them was developed. This seems to indicate very advanced and sophisticated knowledge, which was abruptly lost in antiquity. Joseph Farrell asserts the same and documents how the ancient Babylonians were much more erudite than historians initially believed. He writes, "The Pythagorean theorem was known in Babylon more than a thousand years before Pythagoras.... Traditional stories of discoveries made by Thales or Pythagoras must be discarded as 'totally unhistorical'; much of what we have thought was Pythagorean must now be credited to Babylon."[332] The sexagesimal number system used in ancient Mesopotamia used cuneiform wedge-shaped digits to represent powers of sixty. Farrell believes it could imply a familiarity with extradimensionality:

The very structure of ancient Mesopotamian numerical notation implies a basic familiarity with hyper-dimensional geometries and the basic mathematical techniques for describing objects in four or more spatial dimensions.... It is to be noted that the Sumerian-Babylonian gods may be described by such notation. In other words, the gods were being described as a peculiar union of physics and religion, as hyper-dimensional entities or objects.[333]

According to Asger Aaboe, the origins of Western astronomy can be found in Mesopotamia, and all Western efforts in the exact sciences are direct descendants of the late Babylonian astronomers.[334] These advances suggest the Watchers' influence. If so, then perhaps the notorious tower involved a fantastic angelic technology that would allow Nimrod to actually do the impossible—as the text cryptically implies. More conservatively, it suggests that the "gateway" association was not merely a metaphor. It seems most probable that it opened a channel to the Second Heaven and the abode of the Watchers.

Revealing the Immortals

In response to Nimrod's ambitious structure, Yahweh confused the languages and the peoples dispersed. For that reason, Genesis chapters 10 and 11 constitute what is known as "The Table of Nations." The corresponding nations are the direct result of the Tower of Babel dispersal. According to Jewish tradition, there were seventy original nations after the Flood, corresponding to the seventy names in this chapter. Referring to this era, a strange passage in Deuteronomy reads:

When the Most High gave to the nations their inheritance, when he separated the sons of men, he fixed the bounds of the peoples according to the number of the sons of God [*Bene Elohim*, LXX: "angels"]. For the LORD's portion is his people, Jacob his allotted heritage. (Deuteronomy 32:8–9)

Hebrew Bible scholar Dr. Michael Heiser uses this as the basis for the "Deuteronomy 32 Worldview," a theological construct based on the oldest manuscript's reading of verse 8. Where we read in the King James Bible, "according to the number of the children of Israel," in the Dead Sea Scrolls as well as the Greek Septuagint's more ancient text, this verse reads, "according to the number of the sons of God," which is a clear reference to angels (Deuteronomy 32:8, ESV [the ESV translation used the LXX reading]). The passage (Deuteronomy 32:8) reflects the Jewish belief that the number of the nations is proportional to the number of the "sons of God" mentioned in Genesis 6:2 and Job 2:1, among other passages. This is a more logical reading than "sons of Israel" found in many English Bibles, because when mankind was divided at Babel, Abraham had not yet been born, so there were no "sons of Israel."

The "immortals" are the "sons of God." A Jewish angelology adopts this exegesis as well, stating:

> Another special group of angels are the 70 "princes of the peoples," appointed over each of the 70 peoples of the earth. They are first mentioned in the Septuagint in Deuteronomy 32:8—without their number being given—from which it may be gathered that at this time the number of all angels was thought not to exceed the number of peoples.[335]

In ancient Judaism, it was understood that the dispersal at the Tower of Babel entailed not only the confusion of the languages, but Yahweh's disinheriting of the other nations. God delegated the nations to angelic rule as reflected in the pseudepigraphal book *Testament of Nephatali:*

> And do not forget the Lord your God, the God of your fathers; Who was chosen by our father Abraham when the nations were divided in the time of Phaleg. For at that time the Lord, blessed be He, came down from His highest heavens, and brought down with Him seventy ministering angels, Michael at their head. He commanded them to teach the seventy families which sprang

from the loins of Noah seventy languages. Forthwith the angels descended and did according to the command of their Creator. But the holy language, the Hebrew language, remained only in the house of Shem and Eber, and in the house of Abraham our father, who is one of their descendants. (Testament of Nephatali 8:3–6)[336]

Of the seventy nations in the Genesis 10 table, certain "sons of God" or "powers and principalities" are associated with specific geographic areas and people groups. During the time of Peleg (cf. Genesis 10:25), God descended from Heaven with the seventy angels in order to teach the peoples of the earth their respective languages. Later, Michael, at the behest of God, asked each people to choose its patron angel, and each nation chose the angel who had taught it its language, with the exception of Israel. In order to display distinction, Deuteronomy 32:9 indicates that Yahweh chose Israel as His own. This pantheon of divine beings or angels who were originally to administer the affairs of Heaven and earth for the benefit of each people group became corrupt and disloyal to God in their administration of those nations (Psalm 82). They then began soliciting worship as gods, and because these angels, unlike their human admirers, would continue on earth until the end of time, each "spirit" behind the pagan attributions would become known at miscellaneous times in history and to various cultures by different names. This certainly agrees with the biblical definition of idolatry as the worship of fallen angels, and means the characterization of such spirits as Nimrod/Apollo, Jupiter, Zeus, Isis, and their many other attributions can be correctly understood simply as titles ascribed to distinct and individual supernaturalism.

Jewish lore holds that when the First Temple was destroyed, God turned away and the seventy angels were allowed to hold sway over Israel until the Day of Judgment (Enoch 89:59; 90:22, 25). The seventy nations, with their associate "son of God," is the background behind Jesus' sending of the seventy (Luke 10:1) and adds new relevance to their response: "And the seventy returned again with joy, saying, Lord, even the [seventy fallen angels?] devils are subject unto us through thy name" (Luke 10:17).

The numbers seventy or seventy-two feature prominently in Jewish mysticism and Western occultism. *Ars Goetia* is the first section of a demonological grimoire called *The Lesser Key of Solomon,* which describes how to summon and control the *seventy-two* demons that King Solomon allegedly evoked, employed, and confined when he built the original temple on Mount Zion.[337] After describing the attributes of each of the seventy-two evil spirits, the *Goetia* provides an account of what happened when King Solomon imprisoned them into a brass vessel:

> And it is to be noted that Solomon did this because of their pride [i.e., the pride of the evil spirits], for he never declared other reason why he thus bound them. And when he had thus bound them up and sealed the Vessel, he by Divine Power did chase them all into a deep Lake or Hole in Babylon.[338]

While the Bible does report that Solomon succumbed to idolatry (1 Kings 11:4), there is no historical basis for such fantastic claims about the construction of the Temple and we do not accept the *Goetia's* demonic revisionism. Like most occultism, its demonic magic is based on pseudo history and outright fabrication. It never really empowers the practitioner and inevitably leads one to destruction.

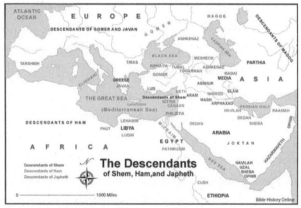

The Descendants of Shem, Ham, and Japeth

In Psalm 82, Yahweh condemns and promises to punish the gods (the seventy fallen angels) who have abused and misled their people:

> I have said, Ye are gods; And all of you are children of the most High.
>> But ye shall die like men, And fall like one of the princes.
>> Arise, O God, judge the earth: For thou shalt inherit all nations. (Psalm 82:6–8)

While anything short of a supernatural interpretation requires externally imposed revision, Heiser was probably the first to point out the most obvious problem with the suggestion that these are Israelites; that is, why does Yahweh condemn them to "die like men" if they actually are men? It only makes sense if you take the text literally when it identifies them as created gods but still called gods nonetheless. The territorial nature of these powers is further supported by Scripture.

Regaining Access to the Angels that War?

In the book of Daniel, the angel Gabriel reports to Daniel that he was delayed twenty-one days due to a battle with the "prince of the kingdom of Persia," and was only able to escape when Israel's champion, the archangel Michael, came to assist (Daniel 10:13–14). Even more, he reports that once he is done battling the Persian spirit, he must then fight the "prince of Greece." In suggesting this is a peek behind the curtain of an extradimensional battle, what immediately comes to mind is that at the time of Daniel's writing, the Persian Empire was in control of most of the world, but it was soon to be conquered by Alexander the Great of Greece. These otherworldly princes appear to be the original seventy divine council members.

After Daniel, the most significant book of end-time prophecy is Zechariah. In the last section of the Zechariah (chapters 12–14), one can parallel the text to fill in details concerning the battle of Armageddon and Jesus' return to the Mount of Olives. He is also shown an angelic paramilitary squad—"These are they whom the Lord hath sent to walk to and fro, through the earth"—which patrols the earth restraining evil and promoting justice (Zechariah 1:10b). Cambridge scholar Iain Duguid writes, "These horsemen are his 'special operations;' forces, not human beings (who could not quickly inspect the whole earth) but angels engaged in secret observation of the world to provide up-to-date and accurate intelligence information for the Lord."[339] Like the divine council, God has chosen to use intermediaries to accomplish His will on earth. What is lesser known, however, is how through Zechariah, God promised Joshua the high priest *access to the heavenly council!*

> Thus saith the Lord of hosts; If thou wilt walk in my ways, and if thou wilt keep my charge, Then thou shalt also judge my house, and shalt also *keep my courts, And I will give thee places to walk among these that stand by.* (Zechariah 3:7, emphasis added)

In context, the persons indicated by the phrase "these that stand by" were the divine council "sons of God," including the angel of the Lord and Satan (3:1). God then promises to bring His servant, the Branch, and to remove the iniquity of the land in one day (a claim singularly explained by Jesus' substitutionary atonement via the cross).

> Hear now, O Joshua the high priest, thou, And thy fellows that sit before thee: For they are men wondered at: For, behold, I will bring forth my servant the BRANCH.
> For behold the stone that I have laid before Joshua; Upon one stone shall be seven eyes: Behold, I will engrave the graving thereof, saith the LORD of hosts, And I will remove the iniquity of that land in one day. (Zechariah 3:8–9)

Interpreting Jesus as "the Branch" is strongly supported by the following: "And there shall come forth a rod out of the stem of Jesse, And a Branch shall grow out of his roots" (Isaiah 11:1). Throughout Isaiah, the

Messiah is consistently symbolized as a branch, shoot or twig (4:2; 6:13; 53:2). The Septuagint contains another fascinating reading concerning Jesus that does not appear in the Masoretic text. The Masoretic reads:

> For unto us a child is born, unto us a son is given: And the government shall be upon his shoulder: And his name shall be called Wonderful, Counseller, The mighty God, The everlasting Father, The Prince of Peace. (Isaiah 9:6)

And the LXX reads:

> Because a child was born to us; a son was given to us whose leadership came upon his shoulder; and his name is called "*Messenger of the Great Council*," for I will bring peace upon the rulers and health to him. (Isaiah 9:6, LES, emphasis added)

Of course, this identifies Jesus as the "Messenger of the Great Council" and reinforces the Deuteronomy 32 worldview. The Septuagint reading is much older and more likely reflects Isaiah's intended meaning for his seventh-century BC reader. It also implies that all who are in Christ have direct access to the CEO and are no longer subject to the council and its territorial princes. Jesus is the High Priest of a new and better covenant that includes all of the nations (Hebrews 8:13).

In Luke 10, Jesus prefigures the Gentile mission by sending seventy disciples to represent the seventy (sometimes seventy-two) nations of Jewish tradition. (Some Greek manuscripts read seventy; others read seventy-two). Similarly, Paul writes of "elemental spirits of the world" (Colossians 2:8) and "principalities, cosmic powers, and rulers of the darkness of this world" (Ephesians 6:12). The prophet Isaiah foretells the future judgment of these so-called gods: "On that day the Lord will punish the host of heaven, in heaven, and the kings of the earth, on the earth" (Isaiah 24:21). Paul was saying as much when he wrote of the cross: "And having spoiled principalities and powers, he made a shew of them openly, triumphing over them in it" (Colossians 2:15). Through

Jesus, all believers "have access by one Spirit unto the Father" (Ephesians 2:18b). Even though these foes are defeated, they still hold sway on the unbelieving world system. Almost certainly, the war in Heaven described in Revelation 12 represents the end game and impending final judgment of the rebel angelic powers.

Even if it seems radically new to the reader, the Deuteronomy 32 worldview is ancient Hebraic theology in its purest form. Despite knee-jerk reactions, it is not really polytheism. The little-'g' gods are created, not eternal. Yahweh is clearly above them all, so monotheism is not challenged. Theological considerations aside, this construct also suggests more interesting explanations for megalithic monuments and the world grid system discussed elsewhere in this book.

Portal Technology in the Cities of the Fallen Gods

After the dispersion from Babel, the Hebrew patriarch Abram's original homeland Ur was in Mesopotamia; Isaac took a wife from there; and Jacob—the ankle grabber—lived there for twenty years. However, Sumer went into a decline. As the book *Nephilim Stargates* notes:

> As the centuries passed, the god and goddess worshipping cities of the Sumerians began to fade away. The flourishing fields of agriculture that provided the underpinnings of the great Sumerian economy were depleted of fertility through over-irrigation, and residues of salt build-up appeared to chaff the surface of the land. The city-states of Sumeria; Kish, Ur, Lagash, and Umma, damaged by a millennium of civil war, finally surrendered to foreign invasion. The barbarian armies of the Elamites conquered and destroyed the city of Ur, and Amorites from the west overran the northern province of Sumer and subsequently established Babylon as their capital. Babylon became the capital of the First Dynasty of Babylon. The renowned sixth king, Hammurabi, an

Amorite, restored the city and expanded its influence. During his reign and that of his son, numerous temples were built.

By B.C.1840, Hammurabi conquered the remaining cities of Sumeria and forged northern Mesopotamia and Sumeria into a single nation. Yet the ultimate demise of the Sumerian people did not vanquish their ideas. Sumerian art, language, literature, and especially religion, was forever absorbed into the cultures and social academics of the nations surrounding Mesopotamia, including the Hittite nation, the Babylonians, and the ancient Assyrians…and something else: the story of flying disks, the gods who flew in them, and gateways through which the evil and benevolent influences sought entry.

Such gateways were represented on earth in Assyrian archways built through elaborate construction ceremonies and blessed by names of good omens. Colossal transgenic creatures stood guard at the gates and palace entries to keep undesirable forces from coming through the portals—important imitative magic thought to represent heavenly ideas—guardians that were often accompanied by winged spirits holding magic devices and magic statuettes concealed beneath the floors.

Sumerian engravings on clay cylinders speak of these flying disks. Very similar winged disks are found throughout Assyrian mythology in association with Ashur, the flying god of war. Ashur is believed to be a later version of Ahura-Mazda, the good god of Zoroastrianism who is opposed by Ahriman. In each case these very ancient beings are depicted coming through or descending from the sky on flying disks. Similar stories are repeated in Egyptian hieroglyphs as well as in the literature of Greece and other cultures around the world.[340]

The city fell to the Hittites in 1600 and then came under Kassite rule. Following attacks by the Assyrians and Elamites, Babylon was restored by Nebuchadnezzar I in 1124.[341] In the books of Daniel, Kings, and Isaiah, we find historically useful material that can be correlated to the Greek and Babylonian writings: "The Babylonian king Mar-duk-apal-iddin II (722–711 BC) sent an envoy to Hezekiah (2 Kings 20:12–13 and Isaiah 39:1), with the intention of fighting against Sargon of Assyria, who however defeated him."[342] Babylon first destroyed Nineveh and then turned its aggression toward the kingdom of Judah. In 605 BC, the Babylonians took Jerusalem, exiled thousands of Israelites including the prophets Ezekiel and Daniel, and installed Zedekiah on the throne (Daniel 1:1–21; 2 Kings 24; 2 Chronicles 36). Jerusalem was finally demolished in 586 BC, Zedekiah's eyes were blinded, and most of the population was exiled to Babylon. This frames the setting of King Nebuchadnezzar's court in the book of Daniel.

Nebuchadnezzar also invaded Egypt and all of the coastal cities of Canaan to secure the borders of his new empire. For more than two decades after the fall of Jerusalem, Nebuchadnezzar reigned over the colossal Babylonian Empire. His architects raised the capital city of Babylon to the height of its grandeur, adorning it with one of the Seven Wonders of the Ancient World, the famed Hanging Gardens.

> There was a conscious effort on the part of the leaders to return to the old forms and customs. It has been said that this period might properly be called the Renaissance of Old Babylonia.[343]

These may have been a reconstruction because Diodorus Siculus and Quintus Curtius Rufus specify that a "Syrian" king originally built the gardens. However, it is not as well known that in addition to the Hanging Gardens and the golden statue of himself, Nebuchadnezzar *rebuilt the Tower of Babel.*

Nebuchadnezzar and the Gateway to the Gods

Nebuchadnezzar immortalized his efforts on a stele—a stone slab, taller than it is wide, erected as a monument, for commemorative purposes.

The Tower of Babel Stele has an interesting history. Today, it belongs to a private collection of Norwegian businessman Martin Schoyen.[344] His book collection contains more than thirteen thousand manuscripts; the oldest book is about five thousand years old. The ancient stele includes the clearest existing image of Babylonian King Nebuchadnezzar II—the king who promoted Daniel—and the earliest images of the Tower of Babel. With narcissistic zeal, Nebuchadnezzar boasts of his construction prowess on the stele and what many scholars overlook is that he specifically claims reconstruction of the Tower of Babylon. A translation of the ancient stele reads:

ETEMENANKI: ZIKKURAT BABIBLI: "THE HOUSE, THE FOUNDATION OF HEAVEN AND EARTH, ZIGGURAT IN BABYLON". NEBUCHADNEZZAR, KING OF BABYLON AM I—IN ORDER TO COMPLETE E-TEMEN-ANKI AND E-UR-ME-IMIN-ANKI I MOBILIZED ALL COUNTRIES EVERYWHERE, EACH AND EVERY RULER WHO HAD BEEN RAISED TO PROMINENCE OVER ALL THE PEOPLE OF THE WORLD— THE BASE I FILLED IN TO MAKE A HIGH TERRACE. I BUILT THEIR STRUCTURES WITH BITUMEN AND BAKED BRICK THROUGHOUT. I COMPLETED IT RAISING ITS TOP TO THE HEAVEN, MAKING IT GLEAM BRIGHT AS THE SUN.[345]

The *stele* is also interesting for diagrams, in this case, the sacred upper room.

The small building at the top, *cella,* was a designated temple.[346] Stan Deyo describes, "The top floor plan has a room for the gods to transit from their world to ours."[347] His proposal is in line with contemporary scholarship. An academic historian explains the image:

He illustrates his great accomplishment with carved images of the gloriously rebuilt Tower: one is a ground plan of the temple showing the outer walls and inner rooms, the other an elevation showing the front of the ziggurat with the relative proportions of each of the seven steps and the temple on top. Unambiguously labeled as "The house, the foundation of heaven and earth, the ziggurat in Babylon," these are the only contemporary images of the tower known to exist.[348]

Tower of Babel stele. Babylon - 604-562 BCE.   Reconstruction   **Tower of Babel Stele**

So within this floor plan was a portal between realms.

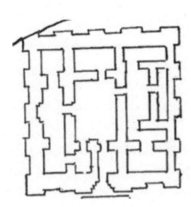

Floor plan

When Deyo was asked if he had a specific opinion concerning which room in the above floor plan hosted the portal, he replied, "I think there could be a portal room where I have the circles."

Stan Deyo's Portal Room

Is it possible that Nebuchadnezzar II opened a gate? The notion offers some explanatory scope for his testimony that the Watchers cursed him to have the mind of an animal for seven years, a disciplinary punishment so that he would acknowledge and worship Daniel's God:

> Let his heart be changed from man's, and let a beast's heart be given unto him; and let seven times pass over him.
> This matter is *by the decree of the watchers*, and the demand by the word of the holy ones: to the intent that the living may know that the most High ruleth in the kingdom of men, and giveth it to whomsoever he will, and setteth up over it the basest of men. (Daniel 4:16–17, emphasis added)

After rebuilding the tower of Babel, he likely experienced the same spiritual transformation as did his predecessor Nimrod. He boasted, "Is not this great Babylon, that I have built for the house of the kingdom by the might of my power, and for the honour of my majesty?" (Daniel 4:30). After his humiliation and arguable conversion, Nebuchadnezzar likely dismantled the pagan portal and the ziggurat began the slow but dependable decline toward deterioration.

Cyrus, King of Persia, conquered the city without a battle in 539 BC. He did this by damming up the Euphrates River, which ran under the city walls, and then marching his army into the city via the dry riverbed. The ancient clay Cyrus cylinder seal preserves his nonviolent victory:

> When I entered Babylon in a peaceful manner, I took up my lordly reign in the royal palace amidst rejoicing and happiness.… My vast army moved about Babylon in peace; I did not permit anyone to frighten (the people of) [Sumer] and Akkad. I sought the welfare of the city of Babylon and all its sacred centers.[349]

Babylon then became part of the Persian Empire serving as secondary capital. During this period, the Greek historian Herodotus visited Babylon immortalizing the tower. In 440 BC, Herodotus wrote:

> In the middle of the precinct there was a tower of solid masonry, a furlong [201 meters] in length and breadth, upon which was raised a second tower, and on that a third, and so on up to eight. The ascent to the top is on the outside, by a path which winds round all the towers. When one is about half-way up, one finds a resting-place and seats, where persons can sit for some time on their way to the summit. On the topmost tower there is a spacious temple, and inside the temple stands a couch of unusual size, richly adorned, with a golden table by its side. There is no statue of any kind set up in the place, nor is the chamber occupied of nights by anyone but a single native woman, who, as the Chaldeans, the priests of this god, affirm, is chosen for himself by the deity out of all the women of the land.[350]

On the twenty-first or twenty-second of October in 331 BC, Babylon was conquered by Alexander the Great, who began to rebuild the venerated but decaying city.[351] At that time, most of the debris was cleared away in preparation for the reconstruction of the Tower. But the construction was abandoned after Alexander's untimely death and then the unmerciful but reliable cycle of neglect, decline, and deterioration continued. By the New Testament era, the Chaldean capital was no more than a famous heap of ruins.[352] We suggest it is likely one of the most haunted places on earth, one that will overflow when "the day of the Lord cometh, Cruel both with wrath and fierce anger, To lay the land desolate: And he shall destroy the sinners thereof out of it" (Isaiah 13:9).

In the early twentieth century, excavations by German archaeologist Robert Koldeway uncovered substantial remains from the Neo-Babylonian Period, including the location of the Tower of Babylon.[353] Interestingly, he was still able to hire local residents to assist with the dig because Babylon had never become the uninhabited wasteland predicted in prophecy (Isaiah 13:20; cf. Jeremiah 51:26).[354] Because Babylon was never destroyed in war as Isaiah and Jeremiah describe, it seems reasonable to expect a future satisfaction. Chuck Missler suggests: "It is illuminating to read—at one sitting—the six principal chapters dealing this topic: Isaiah 13 and 14, Jeremiah 50 and 51 and Revelation 17 and 18."[355] The chart from KHouse displays some of the pertinent issues:

Destruction of Babylon

	Isaiah 13	Isaiah 14	Jeremiah 50	Jeremiah 51	Revelation 17	Revelation 18
Many Nations Attacking	4, 5	2, 26	2, 9 41, 46	7	16	
Israel in the Land, Forgiven		1	4, 20			
Like Sodom & Gomorrah	19		40			
Never to be inhabited Bricks never reused	20	23	13, 26 39	26, 29 37		
During "Day of the Lord"	6, 10 11, 13		25		✓	✓
Literal (Chaldean) Babylon	19	22	50	4, 24 63		
King's fornication Drunk with wine				7	2	3, 9
Scarlet, purple Golden Cup				7	3, 4	6, 16

http://www.khouse.org/images/artpics/chart_500x375.jpg

Before his execution, Saddam Hussein was determined to rebuild the city. Accordingly, premillennial dispensational scholars like Charles

Dyer[356] and Mark Hitchcock[357] argued, convincingly at the time, for a literal Babylon as a future geopolitical force. However, in the aftermath of the US intervention, Hussein is now dead, and today, the "Sacred Complex of Babylon" is a UNESCO world heritage site under protection from the United Nations.[359] As this book goes to press, the situation with ISIS is too volatile to speculate under what conditions Babylon could be rebuilt. Perhaps the arrival of Antichrist holds the answer.

In his fictional series, *Babylon Rising*, told through the eyes of a biblical archaeologist, Tim LaHaye suggested that the UN will eventually move its headquarters to Babylon, Iraq.[359] If so, it provides an elegant solution to the prophetic puzzle, allowing one to resolve most of the troublesome details literally. Chuck Missler responded, "At first this may sound fanciful, but it seems that the UN is highly desirous of moving out of New York for several reasons: they feel too cramped to contain badly needed growth; and, they also have a desire to get out from under the domestic policies there."[360]

With protected UNESCO status, whether or not physical Babylon becomes a geopolitical player may be beside the point. Given the UN's transparent penchant for occultism,[361] it is safe to assume the site is being accessed by the occult elite. The human tendency to underestimate the fallen ones is predictable. For this reason, a Babel portal—opening up to release its denizens of destruction—remains on the table of logical options as a reasonable, if not likely, resolution to the Babylon oracles.

The Return of the Nephilim in Isaiah

Self-proclaimed "bastions of discernment" have ridiculed the "return of the Nephilim" idea popularized by our friend Chuck Missler. While Missler's two-part series focuses on UFOs and a possible connection to Genesis 6, lesser known and completely ignored by the skeptics is that "the return of the Nephilim" has a compelling basis in the Greek Septuagint text of Isaiah.

Isaiah's call to ministry came "in the year that King Uzziah died"

(6:1), around 740 BC, and he lived long enough to record the death of Sennacherib (37:38) around 681 BC.[362] While Isaiah predicted the Babylonian sacking of Jerusalem a century before the event, we believe his prophecy concerning the destruction of Babylon is still to happen. Futurist scholars associate Isaiah 13–14 and Jeremiah 50–52 with Revelation 17–18 because the Mesopotamian city was never actually destroyed in warfare as Isaiah implies.[363] Even more amazing, the ancient Greek translation of this end-time oracle *really does* predict the opening of a gateway in Babylon and the return of the Nephilim.

The Septuagint, from the Latin word *septuaginta* ("seventy"), is a translation of the Hebrew Bible and some related texts into Koine Greek. The title and its Roman numeral acronym LXX refer to the legendary seventy Jewish scholars who completed the translation. It was the Bible of Jesus and the apostles. The New Testament authors show a clear preference for the Septuagint over Masoretic readings.[364] In the early Christian church, the Septuagint was also preferred because it was translated by Jews before the era of Christ, and preserved more Christ-centered readings. It seems that some scribes were attempting to obscure prophetic references to Jesus. For example, Irenaeus pointed out that the Septuagint clearly writes of a virgin that shall conceive (Isaiah 7:14). However the Hebrew text of the second century as interpreted by Theodotion and Aquila was translated as a "young woman that shall conceive." This leads many to prefer the LXX and lends force to a Septuagint reading predicting the return of the Nephilim.

The first oracle against Babylon by the prophet Isaiah opens as the day of the Lord looms over the world (Isaiah 13). The ancient scholars and rabbis who translated the Hebrew into the Greek Septuagint chose the Greek *gigantes* to render the Hebrew *gibborim*, predicting the return of "giants" with "monsters" at the advent of the destruction of Babylon in the final age. From the Septuagint, we read:

> The vision which Esaias son of Amos saw against Babylon. Lift up a standard on the mountain of the plain, exalt the voice to them, beckon with the hand, open the gates, ye ruler. I give com-

mand and I bring them: *giants* are coming to fulfill my wrath.…
For behold! The day of the Lord is coming which cannot be
escaped, a day of wrath and anger, to make the world desolate.… And Babylon…shall be as when God overthrew Sodom
and Gomorrah.… It shall never be inhabited…and monsters
shall rest there, and devils shall dance there and satyrs shall dwell
there. (Isaiah 13:1–3, 9, 19–22, Brenton LXX)[365]

According to the ancient understanding of Isaiah, the end times will
be marked by the destruction of Babylon and the return of the Nephilim
when God commands a "ruler" to "open the gates," unleashing fearsome
titans and cryptids to fulfill His wrath. While the Brenton Septuagint
translation above lists monsters, devils, and satyrs, it skips over an entity
appearing in the Greek text reflected in the newer Lexham English version of the Septuagint: "And wild animals will rest there, and the houses
will be filled with sound; and *Sirens* will rest there, and divine beings will
dance there. And donkey-centaurs will settle there" (Isaiah 13:21–22a,
emphasis added). In this newer version, monsters are rendered "wild animals" from the Greek *therion,* but it is important to note the meaning of
therion can also denote an evil person and is the Greek term behind "the
beast" in Revelation 13. "Sirens" was omitted in the Brenton translation,
but the Greek term *siren* denoted a "demon of the dead living in the
desert,"[366] which almost laughingly appears in modern English Bibles
as "ostrich" or a "desert owl." Where "devils" and "divine beings" are
interchanged, the Greek *daimonai* was in focus (thoroughly discussed
in Putnam's *The Supernatural Worldview*). A satyr is a hairy goat demon
found throughout the Old Testament (Leviticus 17:7; Isaiah 13:21 and
34:14; 2 Chronicles 11:15) and the alternate "donkey centaur" is a
closely related transgenic monstrosity. It seems beyond coincidence that
modern accounts of dimensional portals include similar strange beings.
Also, Isaiah's use of the plural "gates" suggests the possibility of many
locations. Within the present volume, we argue that such portals are
spread throughout the world.

Whereas the Greek reads *gigantes,* the Masoretic text used *gibborim* as reflected in the KJV: "I have also called my mighty ones for mine anger" (Isaiah 13:3). Although it removes "giants" from most English translations, the substitution demonstrates some semantic overlap between the terms *gibborim* and *gigantes* as the LXX and Masorite textual traditions have interchanged them. Isaiah's prophecy is also fascinating given that Nimrod, the builder of the Tower of Babel—the "gate of the gods"— was, perhaps, himself a Nephilim. Reviewing the Hebrew exegesis first presented in our book, *Exo-Vaticana*, we find:

> Genesis 10:8 says about Nimrod: "And Cush begat Nimrod: he began to be a mighty one in the earth." Three sections in this unprecedented verse indicate something very peculiar happened to Nimrod. First, the text says that "he *began* to be." In Hebrew, this is *chalal*, which in its Qal (simple active) stem means "to become profaned, defiled, polluted, or desecrated ritually, sexually or genetically" but in the Hiphil stem (causative) means "begin." It is certainly conceivable that the inspired author's word choice might imply word play for a "profaned beginning." Second, this verse tells us exactly *what* Nimrod began to be—"a *mighty* one" *(gibborim),* possibly one of the offspring of the Nephilim."[367]

That Nimrod had possibly become a "revived Watcher offspring" is supported by Nimrod seeming to abruptly be aware of *where* and *how* to build a tower so that it would penetrate the dwelling place of God or the Watchers. In addition to the possibility of suddenly seeing into the supernatural realm as a result of integration with fallen angels, if Nimrod was genetically modified according to the original Watcher formula, he could have inherited animal characteristics within his new material makeup, and animals, like angels, can perceive "domains" that humans cannot. This includes obvious things, such as wavelengths of the electromagnetic spectrum, but possibly something even more substantial, like the spirit realm. As he became *gibborim,* he would have taken on Watchers' propensities, which, as angels, could see into the supernatural realm including where heaven is located and possibly where to enter it.

The sixteenth chapter of the Book of Enoch also tells of the deceased offspring of Watchers, the spirits of the giants, or Nephilim, as being released at the end of time to bring slaughter and destruction upon man:

> From the days of the slaughter and destruction and death of the giants, from the souls of whose flesh the spirits, having gone forth, shall destroy without incurring judgment—thus shall they destroy until the day of the consummation, the great judgment in which the age shall be consummated, over the Watchers and the godless, yea, shall be wholly consummated. (1 Enoch 16:1)[368]

Of course, this all comes to pass as part of God's Day of the Lord or Great Tribulation, when Satan and his angels punish the unbelieving world before they are resigned to the pit. According to scholars, "This defines the temporal extent of the evil spirits' activity. They will continue their brutality, unabated and unpunished from the death of the giants until the Day of Judgment."[369] This particular prophecy mirrors those of Isaiah and the apocryphal works, which indicate a future date in which Watchers will rise for judgment while the spirits of their giant offspring manifest to wreak havoc upon earth.

The Book of Jubilees—an ancient Jewish religious work that is considered inspired Scripture by the Ethiopian Orthodox Church as well as Jews in Ethiopia—parallels the book of Enoch, which states the deceased Nephilim were damned to haunt the earth (1 Enoch 15:8–10). Jubilees also predicts spirits of the Nephilim erupting upon the earth in the last days.

> And the Lord our God spoke to us so that we might bind all of them [Nephilim spirits]. And the chief of the spirits, Mastema, came and he said, "O Lord, Creator, leave some of them before me, and let them obey my voice. And let them do everything which I tell them, because if some of them are not left for me, I

will not be able to exercise the authority of my will among the children of men because they are (intended) to corrupt and lead astray before my judgment because the evil of the sons of men is great." And he said, "Let a tenth of them remain before him, but let nine parts go down into the place of judgment." (Jubilees 10:7–9)[370]

In this passage, God is ready to destroy all these demons after the Flood, and Noah prays that his descendants be released from their attacks. Mastema (an alternate name for Satan[371]) intervenes, imploring God to allow him to retain and control one-tenth of these demons in order to exercise his authority, because they are needed "to corrupt and lead astray before my judgment." In other words, this corruption will peak just before Satan is judged (Revelation 20:2, 10).

At the fifth trumpet, the abyss opens releasing a demonic horde. Given Isaiah's *gibborim* army, might the abyss include physical giants as well as transgenic demon-locusts? Might the dead walk amongst them? The dual meaning of *rephaim* is the distinction in Job 26:5 found in the LXX and the Masonite tradition. Most English Bibles read, "Dead things are formed from under the waters" in translation of the Masoretic text. However, the LES translation reads, "Are not giants brought forth from beneath the water and its neighbors?" (Job 26:5). Additional biblical references typify the inner earth as a kind of holding tank, or prison, where God has bound certain fallen entities be they angels, demons, ghosts, or giants—or all of the above (2 Peter 2:4; Jude 6; Revelation 9). The black awakening marking the release of powerful fallen ones is associated with Babylon's famous river, "Saying to the sixth angel which had the trumpet, Loose the four angels which are bound in the great river Euphrates" (Revelation 9:14).

It is a matter of record that Saddam Hussein was rebuilding Babylon. He connected himself with Nebuchadnezzar, spending more than $500 million during the 1980s on the reconstruction project. The project included baking over sixty million bricks engraved with the inscription, "To King Nebuchadnezzar in the reign of Saddam Hussein."[372]

Saddam believed he was the reincarnated Nebuchadnezzar[373] and wished to recreate and outdo the feats of the biblical king. Of course, given the Tower of Babel Stele, Saddam also must have planned to rebuild the Tower of Babel. (Discovered hiding like a troll, he was humbled much like Nebuchadnezzar, too).

More than a decade ago, researchers William Henry[374] and Michael Salla[375] implied that there was an esoteric agenda behind the war in Iraq. While we remain undecided regarding occult conspiracies, it is fact that important ancient magical items have never been returned. When the bombs started falling, priceless ancient artifacts were some of the first items to disappear. For example, a news article revealed that the bronze panels from Balawat Gates near the city of Nimrud "stolen in April from the Mosul Museum soon after the fall of Baghdad, are still missing."[376] In 2003, Salla wrote that an interdimensional portal "may lie buried in the desert of Southern Iraq which presumably will play a role in the 'prophesied return of the gods.'"[377] In fact, when Tom Horn was on the popular radio show *Coast to Coast AM* with George Noory during the Gulf War and questioned why George W. Bush had been so stubbornly resolved to take the US into Iraq/Babylon even though Iraq was not connected to the events of September 11, 2001, something interesting happened. Tom made several points, saying some people believed the invasion had to do with creating a strategic placement of US military resources against what the administration saw as a growing threat from Islamic radicals. Then he said others saw it as an effort to seize and maintain control of Iraqi oil reserves; still others believed that 9/11 was itself either a convenient or orchestrated event (false flag) allowing the Bush administration to extend a global domination project. But then, Tom suggested, some may have hit the real nail on the head when they suggested that biblical sites in Babylon—which had been uncovered during Saddam Hussein's reconstruction of the ancient city—possessed something the administration went there to capture. After Tom finished his conversation with Noory and was headed to bed (around 3 a.m.), he suddenly received an email from the "curator" of the National Museum of Iraq (also known as the Iraq Museum, or the Baghdad Museum, which contains many relics from the Babylonian/Mesopotamian civilization), who had been listening to the radio show. This person claimed that Tom's last idea involving the US invading Iraq to capture something Saddam had uncovered was spot on. The emailer then gave Tom a temporary password to the museum's digital backdoor so he could see "proof." The first thing Tom did was verify the email was actually from @theiraqmuseum.com and also that the hidden back page was an extension of the actual museum's website. Once he confirmed that, he clicked the link where he was required to sign in using the temporary password. That is when he saw something he could hardly believe: hundreds and hundreds of step-by-step images of the first day of invasion showing US military personnel and the US ambassador at the museum. Somebody had taken second-by-second pictures of a woman with traditional head-covering greeting and then leading a delegation of US soldiers with the US ambassador to a large, padlocked door in the back of the museum in an area where the public is not allowed to go. This door was unlocked, and the armed soldiers and official American envoy followed the woman down a long flight of stairs into a gigantic underground storage room (something like one might see in an Indiana Jones movie, except this was real). Inside were dozens, if not hundreds, of large wooden cases containing superb gold and silver artifacts, which assumedly the world had never seen, invaluable items obviously dug up by Saddam from the sands of ancient Babylon. These included gold and silver masks of kings, sacred jewelry, cuneiform tablets with unknown secrets, steles bearing mysterious inscriptions and images, papyrus, strange ritual-looking objects, headdresses, vessels, swords, shields, and more. Hour after hour, Tom sat there going through the images one by one.

Then he saw something else. Suddenly, the pictures depicted a change in the observers' demeanors. The crowd appeared agitated, or maybe excited; Tom wasn't quite sure which. This happened as the soldiers began opening several larger-than-coffin-sized crates (actually about three times as large as a full-sized coffin) that were hidden far back in the corners of the concealed room. As the soldiers opened them, they looked inside and gestured for the ambassador. He went and stared inside the boxes, then had them resealed without removing anything (Tom could not tell what was inside the containers). Immediately, the soldiers began carrying these crates and some other ones behind them up the flight of stairs to a transport helicopter outside. Then they quickly departed the city of Baghdad (part of ancient Babylon) with the containers to parts unknown.

Tom was flabbergasted. It was true! Whatever else the US military was doing in Iraq/Babylon, the minute they arrived in the plains of Shinar, they had gone straight to a top-secret room beneath the Babylon Museum where Saddam Hussein had hidden objects of national interest recovered from the ancient world, and they had removed these containers in which *something* the American government wanted—*something* from ancient Babylon—was found! Whatever was inside those large boxes (it took two strong soldiers on each end to carry them out of that room), it was obviously more important to the US military than the irreplaceable golden masks and jewels of ancient kings and queens they didn't bother to seize.

Exhausted, Tom headed to bed with intentions of continuing through the images the following morning. Unfortunately, the next day, he awoke to find his "password" expired and the "curator" never willing to respond again.

So…was there ancient portal technology hidden in Iraq? If so, did the US move it to an undisclosed location? Is it in the hands of the future world leader at this time? What if the US military recovered the remains of ancient giants (with intact DNA?) from Saddam's secret vault that day? Maybe it was the remains of Nimrod himself? Or could it have been golden tablets with secret technology from the Watchers? Maps to a Sumerian stargate? These musings may be more realistic than a casual reader would imagine, as records from antiquity do describe *forbidden knowledge from the Watchers that had been written down and buried in secret places for the express purpose of rediscovery after the Flood!*

The great English theologian, George H. Pember, in his masterpiece, *Earth's Earliest Ages,* records how:

> For nearly a thousand years, immense accumulation of knowledge, experience, and skill must have advanced science, art, and the invention and manufacture of all the appliances of a luxurious civilization, with a rapidity to us almost inconceivable.... And doubtless many of the mighty labours accomplished by the earlier descendants of Noah may be considered to have sprung from reminiscences of pristine grandeur, and fragments of lore, handed down by forefathers who had passed a portion of their existence in the previous age of human glory and depravity. Such may have been the daring conception of a literally cloud capped tower [Tower of Babel]; the stupendous and splendidly decorated edifices of Babylon and Nineveh; and the wondrous structure of the first pyramid, involving, as it apparently does, an accurate knowledge of astronomical truth which would seem to have been at least on a level with the vaunted advances of modern science. For all these great efforts, be it remembered, were in progress during the lifetime of Shem, and probably in that of his brothers also.
>
> Nor must we forget recent discoveries in regard to the primeval civilization of the Accadians, "the stunted and oblique-eyed people of ancient Babylonia," whose very existence was unknown to us fifty years ago. Their language was dying out, and had become a learned dialect, like the Latin of the Middle Ages, in the seventeenth century before Christ. And yet so great had been their intellectual power that the famous library of Agane, founded at that time by Sargon I., was stocked with books "which were either translated from Accadian originals, or else based on Accadian texts, *and filled with technical words which belonged to the old language."* A catalogue of the astronomical department, which has been preserved, contains a direction to

the reader to write down the number of the tablet or book which he requires, and apply for it to the librarian. "The arrangement," says Sayce, "adopted by Sargon's librarians must have been the product of generations of former experience." Could we have a stronger proof "of the development of literature and education, and of the existence of a considerable number of reading people in this remote antiquity"?

According to Berosus there was an *antediluvian "Town of Books" in Babylonia; and Sisuthrus, the Chaldean Noah, "is made to bury his books at Sippara before the Deluge, and to disentomb them after the descent from the Ark."* [We also] have evidence that in very early times there were well-known libraries at Erech, Ur, Cutha, and Larsa [all part of the ancient Babylonian kingdom], to which observatories and universities were attached.

If, then, we give but their fair weight to these considerations, we seem compelled to admit that the antediluvians may have attained to a perfection in civilization and high culture whichhas scarcely yet been recovered, much as we pride ourselves uponour own times.[378] (emphasis added)

Titus Flavius Josephus (usually just called Josephus), the famous and respected first-century Romano-Jewish scholar, wrote his "histories" at the same time the New Testament apostles were alive. He, too, chronicled how pre-Flood knowledge involving tower building and related "secrets of Heaven" were specifically recorded so as to be available to mankind after the deluge. In his *Antiquities of the Jews,* he wrote:

They also were the inventors of that peculiar sort of wisdom which is concerned with the heavenly bodies, and their order. And that their inventions might not be lost before they were sufficiently known, upon Adam's prediction that the world was to be destroyed at one time by the force of fire, and at another time by the violence and quantity of water, they made two pillars; the one of brick, the other of stone: they inscribed their discoveries on them both, that in case the pillar of brick should be destroyed by the flood, the pillar of stone might remain, and exhibit those discoveries to mankind; and also inform them that there was another pillar of brick erected by them. Now this remains in the land of Siriad to this day.[379]

Josephus also recorded how enigmatic knowledge of mathematics, astronomy, and tower construction related to the stars (portals?) was handed down by Adam's son Seth from the earliest post-Flood builders to his children in the plains of Shinar. There, they sought to reproduce construction of a device that caused God to confront and divide them in Genesis 11. But the eighth chapter of the Book of Jubilees specifically mentions the recovery of at least part of this ancient and forbidden Watchers knowledge as having been recovered shortly after the Flood waters abated:

> In the twenty-ninth jubilee, in the first week, in the beginning thereof Arpachshad took to himself a wife and her name was Rasu'eja, the daughter of Susan, the daughter of Elam, and she bare him a son in the third year in this week, and he called his name Kainam. And the son grew, and his father taught him writing, and he went to seek for himself a place where he might seize for himself a city. *And he found a writing which former (generations) had carved on the rock, and he read what was thereon, and he transcribed it and sinned owing to it; for it contained the teaching of the Watchers in accordance with which they used to observe the omens of the sun and moon and stars in all the signs of heaven. And he wrote it down and said nothing regarding it; for he was afraid to speak to Noah about it lest he should be angry with him on account of it.*[380] (emphasis added)

We can only guess what these teachings of the Watchers involved, but if it was about the heavens and possibly locations or methods for piercing the human-angelic barrier, it would go along handedly with what the Bible says happened during Nimrod's tower and technological aspirations.

These observations may be more important than at first we imagine, because the object lesson derived from the Tower of Babel incident is that self-actualization, apart from—and especially in defiance of—the will of God is dangerous. Ziggurats, pyramids, and towers were used to channel false gods—created gods damned to die like men. Thus in coming full circle, we decide the question of whether these ancient portals were (or are) "gates of the gods" or "doorways to destruction" in favor of the latter.

CHAPTER EIGHT

The Science of Portals

By Cris Putnam

> Black holes may be entrances to Wonderlands.
> But are there Alices or white rabbits?
> —Carl Sagan[381]

The 2014 epic space adventure film *Interstellar* features a team of astronauts who leave a postapocalyptic earth and venture through a wormhole in search of a habitable planet to ensure the survival of humanity. In order to make certain the movie's depictions of wormholes and relativity were as accurate as possible, one of the world's leading experts on the astrophysical implications of Albert Einstein's relativity equations, theoretical physicist Kip Thorne, was hired as a scientific consultant for the film. Setting a new precedent, Thorne states that this is the *first* Hollywood film to accurately portray black holes and wormholes the way they would actually appear. Thorne asserts, "This is the first time the depiction began with Einstein's general relativity equations."[382] The visual effects supervisor, Paul Franklin, describes what a black hole looks like up close: "The gravity of a black hole draws in all matter from the surrounding universe and this spins out into a giant disk around the central sphere. As it whirls in towards the center, the gas gets hotter and hotter and the accretion disk around it shines brilliantly."[383] (See illustration.) This chapter will explore these topics and much more, including a new study that suggests the stunning possibility that *all* black holes might be wormholes to untold realms.

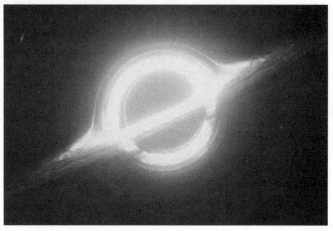

Black hole as depicted in *Interstellar* (2014)[384]

The immortal's path just went down the rabbit hole. As we send this manuscript to press in early 2015, Paolo Salucci, astrophysicist of the International School for Advanced Studies (SISSA), published a groundbreaking paper in *Annals of Physics* entitled "Possible Existence of Wormholes in the Central Regions of Halos." The abstract is rather sensational:

An earlier study has demonstrated the possible existence of wormholes in the outer regions of the galactic halo, based on the Navarro-Frenk-White (NFW) density profile. This paper uses the Universal Rotation Curve (URC) dark matter model to obtain analogous results for the central parts of the halo. This result is an important compliment to the earlier result, thereby *confirming the possible existence of wormholes in most of the spiral galaxies.*[385] (emphasis added)

In other words, if this explanation of dark matter is correct, our spiral Milky Way galaxy likely contains a naturally occurring wormhole tunnel that traverses our entire galaxy. Note that this is specific to *spiral* galaxies. Salucci adds, "We could even travel through this tunnel, since, based on our calculations, it could be navigable. Just like the one we've all seen in the recent film *Interstellar*."[386] Salucci adds, "Dark matter may be 'another dimension,' perhaps even a major galactic transport system."[387] While this begs the question—"A transport system for whom?"—it adds considerable weight to the ideas in this book.

The science of portals may seem intimidating, like a topic only suited for science-fiction aficionados, but everyone is familiar with the "gateway to another realm" concept. Most of us learned it in kindergarten with *Alice in Wonderland* and the *Wizard of Oz*. Interestingly, the era of history (early twentieth century) that inspired those memorable tales was also when those realms moved from fantastic to scientifically plausible. However, the groundwork had been laid centuries before.

The Reverend John Michell and Schwarzschild's Magic Sphere

British polymath John Michell (1724–1793) was rector of St. Michael's Church of Thornhill, near Leeds, Yorkshire, England. A fellow of Queens' College, Cambridge, he taught Greek and Hebrew, and was a Censor in theology. In addition to being a respected theologian, he was "the father of seismology," the science of earthquakes. After the catastrophic Lisbon earthquake of 1755, Michell wrote a book that helped establish seismology as a science. He proposed that earthquakes spread out as waves through the solid earth and related to fault lines. This work earned him Royal Society membership in 1769. In fact, he provided pioneering insights in a wide range of scientific fields, including astronomy, optics, geology, and gravitation.[388] Alasdair Wilkins writes, "A few specifics of Michell's work really do sound like they are ripped from the pages of a twentieth century astronomy textbook."[389] The American Physical

Society has described Mitchell as being "so far ahead of his scientific contemporaries that his ideas languished in obscurity, until they were re-invented more than a century later."[390] Michell's prescience is nearly unmatched, and today he is heralded as one of the greatest unsung Christian heroes of science.

Extrapolating from the laws of physics, Michell even predicted the existence of the black hole. In 1783, he speculated about a star so massive that its gravitational pull would hold back its own light. He reasoned that because all objects have an escape velocity, the velocity required to escape its gravitational pull, then it follows that with super massive objects, like giant stars, very interesting things begin to happen. If the escape velocity equals the speed of light, then light cannot escape; it vanishes and is never to be seen again. It becomes a "dark star."

Michell's speculation was not taken very seriously at the time—that is, not until after 1916, when Karl Schwarzschild, a German physicist, found an exact solution to Einstein's equations for a massive star that suggested Michell's earlier hunch was right. From Einstein's equations, Schwarzschild independently rediscovered Michell's dark star. Schwarzschild conjectured that massive stars were surrounded by a theoretical "magic sphere"—a point of no return, even for light. In honor of his discovery, the radius of a black hole's event horizon is known as the "Schwarzschild radius." In 1939, J. Robert Oppenheimer (of atom bomb fame) proposed that black holes form when an old massive star uses up its nuclear fuel and implodes, compressing to within its Schwarzschild radius. However, how does one prove something that cannot be seen?

Black Holes

The existence of black holes is now considered "settled science." Although it seems fair to ask if anyone has ever actually seen one, such an inquiry misses the point because black holes are by definition invisible. Nobody can directly "see" the dark heavenly dwellers, but they are detectable using various indirect means.[391] Like dark-colored fluid swirling down a drain, the liquid vortex is visible even when the drain's hole is not. Similarly, gas, dust, and space debris form a disk-shaped, spiral pattern up to the edge of the event horizon. Accordingly, astronomers look for the "accretion disk" surrounding a black hole. Using the Hubble Space telescope, space scientists have now collected stunning photographs of these accretion disks. Here is an example of an accretion disk in elliptical galaxy NGC 4261. Likely, this is the closest one will ever get to observe a super-massive black hole.

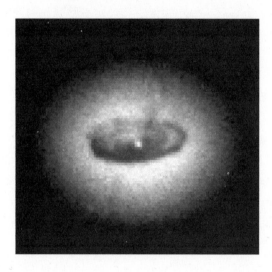

Image taken by Hubble space telescope of what may be gas accreting onto a black hole in elliptical galaxy NGC 4261[392]

The churning vortex of space gases and debris is a tell-tale sign of enormous gravitational suction, but it isn't sufficient for precise identification. In order to distinguish black holes from other super-massive entities, astronomers calculate the size and mass to verify that the matter is compressed in a sufficiently small space. Additionally, as material is sucked in, it is torn apart, releasing vast amounts of heat. As it heats up, the dark star emits copious amounts of detectable radiation, such as x-rays. Providing yet another means of identification, the huge energy transfer can cause matter close to a black hole to be violently ejected in what are called "radio jets." (See image.) Using these established indicators, hundreds of black holes have been detected by the Hubble space telescope and are available for public examination on NASA's website.

Black hole radio jets[393]

The Hubble telescope has also measured black holes rotating at half the speed of light, or 149,896,229 meters per second.[394] This is particularly important to the discussion at hand, because a precisely tuned rotation makes human travel through wormholes—once thought implausible—theoretically possible. In 1963, New Zealand mathematician Roy Kerr found an exact solution to Albert Einstein's previously unsolved equation describing a spinning black hole. The correct spin velocity creates enough centrifugal force to cancel the inward force of gravity, stabilizing the portal that otherwise shreds its passengers into tiny particles. This makes human travel through wormhole portals at least theoretically possible. However, there's a catch. Popular physics author Michio Kaku explains in *Parallel Worlds: A Journey through Creation, Higher Dimensions, and the Future of the Cosmos:*

> The frame of Alice's looking glass, in other words, was like the spinning ring of Kerr. But any trip through the Kerr ring would be a one-way trip. If you were to pass through the event horizon surrounding the Kerr ring, the gravity would not be enough to crush you to death, but it would be sufficient to prevent a return trip back through the event horizon.[395]

While still theoretical (we are told), Kerr-Newman geometry provides a complete description of the necessary gravitational and electromagnetic fields to form a stationary, traversable black hole.[396] It eliminates the crushing gravity near the event horizon, one of the previously thought insurmountable problems associated with wormhole travel. But all of this engineering isn't necessary if braneworld theory is true and the Milky Way galaxy hosts a traversable portal to another dimension.

A spiral galaxy like the Milky Way has three basic components: 1) the spiral-armed disk; 2) the halo of globular clusters; and 3) the nucleus (a large, black hole). These components are labeled in the figure below:

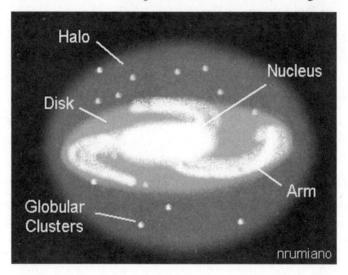

Spiral Galaxy

On Mount Graham, the Large Binocular Telescope (LBT) and LUCIFER are confirming the recent hypothesis that central halo regions of spiral galaxies like the Milky Way contain "stable and navigable"[397] wormholes accessible enough to be labeled a "galactic transport system."[398] The hypothesis is based on the existence of "dark matter" in the halo that makes itself felt by its gravitational influence on the visible matter. The LUCIFER device helps astronomers detect the clouds are typically opaque to visible light.[399] LBT also confirms the invisible dark-matter halo by detecting its angular momentum as with the

Seyfert galaxy Messier 94. The LBT produced this image (reminiscent of *Interstellar*):

The Seyfert galaxy Messier 94[400]

Perhaps even more provocative, a new study suggests that any of the super-massive objects scientists think are black holes could instead be wormhole portals leading to other universes. A recent article reports:

> Though black holes are not seen directly, astronomers have identified many objects that appear to be black holes based on observations of how matter swirls around them.
>
> But physicists Thibault Damour of the Institut des Hautes Etudes Scientifiques in Bures-sur-Yvette, France, and Sergey Solodukhin of International University Bremen in Germany now say that these objects could be structures called wormholes instead.[401]

In other words, *all black holes might be portals* rather than dead ends, and it is impossible to tell the difference.

Wormholes

When the Large Hedron Collider (LHC) first started up on September 10, 2008, director for research and scientific computing at CERN,

Sergio Bertolucci, provoked a whirlwind of speculation with his enigmatic remark that the LHC might open a door to another dimension. During a regular briefing at CERN headquarters, he told reporters, "Out of this door might come something, or we might send something through it."[402] The notion of higher dimensional beings conjures up the denizens of legend, orcs, ogres, elves, fairies, dwarves, and giants. A British military analyst later quipped:

> We're looking here at an imminent visit from a race of carnivorous dinosaur-men, the superhuman clone hive-legions of some evil genetic queen-empress, infinite polypantheons of dark mega-deities imprisoned for aeons and hungering to feast upon human souls, a parallel-history victorious Nazi globo-Reich or something of that type.[403]

While that was amusing, more serious researchers like Richard Bullivant had already connected the dots:

> The most plausible explanation the next time Bigfoot or a lizard man or a flying dragon is sighted—or perhaps even a UFO ascending into the earth and disappearing into the side of a hill—surely has to be that it is evidence that portals to parallel worlds are serving as doorways where strange beings, vehicles and entities occasionally stumble into our universe—and sometimes we in turn stumble into theirs.[404]

It did not help that the LHC was named "Shiva" after the Hindu destroyer of worlds, a fact that prompted a teenage girl in India, Madhya Pradesh, to commit suicide.[405] Whether the scientists responsible for the name believe it or not, wormhole portals are studied very seriously.

In 1935, Albert Einstein and his student, Nathan Rosen, proposed that connecting two black holes would form a tube-like gateway between two regions. This passageway is called an Einstein-Rosen Bridge. The math works. Traversable wormholes provide a valid solution to field equations of general relativity.[406] According to theory, one could enter a black hole and exit a white hole in another universe. A white hole is a region of space-time that cannot be entered from the outside, but from which matter and light may escape. Thus, a black hole serves as the entry portal and a white hole marks the exit portal. Yet, prior to the discovery of spinning Kerr black holes, traversing the magic sphere meant being obliterated down to the atomic level by the enormous gravitational force. Consequently, during Einstein's day, no one took the possibility of traveling through such a gate very seriously.

In the 1950s, John Wheeler, the physicist who coined the term "wormhole," published a paper showing that, rather than connecting to another universe, a wormhole could also bend like the handle on a coffee cup to join two different regions of the known universe. This suggests the possibility of near-instantaneous travel over vast distantness. In 1962, Wheeler and Robert W. Fuller published a paper showing that these wormholes are unstable, and will pinch off quickly after forming, seemingly relegating the hope for a negotiable wormhole to the world of fantasy.

The possibility of truly traversable wormholes was first demonstrated by Kip Thorne of the Theoretical Astrophysics Group at the California Institute of Technology and his graduate student, Mike Morris, in 1988. Thorne devised a wormhole that does not require a black hole and a white hole or that destructive event horizon. He proposed that the throats, or tunnels, could be made large enough for a human in a craft to get through by threading the portal with exotic negative matter. In the film *Interstellar*, aliens (or future humans) from the fifth dimension provide the artificial wormhole. However, according to new theory, we may be getting close.

Interestingly, Thorne's initial attention was sparked when the celebrated physicist, TV personality, and author Carl Sagan asked about the feasibility of his scenario in an early manuscript for the now-famous science-fiction book and movie, *Contact*:

Thorne realized he could design just the sort of wormhole Sagan was looking for. It turned out to be possible in theory to have a link between two parts of the Universe that looked, schematically, just like Wheeler's quantum wormholes of thirty years earlier. But this time the tunnels would be large enough for humans to travel through in a spacecraft without feeling any discomfort. For instance, a traveler could enter one mouth of the wormhole near Earth and within a short time he or she would emerge from the other end on the opposite side of the Galaxy. The traveler would then be able to return through the wormhole and report back. This "connection" was thus dubbed a "traversable wormhole" to distinguish it from non-traversable ones like the Einstein-Rosen bridge.[407]

The Morris-Thorne traversable wormhole they proposed is held open by a spherical shell of exotic matter. This theoretical element would prevent the pinching off Wheeler discovered and stabilize the wormhole for travel. Unfortunately, "exotic" entails hypothetical properties that violate the known laws of physics. Not to be confused with antimatter, negative matter has negative mass, not a reverse electrical charge from matter. Unfortunately, it is only theoretical. As far as the public is told, the closest known example of such exotic matter is the region of pseudo-negative-pressure density produced by the Casimir effect. This effect occurs when quantum vacuum fluctuations of the electromagnetic field between two close, parallel, uncharged, conducting plates create a small attractive force.[408] Stephen Hawking,[409] Kip Thorne,[410] and others[411] argue that such effects might make it possible to stabilize a traversable wormhole. The work is ongoing.

In 2008, Matt Visser refined the basic design in order to "minimize the use of exotic matter. In particular, it is possible for a traveler to traverse such a wormhole without passing through a region of exotic matter."[412] Additionally, physicists have now identified scenarios in which wormholes could have naturally formed with stabilizing forces preventing such a collapse.[413] Several new types of traversable wormholes have been suggested, including a wormhole that does not require exotic matter.[414] The best minds in astrophysics and quantum mechanics increasingly breathe scientific plausibility into previously thought fanciful descriptions of mystical portals, heavenly gates, visionary ladders, and vile vortices.

A simulated traversable wormhole that connects Tübingen University, Germany, and the sand dunes near Boulogne sur Mer in the north of France[415]

Four Levels of Multiverse

All this talk of wormholes and otherworldly realms demands a discussion about the multiverse idea. While the term "multiverse" is used in several different ways, they all denote a hypothetical cosmos that contains our known universe as well as numerous other regions. Frankly, the word "universe" has traditionally included the totality of all matter. In *Merriam-Webster's Collegiate Dictionary,* 11th edition (2003), "universe" is defined as: "The whole body of things and phenomena observed or postulated." That would seem to preclude more than one, would it not? Coherence aside, some multiverse advocates even propose different laws of physics in their hypothetical nether regions.

An important precursor to understanding multiverse reasoning is the theory of inflation. Cosmic inflation theory posits that there was a period of faster-than-light acceleration during the expansion of the early universe after the Big Bang. In March of 2014, the Internet was buzz-ing with articles like "First Direct Evidence of Cosmic Inflation"[416] and "Direct Evidence of Big Bang Inflation,"[417] yet less heralded were the retractions a few months later, like "Big Bang Inflation Evidence Incon-clusive."[418] While the jury is still out, cosmological inflation is simply assumed in multiverse reasoning—the big idea being that in the first fraction of a second after the Big Bang, the universe expanded exponen-tially, stretching far beyond the view of the most powerful telescopes.

MIT cosmologist Max Tegmark has provided a simple, four-level classification of these regions beyond the observable universe.[419] The lev-els can be understood to encompass and expand upon previous levels and are increasingly speculative. While many prominent scientists and philosophers are openly critical of Levels III and IV, Level I is relatively uncontroversial in science.

Level I

This level simply entails regions so distant that they are not able to be observed. In other words, even at the speed of light, there has not been enough time for light to traverse the enormous distance. Scientists gener-ally agree that all regions of the Level I multiverse exhibit the same physi-cal laws and the same constants. Astrophysicist Jeffrey Zweerink writes, "Calling Level I a 'multiverse' is somewhat of a misnomer because all of the observable volumes are really part of the same large universe."[420] This one really offers no serious challenge to anthropic reasoning. Accord-ingly, many reserve the term "multiverse" for the more conjectural sce-narios that follow.

Level II

The second level entails otherworldly realms with far-reaching implications. While the limits of observation of a single universe define the first level, the Level II multiverse entails true multiple universes ostensibly with different physical laws and constants. This idea springs from chaotic inflation theory, in which the multiverse as a whole is endlessly stretching, but some regions stop enlarging and form distinct bubbles, like the foam in a glass of soda. According to this model, our universe is merely a single bubble of the cosmic foam. It finds some support in that some versions of String Theory indicate that there are many different arrangements of physical laws and constants. Accordingly, the uniformity we observe in our universe is limited to our one bubble. Stephen Feeney at University College in London believes that evidence for these other bubble universes is present in the cosmic microwave background radiation, the heat signature "echo" of the Big Bang.[421]

Level III

Inspired by the many-worlds interpretation of quantum mechanics, this level seems inordinately fantastic to most folks. In quantum mechanics, certain observations (like the position of an electron) cannot be predicted absolutely. Instead, there is a range of possible positions, each with a different probability.

Quantum mechanical uncertainty can be explained in terms of every possible position or state being represented in some possible world. According to the many-worlds interpretation, each possibility generates a different universe. For example, rolling a six-sided die has six possible outcomes, such that each time the die is rolled, it lands on every number, in effect, birthing five new universes in addition to the one from which it was originally thrown. Thus, every decision creates parallel realities where every possible outcome plays out. The sheer magnitude of quantum mechanical events seems prohibitively absurd—but perhaps, fun, nonetheless. According to this model, one might imagine a universe where Richard Dawkins is a young-earth creationist or President Obama is a legitimate, natural-born American citizen. Even so, it seems that all of these wacky parallel realities occur within the same universe entailing the same physical laws and constants, so Level III is not particularly useful for describing a proper multiverse.

Level IV

Most Level II multiverse advocates allow that any possible manifestation of physical laws will appear in at least one bubble. Thus, Level IV entails the existence of every mathematically consistent possibility. If universes with every mathematically consistent set of physical laws actually exist, then no explanation is needed for the fortuitous, life-supporting universe we find ourselves in. Critics see this as a convenient ploy to escape the theistic implications of fine tuning and the anthropic principle. The Albert Einstein Professor in Science at Princeton University, Paul J. Steinhardt, called this "a pervasive idea in fundamental physics and cosmology that should be retired"[422] and voiced his opposition to the reasoning behind the Level IV multiverse:

> According to this view, the laws and properties within our observable universe cannot be explained or predicted because they are set by chance. Different regions of space too distant to ever be observed have different laws and properties, according to this picture. Over the entire multiverse, there are infinitely many distinct patches. Among these patches, in the words of Alan Guth, "anything that can happen will happen—and it will happen infinitely many times." Hence, I refer to this concept as a Theory of Anything. Any observation or combination of observations is consistent with a Theory of Anything. No observation or combination of observations can disprove it. Proponents seem to revel in the fact that the Theory cannot be falsified. The rest of the scientific community should be up in arms since an unfalsifiable idea lies beyond the bounds of normal science. Yet, except for a few voices, there has been surprising complacency and, in some cases, grudging acceptance of a Theory of Anything as a logical possibility. The scientific journals are full of papers treating the Theory of Anything seriously. What is going on?[423]

We believe Steinhardt has the correct analysis of the Level IV multiverse, but that doesn't mean that something like the Level II is not possible. In fact, Steinhardt is leading advocate of braneworld theory (as introduced to our readers in *Exo-Vaticana*).

Braneworld

Braneworld cosmology posits that our four-dimensional space-time is like the sheet of paper, a membrane or "brane" that is simply a subspace of a larger, multidimensional space. The big idea is that our visible, four-dimensional space-time universe is restricted to its own membrane inside a higher-dimensional space called "the bulk." The bulk could contain other branes that are, for all intents and purposes, parallel universes. Within the bulk, a parallel universe might be only a hair's width away from this universe. Matter cannot transcend its brane, but gravity does. Thus, other branes are invisible (like black holes) because its photons of light are stuck to the brane. Despite that, scientists theorize that gravitational forces *can* reach from one membrane-universe to another. If so, dark matter suggests the existence of other braneworlds.

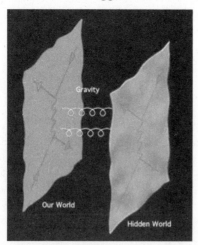

Dark matter: Gravity from a parallel world?

Steinhardt explains, "Our three-dimensional world can be viewed as a membrane-like surface embedded into space with an extra, fourth spatial dimension."[424] Thus, our universe is one "braneworld" and there exists another braneworld, a parallel universe, less than an atom's width away. This is likely a strange domain where the laws of physics might be entirely different. Does this seem too much like a science fiction novel? Not so fast; Steinhardt believes we already have quantifiable evidence for it.

He argues, "Although we can't touch, feel, or see any matter on the other brane, we can, nevertheless, sense its existence because we can feel its gravity."[425] He is arguing that there is no dark matter within our universe after all; rather, it is matter existing in a parallel universe. A nearby parallel reality, immune from our light, is producing gravitational effects. This readily explains dark matter, an otherwise cosmological conundrum. More interestingly, Steinhardt proposes that these two membranes might even touch at points, transferring matter and radiation from one to the other. This suggests that black holes may, in fact, be points of connection between parallel braneworlds. If an excess of matter collects at one point on either brane, its gravitational field becomes so strong that it draws the other brane towards it, and what is a black hole on one side is a white hole on the other. In this way, some black holes might be gateways to a parallel universe. This idea offers a solution as to the perplexing origin of UFOs and some paranormal phenomenon. UFOs do not seem to be propelled by conventional means.

Mind over Matter

Ben Rich was the director of Lockheed's Skunk Works from 1975 to 1991. In 1993, Rich shared some amazing insight with Jan Harzan, director of the Mutual UFO Network. When asked about incredible feats of UFO propulsion:

> Harzan says Rich stopped and looked at him, then asked Harzan if he knew how ESP worked. Jan says he was taken aback by the question and responded, "I don't know, all points in space

and time are connected?" Rich replied, "That's how it works." Then he turned around and walked away.[426]

This works nicely with J. Allen Hynek's idea: "I hypothesize a 'M&M' technology encompassing the mental and material realms."[427] But how can the mental propel the material? It turns out that mental events do profoundly impact physical reality.

Wave-Particle Duality and the Two-Slit Experiment

Photons of light sometimes behave like a wave and at other times appear to be a particle. When a light photon passes through a slit, it can take the form of a wave or particle. Before it is observed, it is literally *both* a particle and a wave. Status is observed as a particle produces two bands on the back wall and a wave creates an interference pattern (as seen in illustration). The status is called "super position," which literally means that all possible outcomes exist in tandem. Once observed, a photon assumes the perceived state irrevocably. If this is the first you've heard of this famous experiment, please watch the brief video explanation available on YouTube.[428]

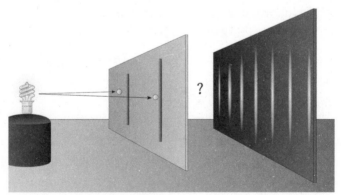

Two-slit wave interference pattern

The observer-dependent status of light photons introduces the mysterious element of intelligent consciousness into the building blocks of reality. Dr. Robert Lanza explains the metaphysical implications:

Consider the famous two-slit experiment. When you watch a particle go through the holes, it behaves like a bullet, passing through one slit or the other. But if no one observes the particle, it exhibits the behavior of a wave and can pass through both slits at the same time. This and other experiments tell us that unobserved particles exist only as "waves of probability" as the great Nobel laureate Max Born demonstrated in 1926. They're statistical predictions—nothing but a likely outcome. Until observed, they have no real existence; only when the mind sets the scaffolding in place, can they be thought of as having duration or a position in space. Experiments make it increasingly clear that even *mere knowledge in the experimenter's mind* is sufficient to convert possibility to reality.[429]

Introducing consciousness as a determinative factor in the structure of physical reality suggests that mind is more fundamental than matter, offering a way to merge physics and consciousness. Although he embraces a monistic cosmology, B. Allen Wallace has offered a "general theory of ontological relativity" suggesting that mental phenomena supersede the material.[430] Of course, a biblically consistent alternative is offered in my book, *The Supernatural Worldview.*[431] If consciousness really is primary, the heavenly voyages described in ancient texts like Revelation and Enoch acquire a new sense of objectivity. Anthropologist Lynne Hume writes:

> It may be that "consciousness" is as close to the notion of "spirit," and "levels of consciousness" is as close to the notion of "different realms of existence," as empiricists are willing to accept. In the end, this may be just a matter of semantics and not important to the essence of what people say they experience. Indeed, if we replace one term for another, we might end up with the same argument.[432]

She also notes that worldwide belief in accessing a "portal or doorway to access another type of reality is widespread."[433] Perhaps descriptions of the "spirit realm," "second heaven," or "astral plane" are descriptions of what science deems a parallel universe?

Based on the discussed science, paranormal researchers suggest a possible explanation of apparitions:

> If there are other universes that have their own separate time and space that expand and contract on their own apart from our universe, isn't it conceivable that at some point they would intersect with our universe/dimension and produce a phenomenon that we would view as being a ghost or spirit?[434]

If so, then perhaps apparitions appear as misty vapors because our thin membrane of reality only overlaps with theirs momentarily, and then, "poof," they're gone.

The former research professor of astronomy and of the history of science at Harvard University, Owen Gingerich, has authored books defending *God's Universe* (2006) and *God's Planet* (2014). He famously observed that "anyone who can believe in multiple universes should have no problem believing in heaven or hell."[435] We believe his comment frames the discussion of portals and otherworldly realms in a sobering light for the believer as well. The reverse holds true as well: "If one can believe in heaven and hell, then one should be able to believe in other universes." Because the Bible mentions portals to netherworlds (Revelation 9:1) as well as Heaven (Genesis 28:12), one cannot be a consistent Christian (or scientist) while summarily dismissing the subject matter of this book.

Essential Points

- Black holes are detected by the accretion disk of vortex energy.
- An Einstein-Rosen bridge forms when a black hole connects to another, forming a white hole.

- All spiral galaxies might contain centralized, galactic wormhole transport systems.
- It is theoretically possible that all black holes are wormholes.
- It is theoretically possible to create a traversable wormhole.
- The multiverse stems from inflation theory (that the universe expanded exponentially in the first nanoseconds after the Big Bang).
- The Level I multiverse is uncontroversial.
- The Level II multiverse entails distinct "universes."
- The Level III multiverse is based on the many-worlds interpretation of quantum mechanics and is fancifully speculative.
- The Level IV multiverse has been criticized as unclassifiable.
- Braneworld theory posits true "parallel universes" and may explain dark matter.
- VATT, LBT, and LUCIFER are confirming dark matter and wormhole theories.
- Photons seem to be a wave and a particle.
- Positions of quantum particles are expressed as probabilities, but once observed, they assume a position collapsing the field of probability.
- The observer introduces the esoteric element of consciousness into physics.

CHAPTER NINE

Secrets of the CERN Stargate

By Tom Horn

The Large Hadron Collider could open a doorway to an extra dimension and out of this door might come something, or we might send something through it.

—Sergio Bertolucci, director for research and scientific computing at CERN

The idea of multiple universes is more than a fantastic invention and deserves to be taken seriously.

—Aurelien Barrau, French particle physicist at CERN

Tom Hanks is to appear in the movie of Dan Brown's *Angels and Demons*, which involves scientists at CERN making anti-matter. But the new experiment at the LHC to understand anti-matter cost less than Tom Hanks will earn from the movie.

—Dr. Chris Parkes, Glasgow University, UK, CERN

CERN's governing council wanted to build a kind of time machine that could open a window to how the Universe appeared in the first microseconds of its existence.... We might even find evidence of the existence of other dimensions. But to conjure up these conditions, the CERN council knew it needed to perform an engineering miracle.

—James Morgan, BBC science reporter

The laboratory we know as CERN was born in 1952, not long after World War II and the emergence of the nuclear bomb. Since that time, some of the research at CERN has entered the public lexicon and nearly become a household word. This European facility began as a post-war physics project and blossomed into an international cabal searching for nothing less than God.

CERN is a French acronym based on the name of the working committee that imagined the possibilities for a physics laboratory governed by another emerging body, the Common Market, which would eventually rise as the revived Roman Empire, the European Union. The name for the committee was the *Conseil Européen pour la Recherche Nucléaire* (European Council for Nuclear Research). Just two years later, in 1954, the working committee disbanded, the formal organization commenced work, and the official name was changed to *Organisation Européenn pour la Recherche Nucléaire* (European Organization for Nuclear Research).[436] Oddly enough, when the official name changed, the acronym should have changed as well—after all, the earlier "committee" had been a temporary entity that had helped birth a major research laboratory; the CERN acronym and the French designation *Conseil Européen pour la Recherche Nucléaire* hadn't yet propagated enough that renaming it would have proven problematic. So why didn't the founders change the acronym along with the name?

Enter Werner Karl Heisenberg, a renowned German Nobel laureate physicist who is often called "the founder of quantum mechanics." He served as head of the Kaiser Wilhelm Institute during World War II, heading up the Nazi push to create an atomic weapon. Many in the West say that the Allies owed much to Heisenberg, for it is believed that he actually stalled and intentionally misled the Nazis, hoping the Allies would win the race to "find the bomb." Lew Kowarski, one of Heisenberg's colleagues, claims that Heisenberg had inexplicably insisted that the original acronym CERN remain in effect.

Werner Heisenberg understood quite well what quantum physics implied for humanity. Inherent within this theoretical realm, populated by obtuse equations and pipe-smoking scientists, lies what I call the "Babylon Potential." This is the "secret knowledge"—the scientific imperative, informed and driven by spiritual advisers—that the Bible cites as the key to opening a gateway for the "gods." It is Entemenanki, Baba-alu, the opening of the Abzu, the doorway to Hell.

How is the Babylon Potential related to a simple acronym—CERN? Here's the answer: Although Heisenberg may not have known it, CERN is an abbreviated title for the ancient god worshipped by the Celts: Cernnunos. The name means "horned one," and his stern image appears in various forms, usually wearing "stag's horns" upon his head, and he is oftentimes accompanied by a ram-headed serpent. His worshippers celebrated Cernunnos' birth in December during the winter solstice. As the Celtic god of the underworld, he parallels Hades and Pluto. Cernunnos controls the shadows, and he is a dying/rising god after the order of Osiris and Horus. Cernunnos alternates control of the world with the moon goddess Danu (another form of Diana/Isis/Semiramis). This intertwined and sometimes antagonistic relationship is similar to that of Shiva and Kali—an important point to make because it is Shiva's statue that welcomes visitors to CERN's headquarters in Geneva.

Cernunnos, Celtic god of the underworld

The Shiva statue depicts the Hindu god in his "nataraja" position, a cosmic dance that destroys the old universe in favor of a new creation.[437]

This ritual is performed on the back of a dwarf, a demon named Apasmara who is said to represent ignorance. Much like the mystery religions and secret societies (of which Freemasonry is a prime example), the initiates receive hidden knowledge that is passed down from mentor to apprentice, and each level achieved brings with it additional clarification as to the true purpose of the organization (or cult). Members are considered "enlightened," while all those who do not belong are mundane and walk in darkness. We are ignorant. Therefore, the Shiva dance illustrates the superposition of the enlightened over the backs and souls of the blind. Of course, to the Illuminati, the truly ignorant are the foolish Christians. As I've said many times in my previous books, the lowest-level members of these mystery religions and secret societies rarely know the truths reserved for the few who actually run the show.

Shiva has been compared to Dionysus,[438] another fertility god associated with vegetation, forest, streams, and dancing—powers also attributed to Cernunnos. All three have dominion over the underworld: Dionysus, the son of Zeus and the mortal Semele, is a type of beast-god (one who inspires his followers to behave as "beasts"—witness the Maenads, the mad women who followed and tended to the needs of Dionysus, who is called Bacchus in the Roman pantheon. The Maenads danced and drank themselves into an ecstatic frenzy, usually dressing in fawn skins (something the followers of Cernunnos also do), carrying a long stick or staff adorned with a pine cone (symbol of the pineal gland, itself considered a doorway into another realm). As with Osiris and Nimrod, Dionysus journeyed to the underworld—in this case, to rescue his mother. Semele is yet another moon goddess, and she fits the Semiramis/Isis/Danu/Diana model.

It also seems fair to examine indigenous spiral petroglyphs (described elsewhere in this book) that very often feature horned humanoid figures in close proximity to a vortex. While scholars admit to speculating as much as anyone else, they typically interpret these spirals as symbolizing the portal to a long journey.[439] Could these ancient petroglyphs also be omens of the horned beast god emerging from a vortex spiral?

Ancient Native American
petroglyphs

What is my point? With its name and by placing a bronze Shiva sculpture prominently in front of its headquarters, CERN is indicating to those with "eyes to see" that the collider's true purpose is to open a portal to the underworld—to create a stargate or "god-gate," which would serve as a doorway between worlds. *Ordo ab chao*, "order out of chaos," has been the plan for millennia, and the invasion commences when the Abyss is finally opened, and its monstrous inhabitants are set free.

Sound far-fetched? Did you know that the Large Hadron Collider is the second attempt by Western scientists to create such a portal? That first massive Hadron Collider, built in Waxahachie, Texas, was shut down after Congress poured nearly $3 billion into its infrastructure. Known colloquially as Desertron, the planned circumference for the main ring was more than fifty-four miles, approximately 3.3 times larger than the CERN facility. Desertron's construction would have allowed energy levels of up to forty TeV per proton! CERN's largest energy output to date is just over eight TeV with plans to increase that this year to an intriguing thirteen TeV.[440] If the Waxahachie collider had the potential to outperform CERN back in the 1980s, then why was it defunded and construction stopped? Well, picture the scene in *Raiders of the Lost Ark*. After hearing Indiana Jones state that Bolloq (the rival archaeologist who working for the Nazis) has been using a staff of the wrong length, Sallah and Indiana both proclaim, "They are digging in the wrong place!"

Location, Location, Location

Saint-Genis-Pouilly is a township within the county of Ain in eastern France. It lies on the border with Switzerland, nestled into the foothills of the Jura Mountains and Lake Geneva (Lac du Leman to the French)—and, because of its unique location, it is governed by the cross-border area of Geneva. The ALICE, ATLAS, and MERYN experiments lie within this region. The township consists of four towns: Saint-Genis (sometimes spelled Saint-Genix), Pouilly, Pregnin, and Flies. "Jura," in Old Norse, means "beast." Dionysus, Cernunnos, and, to a degree, Osiris are all "beast" gods. Osiris, with his "green" skin, reflects the forest nature of Cernunnos and Dionysus. But, more to the point, if this CERNunnos Illuminati experiment succeeds, it will open the gateway to a beast. However, the term "Jura" also refers to the Latin word for "law." This is another reflection of the ancient goddess Columbia, Athena, Maat, Themis, Dike, and all those who are "Lady Justice," a deity that weighs our souls in the balance. The Jura Mountains loom over the CERN campus like ancient judges who oversee the construction and implementation of the new Babylon Portal. The book *Zenith 2016* explains the occult significance of these deities with Lady Justice:

> According to Virgil and the Cumaean Sibyl, whose prophecy formed the *novus ordo seclorum* of the Great Seal of the United States, the New World Order begins during a time of chaos when the earth and oceans are tottering—a time like today. This is when the "son" of promise arrives on earth—Apollo incarnate— a pagan savior born of "a new breed of men sent down from

heaven" when "heroes" and "gods" are blended together. This sounds eerily similar to what the Watchers did during the creation of the nephilim and to what scientists are doing this century through genetic engineering of human-animal chimeras. But to understand why such a fanciful prophecy about Apollo, son of Jupiter, returning to Earth should be important to you: In ancient literature, Jupiter was the Roman replacement of Yahweh as the greatest of the gods—a "counter-Yahweh." His son Apollo is a replacement of Jesus, a "counter-Jesus." This Apollo comes to rule the final New World Order, when "Justice returns, returns old Saturn's [Satan's] reign." The ancient goddess Justice, who returns Satan's reign (Saturnia regna, the pagan golden age), was known to the Egyptians as Ma'at and to the Greeks as Themis, while to the Romans she was Lustitia. Statues and reliefs of her adorn thousands of government buildings and courts around the world, especially in Washington D.C., as familiar Lady Justice, blindfolded and holding scales and a sword. She represents the enforcement of secular law and is, according to the Sibyl's conjure, the authority that will require global compliance to the zenith of Satan's dominion concurrent with the coming of Apollo. What's more, the Bible's accuracy concerning this subject is alarming, including the idea that "pagan justice" will require surrender to a satanic system in a final world order under the rule of Jupiter's son.[441]

This excerpt from *Zenith 2016* and the CERN relationship with the Jura Mountains becomes even clearer when we examine the second of the towns mentioned earlier—Pouilly, established by the Romans as Apolliacum, which reportedly served as the location for a temple to Apollo. Apollo, or Apollyon, is listed in the book of Revelation as belonging to the king of the hybrid-fallen angel creatures that rise up from the pit—Abyss—when it is unsealed. It should also be mentioned that at the time of the Roman occupation of the area, the predominant inhabitants were the Celts, which takes us back to Cernunnos. In a roundabout way, pun intended, the rings of CERN encompass a variety of ancient deities who are all connected to the underworld:

> And the fifth angel blew his trumpet, and I saw a star fallen from heaven to earth, and he was given the key to the shaft of the bottomless pit.
>
> He opened the shaft of the bottomless pit, and from the shaft rose smoke like the smoke of a great furnace, and the sun and the air were darkened with the smoke from the shaft.
>
> Then from the smoke came locusts on the earth, and they were given power like the power of scorpions of the earth.
>
> They were told not to harm the grass of the earth or any green plant or any tree, but only those people who do not have the seal of God on their foreheads.
>
> They were allowed to torment them for five months, but not to kill them, and their torment was like the torment of a scorpion when it stings someone.
>
> And in those days people will seek death and will not find it. They will long to die, but death will flee from them.
>
> In appearance the locusts were like horses prepared for battle: on their heads were what looked like crowns of gold; their faces were like human faces,
>
> their hair like women's hair, and their teeth like lions' teeth;
>
> they had breastplates like breastplates of iron, and the noise of their wings was like the noise of many chariots with horses rushing into battle.
>
> They have tails and stings like scorpions, and their power to hurt people for five months is in their tails.
>
> They have as king over them the angel of the bottomless pit. His name in Hebrew is Abaddon, and in Greek he is called Apollyon. (Revelation 9:1–11)

Both Apollyon (Greek) and Abaddon (in the Hebrew) mean "the destroyer," just as Shiva is the destroyer. These "gods," these fallen angels from the pit, intend to set up a *new world order* on the ash heap of the old—on the backs of "ignorant dwarves" like you and me. Peter Good-game sheds further light on the identity of this "king" locust:

> And just who is this Greek god Apollyon who makes his strange appearance in the book of Revelation? Charles Penglase is an Australian professor who specializes in ancient Greek and Near Eastern religion and mythology. In his book, *Greek Myths and Mesopotamia: Parallels and Influence in the Homeric Hymns and Hesiod*, Penglase carefully and methodically demonstrates that the Greek myths and legends of Apollo were simply Greek retell-ings of the Babylonian myths involving the rise to power of the god Marduk, which were themselves based on earlier legends of the Sumerian hunter/hero known as Ninurta. Furthermore, according to David Rohl, the original name for Ninurta was in fact Nimurda, whose historical identity can be traced back to King Enmerkar of Uruk, the very same figure who is known in the Bible as Nimrod.[442]

Is it not astonishing that, following upon the heels of two world wars in which millions upon millions of human lives were sacrificed—and upon the discovery of a mighty weapon that changed history forever, that being the atomic bomb—the victors in both wars would come together to form a scientific endeavor that would unlock the secrets of the universe? And is it not even more astonishing that this collective of the world's finest minds mirrors one of the darkest events in biblical his-tory, that of the Tower of Babel?

It is said that one possible location for the tower was directly over the presumed location of the Abzu, the Abyss! Was Nimrod actually trying to unleash the locusts in defiance of God's ultimate timing? Nimrod, deified as Apollo by the Greeks and Osiris by the Egyptians, is consid-ered by many theologians to be the same "spirit" that will return to earth in the last days as the Antichrist. In fact, in the New Testament, the identity of the god Apollo (repeat-coded on the Great Seal of the United

States as the Masonic "messiah" who returns to rule the earth in a new Golden Age), is the same spirit—verified by the same name—that will inhabit the political leader of the end-times New World Order. Again, from *Zenith 2016* we read:

> According to key Bible prophecies, the Antichrist will be the progeny or incarnation of the ancient spirit, Apollo. Second Thessalonians 2:3 warns: "Let no man deceive you by any means: for that day shall not come, except there come a falling away first, and that man of sin be revealed, the son of perdition [Apoleia; Apollyon, Apollo]" (emphasis added). Numerous scholarly and classical works identify "Apollyon" as the god "Apollo"—the Greek deity "of death and pestilence," and Webster's Dictionary points out that "Apollyon" was a common variant of "Apollo" throughout history. An example of this is found in the classical play by the ancient Greek playwright Aeschylus, The Agamemnon of Aeschylus, in which Cassandra repeats more than once, "Apollo, thou destroyer, O Apollo, Lord of fair streets, Apollyon to me." Accordingly, the name Apollo turns up in ancient literature with the verb *apollymi* or *apollyo* (destroy), and scholars including W. R. F. Browning believe apostle Paul may have identified the god Apollo as the "spirit of Antichrist" operating behind the persecuting Roman emperor, Domitian, who wanted to be recognized as "Apollo incarnate" in his day. Such identifying of Apollo with despots and "the spirit of Antichrist" is consistent even in modern history. For instance, note how Napoleon's name literally translates to "the true Apollo."
>
> Revelation 17:8 likewise ties the coming of Antichrist with Apollo, revealing that the Beast shall ascend from the bottomless pit and enter him:

> > The Beast that thou sawest was, and is not; and shall ascend out of the Bottomless Pit, and go into perdition [Apolia, Apollo]: and they that dwell on the Earth

shall wonder, whose names were not written in the
Book of Life from the foundation of the world, when
they behold the Beast that was, and is not, and yet is.[443]
(emphasis added)

Many prophecy scholars equate Nimrod with Gilgamesh, the hero
of the ancient Sumerian creation story composed circa 2000 BC. Gilgamesh claimed to be two-thirds "god," which seemed impossible until
today, when babies are born every day with three parents (a process
where one "parent" is a woman who donates her enucleated ovum as
carrier for the DNA of the other two parents). But Genesis refers to
Nimrod as a man who "*began to be* a mighty one in the earth" (Genesis
10:8 emphasis added). The Hebrew word translated as "began to be"
is *khalal,* which implies sexual profanity or genetic pollution—and a
process. Nimrod was *becoming* a *Gibbowr* (mighty one), which is most
often used when referring to giants. Nimrod most likely was a product
of a profane mating of fallen angel (god) and human. He is Apollo,
Cernunnos, Abaddon, Osiris, and Horus, and he is returning as king of
the locusts (hybrid fallen angels) from the pit! And CERN may be the
stargate that will open this unholy portal!

The race to discern the atom's secrets has been part of the millen-
nia-old plan of the ages: to unseat God through secret knowledge and
rituals. The very logo chosen for CERN, representing the rings of the
colliders, forms a "666." This is semiotic subterfuge. The overt symbol,
we are told, merely represents the rings, but Bible scholars who know
prophecy—those with "eyes to see" can discern the truth. Yet this semiotic veil may hide much more. The opening to this chapter includes
a quote from Sergio Bertolucci, director of CERN, implying that the
real purpose of the colliders is to open a gateway to other dimensions.
CERN is using its massive rings to study and create anti-matter, anti-
gravity, and perhaps even torsion fields,[444] which have been theorized as a
means to travel through time and space (and perhaps dimensions). Torsion fields—if they exist—are like wormholes into another dimension.

A curious passage occurs in the Old Testament:

And it came to pass, when the LORD would take up Elijah into heaven by a whirlwind, that Elijah went with Elisha from Gilgal. (2 Kings 2:1)

Gilgal is the location of an ancient stone circle, after the pattern of Stonehenge. According to author Barry Chamish, the full name of this installation is the "Circle of the Giants" (Gilgal-Rephaim):

The Israeli UFO experience is unique and very complicated. I have touched on just one aspect of it; but it is vital to understanding the Israeli puzzle. Of the seven best documented close encounters with alien beings provably connected to UFOs, six involved giants. These giants were determined to leave evidence of their arrival in the form of cadmium-imbued landing circles, miles of impossible boot tracks and deliberate communication with witnesses. Indeed, the abundant evidence more than indicates that there are giants roaming Israel today.

As there were 5,000 years ago and they also left proof of their existence. The giants were descended from the Nephilim, literally the fallen ones. In ancient time, entities fell on Israel from the heavens and later became the mortal enemies of the Hebrew nations.

The Circle of the Giants—Gilgal Rephaim. 5200-year-old monument believed by some to have been built by the biblical giants, also called Nephilim.

One giant king was Og of Bashan. The bible records that his bed was thirteen feet long. Bashan's territory included the Golan Heights. Sitting on the Golan Heights is the Israeli version of Stonehenge. Called Gilgal Rephaim, the Circle of the Rephaim or giants in English, this site consists of five concentric rings whose beauty can only be appreciated from above. Unfortunately, there was supposedly no way for the simple nomads of 5000 years ago to see the circles from above.

The site is enormous. The outside circle has a diameter of

159 meters and over 37,000 tons of rock went into the construction of the complex. Two openings in the circles may have
been used to measure the solar solstice and the rising of Sirius in
3000 BCE.

The fact remains that Israeli archaeologists are totally mystified by the Gilgal Rephaim. No other complex built in the
Middle East resembles it and it predates the pyramids by over
500 years. The indigenous nomads of the time did not engage
in this kind of megalith building, so outsiders were probably the
builders. According to the Bible, the only outsiders living on the
Golan Heights back then were giants.

Maybe it's a longshot, but no one has come up with a better
explanation for Israel's current UFO wave. I believe the ancient
giants may be coming home. I conclude on a somber note. The
biblical giants were God's enemy and Israel's armies were the
means to their utter destruction. There is a legitimate reason to
contemplate the recent rearrival of giants in Israel with a good
measure of dread.[445]

It's intriguing that Elijah was at this very location when he received
the message from the Lord that he would soon be taken to heaven by a
whirlwind. Had Elijah remained there waiting for God to send for him,
the local pagans may have attributed the supernatural event to the Prince
of the Power of the Air—Baal, the god of storms, or perhaps Dagon, the
god of the wind. Jesus calls Satan "the Prince and Power of the Air." The
whirlwind has a shape similar to that of a torsion field, or wormhole.
God Almighty works with His universe using His rules and methods, so
what appears to us humans, who are confined to a limited perception of
space/time as a whirlwind, may actually be a wormhole. Elijah heard the
promise of the Lord, and he left Gilgal.

In fact, Elijah kept traveling for days—much to Elisha's surprise and
befuddlement—finally arriving in Bethel, then Jericho, then crossing
over the Jordan river (by striking it with his garment and parting the
waters, mind you!). It was only then that a "chariot of fire" drawn by

horses of fire appeared, and Elijah was taken by a whirlwind. Was he translated to another dimension—to heaven—via a wormhole? These "chariots of fire"—were they heavenly messengers or another manifestation of God's methods as they appear to human senses?

As Above, So Below

The circular tracks at CERN create enormous amounts of energy as the particles collide, and some researchers fear that this energy, plus the torsion fields that arise from the electromagnetic interactions—coupled with the notion of dark matter, which is theorized as a massive, unseen web that connects all the universe—may combine to form the god-gate that is called the key to opening the Abyss.

The description of the entities rising up from the Abyss in Revelation 9 states that they will rise "like smoke from a great furnace." This is not a picture of smoke gently rising from a fire, but dense, black smoke as it is belched from a massive conflagration. This smoke is so dense that it covers up the sun! The momentum requires an "engine" to propel it upwards, and a torsion field may aid in that endeavor. As this occurs, the four angels bound in the Euphrates are loosed (Revelation 9:13), and these four lead a hybrid army of two hundred million, given the power to kill a THIRD of mankind!

Order out of chaos, the dance of Shiva, the overturning of an old order replaced by a new one—intended by the spiritual enemy of mankind, the destroyer Apollyon, to preempt Christ's millennial reign and forever hold back the TRUE KING's return. This is what the initiates of the mystery religions, the scientists and politicians who trust in rituals and "knowledge" as god rather than God Almighty—this is their ultimate plan. It is no coincidence that CERN was established at almost the exact same time as the Bilderberg group.

The tracks for the ATLAS ring at CERN have an occult signature built within their design: they are octagonal. The occult "cross" has eight points. The primary cross represents the four corners of the "clock," also called the "cardinal points." These are the vernal equinox, summer solstice, autumnal equinox, and the winter solstice. Within the heavens (the constellations that encircle the earth that God told us would serve as signs and seasons), and according to Michael S. Heiser, these primary directions correspond to the faces of the cherubim. In part 2 of Dr. Heiser's essay on Ezekiel's vision, he quotes the work of Bible scholar Dan Block:

> Speaking of the vision of ch. 1, Dan Block, in his massive two volume commentary on the text of Ezekiel makes the following observation: "Since the inaugural vision came to the prophet from the north, the frontal view (south) would have had a human face, with the other three being arranged as follows": [this text is based on Heiser's graphic] North (Eagle/Phoenix), East (Ox/Taurus), South (Human/Sagittarius), West (Lion/Leo).
>
> Block adds, "If the faces in 10:14 are also listed in clockwise order, the sequence is identical, and the cherub is identified with the bull." Other scholars (like Leslie Allen in the Word Biblical Commentary, vol. 1, of Ezekiel) note that the four faces suggest the four directions, or the cardinal points. He's right—and what's more, the faces of the creatures (cherubim) correspond to the four cardinal points of the zodiac. Scholars of ancient astronomy will tell you that the zodiac has a Babylonian derivation—which is precisely where Ezekiel is living and writing from.[446]

These four points are represented in the main cross of the occult octagon. The second set of four are cross-quarter points, representing Imbolc, Beltane, Lammas, and Samhain. While the first four are reflected in God's creation of both the cherubim's faces and the constellations, this second set of four is not—these are occult festivals that celebrate fallen angels and gods. Imbolc celebrates Diana, Brigid, and other fertility goddesses. Beltane, also known as Walpurgisnacht, is a lustful time of chaos and fertility rites, celebrated on May Day. Lammas is a festival of harvest, meaning "loaf mass," and it actually corresponds neatly with Thanksgiving. Samhain celebrates all demons and evil spirits, and we reenact a watered-down version of the ancient rites during Halloween.

But aside from pagan celebrations, the octagonal shape is revered by secret societies. The eight-sided star is sometimes called the Chaos Star (I-Ching), Ishtar's Star, the Dharmacakra, the 8 of Wands in Aleister Crowley's Thoth Tarot Card deck, and it is even pictured representing the sun in the Piazza San Pietro in the Vatican. The Masonic Chaos Star is shown within an Ouroboros Circle (a snake that is eating its tail is called an ouroboros, and it sometimes represents Leviathan) that includes a crown over the head of the snake! Chaos stars can also be discerned with the "semiotic" (hidden meaning) logos of the CIA, the ancient flag of Chaldea, the Annapolis Middle East Peace Conference—but this star is sometimes hidden within a many-pointed star known as the "black sun." The black sun is particularly pertinent to this essay, because it also represents a black hole, but can also represent what Helena Blavatsky of the Theosophy Society claimed was a burned-out sun that had been defeated by Sol.

The octagon is a revered form, and the number eight appears in Freemasonic architecture. David Bay of Cutting Edge Ministries, when noting that the Washington Monument has eight windows, says this:

> And, also remember the importance of the Number 8 in Occultic Numerology, for it carries the meaning of "New Beginnings." Combined with the meaning of Number 13, as "Extreme Rebellion," you get the total message that this "New Beginning"(New World Order) is to be carried out in "Extreme Rebellion."[447]

When President Gerald Ford's coffin was brought in to the funeral service, it was placed upon an octagonal base. The logo for the Dharma Initiative in the television series *LOST* is an eight-sided "chaos star." The

Dharma Initiative had set up a series of bunkers on the mysterious island to study the many anomalies there, especially the ability of the island to contort time and space. The reimagined *Battlestar Galactica* science-fiction series used octagons for many shapes within the ship, including all books and documents. The Templar cross is in fact an octagon, perhaps referring to the Chaos Star, but many believe it is a reflection of the "craft" related to Templars, that of Freemasonry. Much of the higher degrees use Moorish architecture and names; are these imitating the octagonal construction of the interior of the Dome of the Rock, which many say sits upon Mount Moriah?

The final series of collisions for the "first run" at CERN ran from December 17–December 21, 2012, the very date when the Mayan calendar rolled over and supposedly opened a mystical portal in heaven and inside earth, marking the end of an era and the beginning of a new and final age of man (and, as documented in the book *Zenith 2016*, this is the same date predicted by numerous ancient societies as well as turn-of-the-century preachers who believed the Antichrist and False Prophet would arrive on earth between 2012–2016 and thereafter make themselves known to the world). Following that run, the LHC shut down until this year, when the scientists at CERN plan to run collisions at much higher energy levels. The ATLAS ring, one of seven detector experiments with the forced acronym that we're told means "A Toroidal LHC Apparatus" ("toroidal" refers to a donut-shaped object, like a whirlwind), may actually be a "nudge, nudge, wink, wink" reference to Atlas, the god who was sentenced to forever hold the heavens on his shoulders. Atlas was a Titan who sided with the losers in the Titanomachy, the battle for dominance between the Titans and the Olympians. His punishment is often listed as carrying the heavens, but in fact he was commanded to hold up Uranus, the "heavens or sky," so that he could never again mate with Gaia, the earth mother. Using ATLAS to open a portal so that fallen angels could once again mate with human females and torment mankind is a MAJOR nudge and wink to the Illuminati.

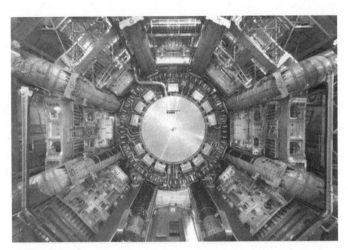

The 7000-ton ATLAS detector is probing for unknown realities from a cavern 100 meters below the ancient Apolliacum.

ATLAS is composed of eight-sided sections that look very much like the pagan Wheel of Time and the Chaos Star. Is there something about this configuration that has power in the spiritual realm? The Jewish Kabbalah sees the number eight as one step beyond perfection, where seven is the number of perfection and completion:

> Eight, on the other hand, is symbolic of an entity that is one step above the natural order, higher than nature and its limitations. That's why Chanukah is eight days long—the greatly outnumbered Maccabees' resolve to battle the Greeks wasn't logical or natural. They drew on reservoirs of faith and courage that are not part of normative human nature. They therefore merited a miracle higher than nature—a miracle that lasted eight days—and to commemorate this, we light on Chanukah an eight-branched menorah. In a similar vein, we circumcise our children when they are eight-day old babies, because the *brit milah* symbolizes our nation's supernatural and logic-defying covenant with G-d.[448]

In this light, the Messiah's number is often listed as eight, but when referring to the opening of the Abyss, this would be the anti-Messiah,

Apollyon! I've mentioned "semiotics," (the art of hiding meaning within symbols), and the NASA space program is rife with them. Apollo 8 was originally supposed to be the Apollo 9 Mission, but when the lunar lander failed to be ready for low-earth orbit, it was decided that NASA would send up the team that was ready and call it Apollo 8. The three astronauts, Frank Borman (a Freemason), James Lovell, and William Anders were catapulted into space on December 21 (there's that mystical date again), 1968—the winter solstice, when CERNunnos, the god of the Celts, is celebrated by his followers.

But there is another, little known component of CERN that dovetails neatly with God's prophecies about the coming *beast system*. The amount of data being produced by the collider experiments is monumental in size and scope. More than fifteen petabytes of data are produced, stored, and analyzed every year, and that amount will grow exponentially as the LHC begins operating at higher energy levels throughout this year. How can one location handle all this information? It can't. In 2002, visionaries from CERN created the Worldwide LHC Computing Grid (WLCG):

> The Worldwide LHC Computing Grid (WLCG) is a global computing infrastructure whose mission is to provide computing resources to store, distribute and analyse the data generated by the Large Hadron Collider (LHC), making the data equally available to all partners, regardless of their physical location.
>
> WLCG is the world's largest computing grid. It is supported by many associated national and international grids across the world, such as European Grid Initiative (Europe-based) and Open Science Grid (US-based), as well as many other regional grids.
>
> WLCG is coordinated by CERN. It is managed and operated by a worldwide collaboration between the experiments (ALICE, ATLAS, CMS and LHCb) and the participating computer centres. It is reviewed by a board of delegates from partner country funding agencies, and scientifically reviewed by the LHC Experiments Committee.[449]

Forty countries. One hundred seventy million computing centers. Two million jobs run every day.[450]

The grid was used to announce the discovery of the Higgs Boson on July 4, 2012. The grid is humming all around us—moment by moment, second by second—communicating with data produced by the rings of Saturn. Yes, I said Saturn. In a very real way, this can be said because Saturn is yet another name for the Destroyer, Abaddon, Apollyon, Nimrod, Osiris, Shiva, Dionysus, and CERNunnos. And Saturn is to play a very important role, according to the prophecy of Apollo/Nimrod's ancient and most powerful Sibyl (the Cumaean, also known as Amalthaea), who predicts the return of the god Apollo on the Great Seal of the United States. As the oldest of the Sibyls and the seer of that underworld, Apollyon opens in the end-times, she prophesied Apollo would return to earth through mystical "life" given to him from the gods when the deity Saturn (Satan?) returns to reign over the earth in a new pagan golden age.

From the beginning of the Novus Ordo Seclorum prophecy, we read:

Now the last age by Cumae's Sibyl sung Has come and gone, and the majestic roll Of circling centuries begins anew: Justice returns, *returns old Saturn's reign*, With a new breed of men sent down from heaven. Only do thou, at the boy's birth in whom The iron shall cease, the golden race arise, Befriend him, chaste Lucina; 'tis thine own Apollo reigns.

He shall receive the life of gods, and see Heroes with gods commingling, and himself Be seen of them, and with his father's worth Reign o'er a world....

Assume thy greatness, for the time draws nigh, Dear child of gods, great progeny of Jove [Jupiter/Zeus]! See how it totters—the world's orbed might, Earth, and wide ocean, and the vault profound, All, see, enraptured of the coming time![451] (emphasis added)

The Cumaean Sibyl, who, in the *Aeneid,* gave Aeneas a tour of the infernal region, is also honored by the Vatican as a "vessel of truth" on their altars and illustrated books and even upon the ceiling of the Sistine Chapel, where five Sibyls including the Delphic (like the one Paul cast a demon out of in the New Testament) join the Old Testament prophets in places of sacred honor.

Will the power of Saturn's rings and Apollo's (Apollyon's) coming join the dancing image of Shiva, which at CERN has a mighty ring behind his back as if he uses this magic circle (a chaos star?) to initiate the ultimate death and rebirth cycle? Rings as in a torsion field or a *whirlwind?* Rings as in a vortex, a time tunnel, a gateway to another dimension? The grid may be thought of as the brain for this mighty machine as it commands and collates—transmits and receives. And it reverberates across the globe, courtesy of the connected computers in fortycountries! CERN and its rings lie at the heart of a massive data cloud that may soon drive a mighty smoke column that will block out the sun and even attempt to block out the SON.

CHAPTER TEN

Patterns, Portals, and 3, 6, 9

By Tom Horn

I created the Event Horizon to reach the stars, but she's gone much, much farther than that. She tore a hole in our universe, a gateway to another dimension. A dimension of pure chaos. Pure...evil. When she crossed over, she was just a ship. But when she came back...she was alive! Look at her, Miller. Isn't she beautiful?
—Dr. Weir to Dr. Miller in the film *Event Horizon*

The thing's hollow! It goes on forever, and...
oh My God, it's full of stars!
—Arthur C. Clarke, *2001: A Space Odyssey*

"The gates of Hell are open night and day; smooth the descent, and easy is the way: but, to return, and view the cheerful skies; in this, the task and mighty labor lies.
—Virgil, *The Aeneid*

If you only knew the magnificence of the 3, 6 and 9, then you would have the key to the universe.
—Nikola Tesla

You know, I will never be called a "mind reader" by anyone, but even *I* can predict with a strong degree of accuracy that *at this moment*, as you read this, the theory of "vortex-based mathematics" is probably *not* on your mind—but it should be. As we've researched mythologies, symbols, artwork, biblical references, and even fictional representations of wormholes and stargates, both Cris Putnam and I have sought to bring you the secrets about parallel dimensions and the multiverse, and how—beginning in the late nineteenth century—scientists began to unlock the mysteries of the atom, and with them, the Pandora's Box of quantum physics.

Nikola Tesla, a pioneer whose work has been stolen, copied, lauded, and sometimes praised since his death, is quoted as saying that the numbers 3, 6, and 9 hold the key to the universe. Recently, a science maverick named Marco Rodin delivered a curious talk at Charlotte, West Virginia's, TEDx conference. If you've not heard of the TED talks, allow me to spend a paragraph or so explaining the history behind this collective of technology movers and shakers.

The friendly little acronym TED stands for "technology, entertainment, and design." It is the brainchild of graphic designer Richard Saul Wurman, who saw early on that the three disciplines had begun to converge into a massive new form of medium. Not surprisingly, the kickoff conference occurred in 1984, the year the Apple Macintosh burst onto the world stage with its now-famous Super Bowl commercial that portrayed IBM as a type of Big Brother. Ironically, Apple and its hand-held enterprise collect vast amounts of data for the massive though "hidden" Big Brother artificial intelligence (AI) growing inside the Internet—but that's a topic for another book and another day.

TED has been hailed as innovative but criticized as being a closed club for rich insiders. One cannot simply contact TED and ask to be placed on the roster of presenters. Let's just say, I will never make its list. Here's how Sarah Lacy, a former "insider" who found herself suddenly delisted, explained it:

Business conferences have good reasons to be elitist; deals are getting done and high-level conversations need to be private sometimes.

But when credentials are revoked at the last minute based purely on the whim of a more important member of the TED community, the inner workings are just too much like a country club for an organization whose stellar content is all about pluralism and uplift. It's the Sarah Silverman incident all over again. Oh you made one of the more important people feel uncomfortable? Then you're out of here.[452]

If you watch a lot of these talks, you'll soon notice a pattern. Global agendas like overpopulation, animal rights, transhumanism, singularity, meditation, climate change, and augmented thinking are but a few of their topics. Attendees pay tens of thousands of dollars for the privilege to "be seen" and "see," and speakers must adhere to those of the Sapling Foundation, the event's parent company and organizer.

Now that you have that reference in your back pocket, let's return to Marco Rodin. His presentation at TEDx brought a new way of thinking about numbers and the universe—and even quantum physics—to the forefront. Rodin's theory rests upon the mysterious number 9. Here's an excerpt from one of Rodin's newsletters:

The last number left to be explained from The Mathematical Fingerprint Of God is the number 9. The number nine is Energy being manifested in a single moment event of occurrence in our physical world of creation. It is unique because it is the focal center by being the only number identifying with the vertical upright axis. It is the singularity or the Primal Point of Unity. The number nine never changes and is linear. For example all multiples of 9 equal 9. $9 \times 1 = 9$, $9 \times 2 = 18$, but $1 + 8 = 9$, $9 \times 3 = 27$, but $2 + 7 = 9$. This is because it is emanating in a straight line from the center of mass out of the nucleus of every atom, and from out of the singularity of a black hole. It is complete, revealing perfection, and has no parity because it always equals itself. The number nine is the missing particle in the universe known as Dark Matter.[453]

Rodin asserts that bisecting a circle (360 degrees, which reduces to the number 9) gives an infinite number of hidden 9s, leading to an ultimate singularity. Bisect it once and you get two 180-degree angles, with each one reducing to 9. Quarter sections give four 45-degree angles, each one reducing to 9, and so on *ad infinitum*. Rodin calls this an internal progression. Inserting polygons into a circle yields another set of 9s. A pyramid within the circle gives you three 60-degree angles; 6 x 3 = 18, which reduces to 9. A square gives four 90-degree angles; 4 x 9=36, reducing to 9, and so on—a progression he calls a "vacuum." The Singularity and the Vacuum. Rodin calls this an external progression, and the two combined—he claims—form the secret fingerprint of God in the form of a torsion field. A spiral. The angel in the whirlwind, one might say. According to Rodin, his work in this field has been praised by Microsoft senior researcher Russell Blake:

> As Russell Blake, senior researcher from Microsoft, has said of Marko's work, This fantastic coherence has existed since the beginning of time but has yet to be harnessed by mankind and the potential is truly mind-boggling! Not only is the Rodin Torus three dimensional, but actually fourth dimensional and higher![454]

Since Rodin spoke at TEDx, his video presentation has been removed from the TED website and all official YouTube channels, and it may soon disappear from the Web, so you might want to head to the link in the endnotes for a simplified version of Rodin's basic theory of the mysterious number 9.[455]

Is Rodin onto something? Has he discovered the "Philosopher's Stone" of quantum mechanics and the secret to God's Fingerprint, perhaps hinted at by Nikola Tesla? It's quite possible that his mathematics unveil a mystery known to many ancient pagan religions, based upon esoteric knowledge given to Nimrod, which the world leader used to build a godgate.

As Dr. Michael Lake explained in his blockbuster book, *The Shinar Directive*, Nimrod's tower was much more than just a tall building:

> Perhaps Nimrod was diligently laboring to create more than just an interdimensional landing pad; it is quite possible that he was building an ancient interdimensional portal generator. It is quite possible that the wrath of God came because mankind was "of one mind" to create a mechanism to storm heaven itself![456]

Nimrod's uncompleted work continues today, hidden within the lore of mystery religions and secret societies, and a day is coming when the portal generator may rev up anew. If Rodin is correct, then his presentation may have startled members of the elite TED group. Knowledge, when released too soon, can prove dangerous. Timing is everything, and the gateways and portals that exist in various places across the globe await the signal for the return of the "ancient gods" of Noah's day.

So where are these portals? A quick Google search will bring up thousands of websites that list the presumed locations of the "gates to Hell" sometimes called "portals to other dimensions," but a dozen or so recur on just about everyone's list. We'll begin with the one nearly every reader must have already blurted out (at least mentally).

The Bermuda Triangle

The coordinates of this curious section of the Atlantic Ocean are 25.0000 degrees North, 71.0000 degrees West, and the area forms an almost equilateral triangle with Bermuda, Puerto Rico, and the southern tip of Florida as the points. Records of strange occurrences reach back at least to when Christopher Columbus experienced the "compass variations" that are often reported even today. He wrote in his log:

Thursday 13 September 1492

On this day at the beginning of night the compasses north-wested and in the morning they northeasted somewhat.

Monday September 17,

The pilots took the north, marking it [North Star], and found that the compasses northwested a full point [11 and one quarter degrees]; and the sailors were fearful and depressed and did not say why. The Admiral was aware of this and he ordered that the north again be marked when dawn came, and they found that the compasses were correct. The cause was that the North Star appears to move and not the compasses.

Sunday 23 September

Since the sea had been calm and smooth the men complained, saying that since in that region there were no rough seas [Sargasso Sea], it would never blow for a return to Spain. But later the sea rose high and without wind, which astonished them, because of which the Admiral says here that the high sea was very necessary for me, a sign which had not appeared except in the time of the Jews when they left Egypt and complained against Moses, who took them out of captivity.

Sunday, 30 September

Also the Admiral says here when night comes the compasses northwest one quarter, and when dawn comes they coincide with the North Star exactly.[457]

On October 11, Columbus and his men reported seeing an unexplained "light on the horizon."

A chronological listing of the most well-known "disappearances" can be found at the website www.bermuda-attractions.com, which includes the Columbus event, plus:

1609—The Sea Venture

1812—Theodosia Burr Alston, the daughter of former United
        States Vice President Aaron Burr. She was a passenger
        on board ThePatriot, which sailed from Charleston,
        South Carolina to New York City on December 30,
        1812, and was never heard of again.

1814—The USS Epervier and her crew disappeared while
        carrying the peace treaty to end the war between
        America and the North African Barbary States.

1872—Mary Celeste

1881—The Ellen Austin on its voyage in 1881 came across
        another ship that was sailing without a single soul on
        board. Ellen Austin transferred some of its crew onto
        the other ship and attempted to sail with it to New
        York. The other ship suddenly disappeared. Later it
        re-appeared, but again without a person on board.
        Then it again disappeared without trace.

1918—USS Cyclops: This navy ship disappearance **resulted
        in the single largest loss of life in the history of the
        US Navy.** It went missing without a trace with a crew
        of 309, sometime after March 4th 1918 and after
        departing the island of Barbados.

1941—The USS Proteus and the USS Nereus vanished, just as
        their sister ship the USS Cyclops previously did along
        the same route.

1945—Flight 19: They were training aircrafts of TBM Avenger
        bombers of US Navy that went missing on Dec 5,
        1945 while flying over the Atlantic. Adding to the
        mystery, two rescue Martin Mariner aircraft with
        13-man crew were sent to search for the missing flights.
        But one of the Martin Mariners itself did not return
        and was never traced again.

1945—PBM Martin Mariner: Two Martin Mariner planes

were sent on the 5th of December 1945 to search for the Flight-19. One did not return. Find out the full story.

1948—Tudor Star Tiger: A Tudor Mark IV aircraft disappeared in Bermuda Triangle shortly before it was to land in Bermuda airport in January 1948.

1948—Fight DC-3 Disappearance: The flight Douglas DC-3 NC16002 disappeared in Bermuda Triangle when it was only 50 miles south of Florida and about to land in Miami on December 28, 1948.

1954—Flight 441 Disappearance: The flight 441, a Super Constellation Naval Airliner, disappeared in Bermuda Triangle on October 30, 1954

1963—Marine Sulphur Queen: This 524-foot carrier of molten sulphur started sail Feb 2, 1963 from Beaumont, Texas with 39 crew. It was reported lost in Florida Straits on Feb 4.

1967—Witchcraft: A 23-foot cabin cruiser went missing for ever in Bermuda Triangle area on the night of December 22, 1967. The owner took it offshore only to watch the lights of Miami shoreline.

1968—USS Scorpion: (SSN-589) a Nuclear powered submarine of United States Navy that disappeared in Bermuda Triangle in May 1968.

1971—Sting-27, a USAF Phantom jet, vanished completely without a trace. Official reports indicated it may have suffered an impact, but the details were never revealed.

1976—The Sylvia L. Ossa, a 590-foot ore carrier with a crew of 37 disappeared 140 miles from Bermuda.

1991—The pilot of a Grumman Cougar jet made a routine radio request to increase altitude. While ascending, the aircraft gradually faded from radar and vanished.

1999—The cargo freighter Genesis sent a radio signal to a nearby vessel, indicating a problem with the bilge pump. Despite extensive searches by the Coast Guard, the ship and crew were never seen or heard from again.

2003—A newly married couple Frank and Romina Leone went for fishing on their brand new 16-foot boat on June 18, 2003. They left from the Boynton beach inlet in Florida but never returned. The US Coast Guard eventually gave up the search & rescue operation after having combed a large part of the sea area for several days.

2005 &

2007—On two separate incidents, two Piper-PA planes disappeared in the Bermuda Triangle area. One on June 20, 2005 between Treasure Cay island of Bahamas and Fort Pierce of Florida. There were three persons on board. The second incident took place on April 10, 2007 near Berry Island. Only the pilot was on board and no passengers.

2008—A Britten-Norman Islander (also known as 3-engine Trislander) took off from Santiago for New York on December 15, 2008 at around 3:30pm with 12 persons on board. After about 35 minutes from take-off, the aircraft fell off the radar. A massive search operation was launched by US Coast Guards, but the aircraft was never traced again. Its last known location was about 4 miles west of West Caicos Island. No debris has been found until now.[458] (emphasis added)

Opposite the Bermuda Triangle, in the Devil's Sea, is an area known as the Dragon's Triangle. Its history runs parallel to that of its antipodal sister, including long lists of missing fishing vessels, airplanes, and even the crew of USAF C-97, who disappeared on March 22, 1957. Recently, however the Dragon's Triangle popped up again recently when Malaysia Airlines Flight MH370 disappeared from radar. An article published online at Liveleak.com[459] hints that this mysterious region might be to blame for the tragedy. Certainly, authorities and rescue pilots in the weeks following the plane's disappearance seemed to have little to no idea exactly where the airliner may have traveled during its time off radar, but it had apparently strayed off course prior to its presumed crash. No debris has been found as of this date.

Mountains and Gateways

Mountains—and, in particular, volcanoes—have long been associated with portals. The Superstition Mountains, covered in another section of this book, are but one example. The Cascade Range in the western United States is another. Mount Shasta, a stratovolcano, is one of Cascade's mighty peaks, rising over fourteen thousand feet above sea level. Writer and adventurer Frederick Oliver wrote a book about the "sacred mountain" in 1884, claiming that beneath Shasta's heights lay a massive network of tunnels and hallways where the descendants of Atlantis lived. According to the website mtshastaspirit.org, more than one hundred New Age sects revere the "sacred mountain." An article written by Pam Huher and posted to a site called Mt. Shasta Spirit[460] tells of Bigfoot sightings, UFO activity, dwarves, robed "humanoids," and even angels. If Mount Shasta is indeed a portal location, then none of these reports comes as a surprise.

Point Pleasant, West Virginia, is a sleepy little town that lies just opposite Gallipolis, Ohio, near the T-junction of the Ohio and Kanawha Rivers. Though the name of the town might not ring any bells, the movie and book about the town's silver bridge will: *The Mothman Prophecies*. John Keel, the book's author, begins his tale in 1967, when the silver bridge collapsed, but an online blogger who calls herself "The Appalachian Lady" begs to differ with his conclusions. She claims the real cause of the bridge's collapse lay in a curse voiced by Chief Cornstalk:

I was the white man's friend. Many times I have saved the white man and his people from harm. I never made war with you, except to protect our land. I refused at the peril of my own people to join your enemies in the red coats. I came to this fort as your friend, and you have murdered my young son, who harmed no one, and you have murdered me when I came only to save you. For this, may the curse of the Great Spirit rest upon this land and its inhabitants. May it be blighted by nature, and may it be blighted in its hopes. May the strength of its people be paralyzed by the stain of our blood.[461]

Here is what the Appalachian Lady recalls hearing from her Shawnee grandmother:

For millennia, the abundant Ohio River Valley around Point Pleasant was home to multiple Native American tribes, including the Shawnee. Their leader in the late 1700s was Chief Kiteug-gua (translated to Cornstalk), and their rock drawings exist even today. Among those drawings are depictions of a large bird-like creature with large saucer-like eyes, known as the Thunderbird. So the Mothman wasn't a new thing at all, really. It was actually something known to Native Americans for hundreds if not thousands of years, long before the Mothman ever appeared.

The Thunderbird was a servant of The Great Spirit, and it lived atop the hills and mountains. It was huge, and according to legend, could cause wind and the sound of thunder with its wings, and lightning by blinking its huge eyes. It is said that the Thunderbird could change its appearance to that of a man, by pulling back its beak and removing its feathers. It was a very dangerous and wrathful spirit, and its power could be summoned through The Great Spirit, to avenge the Native Americans against their enemies.

She goes on to make her case, connecting the Mothman sightings to ancient legends of the Thunderbird:

There were over 100 witnesses to the Mothman phenomenon, and most were considered to be credible. They would talk of being chased by a large, approximately seven-foot-tall birdlike creature with large glowing red eyes, sometimes at **speeds of over 100 miles per hour**. They would also talk of this same creature appearing before them on remote roads or even in their own yard, sometimes peering with its large red eyes into their homes. (emphasis added)

Witnesses disagree as to whether or not this Mothman, a creature that bears an uncanny resemblance to a winged and red-eyed form of "Slender Man" now being reported in Staffordshire, England,[462] was trying to warn citizens of Pleasant Point about an impending disaster or actually caused it, but the spiritual and perhaps "interdimensional" being reported may have been visiting the area as far back as the Shawnee tribe and even before.

Another anomalous region is Lake Anjikuni in Canada. Wikipedia says this:

In 1930, a newsman in The Pas, Manitoba, reported on a small Inuit village right off of Lake Angikuni. The village had always welcomed the fur trappers who passed through occasionally. But in 1930 Joe Labelle, a fur trapper well known in the village, found that all the villagers had gone. He found unfinished shirts that still had needles in them and food hanging over fire pits and therefore concluded that the villagers had left suddenly. Even more disturbing, he found seven sled dogs dead from starvation and a grave that had been dug up. Labelle knew that an animal could not have been responsible because the stones circling the grave were undisturbed. He reported this to the Royal Canadian Mounted Police (Kelleher refers to them using the anachronism North-West Mounted Police), who conducted a search for the missing people; no one was ever found.[463]

The Lacus Curtius in Rome, the Cave of the Sibyl in Naples, and the Cape Matapan Caves are three more "portals" that often appear on the lists. The first involves a little-known monument in the Roman Forum, which depicts a Roman soldier and his horse, descending into the ground. The story is told by Livy that in 362, a great chasm opened up on the forum, threatening the entire city. Upon consulting the seers, the townspeople were told that only the sacrifice of "the greatest strength of the Roman people" could forestall the disaster. A warrior named Marcus Curtius is said to have offered his life by mounting his horse and leaping into the chasm, which immediately closed in upon him.[464]

The Sibyl Cave is where the oracle of Apollo known as the Cumeaen Sibyl presided over a cult of women. Sibyl means "prophetess" in Latin. The Cumeaen Sibyl is perhaps the most famous, for she is said to have written nine (there's that number again) books of prophecy, which she offered to the ruler of Rome, King Tarquin. Wikipedia has this entry:

> Centuries ago, concurrent with the 50th Olympiad not long before the expulsion of Rome's kings, an old woman "who was not a native of the country" (Dionysius) arrived incognita in Rome. She offered nine books of prophecies to King Tarquin; and as the king declined to purchase them, owing to the exorbitant price she demanded, she burned three and offered the remaining six to Tarquin at the same stiff price, which he again refused, whereupon she burned three more and repeated her offer. Tarquin then relented and purchased the last three at the full original price, whereupon she "disappeared from among men."[465]

In the introduction to her little-known novel, *The Last Man*, about a plague ending mankind, horror writer Mary Shelley claims to have found prophetic writings written upon leaves by the Sibyl in a cave near Naples. The Cumeaen Sibyl's cave may have communicated with underground tunnels that linked to a vast underworld. The caves at Matapan are another example.

Sitting atop a hill just above the area of Mani, Greece, known as Cape Matapanlie, are the remnants of an ancient temple to Poseidon. Just below the cliff is a cave that the ancient Greeks believed led directly into the realm of Hades, god of the dead. Local stories say that both Orpheus and Heracles used the cave's portal to access Hell.

While such concepts may seem strange to a few readers, the Bible supports the notion that the earth is a "holding tank" and that intelligent beings exist beneath its surface and sometimes move between its interior and exterior through "gates." We know the location of the Old Testament Paradise as well as Shoel-hades lies beneath the crust of the earth. Other places in the Bible depict an underwater reality, including where "the four angels are bound in the great river Euphrates" (Revelation 9:14), as well as where God has imprisoned until the day of Judgment those Watcher angels that so famously fell (2 Peter 2:4; Jude 6). Job 26:5 also speaks of "dead things" that move beneath the waters, and when the woman of Endor communicated with underground spirits, they ascended up from "out of the earth" (1 Samuel 28:13).

Thus the ancient belief that beings and underworld regions were under the control of a supernatural "gatekeeper" associated with Hades is both fascinating and enlightening when compared to these Scriptures, especially when we consider the words of Jesus in Matthew 16:17–18: "Blessed art thou, Simon Barjona [son of Jonah]…thou art Peter, and upon this rock I will build my church, and the *gates* of hell shall not prevail against it" (emphasis added). We do not believe it is coincidental that Jesus referred to Jonah when tying Peter's confession to gates and the ultimate victory of the church. In the Old Testament, Jonah 2:6 tells of his journey to the bottom of the sea to a "city of gates" (Hebrew *běriyach*, "a fortress inside the earth, a prison") from which God delivered him. There is doubt about where Jonah was, as he prayed to God out of the "belly of hell"—the underworld prison of the dead. Jesus made the same connection to earth gateways, Jonah, and His mission for the church again in Matthew 12:40 when He said: "For as Jonas was three days and three nights in the whale's belly; so shall the Son of man be three days and three nights in the heart of the earth." This type of reasoning—that the physical planet serves as a repository in which intelligences reside—is and was fundamental to ancient biblical interpretation.

But could it be, as science advances, that we may uncover some kind of "proof" of life beneath our feet? Recently, there have been stories of strange sounds coming up from (what seems like) the ground, including a "hum" that numerous newscasters around the world have said is driving some people crazy. Upon reading one of those stories recently, I forwarded it to a very well known and popular prophecy teacher for his opinion. He emailed back: "Tom, they're busy down there, aren't they. Those pesky subterranean dwellers must know that something's up! The word is out that they'll soon be released to the surface of the earth, and they're getting excited!"

Just a few days after that email exchange, NASA and the European Association of Geochemistry published research by a team of Harvard scientists who are now "confirming evidence" of the remnants of an ancient earth, dating back to a time when something impacted the earth with such force (they surmise it was an earth-sized object, but could this have been the fall of Lucifer?) that it collided with our planet and produced our moon. They believe when that happened, part of the surface of the earth and its life forms were crushed down into the mantle and covered by the current surface material. Huge chasms could exist in this area hosting remnants of that ancient world. The scientists say they are registering unexplained isotopic ratios from deep within the planet that could be coming from this earlier earth—an echo of an ancient world that existed prior to the proposed collision some 4.5 billion years ago. According to lead researcher, Associate Professor Sujoy Mukhopadhyay of Harvard:

> The energy released by the impact between the Earth and Theia [interesting that they give this other earth-size object, which they believe impacted the earth, the name "Theia," as this is the ancient female equivalent of Lucifer—the female "light bearer" or "shining one"] would have been huge, certainly enough to melt the whole planet. But we believe that the impact energy

was not evenly distributed throughout the ancient Earth. This means that a major part of the impacted hemisphere would probably have been completely vaporised, but the opposite hemisphere would have been partly shielded, and would not have undergone complete melting….

The geochemistry indicates that there are differences between the noble gas isotope ratios in different parts of the Earth, and these need to be explained. The idea that a very disruptive collision of the Earth with another planet-sized body, the biggest event in Earth's geological history, did not completely melt and homogenize the Earth challenges some of our notions on planet formation and the energetics of giant impacts. If the theory is proven correct, then we may be seeing echoes of [an] ancient Earth [somewhere within our current world signaling an ongoing existence], from a time before the collision.[466]

Just a couple of weeks before the press release above, another team of scientists announced discovery of a massive "ocean" towards the earth's core. The reservoir of water there is three times the volume of all our surface oceans, they say, and in confirmation of Genesis 7:11, they even believe this underground ocean—seven hundred kilometers beneath the mantle (the layer of hot rock between earth's surface and its core) could have provided all of the waters that make up the earth's seas today![467]

Could it be that life is there now? Perhaps something substantiating the "Hollow Earth" theory and offering that, inside this pale blue dot, there are plants, animals, and perhaps even some form of intelligent life?

X Marks the Spot—Where Gateways Are Reportedly Located

England is replete with henges, standing stones, and tales of gnomes, faeries, and giants. When mentioned, most spiral hunters look to Stonehenge for inspiration, and it's more than possible that the stones were set in place to "mark" the occurrence of a gateway opened either spontaneously or intentionally. However, the Settle Sundial is an ancient site often missed by those who compile the major portal lists. Located in Settle, North Yorkshire, in England, the hillside known as Castleberg Rock, now covered with seventeenth-century trees, is, according to paranormal researcher Nigel Mortimer, the location of a circle of standing stones. Mortimer is convinced that up until 1779, a ring of "rude" standing stones formed a now concealed and obscured "portal." Like many of his colleagues, Mortimer believes that—rather than the stones creating a portal—the formations were erected to "mark" portals linked to that location on earth. This belief is consistent with the theory of "ley lines" made famous by Alfred Watkins in in his books *Early British Trackways* and *The Old Straight Track*. Watkins believed these were Roman trade routes.

Today, ley lines are used to describe a matrix of geometric lines across the face of the earth that indicate geomagnetic anomalies like the Marysburgh Vortex located in Lake Ontario. Some one hundred vessels have "disappeared" within the borders of this vortex. According to Dr. Richard Lefors Clark:

> The Canadian National Research Council and U.S. Navy began Project Magnet in 1950 to investigate the area's magnetic anomalies and possible magnetic utility. This has been the only known official governmental research program into the Earth Grid system. A considerable number of planes and ships had mysteriously vanished from this region, while many UFO sightings were reported, and other bizarre and unearthly phenomena were noted.[468]

Proponents of the "ley line" paradigm assert that invisible connections intersect and form gateways into another dimension, realm, or perhaps even Hell itself. Many of these portals are associated with water, like St. Ann's Well mentioned above, the various water-based "triangles" like the Bermuda and Dragon's Triangles. But recently, everyone who follows the Internet news found themselves staring at an anomaly that baffled scientists: the Norway Spiral.

On December 9, 2009, one night before President Obama, the leader of the "free world," was to receive his Nobel Peace Prize (a much-debated accolade, made all the more ironic by President Obama's massive anti-terror operations throughout the Middle East and North Africa), a gigantic spiral appeared in the skies over Norway, the site of the awards ceremony. Forming just above the city of Tromso, romantically called the "Paris of the North."[469] The phenomenon began as a twisting spiral of light that shone into the sky from a point near Tromso. Over a matter of minutes, this beam of light expanded in the inky black sky as a massive and expanding spiral that appeared to rotate clockwise. The center point of this spiral was white, but shortly turned dark, taking on the appearance of an expanding "black hole." Now, here's what most do not know about this spectacular mystery. According to well-known paranormal researcher Richard C. Hoagland:

> Is it another "coincidence" that, just over the hill from Tromso, lies a high-tech Norwegian "HAARP antenna farm"—the EISCAT Ramfjordmoen facility (below)—specifically designed to broadcast powerful beams ofmicrowave energy high into space...thereby also creating blatantHD/torsion side-effectsin the Earth's highly-electrified upper "plasma" atmosphere (ionosphere)? The facility is officially supported by Norway, Sweden, Finland, Japan...China...the United Kingdom...and Germany.[470]

Thanks to the instantaneous nature of the World Wide Web, within minutes of the event, new sources, bloggers, and social media lit up with reports, theories, pictures, and even videos. There was no denying this one. The entire world saw it! Due to its conjunction with President Obama's scheduled acceptance of the Nobel Prize, prophecy scholars and even the *Christian Science Monitor* began to connect the sky portal with some cosmic approval or prophetic significance. The *CS Monitor's* article[471] on October 10, 2009, asked whether "Space aliens" were "welcoming Obama"!

Theories began to populate the Internet within minutes. One blogger noted that the spiral appeared precisely 1,260 days before May 22, 2013, and thereby predicted a cosmic event to come. Others claimed the phenomenon fulfilled a Fatima prophecy, this being the "second prophecy," which states, "when you shall see a night illuminated by an unknown light, know that it is the great sign that God gives you that He is going to punish the world for its crimes by means of war, of hunger, and of persecution of the Church and of the Holy Father."[472]

Incidentally, I will tell you now that I do not ascribe to these Fatima "secrets" as being from God Almighty; rather, the apparitions of "Mary" must rather be attributed to a sinister source from the enemy of Christ and His followers. However, knowing the enemy's tactics and twisted prophecies can help those with "eyes to see" to discern His traps and lies.

Was the Norway Spiral created by a Russian missile? Some claim it was, though Russia denies conducting any tests that night. Is Hoagland's theory that a HAARP installation created it feasible? Hoagland is a scientist and theorist, therefore, his statement may be correct. Is it possible that either a HAARP installation or even CERN's underground collisions created this portal, an opening or gateway with the intention of "inviting" entities into our world? Perhaps not coincidentally, beginning just after the Norway portal's opening, Scandinavians and soon people throughout the world reported strange sounds emanating from the heavens.[473]

Skeptics ask for scientific proof of the existence of portals and dimensional gateways. Perhaps the best known space agency in the world is the National Aeronautics and Space Administration, NASA. It took a bit of sleuthing, but I managed to find a document on NASA's own website discussing the topic. Here's an excerpt:

> A favorite theme of science fiction is "the portal"—an extraordinary opening in space or time that connects travelers to distant realms. A good portal is a shortcut, a guide, a door into the unknown. If only they actually existed....
>
> It turns out that they do, sort of, and a NASA-funded

researcher at the University of Iowa has figured out how to find them.

"We call them X-points or electron diffusion regions," explains plasma physicist Jack Scudder of the University of Iowa. "They're **places where the magnetic field of Earth connects to the magnetic field of the Sun**, creating an uninterrupted path leading from our own planet to the sun's atmosphere 93 million miles away."

Observations by NASA's THEMIS spacecraft and Europe's Cluster probes suggest that these magnetic **portals open and close dozens of times each day.**[474] (emphasis added)

Now, let's unpack the language NASA is using. It echoes much of the imagery found in statues, buildings, and all manner of architecture—even paintings!—throughout history and across the globe. Much of this imagery can be found in Freemasonic Lodges and in fountains, edifices, and interior designs constructed by Masonic members. One major hallmark of these symbols in brick and stone is that they echo what Nimrod tried to do—in stone and brick. Perhaps the Masonic semiotics tell a story—an ancient story. I trust that almost all reading this chapter know how a Masonic lodge floor is designed: as a black-and-white "checkerboard." Around these floors, one often sees a rope motif, connected at the four corners of the floor with tassels. Within the center of the floor, you will often find the five-pointed star, many times inscribed within a circle. Most assume this represents the Eastern Star, but a YouTube blogger who calls himself "halfasheep'" has documented hundreds of symbols in Australia that link Masonic imagery to "sun wells."

This takes us back to the first part of this chapter, the mathematics of 3, 6, 9, which indicates that a subdivided circle will—when taken to infinity—reveal a hidden 9 and lead to a singularity or a vacuum. In the video game World of Warcraft, a sun well is a portal used by a "mage" to summon entities. The video blogger halfasheep contends that the floor "stars," the "one surrounded by four" repetitions in stone and marble, the gargoyles, and the pillars (representing pillars of light, aka portals) are used by "'the builders" to represent and perhaps even communicate with gateways to "the sun."

The sun has been worshiped since the dawn of time, and many "riddles in stone," as Chris Pinto would call them, are coded messages that call to the ancient "gods." Jupiter, Zeus, Thor, Odin, Tonatiuh of the Aztecs, Taiyang Shen of China, Ra/Isis of Egypt, Solar Logos of Theosophy, and even Sol Invictus (the undefeated Sun) reflect an ages-old story of an entity that sought to rise into the heavens and become a god—Nimrod, the rebel builder who deigned to assault God's throne by building a stargate. When the languages were confused at Babel, and the enslaved and entranced citizen builders scattered into the four corners of the globe, each group retold the story of Nimrod and of the pre-Flood Nephilim "gods" and fallen angels—but with their own new names, according to their new languages. Spirals in stone, sacred places like Stonehenge, the Sundial of Settle, the mounds of the Americas, even the massive pyramids and the very layout of our nation's capital tell the story and whisper secrets into the void.

One final note before I close this chapter: I've just learned about an "augmented reality" (AR) game called Ingress. AR uses a computer interface (generally a handheld phone but also a head-display like Google glass) to overlay "secret" information upon real world objects using GPS coordinates. Ingress defines itself as a "portal game." The back story is this:

> Physicists at CERN have discovered that the Earth has been seeded with "Exotic Matter," or XM, associated with the Shapers, a mysterious phenomenon or alien race which is neither described nor seen (and which thus functions as a MacGuffin). **The in-universe motivation for the Enlightened faction is their belief that the Shapers are working toward a powerful enlightenment which will uplift all mankind.** The **Resistance believes that it is protecting humanity from Shaper ingression.** The factions have, however, been occasionally observed to ignore the back-story and to co-operate for the sake of real-life

gameplay and game balance, for example by establishing neutral zones and rules of engagement.[476] (emphasis added)

When Nimrod and his minions attempted to open a portal, the Lord God Himself said that as they were "of one mind"—nothing would be impossible for them. With the Internet forming these players into "one mind," this "game" becomes all too real! Of course, the "resistance" faction in the game represents you and me and all who oppose the nefarious plans of the new Nimrod and his Illuminati forces. How incredible that the makers of this game actually portray "Shaper" aliens as the good guys! The world has truly entered a dangerous time period.

The mystery religions and secret societies seek to open the old portals and welcome back the ancient gods. Only the perfect plans of Almighty God, foretold to us in the Bible, stand between mankind and the twisted plans of evil men and the hordes of Apollyon. Christians look to Him, not to spiritual powers and principalities, for protection. Jesus Christ is our Champion, King, and High Priest. He is our Savior, and no hidden hand of man or spirit can hold back His coming.

Thank God for that!

CHAPTER ELEVEN

The World Grid, Megaliths, and the Axis Mundi Decision

By Tom Horn and Cris Putnam

The novel *Foucault's Pendulum* by Umberto Eco revolves around an occult conspiracy theory concocted by three greedy book publishers. Their creation called "The Plan" is represented as a real conspiracy by secret societies to control the world. In physics, the Foucault pendulum is a simple device, named after the French physicist Léon Foucault, that demonstrates the rotation of the earth. The book is divided into ten sections represented by the ten Sefiroth of Kabbalah. It is packed full of esoteric references to magic, alchemy, and conspiracy theory. In particular, Eco borrows heavily from a particular type of world grid theory, primarily popularized by ancient astronaut theorists, entailing that in the deep past there was a civilization like Atlantis and a global power grid supplying free, clean, earth energy.

A leading proponent of that version of world grid theory, David Hatcher Childress, explains, "Earth energy, organized into a precise web, was once, and can be again, the source of a free and inexhaustible supply of power, once empowering older civilizations of high technological achievement."[477] However, the evidence for such a fantastic claim is less than persuasive, because it imposes a post-Enlightenment scientific worldview onto ancient people who were thinking much more in terms of ritual magic than the language of calculus, physics, and chemistry. Although it might indeed have a scientific basis, one should never presume a conventional analog to today's concepts and technology like electricity. When ancient people conceived of a power center, it wasn't like an electrical power-grid substation for their city's neighborhoods and schools; it was magical energy for opening portals to the higher and lower realms to communicate with the immortals.

In simple terms, the world grid is a web-like division of the earth's surface into a geometric model. In cartography, such a practice is necessary and assumes the longitude and latitude convention involving vertical and horizontal straight lines. The equator is set at 0 degrees latitude and the prime meridian is a line of longitude defined to be 0 degrees. This assignment places an *axis mundi*, or "world center," arbitrarily in the Gulf of New Guinea off the west coast of Africa in the Atlantic Ocean. While any Cartesian coordinate could be set as the *axis mundi*, some world grid theorists assert that ancient megaliths functioned in a similar way, often centering on the Great Pyramid at Giza.

In most spiritual traditions, the axis mundi—also called the *umbilicus mundi* (Latin: "the navel of the world") and the "world pillar" or "world tree"—is the numinous center of the earth and a portal between the heavenly and underworld realms.[478] In the Hebrew Bible, Bethel, the place where Jacob saw "the gate of heaven," was for a time considered the center, but later moved with the Ark of the Covenant to the Temple in Jerusalem by divine decree. In Islam, the Al-Masjid al-Haram mosque in Mecca, Saudi Arabia, is the axis mundi, and the umbilicus mundi is a very strange black meteorite housed within a bricked, granite cuboid structure called the Kaaba. In Catholicism, the Egyptian Obelisk in its plaza of St. Peter's Basilica in Rome, Italy, is the axis mundi, and it is designed to function as a spiritual center in a surprising, yet revealing, manner (more on that later).

In Eco's novel, the axis mundi is the location from where one can control the telluric energies of the earth. Although telluric energy, or "earth current," is an actual low-frequency electric current moving underground and through the sea, the novel takes this much farther by suggesting that monuments like the Eiffel Tower are giant antennae clandestinely designed to magnify and route these currents. While Eco makes sport of the idea, theorists like Childress and Joseph Farrell are serious. For example, Farrell asserts a vast global conspiracy to explain the appearance of megalithic structures.

> Nobody sets out to build 50,000-plus pyramids and mounds around a planet just for the hell of it, or want of something to do. History teaches that these primitive people were hunter-gatherers who spent their waking hours running down their next meals. If that's true, then who built these monuments? These people didn't have the time...these things were not built at the whims of medicine men. There was enormous global planning behind it all.[479]

He jumps to a materialist conclusion by imposing modern thinking rather than a context-proper supernatural worldview. Of course, it wasn't the whims of the priests and medicine men. After all, they told us that it was dictated to them by the immortals!

Enoch's Portals meets Sanderson's Vile Vortices

The twelve "vile vortices" are geographic areas that are alleged to be the sites of mysterious disappearances and other high profile anomalies. The twelve areas were first proposed by biologist and UFO researcher, Ivan Sanderson, in the article "The Twelve Devil's Graveyards Around the World," first published in *Saga* magazine. He credited Charles Hapgood, who referred to them in his book, *The Maps of the Ancient Sea*

Kings. Five of the vortices are on the same latitude to the south of the equator; five are on the same latitude to the north. Sanderson enlisted the help of a geometer who determined that these lie precisely opposite of each other directly through "the exact center of the earth."[480] The other two are the north and south poles.

The best-known vile vortex area is the Bermuda Triangle. Others include the "Devil's Sea" near Japan, the Indus Valley in Pakistan, the Algerian Megaliths just south of Timbuktu in the West African nation of Mali, and the Hamakulia Volcano in Hawaii and the North and South poles. Sanderson felt the weakest example, the area in the southeast Indian Ocean, was rationalized by the "very simple reason that hardly anybody ever goes there, and there are no records."[481]

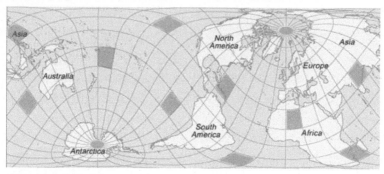

The twelve Vile Vortices

Even more fascinating is that Sanderson's theory is supported by the ancient Book of Enoch, which also speaks of twelve portal areas on the earth:

> And at the ends of the earth I saw twelve portals open to all the quarters of the heaven, from which the winds go forth and blow over the earth. Three of them are open on the face i.e. the east of the heavens, and three in the west, and three on the right i.e. the south of the heaven, and three on the left i.e. the north. And the three first are those of the east, and three are of the north, and three after those on the left of the south, and three of the west. (Enoch 76:1–3)

According to Enoch, four of these heavenly portals bring prosperity, and eight of them wreak destruction. Recent research suggests that there might be a scientific basis for these portal areas.

A team of three Russians—historian Nikolai Goncharov, engineer Vyacheslav Morozov, and electronics specialist Valery Makarov—wrote an article titled "Is the Earth a Large Crystal?" for the USSR-sponsored scientific journal *Chemistry and Life*. Based on the planet's crystalline properties, they proposed the earth projects from within a "geometrically regularized grid."[482] According to their theory, that grid is projected as a dodecahedral-isochedron that delineates the earth's energy structure or skeleton.

Based on Sanderson's work and that of the Russians, a husband and wife team consisting of William Becker (professor of industrial design at the University of Illinois, Chicago) and Bethe Hagens (professor of anthropology at Governors State University) offered "The Planetary Grid: A New Synthesis" in 1984.[483] The essay proposed a new projection of the grid as a polyhedron with 121 "great circles" (circling the entire planet) and 4,862 points, including the vortex areas. It is the same polyhedron used by futurist architect Buckminster Fuller for his geodesic domes (half of a geodesic sphere).[484] Becker and Hagens call it the "Unified Vector Geometry (UVG) 120 Sphere."[485] Their work is ongoing and they have provided a grid overlay plugin for Google Earth, allowing one to investigate this UVG grid at leisure (follow the end noted link for instructions).[486] Another version of the world grid has been suggested based on observed alignments of UFO appearances and disappearances by highly trained observers.

The French ufologist Aimé Michel detected remarkably straight alignments during a 1954 UFO flap that corresponded to large circles around the earth separated by 54.46 kilometers.[487] His work caught the attention of New Zealand airline pilot Bruce Cathie who, after a few of his own sightings, had noticed similarly aligned patterns. Cathie discovered that 54.46 kilometers converted to 30 nautical miles or 30 degrees of arc.[488] The fact that thirty is a fundamental frequency number, combined with his study of harmonics, led Cathie to propose an elaborate theory of harmonic energy propulsion in the books *Harmonic 695, the UFO and Anti-gravity* and *The Pulse of the Universe, Harmonic 288,*which were combined into *The Energy Grid.* Of all the energy grid theories associated with ufology, Cathie's demands more serious attention.[489] He might have actually discovered a form of "technology" employed by the immortals.

Geomancy, Feng Shui, and Ley Lines

Geomancy is often defined as "earth magic" and gets grouped in the same category as grid theories about alignments and energy flows. The term is derived from the Greek words *geo*, "earth," and *manteia*, "divination." It was a popular way of foretelling the future based on a chance set of symbols based on dot patterns, like dominoes. "Geomancy was among the most popular of all divinatory methods during the last great magical revival in the Western world, the time of the Renaissance."[490] Although it has come to be used for different topics from feng shui to world grid theories involving ley lines and megaliths, those subjects have nothing to do with true geomancy.[491]

Feng shui, Chinese for "wind and water," is the ancient Chinese system of earth magic and sacred geometry. The Victorian missionary Ernest J Eitel wrote of the feng-shui practitioner: "They see a golden chain of spiritual life running through every form of existence and binding together, as one living body, everything that subsists in heaven above or earth below."[492] While such oneism finds open armed acceptance in modern paganism, feng shui traces back four thousand years. According to legend, the practice of feng shui began with the shaman-kings who led the early Chinese tribes.[493]

Chi is the Chinese term for life energy that flows through our bodies and the earth. Whereas the martial arts and acupuncture manage chi at the bodily level, feng shui seeks to do so at the geographic level. The goal is to manage chi energy by spatial design so that it accumulates at a location without becoming stagnant. When applied to the planet, it sounds much like the telluric currents previously discussed. Devereux writes, "Feng-shui identifies precisely the same kinds of forces or energies as we find referred to by the Indians of the American south-west or the Aborigines of the Australian Outback."[494] The concept of chi is analogous with the "earth energy" of Western earth magic and sacred geometry. Modern proponents believe that this energy travels along lines discernable in the alignments of various sacred sites.

Englishman Alfred Watkins (1855–1935) noticed that an uncanny number of ancient hilltop ruins in Herefordshire formed "old straight tracks." As he became intrigued, he discovered that all over the English countryside, stone circles, standing stones, burial mounds, and megalithic sites were also aligned. He called the straight alignments "leys" and published his ideas in the book *The Old Straight Track* in 1925. Watkins wrote, "A genuine ley hits the cross-roads or road junctions as if by magic."[495] Even so, he was more a rationalist than a spiritualist, and he concluded that the alignments were best explained by Roman trade roads from deep antiquity.

In the paranormal world, the term "ley" has come to denote a line where spirits or telluric currents travel. Modern ley proponents attempt to recreate them by tracing alignments of ancient sites. It seems fair to assert that random patterns are almost as likely to be as straight as planned alignments because of the large amount of mounds, ruins, stones, hilltops, sacred sites, and other potential items to be considered. The real question concerning leys is not whether the sites fall on a truly straight line, but rather, one of detecting intelligent design. In this case, one must seek to determine whether the sites aligned from random connection or were designed to form a line. Some alignments, like the obelisk at St. Peter's Square, have significance that cannot be written off.

The Vatican's Alignment with the Dome of the Rock

The Egyptian obelisk in the center of the plaza at St. Peter's Basilica represents the axis mundi of Roman Catholicism. Romanian historian of religion, Mircea Eliade, wrote of the axis mundi that "it is only in such a Centre that communication between Earth, Heaven and Hell is possible."[496] The plaza works like a giant compass built on the ground of the square. The obelisk is surrounded by sixteen markers in 22.5-degree increments labeled "N" for north, "NNE" for north-northeast, and so on.[497] Graphically, it looks like a "wind rose," a tool that shows wind speed and direction, but in this case, representing ley lines to places that are important to Romanism. These sixteen leys all have a Latin designation for the region in which they intersect, like *Scirroco Levante* for the "wind of the Levant."[498] "Levant" is another name for the ancient Holy Land, comprising modern-day Israel, Jordan, Lebanon, and Syria.

Vatican obelisk Wind Rose

The Vatican's axis mundi aligns with the Dome of the Rock in Jerusalem in a surprising way. Credit for the discovery of this alignment belongs to researcher Cort Lindahl, who publishes on the web as Geomantic Information Systems, as well as producing YouTube videos showcasing his discoveries. Lindahl explains this astonishing alignment (and note that the number 111.11 as discussed below that was intentionally linked with the Vatican's obelisk is astonishing, given how the Freemasons who designed the Washington, DC, obelisk also incorporated the very same numerology into the monument dedicated to America's first president in the capital city [111], which, as occultists know, is related to the magic 666 square and ceremony used to raise Osiris from the underworld. We discuss this in the final bonus chapter in this book—*The Most Powerful Stargates in the World? America, the Vatican, and the Portals of Apollo-Osiris*):

> From the obelisk at the center of St. Peter's Square through the ESE "Levante Scirocco" windrose marker at 111.11 degrees true north lies the octagonal shaped structure of the Dome of the Rock on the Temple Mount in Jerusalem (Jordan). Not only does this line transect exactly to the Dome of the rock but it matches the angle and orientation of the northeast facet of the octagonal structure of the building itself! More amazing is the fact that an azimuth or line created using the angle of this facet of the Dome of the Rock's octagon (305.55 deg. TN) creates the exact same line that transects back across the windrose marker to the obelisk in St. Peter's! [499]

An absolutely perfect straight line, named the *Levante Scirocco*, falls precisely on the wall of the octagonal base of the Dome of the Rock. The exterior octagon consists of eight stone walls 20.59 meters long and 9.5 meters high. [500] The precision of hitting this octagonal angle goes well beyond a straight alignment of points and such precision has to be intentional. It implies an intentional association with Islam. One cannot assert it merely aligns with the Temple Mount because the octagonal base is a feature exclusive of the Islamic structure.

To view this alignment, watch Cort Lindahl's video, *Stargate Vatican: The Axis and Templum of Rome*, at 7:56:http://youtu.be/w_isGhysLWc?t=7m56s.

In *Petrus Romanus*, our first work of what has now become a cowritten trilogy, Tom Horn and I wrote about the Vatican's ambition to sit on the Temple Mount in Jerusalem. The Dome of the Rock alignment, likely dating back to the seventeenth century, hints that the Vatican has its eyes on one of Islam's most sacred structures, the Dome of the Rock, as well as the Cenacle on Mount Zion and the Garden of Gethsemane at the foot of the Mount of Olives in Jerusalem.[501] Pope Francis has already made unprecedented overtures to Muslims. In 2014, the *Washington Times* reported, "For the first time in Vatican history, the pope allowed for the reading of Islamic prayers and Koran readings from the Catholic facility. The readings and prayer came as Pope Francis met with Israeli President Shimon Peres and Palestinian Authority President Mahmoud Abbas in Vatican City, a gathering designed to pray for Middle Eastern peace."[502] Now the alignment speaks to a spiritual reality predicted in Bible prophecy as "the great whore" (Revelation 17:1–18).

The counter-reformation Jesuit priest Athanasius Kircher (1602–1680) is likely responsible for the alignment. The Vatican plaza was redesigned by Gian Lorenzo Bernini from 1656 to 1667, under the supervision of Pope Alexander VII. In a report to that pope, the Jesuit Kircher suggested the Vatican obelisk be used as a sundial by inserting markers in the pavement of Saint Peter's Square.[503] Kircher was a polymath known as "master of a hundred arts" and familiar with esoteric knowledge.[504] At the time, Pope Alexander was too ill to accomplish the task, which places the report near the year of his death in 1667. One hundred and fifty years later, circular stones were set to mark the obelisk's shadow as the sun entered each of the signs of the zodiac.[505] Of all those involved, the Jesuit Kircher seems the most likely culprit for the curious alignment. The Jesuits well know that *Jerusalem is the real axis mundi*—the future capital from which Jesus Christ will rule and reign.

In Judaism, Christianity, and Islam, Jerusalem has been described as a portal between Heaven and Earth—represented respectively by the Jewish Temple, the resurrection and ascension of Christ, and Mohammed's heavenly journey on a strange, donkey-like beast named Buraq.[506] Also, Jerusalem plays a major role in the eschatology of all three religions. We expect that the Antichrist will soon sit in Jerusalem with the False Prophet, offering the pluralistic platitudes that have already made him famous.

In the Vatican-suppressed ancient text known only as the *Angel Scroll*, Jerusalem is the predicted site for an invasion of immortals. We know a little about this text from its brief surfacing in the late 1990s at the guilt-laden request of a Benedictine monk named Mateus, who left a note to make it public upon his death.[507] The Dead Sea Scrolls scholar who initially examined and authenticated it, Stephen Pfann, wrote that it contains "divine chariot-throne themes with elaborate details of angels ascending heaven's multiple gates."[508] In other words, it's about the immortals and their heavenly gates. Unfortunately, Pfann only got a peek before the scroll vanished. Once it made the national news (implying the Vatican found out), the monks who promised to turn over the originals to Pfann were never heard from again. Michael Heiser, who also got a glimpse of the text, called it the "Apocalypse Scroll" in his novel *The Façade* and quoted it as depicting Jerusalem besieged by "thousands of sun disks."[509]

Earth Portals

What if something like "The Plan" in *Foucault's Pendulum* by Umberto Eco turned out to be true? Could there really be secret societies locating axis mundi sites in order to open gateways for the return of the fallen immortals? Opening new earth portals requires arcane knowledge. It's a task requiring years of preparation, plentiful resources, and, when it gets down to brass tacks, a human sacrifice. Sorcerers capable of opening a permanent earth portal are born into it.

Brazilian author Daniel Mastral claims to be such an individual who converted to Christianity. In the book *Rastros do Oculto* ("Traces of the Occult"), Mastral revealed that opening new earth portals is a primary objective for Satanists. He stated that out of ninety possible earth portals, only seventy-two were open in 2001 when the book was first published. If Mastral is genuine—and he seems to be so—his assertion that opening these gates requires human blood sacrifice offers an interesting rationale for the immortals' gruesome demands. Patristics scholar Joseph P. Farrell writes:

The appearance of an organized spiritual technology, controlled by the priests, was attended in every country by a massive increase in human sacrifice. The Aztec massacres are notorious; the Druids in Ireland are said to have decimated the population.[510]

It seems likely that the ancients' bloodletting was, at least in some cases, related to opening permanent earth portals accessible to the fallen ones. Many of the gates opened by the ancients are marked by megaliths and sacred constructions.

Ancient, mysterious rock foundations, structures, and temples across the globe have not ceased to baffle observers, and those who have dedicated their entire life's work to studying these ruins have often raised more questions than they have answered. Not the least of these questions are frequently who built these structures, for what purposes they were built, and, most importantly, how they could have possibly been built. The size of the monolithic stones found in these locations, as well as the archaic building technology of that period, would have made the transportation and positioning of these stones a logical impossibility. And yet, these monoliths and constructs not only exist out in the open for any and all to see, they are frequently assembled with such expert precision that you cannot place a needle or a human hair between the stones. Collectively, these stones are proof that planet earth, at some point in its history, was home to a people or race much more intelligent and proficient than the slaves-with-pulley-carts civilization that our modern history books reflect. These include gigantic edifices built from the largest stones ever cut and put into place, and that seem to indicate manufacturing skills well beyond what we know of primeval man. Examples of such herculean slabs weighing hundreds of tons can be found above Lake Titicaca in Peru, others in Tiahuanaco, twelve miles south of Lake Titicaca in Bolivia, South America, and even larger stones at the southern entrance of Baalbeck, a city in eastern Lebanon famous for its magnificent temple ruins. What follows are a few examples of the many megalithic and mysterious structures some believe predate the great Flood. We could add to this list the Great Pyramid of Giza and more, but for the sake of time, let us briefly summarize here just four examples:

Puerta de Hayu Marca ("Gate of the Gods")

Just off the shores of Lake Titicaca, Peru, rests a peculiar wonder that defies explanation. In a region known by the Peruvian Indians as "The City of the Gods," measuring in a perfect, twenty-three-foot square, is the *Puerta de Haya Marca*—the "Gate of the Gods"—an absolutely bizarre stamp embedded in the side of a flat, natural rock formation on the border of Bolivia. Inside the square, at the bottom center, is another recessed impression within the rock (standing just under six feet high), which, from a distance, resembles a kind of keyhole.

Gate of the Gods, near Lake Titicaca, Peru, at the border of Bolivia[511]

Upon closer inspection, the "keyhole" appears more like a door, and in the very center of it is a small, circular dent/depression in the back wall. Local legend says that the Amaru Meru (sometimes "Amaru Muru"), the Incan priest of the "Temple of the Seven Rays," ran away into the mountains to flee the Spanish Conquistadors who had come to rob and plunder the Incan tribes. With him, he held a small disc, the "Key of the Gods of the Seven Rays." Once a safe distance from the temple, the Amaru Meru conducted a ritual with his fellow priests, using the small disc to open a portal within the flat rock, through which he completely disappeared. (Some versions of this tale claim that the Amaru Meru was fleeing alongside several familiar priests of the Temple of the Seven Rays. Others say he fled alone, discovering the doorway while in hiding, and happened upon shamans guarding the doorway, who thereafter agreed to perform a portal ritual with him when they saw the disc he held. Either way, both versions of the tale suggest that the doorway was a giant image carved into the mountains well before the priest fled the temple.) This event, the legend says, turned this solid rock into a "stargate." According to local lore, this priest was the first of other "kings" who came to earth from heavenly locations specifically associated with the Pleiades (Apollo) and Orion (Osiris).

Closer view of the Gate of the Gods.[512] Observe the small black mark in the center of the photo. This is the depression into which the Amaru Meru was said to have inserted the Incan relic disc or "key," opening the legendary portal.

Other folklore offered by the Native Indians say the site is "a gateway to the lands of the Gods" through which, in their ancient past, great heroes arrived and then departed with a "key" that could open the mysterious doorway. In some adaptations, these ancient men had left this world to begin life anew amidst other interdimensional heroes, occasionally returning to "inspect the land of the kingdom."[513]

Nobody knows who crafted this door-shaped marvel. Theories abound as to its origin, and for as many archaeologists who claim the site is merely an abandoned building project by the Incas, just as many archaeologists have reason to believe the site predates Incan occupancy—and some note the doorway carving is not typical of sporadic Incan design. Because the site is considered an ancient archaeological site, and because it is protected by the Peruvian government, further excavations potentially revealing its secrets and origin have not yet occurred.[514] However, as of this writing, similar to the Göbekli Tepe site we will briefly discuss, there has never been any evidence of an earlier/ancient settlement nearby.

(As an interesting sidebar, the mysterious Gate of the Gods exists within close proximity to the "Stone Forest" of the Markawasi [*Marcahuasi*] plateau in the Andes Mountains. The Stone Forest is a wealth of oddities in and of itself, sporting gigantic carvings and sculptures strongly resembling human faces and heads [as well as many animals], many of which could easily be interpreted to represent various ancient world cultures. Among which is one sculpture that mirrors the Face on Mars. Another, the famous "Monument of Humanity" at Markawasi, is so named for the "four distinct races of humanity which can be found on this 85-foot-high monument."[515] It is especially fascinating that four different races of people would be sculpted from the same rock so nearby the gate that legendarily became the portal for "ancient heroes" that had the access to seeing whatever "races of humanity" they wished to all at once. There doesn't seem to be many available explanations for how an ancient civilization would be so familiar with other races of people—*and consider them important enough to carve onto giant stones*—all within the same timeframe and location. Yet, assuming there is validity to the portal theories, interdimensional traveling, and carving as a way of "documenting" such an event, it is worthy of note.)

To this day, rumors abound that light can often still be observed behind, or emanating through, the disc-shaped dent within the Gate of the Gods. Many of the local residents "refuse to go near it."[516] Some travel great distances to lay hands on the back wall or inside frame of the small door, "a feeling of energy flowing [through them]" upon contact, "as well as strange experiences such as visions of stars, columns of fire, and the sounds of unusual rhythmic music."[517]

Not far away from this gate is another notable "portal," as they say, known as the Gate of the Sun.

Tiahuanaco and the Gate of the Sun

The archway (or "gate") of Tiahuanaco (often spelled alternatively: "Tiwanaku"), near La Paz, Bolivia (and like the Gate of the Gods, located close by Lake Titicaca) is a puzzling discovery on many counts. To begin, it raises the same questions as Baalbek and Göbekli Tepe regarding the hows and whos of its megalithic size and expert composition. The gate is 9.8 feet tall, 13 feet in width, and weighs approximately 10 tons (20,000 pounds). Though split into two at some point in history, it was originally constructed from a single stone. Many sources online say this stone could date to around 12000 BC.[518]

But the iconic Gate of the Sun piece is not by any stretch the largest stone moved at the surrounding archaeological site, an area said to be an "oxygen-deprived" and "inhospitable" thirteen-thousand-foot elevation, housing two-hundred-ton monoliths in the structures some *ten miles* away from the quarry.[519] These ruins are unique in their cutting-edge geometric design, the techniques of which have only *just* been acquired within the last one hundred years by our modern-day builders.

ViewZone journalist Dan Eden documents:

Some of the stones show evidence of tooling that simply could not have been done with any known ancient technology.…

[And much lower in the article:] There is no known technology in all the ancient world that could have transported stones of such massive weight and size. The Andean people of 500 AD, with their simple reed boats, could certainly not have moved them. Even today, with all the modern advances in engineering and mathematics, we could not fashion such a structure.[520]

Unlike previously mentioned sites, there is enough evidence here of settlement, resources, intelligence, and planning, that the question of "who" becomes an all-new opposite extreme. Whereas we might wonder how Neolithic, nomadic, wandering wheat-ploughers could possibly comprehend the Göbekli Tepe structures we discuss later in this chapter, at the Tiahuanaco site we find ourselves asking how a race of humans that prove to be in some ways more intelligent than we are today could possibly have lived an estimated ten thousand to sixteen thousand years before Christ walked the earth.[521] Although archaeologists and historians agree that this site was built by "Tiahuanacans," there is no easy explanation for what kind of people—or race—they were, exactly. Set apart from other ancient civilizations as a result of their advanced intelligence, it is no surprise that many individuals associate them with extraterrestrials.

Extraterrestrial connections were first suggested by Eric von Daniken and have been perpetuated by discoveries of the apparent advanced knowledge that Tiahuanacan engineers seemed to possess—thousands of years ahead of other cultures.

Analysis of this culture has shown that ancient Tiahuanacan scientists knew that the earth was a globe which rotated on its axis and they calculated exactly the times of eclipses—even those not visible at Tiahuanaco but visible in the opposite hemisphere.

Scientists have also ascertained that the Tiahuanacans divided the circle mathematically into 264 degrees (rather than 360 as was initiated by the Babylonians); they determined the correct ratio of pi (22/7), and they could calculate squares (and hence, square roots).[522]

But despite the speechlessness that such irrefutable brainpower hidden away in the hills of the sun would cause, the innate yearning within human nature to solve the unsolvable inspires many to speculate:

> Many theories for the skill of Tiwanaku's architectural construction have been proposed. One is that they used a *luk'a*, which is a standard measurement of about sixty centimeters. Another argument is for the Pythagorean Ratio. This idea calls for right triangles at a ratio of five to four to three used in the gateways to measure all parts. Lastly Protzen and Nair [authors of "On Reconstructing Tiwanaku Architecture," in *The Journal of the Society of Architectural Historians*]argue that Tiwanaku had a system set for individual elements dependent on context and composition. This is shown in the construction of similar gateways ranging from diminutive to monumental size, proving that scaling factors did not affect proportion. With each added element, the individual pieces were shifted to fit together.[523]

Regardless of the methods used for building, there is absolutely no evidence that this culture had experimented up to the ingenuity we see today. It is as if they knew exactly how to execute their building aptitude by instinct from the very first attempt, instead of showing any evolutionary phases of skill.

Not surprisingly, their ability to survive and maintain food/plant resources—in an atmosphere and climate hostile to vegetation—had the world baffled. When their secret was finally discovered, it proved cleverer than what many farming communities could organize today. Canals were fixed into the soil at exactly the correct depth in grids around the plants; when the sun bore down on the canals, the water would heat to the point that after dark, the water would cool slowly overnight, dissipating heat in a steam or mist that wrapped the plants like a blanket, the surrounding air never dipping to below-freezing temperatures typical of this area. And as if this strategy in and of itself wasn't sophisticated enough, this tactic doubled as an early irrigation system.

As a point of further intrigue, the site tells excellent stories and displays impressive religious implications within its artwork. The deity at the center and top of the Gate of the Sun has been identified by some historians and archaeologists as the god Viracocha, who created the "race of giants."

Gate of the Sun in Tiahuanaco, Bolivia, near Lake Titicaca, 2006[524]

Gate of the Sun, as photographed in 1903[525]

Close up of the Gate of the Sun, as photographed in 1903[526]

The following is an excerpt from the Wikipedia page on the god Viracocha (note the similarities between the Viracocha myth and that of the story of Genesis):

According to a myth recorded by Juan de Betanzos, Viracocha rose from Lake Titicaca (or sometimes the cave of Paqariq Tampu) during the time of darkness to bring forth light. He made the sun, moon, and the stars. He made mankind by breathing into stones, but his first creation were brainless giants that displeased him. So he destroyed it with a flood and made a new, better one from smaller stones. Viracocha eventually disappeared across the Pacific Ocean (by walking on the water), and never returned. He wandered the earth disguised as a beggar, teaching his new creations the basics of civilization, as well as working numerous miracles. He wept when he saw the plight of the creatures he had created. It was thought that Viracocha would re-appear in times of trouble. Pedro Sarmiento de Gamboa noted that Viracocha was described as "a man of medium height, white and dressed in a white robe like an alb secured round the waist, and that he carried a staff and a book in his hands."[527]

An illustration of the deity Viracocha[528]

A description/explanation of the illustration of the deity Viracocha, pictured, provides insight on what may have been carved upon the Gate of the Sun:

Viracocha was one of the most important deities in the Inca pantheon and seen as the creator of all things, or the substance from which all things are created, and intimately associated with the sea. Viracocha [was said to have] created the universe, sun, moon, and stars, time (by commanding the sun to move over the sky) and civilization itself. Viracocha was worshipped as god of the sun and of storms. He was represented as wearing the sun for a crown, with thunderbolts in his hands, and tears descending from his eyes as rain.[529]

Göbekli Tepe

Perhaps one of the most debated locations on earth today is the Göbekli Tepe structures in Turkey, just north of the Syrian border. However, it should be noted that with as much discussion as this site inspires, it has so far provided much less plausible human-hands theories than even that of Baalbek, which we will mention in this chapter.

Göbekli Tepe is unique from other archaeological sites in that the oldest and deepest layer of the structure excavated dates to Pre-Pottery Neolithic A (or "PPNA"; 8000–7000 BC;[530] though radiocarbon dating suggests this first layer could be as old as 9600 BC), yet it is home to almost two hundred T-shaped pillars (according to geophysical surveys; they have not all been excavated as of this writing), standing at up to twenty feet (six meters) and weighing up to twenty tons (forty thousand pounds). (Note also that there is one stone in the nearby quarry weighing fifty tons.) Many of the pillars have ornate carvings on one side involving animals—both docile and predatory, insects, reptiles, birds, etc.—but not surprisingly in relation with Neolithic cave paintings and very few humanoid shapes. The largest pillars stand in the center of mysterious circles made up of smaller pillars and stones. The contrast of such magnificent stones being dated to within the PPNA era draws serious attention from archaeologists and historians because of the implications this combination has upon everything we know of early human civilization development, which is what links this site to its fame.

Prior to modern farming settlements, which created the blank grounds we see today, this area would have been an ideal plant/animal source for the nomadic hunters/gatherers of the Pre-Pottery eras. Chief German archaeologist Klaus Schmidt, who has devoted well over ten years of his life to the mysteries of the Göbekli Tepe site, has been able to rule out that the summit, itself, was ever a permanent residence to any early inhabitants. That would suggest, to Schmidt, that this eleven-thousand-year-old location—*said to predate Stonehenge by six thousand years*—was a place of worship; the "first human-built holy place;"[531] "humanity's first 'cathedral on a hill.'"[532]

Because only approximately 5 percent of the site is currently unearthed (about one acre), many secrets may yet remain beneath the soil. However, despite the minimal unveiling that has been accomplished as of this moment, there is good reason for such global attention toward this hill.

According to *Smithsonian Magazine*, "Scholars have long believed that only *after* people learned to farm and live in settled communities did they have the time, organization, and resources to construct temples and support complicated social structures."[533] But with no evidence of settlement ("no cooking hearths, houses or trash pits, and none of the clay fertility figurines that litter nearby sites of about the same age"[534] among other items), the only human explanation for these monumental complexes would attribute the building, stacking, lifting, shaping, and conceptualization of these pillars to the travelers of that time. Because the site is dated to PPNA, we are left to believe the site was created by people without even the "time, organization, and resources" to construct a clay pot. Not to mention, as the constantly moving/relocating/survival lifestyle of these pre-sedentary-society nomads suggest, they would have had to accomplish these tasks overnight, so this theory isn't even taken seriously by most archaeologists. "Schmidt says the monuments *could not have been* built by ragged bands of hunter-gatherers. To carve, erect and bury rings of seven-ton stone pillars would have required hundreds of workers, all needing to be fed and housed."[535]

Pillar 27, Enclosure C, Layer III (the oldest/ deepest of the three layers).[536] Sculpture displays a predatory animal, which most interpret to be a depiction of a short-mouthed crocodile or large-breed feline, with teeth bared and tail swerving at an extreme angle. This carving "has excited particular interest for being carved almost in the round, hinting at a degree of artistic training and division of labor that is again surprising, if not impossible, in a hunter-gatherer society."[537]

Layer II, consisting of structures in, on, and around Layer III, is dated to the PPNB Age, and involves the installation of small window-less rooms and smaller T-shaped pillars. Layer I is the youngest of the layers, located at the topmost portion of the hill (ground level prior to excavation) and only offers loosened sediments from erosion gathered since the hill had been intentionally backfilled (ca. 8000 BCE, the Stone Age, as per carbon dating; reason for deliberate backfill unknown), as well as other small stone tools and limestone fragments from the refuse that was used to fill. *National Geographic* explains the layers in a way that is, perhaps, easier to understand: "Bewilderingly, the people at Göbekli Tepe got steadily worse at temple building. The earliest rings [Layer III] are the biggest and most sophisticated, technically and artistically. As time went by, the pillars [in Layer II] became smaller, simpler, and were mounted with less and less care. Finally the effort seems to have petered out altogether by 8200 BC [when the site was backfilled; Layer I]. Göbekli Tepe was all fall and no rise."[538]

One leading theory as to the purpose of Göbekli Tepe proposes that the pillars and circles were intended as a pilgrimage site, and to welcome the deceased as a final resting place. This is supported by the carvings, primarily predatory animals; some suggest that the early handiwork was made to drive away evil spirits from tampering with the bodies of lost loved ones. Because vultures appear often amongst the ancient art-work—as well as chipped, human bone fragments found in the area—this points to the possibility of early sky burials, in which the travelers would have left their loved ones' remains behind at the pillars for the carrion birds to scatter. Butchered animal bones were also discovered, despite the lack of housing edifices or cooking constructs, which suggest that the congregants would share a brief meal (prepared elsewhere or aboveground outside of the circles) before their departure from the hill. That seems like a logical "why" for the equation, but what remains unanswered is "how." Even if religion or burial was the original intent of the site, how would these pillars have been erected by people who lacked the resources, housing, time, and intelligence to do so?

There is a whisper among several involved in the debate that this may have been one of the world's first farming initiatives, originating from desperation, as opposed to ingenuity and planning. If this were true, the story, as hypothesized by archaeologists, would unfold like this: Neolithic hunters/gatherers set out to create a holy place. They found a quarry, and began digging up multi-ton megaliths with flint flakes (sharp-edged, palm-sized, flaky stones used by early settlers for varying uses, often appearing similar to obsidian arrowheads or the like, except much lighter in color). Quickly, their resources ran out as they realized that their building site would take much longer than planned, so they began to gather the wheat from the surrounding fields to survive, which slowly became the first domesticated wheat farm. As they continued to dig up the stones and build their holy site, they learned simultaneously about planting and harvesting, the knowledge they gained based more on lucky happenstance and the sheer will to survive than by planning. They continued to apply their intelligence toward the goal of remaining in one place, their dedication to the holy site forcing them into a new way of life, and the hunters/gatherers eventually became the earliest farmers/settlers.[539]

Another more believable version of this story was conceived by Schmidt:

Such scholars suggest that the Neolithic revolution, i.e., the beginnings of grain cultivation, took place here. Schmidt believed, as others do, that mobile groups in the area were compelled to cooperate with each other to protect early concentrations of wild cereals from wild animals (herds of gazelles and wild donkeys). Wild cereals may have been used for sustenance more intensively than before and were perhaps deliberately cultivated. This would have led to early social organization of various groups in the area of Göbekli Tepe. Thus, according to Schmidt, the Neolithic did not begin on a small scale in the form of individual instances of garden cultivation, but developed rapidly in the form of "a large-scale social organization."[540]

We know that human domestication had to have happened at some point in history, so why not there and then? Again, the theory could make sense, and has even been supported by recent DNA analysis linking the modern domestic wheat strands with the wild wheat strands of Mount Karaca Dağ, only twenty miles from Göbekli Tepe, evidence that modern wheat likely could have originated from wheat domestication experiments just like the one in Schmidt's theory.[541] Yet, the farther we get into this story, *again*, the more questions surface. How could there have been an early farming initiative without a nearby settlement (the nearby towns were not built until centuries later)? These ten- to fifty-ton stones are estimated to have required five hundred men to pull them from the quarry a quarter mile to the pillars and circles. As *Archaeology Magazine* puts it, "How did Stone Age people achieve the level of organization necessary to do this?" The article goes on to say that some archaeologists speculate that "an elite class of religious leaders supervised the work and later controlled the rituals that took place at the site."[542] Were these the reptilians of Genesis 6, the Watchers who descended as "flying geniuses"? I ask this because the so called Pre-Pottery Neolithic types that would have existed in Göbekli Tepe were within migrating distance from the ancient town of Jericho, and at approximately the same time the massive building project was underway in Turkey (Göbekli Tepe is an archaeological site in the Southeastern Anatolia Region of Turkey), the Pre-Pottery Neolithic A culture at the famous biblical site of Jericho started something in haste that could be telling. The hunter-gatherers there who had been living in the mud huts and tents and following the seasons wherever it led them, suddenly stopped migrating and started a massive building project of their own—and it was purely defensive. Very quickly a people who up until then would have simply run away from any superior army abruptly reacted as if they perceived something they could not outrun, a need to surround their settlement with a massive wall that was ten feet thick and nearly a half mile long around the inner city. As part of the wall, they also erected a gigantic stone lookout tower thirty-three feet in diameter and about that high. The wall was surrounded by a moat of sorts, cut out from solid bedrock and filled with mud. It was approximately nine feet deep and twenty-seven feet wide, with another wall outside that perimeter. The purpose of the moat was to restrict an enemy's ability to get to the wall with scaling gear (or, more likely, to stop something that could jump over the wall, as in giants). Of course, I am theorizing here, but clearly something suddenly was confronting the inhabitants of what would become the city of Jericho, and this at the same time the apocryphal Book of Enoch records serpentine Watchers—the immortals we are studying—who descended in the days of Jared and created mutant life forms called Nephilim.

Yet while these mysterious portal-traversing entities were coming under the judgment of God throughout the Middle East, at Göbekli Tepe, the people rushed to bury the construction site under tons and tons of earth-fill for reasons that remain unclear. Was it so this site could be uncovered after the Flood (which had been prophesied and then the world was aware)? Or is there something in Turkey yet to be discovered that might explain why it was—like the Anasazi dwellings in the United States would later be—abruptly abandoned? Something that might even be used by those giants who are prophesied to return, or some part of great deception in the end times? Even more so perhaps than Baalbek (summary follows), Göbekli Tepe remains a mystery. We can't say for sure who, how, or for what purpose it was built; *nor* can we even begin to guess why it was ever ordered to be backfilled, *or* why each generation of builders became *less* proficient and impressive than the previous, instead of the other way around, which is what natural evolutionary intelligence would suggest. One thing we know for sure: If Göbekli Tepe was the result of human hands, then, at the very least, it erases everything we *thought* we knew about early human development, agricultural efficiency of nomadic persons, and settlement domestication.

Baalbek

Since 1956, Baalbek (often spelled "Baalbeck" or "Baalbec") has been home to "the oldest and most prestigious cultural event in the Middle East,"[543] known simply as the "Baalbeck International Festival." Although this annual summer event suffered great decline, followed by temporary cessation between the years 2006 and 2007 as a result of political instability, by 2008, it had "regained its place in the line of the most prestigious international festivals with varied and excellent [Lebanese] cultural quality programs performed by great artists inside the magnificent Baalbeck Acropolis."[544] A curious outsider traveling major Roman historical sites for the first time will find the attention-grabbing sights, sounds, celebrations, and almost explosive energies bursting forth from the seams of this small location—spanning less than three square miles—a tourism force to be reckoned with. Amongst the appearances and performances of internationally acclaimed stars of the music, television, and film industries as well as many celebrated stage performers, one might struggle to find time to breathe, let alone rest, in this town that never sleeps every June through August.

However, when September rolls around, the tent stakes are pulled, and the vacationers all return home from the lively festival. Even then, and despite how deserted and forgotten the area looks in pictures of crumbling temple ruins, Baalbek continues to welcome an almost never-ending line of spectators all year round. Professional scholars, historians, architects, and archaeologists continue to name Baalbek one of the greatest mysteries in world history for its monumentally scaled temple ruins and enigmatic findings at the nearby quarry.

Known by early inhabitants (ca. 334 BC after Alexander the Great's victory in the Near East) as "Heliopolis"—which translates to "City of the Sun" from the Greek *helios* ("sun") and *polis* ("city")—Baalbek was one of the most prevalent sanctuaries in the Roman Empire, and its structures are some of the most well preserved standing today. Much discussion has centered around theories that the town may have been an ancient settlement predating Roman rule by centuries at least, and recent pottery fragment finds along the trench channeling the Jupiter temple now date the site to between the "Pre-Pottery Neolithic B Age" (or "PPNB," representing the latter stages of the Stone Age before mankind could craft pottery, approximately 8000 BP ["Before Present"] and 6000 BCE) and the Iron Age (approximately 1200 BC–AD 550).[545] Several skeletons and some pottery from Persia were discovered under the Roman flagstones, indicating additional settlement evidence dating to around 550 BC.[546]

The largest confirmed ancient stone building block on earth at the time of this writing (see note about Mount Shoria later in this chapter) was found in Baalbek by German archaeologists in the middle of 2014 at the quarry of a building site from which gigantic stones had been used for the podium of the enormous "Temple of Jupiter" (built later on by the Romans atop the original mound construction, "Tel Baalbek"). This unfathomable monolith measures in at 64 feet (19.6 meters) in length, 19.6 feet (6 meters) wide, and 18 feet (5.5 meters) high, and is estimated to weigh 1,650 tons (3,300,000 million pounds).[547]

Prior to the unearthing of this giant rock last year, one of the largest quarried stones on earth had been the "Stone of the Pregnant Woman" (*Hajjar al-Hibla*), also located in Baalbek, which protrudes out of the ground at a sloping angle directly alongside the even larger stone found last year. There are several stories and claims behind the naming of this rock. One tells of a pregnant woman who duped the Baalbek inhabitants into believing she held the secret behind lifting and moving the rock in one piece. In trade for her secret, they would feed her and the baby in her womb and take care of all her prenatal needs, but after her child was born, no hidden truths emerged, and the stone has remained tilted out of the ground ever since.[548] Another story suggests that jinn—the Arabian and Islamic mythical beings made of smokeless, yet corporeal, fire—assigned their pregnant women to move the stones, and when one such jinn heard the news that Solomon had died, she excitedly dropped it to the ground where it still lay.[549] Yet another rumor lingers around the local area that the name originated from the stone's ability to increase the fertility of any woman who touches it.[550] Whatever the true origin of its name, the Stone of the Pregnant Woman (weighing just over 1,000 tons [approximately 2,205,000 pounds]) is estimated to have required more than forty thousand laborers to move it,[551] though the sources that suggest this number seldom seem to provide a convincing answer as to *how* that would have been accomplished with the building technology of the time regardless of the number of available work hands. It is so close to its newly found and massive counterpart that a fascinated voyager to Baalbek can reach out and touch two of the largest stones on earth at the same time. (Note that there is a third stone across the road from these, more vast than the Stone of the Pregnant Woman, but not as enormous as the most recent find by the Germans in 2014.)

There are many theories in existence, sometimes heatedly debated, regarding who carved the monoliths of Baalbek (both those left at the quarry, and the base stones of the Temple of Jupiter known as the "trilithon"), when they were created, for what purpose, and how they were transported. The mind-boggling reality is that almost every explanation relying on the hands of human men seem to reveal numerous flaws.

Because we know that the Romans were responsible for the building of the uppermost portions of the Temple of Jupiter (as well as the *Heliopolis* temples of Bacchus and Venus in the Baalbek temple complex over the period of two centuries) based on biographical Roman engineering documentation ordered during the Roman Empire, it seems, for many, quite rational to assume that the Romans were responsible for the larger stones in this area as well.

Baalbec, Great Monolith [the Stone of the Pregnant Woman] from *The Holy Land Photographed* by Daniel B. Shepp, 1894.[552] Shepp's original caption under the photo captured over one hundred and twenty years ago is as follows: "Taken as a whole, the ruins of Baalbec are among the grandest in the world. Nowhere is there evidence of more exquisite workmanship. To an antiquarian they are the study of a lifetime.... Before us is one lying in the quarry, whence it had been hewn. It measures sixty-nine feet in length, thirteen feet in breadth and thirteen feet three inches in thickness.... It is accurately squared and trimmed on three sides, showing that it was the custom of the people to dress the stones while quarrying them. There has been much speculation as to how stones like this were quarried and moved into their positions, but no satisfactory theory has been advanced. There is a peculiar absence of inscriptions in connection with all these massive ruins, hence we are left in much doubt and darkness." Note that this image is dated, and therefore shows no evidence of the recently excavated mammoth stone within the soil just on the other side of it.

Visiting that possibility, and focusing only on the Temple of Jupiter, we will start at the top and work our way down. In order to understand these authors' take on the Romans' involvement with the monoliths, some knowledge is needed of their usual building practice.

Columns and Corner Stones

There were fifty-four columns raised in the original Temple of Jupiter structure, involving blocks weighing up to sixty tons each (120,000 pounds). Each corner stone weighed over 100 tons (200,000 pounds), and they were hoisted to 62.34 feet (19 meters) above ground surface.[553] The method used for the top of the temple construction could *in part* be attributed to the Greco-Roman man-operated treadwheel pulleys (*pentaspastos* or *polyspastos*, depending on the number of men required to operate), the tools and techniques of which were well documented by engineers Vitruvius (*De Architectura* 10.2, 1–10) and Heron of Alexandria (*Mechanica* 3.2–5).

The maximum weight that these early cranes could lift and carry when operated to the absolute maximum capacity of their design and with a full crew did not usually exceed 6,000 kilograms (13,228 pounds).[554] Mathematically, this would mean that the cranes—when used alone—fell shy of the capability to lift a single corner stone of the Temple of Jupiter by approximately a little under a staggering 200,000 pounds.

The most likely explanation for the additional weight lifting and maneuvering for the top of the Tower of Jupiter—often mentioned by historians and architectural professionals today (and discussed in historical accounts associated with the raising of the Lateranense obelisk of the Circus Maximus [*AmmianusMarcellinus* 17.4.15] ca. AD 357)—points to the installation of lifting towers (*Mechanica* 3.5), used in tandem with early capstans (horizontal rotators) fixed upon the ground around the lifting tower. The capstans each contributed less weight-lifting efficiency than did the treadwheel pulleys, but they required fewer men (or animals) to function, and more of them could be placed upon the ground when needed, offering increased leverage overall than the pulleys alone. If more weight was required for the lift of an individual stone, more capstans would be installed on the ground around a lifting tower, and so on.

The average capacity of the joined capstans in tandem with a lifting tower of this era has been estimated at 7.5 tons per capstan,[555] and the method of lifting by capstan was via attachment to lewis iron holes in each stone. For example: a 60-ton architrave block (one of the stones placed near the top of the Roman columns) from the Tower of Jupiter, discovered with 8 lewis iron holes, delivers this equation: 8 capstans x 7.5 tons per capstan = 60 tons capacity. The architrave blocks in the

Jupiter tower weighed *up to* 60 tons, so the capstan/lifting tower combination theory is certainly feasible for the tower stones when inflated for
more weight, even for the over-100-ton cornerstones.

With enough capstan and lifting tower installations scattered about,
and with the assistance from treadwheel pulleys on the lighter stones, the
achievement of the Tower of Jupiter columns above the original and far
more ancient foundation stones could be explained and easily attributed
to Roman ingenuity.

Below the columns, however, is the trilithon (three extremely large
and heavy monoliths, lying between the Tower of Jupiter and the Tel
Baalbek mound). This is where we first begin to run into the heated
debate regarding the whos and hows of this so-called Roman architecture.

Trilithon

The first theory (more often this theory is merely associated with Arabian lore involving the "magician" works of Solomon, and is therefore
taken less seriously than theories involving Roman origin) can be seen in
the following image on the next page from Daniel B. Shepp's *The Holy
Land Photographed.*

Yet, it goes without saying that most great minds that approach the
mystery of the trilithon secularly will disregard the idea that Solomon
transported the stones by magic. Considering other mainstream theories, one will almost immediately land on the arguments put forth by
French archaeologist Jean-Pierre Adam, author of the 1977 scholarly
article, *A Propos du Trilithon de Baalbek. Let transport et la miseen oeuvre
des megaliths*[557] ("Concerning the Trilithon of Baalbek: Transportation
and the Implementation of the Megaliths"). Adam's approach to the
mystery involves a look at the "Thunder Stone," a giant boulder (one
and a half times the weight of the trilithon blocks of Baalbek [1,250,000
kilograms; 2,755,778 pounds])[558] that makes up the base of the "Bronze
Horseman" (*aka* the "Statue of Peter the Great") in Saint Petersburg,
Russia.

Baalbec, Monolith in Wall [trilithon] from The Holy Land Photographed.[556] Shepp's original caption under the photo is as follows: "Even more wonderful to many than the ornate ruins of the temples, is the masonry of the outer walls of Baalbec. Here are the three largest stones ever used in architecture.... One of these is sixty-four feet long, another sixty-three feet eight inches, and the third sixty-three feet. Each is thirteen feet high and thirteen feet thick. To these dimensions must be added the fact, that they have been built into the wall fully twenty feet above the ground [note that Shepp is referring to the measurement from the stones to the ground as it lay in 1894, prior to further depth revealed in archeological digs, which increased that measurement later], and the further fact that the quarry from which they were taken is fully a mile distant. Those who identify Solomon with the buildings of Baalbec, connect these stones with the narrative in I Kings VII: "And the foundation was of costly stones, EVEN GREAT STONES, stones of ten cubits, and stones of eight cubits." The Arabs believe that Solomon was a magician, and by a magic word, moved these giant slabs.

The composition of the Bronze Horseman statue was ordered by Catherine the Great in an attempt to inflate her position as Peter the Great's rightful heir. Beginning the planning for the statue in 1766, the Thunder Stone was found in the deep marshlands of Lakhta, just a few miles from the Gulf of Finland, in 1768. Greek engineer Marinos Carburis agreed to oversee the moving of the stone, and began the intimidating trek as soon as manpower resources were in place. The stone was moved approximately four miles (six kilometers) within two years over both land and water. Most land transportation occurred in a nine-month period by four hundred men using ingenious roller tracks and capstans, and water transportation required a gigantic barge built specifically for carrying the Thunder Stone, with the additional requirement of a warship on each side of the barge for further support.

The Transportation of the Thunder-stone in the Presence of Catherine II, Engraving by I. F. Schley of the drawing by YuryFelten, 1770.[559] In the picture: On the ground at the far left are the capstans in operation by only human hands; no oxen or cattle of any kind were used for the moving of the Thunder Stone; the operation was observed in person by thousands of witnesses in the company of Catherine the Great, herself. The boulder sits atop the ballbearings-like roller tracks designed by Marinos Carburis. The tracks would be assembled in front of the stone, the stone would be pulled by the crews at the capstans to the front of the tracks, and simultaneously the tracks at the back would be disassembled and carried to the front where they were reassembled for further transport, one centimeter at a time.

Here we can observe the finished Bronze Horseman statue as it sits in St. Petersburg today.[560] At the bottom right of the photo, tourists stand probably ten or fifteen feet just behind the boulder.

Because the distance between Lakhta and the Senate Square of St. Petersburg is about four miles, and the distance from the trilithon to the quarry in Baalbek is only about 2,600 feet (800 meters), and because the Thunder Stone is larger than the trilithon stones, Adam finds the moving of the trilithon stones an even lesser feat than that of the Thunder Stone when hypothetically applying the same or similar transportation methods.

Understandably, this comparison inspires that "aha" moment for many researchers, and is considered a feasible explanation for the potentially applied physics of the brightest minds in ancient Roman engineering toward the trilithon stones of Baalbek. Adam's is an interesting theory, for sure, and one that has gained immense following as a result of the Temple Mount structure ordered by Roman client King Herod the Great in Jerusalem, Israel, which is home to base stones weighing close to the same weight as those of the trilithon at Baalbek. These Temple Mount stones (the largest of which is 630 tons) remain unchallenged as Roman origin, so many suggest with good reason that the stones of Baalbek would have only required a slight increase in construction efforts to accomplish. Further, many assume that the three monoliths left at the nearby quarries represent a point at which the Romans bit off more than they could chew, so to speak, cutting and shaping stones that ended up later to be more than their cranes, lifting towers, capstans, etc., could move. This would not only explain why the stones were abandoned at the quarries, it would also explain why the monolith across the road from the Stone of the Pregnant Woman shows deep, squared cuts in one end, as if the Romans acknowledged their inability to move the stone, and therefore decided to cut it down into smaller stones until the monolith was of manageable moving size. (Note, however, that the stone with the rivets cut on one end has also been acknowledged to have imperfections within the stone, so for just as many people asserting that the Romans were cutting it down to a size they could lift, there is an equal number who claim the stone was merely being cut by its original dressers to preserve quality and avoid the evident risk of a crack quickly appearing in a foundation stone.)

Left wanting, however, is any documentation whatsoever by the Romans that they would have used this Thunder Stone method of transportation for the trilithon stones when all other building practices were so well documented during their heyday. The Romans were a proud and brilliant people who left our world with so many records of what they accomplished and, in so many cases, how they accomplished it. Those records have been thoroughly researched and studied for hundreds of years. We cannot attribute this stone-moving method (as well as the other methods mentioned by Adam in his study) to their book of tricks without also asking why they wouldn't have been intelligent enough to record such an accomplishment at Baalbek. Even more important, as stated earlier in this chapter, there have been discoveries from the Pre-Pottery Neolithic era within the soil along the channels of the Temple of Jupiter that point to this site predating the Romans by centuries.

On the tails of the most prevailing theories of Roman attribution come thoughts perpetuated by archaeologists that the trilithon stones were of Greek origin for use as a retaining wall in soil-erosion circumstances. And whereas, again, we have no record of this, we also have no reason to believe the Greeks—despite their impressive amphitheater ingenuity—would be capable of achieving more than the Romans in relation to moving stones that weigh hundreds and hundreds of tons.

Other ideas have surfaced throughout the preceding decades. Some are both sensational and altogether incredible. For instance, the idea that the Romans would have built a Nile-like river that carried the trilithon stones by boat when there doesn't seem to be enough solid evidence that a river of that magnitude could have ever existed that close to these structures. On and on the Roman-origin explanations seem to arrive, each one supported by its own list of archaeological professionals, and each one eventually challenged by just as many or more archaeological personalities well respected in the field. Skeptics chastise those who attribute the monoliths to ancient extraterrestrial activity or the giants of Genesis, saying that just because one cannot find origin in human life, he or she will turn all too quickly to the supernatural for explanation.

Sometimes these comments are delivered in extreme sarcasm, flowing to the tune of: "We can't understand how ancient humans could have done it, so it must have been aliens." Believers in the supernatural chastise the skeptics in turn, questioning their outright denial of the possibility of supernatural activity or ancient humanoid hybrid beings when there remains to be found any other solid, irrefutable explanation as to how ancient humans could have accomplished more than our historical records have *ever* been able to attribute to them.

But whatever the theory, the fact remains that the origins of the trilithon and quarry stones at Baalbek remain unknown and have served to baffle researchers and archaeologists for centuries. Without documentation by a race or people as to the materials and methods used, as well as the purpose behind the structures in Baalbek, the answers may always be obscured, and speculation may always result in the posing of even further mystery.

Note, however, that there is one historical document we have yet to visit in this chapter, which seems to give just as likely an explanation as the speculated "ancient humans." The Bible is respected, even by many nonbelievers of the Christian faith, as a historical document, and one that has proven time and time again to connect the dots where other sources have failed, and this was the source reflected in the 1860 diary of the Scottish diplomat and writer David Urquhart, whose mind was "paralyzed" by "the impossibility of any solution" involving how, why, and by whom the original construction at Baalbek (whose much older ruins were built upon by the Romans, who used it as foundational substructure on which they built the "Temple of Jupiter"). Urquhart's only conclusion was that the temple had to have been built by those megalithic masterminds of the days of Noah.

> There was here, therefore, not one of the elements combined at Memphis, Babylon, Nineveh, or any of the seats of empire, of the ancient or modern world [but] ruins, surpassing in their indications and evidences of greatness anything to be found in

those ancient capitals, to an extent which defies all calculation, leaving the imagination itself stranded on a bank of mud.

On the top of this comes a third riddle; how these works were interrupted. They are not merely not concluded, but they are stopped at the very beginning....

Was it a foreign invasion? Was it an irruption of savages? Was it a "confusion of tongues?" What could it have been?...

My first exclamation, on looking down into the quarry, had been "There were giants in the earth in those days."...

The builders of Baalbeck must have been a people who had attained to the highest pinnacle of power and science; and this region must have been the centre of their dominion. We are perfectly acquainted with the nations who have flourished here or around, and their works; they are the Assyrians, Chaldeans, Medes, Persians, Egyptians, Canaanites, and Jews. These complete the catalogue of ancient empires, and this work is none of theirs....

It was only on my way back, and when the tomb of Noah was pointed out to me by the wayside, that it occurred to me that there might be something in Emir Hangar's story, and that the stones of Baalbeck had to be considered as some of "those sturdy fellows that the Deluge could not sweep away." This, then, was a remnant of that pride and presumption, which had brought the waters over the face of the earth.[561]

Could there be something to Urquhart's train of thought that actually provides more "answer" than it does pose further inquiry?

Russian Megaliths May Provide the Biggest Proof Yet

Lastly, supposing the mysteries of Baalbek were finally cracked, attributing the movement of the trilithon stones and the existence of the quarry stones to human hands, a more recent discovery could potentially erase all of that decryption progress and render it largely irrelevant in comparison to the latest thrill: As mentioned prior, the largest stone in the world confirmed for the purposes of building at the time of this writing currently rests in the quarry of Baalbek, weighing an estimated 1,650 tons. However, last year, stones estimated to weigh *an astounding 3,000–4,000 tons* have been discovered on Mount Shoria in Siberia. At this present time, the site is such a young find that little is known about these stones, so theories haven't yet begun to surface. Before this site officially launches all the who and how questions that our world has attempted for centuries to answer about Baalbek, further study on the megaliths of Mount Shoria must rule that the stones were, in fact, dressed by hand, and therefore not a product of natural formation. That said, pictures of the stones can be viewed online, and archaeologists are already buzzing about the proof that the stones are much more than that:

> An ancient "super-megalithic" site has been found in the Siberian Mountains. Found recently in Gornaya Shoria (Mount Shoria) in southern Siberia, this site consists of huge blocks of stone, which appear to be granite, **with flat surfaces, right angles, and sharp corners.** The blocks appear to be stacked, almost in the manner of cyclopean masonry, and well…they're enormous!
>
> Russia is no stranger to ancient megalithic sites, like Arkaim or Russia's Stonehenge, and the Manpupuner formation, just to name two, but the site at Shoria is unique in that, if it's man-made, the blocks used are undoubtedly **the largest ever worked by human hands.**[562] (bold emphasis in original)

Needless to say, Mount Shoria is about to become the source of much news. Should these square, stacked stones prove to be dressed by tools and not by weather conditions (which seems a preposterous thought when viewing the photos of their precise shapes), Baalbek will no longer hold the heavyweight title for the world's greatest archaeological monolith mystery.

The Axis Mundi Decision

As of the 2008 edition of *Rastros do Oculto* from which Putnam translated, ex-occultist Daniel Mastral believed that only nine portals remained to be opened.[563] He originally believed the opening of the final portals would culminate in 2013, but since he had been out of Satanism for many years by that time, it is hard to know if that timetable, he first disclosed in 2001, is still on track. Even with some delay, it speaks to the lateness of the hour in terms of end-time prophecy. At the time we go to press the only English language article about Mastral's exposé, offers this explanation:

> Satan's hope is that with the opening of the last portals, power-ful demons from lower dimensions will be able to come to earth and eventually, interact with humankind. They will not pres-ent themselves as demons, but as benevolent aliens and evolved spirits of light.[564]

Of course, that rationale corroborates the hypothesis we offered in *Exo-Vaticana*. The immortals are coming! If one is unsure of where they stand with God, that's a chilling proposition given the information covered in *On the Path of the Immortals*.

In closing this chapter, our confidence comes from Christ alone but everyone reading this will make a decision concerning their personal axis mundi. We believe three items are essential: Jesus Christ is the ultimate cosmic center, He is returning soon, and that you can enjoy being with Him forever in heaven and on the new earth. We believe we have presented a case thus far for the second point within, and the third is based upon a decision concerning the first—YOUR axis mundi decision. The right answer comes by faith alone (Romans 3:28), by sincerely believing that Jesus lived a perfect life, died for your sins and resurrected from the dead (1 Corinthians 15:3-5). It is a free gift from God (Romans 5:15; 6:23), that can only be received by faith, apart from any sacrament, papal indulgence, or earned merit on your part (Ephesians 2:8–9). The "axis mundi decision" is presented to all, "That if thou shalt confess with thy mouth the Lord Jesus, and shalt believe in thine heart that God hath raised him from the dead, thou shalt be saved" (Romans 10:9).

Only one chapter remains, and it is the most disturbing. It is a bonus chapter with large excerpts from *Zenith 2016* that had to be included in this work. Why? Because the information lays out who the chiefs of the immortals are, and the American and Roman gateways that were built specifically for—and are ready for—their return.

The Most Powerful Stargates in the World?

America, the Vatican, and the Portals of Apollo-Osiris

By Tom Horn

S ome years ago I was on my way to Roswell, New Mexico, to meet with David Flynn and some other fiends. As I recall, we were join-ing up to support David, who was scheduled to give a presenta-tion during the famous International UFO Festival. While driving, my cell phone rang, and on the other end of the line was another friend, filmmaker Chris Pinto. He wanted to know if I would be interested in meeting with him in Washington, DC, in just two days from then to be part of the History Channel's *Brad Meltzer's Decoded* series. Nor-mally, I decline all such invitations, as I have witnessed too many times how these programs twist the Christian's worldview, and I'm typically uninterested in sacrificing myself to help somebody's secular ratings. Yet, because it was Pinto, and the project sounded like it was right down his alley (the Brad Meltzer's team was going to "investigate the histori-cal mystery as to what happened to the White House Cornerstone"), I agreed to participate. The History Channel (HC) wanted me to speak to the issue of the Washington Monument, why and how it was built, and whether the missing White House cornerstone may lie hidden beneath it. It sounded harmless enough, and so I agreed to turn around and head that way.

Two days later—while Pinto was somewhere across town having already been filmed for the program—I met up with Meltzer's two main field investigators (who can be seen running around the world in the HC series checking into whatever the producers pretend to investigate) in DC—Christine McKinley and Scott Rolle. Christine has a mechanical engineering degree from California Polytechnic University, and Scott is a circuit court judge in Frederick County, Maryland (and an actor), so I was interested especially in what Christine might think of the engineering feat that the Freemasons had employed in building the largest obelisk of its kind in the world (the Washington Monument). A special permit had been secured for the film project, and besides Christine and Scott, there were at least five camera operators, two producers, a team of technicians, and a huge crowd of people who had gathered to see what was going on. The producer wanted to film Christine and Scott (the "investigators") walking up (with the Capitol dome in their background) while I approached the obelisk from the other direction, and then we would meet up at the base of the monument, greet each other, and begin talking about the mysterious construction project, why it was built, and finally whether I believed the stone was buried beneath it.

But something else happened.

As I started describing the obelisk facing the dome and the rich Egyptian symbolism involving Osiris, Isis, the Freemasons, and how the mechanics of these magical devices were specifically designed to open a doorway or "stargate" that allows Osiris to arise from the underworld to take his rightful place inside every US president (more on that in a bit), the producer became enthralled with the storyline and wanted to continue filming me (for almost two hours), basically describing the plotline from my book *Zenith 2016*. Then Christine McKinley went off script too, explaining that her father had been a 32nd-degree Freemason, and she wanted to know if I thought he had been part of an occult organization. That led to another half-hour of discussion and, well, we never did get back to the original reason for my being there. The producer then approached me to ask if they could use the film they had shot to pitch a different project to the History Channel, which I agreed to but never heard any more about.

When the *Decoded* episode on the missing White House cornerstone played on television, I was—once again—happy that my face was not included in a History Channel production (and I have since turned them down several times, most recently for their *Search for the Lost Giants* program in which they practically begged me to appear to discuss how transhumanism and the genetics revolution may be repeating what the ancient Watchers did in creating Nephilim). They did, however, include Chris Pinto's interview in the *Decoded* episode filmed that day, followed by the "investigators" at a bar or pool hall somewhere afterward, defending the Freemasons as American heroes and depicting Pinto as a nut-job conspiracy theorist. I only had to watch a couple other episodes of *Decoded* to get that it's a ruse meant for entertainment, ratings, and sales, but not a whit about serious investigative work or about "decoding" anything.

That said, I do have to thank the History Channel and Brad Meltzer for that Washington, DC, experience and their disgraceful treatment (frame-up) of award-winning and *real* exploratory filmmaker, Chris Pinto. They unintentionally provided me one of the "thousand points of light" that eventually convinced us to launch SkyWatch TV and to make bona fide investigative reports an integral part of our future media endeavors. In fact, the book you now hold in your hands is only a part of what will be followed by a documentary film and four-part television special into this subject, including (to return to my point) fresh insights into the most powerful stargates in the world—America, the Vatican, and the portals of Apollo-Osiris

How many people know that located right inside Washington, DC, is: 1) a stargate; 2) seventy-two (72) pentagrams at the base of the stargate to control the "immortals"; 3) powerful generators (dome and obelisk) designed from antiquity to make the stargate work; and 4) ancient prophecies connected to this device that make it clear exactly who will be coming through the mystical doorway in the future? How many also know that similar devices and prophecies are built into the Vatican's headquarters in Rome? We decided this information was so important that we have included it as bonus material in this chapter, which is excerpted from *Zenith 2016*.

The Dome and Obelisk

Undoubtedly the vast majority of people, when looking at Washington, DC, and at the Vatican, never comprehend how these cities constitute one of the greatest open conspiracies of all time. There, reproduced in all their glory and right before the world's eyes, is an ancient talismanic diagram based on the history and cult of Isis, Osiris, and Horus, including the magical utilities meant to generate the deity's return.

The primeval concept—especially that of sacred domes facing obelisks—was designed in antiquity for the express purpose of regeneration, resurrection, and apotheosis, for deity incarnation from the underworld to earth's surface through union of the respective figures—the dome (ancient structural representation of the womb of Isis) and the obelisk (ancient representation of the erect male phallus of Osiris).

This layout, as modeled in antiquity, exists today on the grandest scale at the heart of the capital of the most powerful government on earth—the United States—as well as in the heart of the most politically influential Church on earth—the Vatican. Given this fact and the pattern provided by the apostle Paul and the Apocalypse of John (the book of Revelation) that the end times would culminate in a marriage between political (Antichrist) and religious (False Prophet) authorities at the return of Osiris/Apollo, it behooves open-minded researchers to carefully consider this prophecy in stone, as it defines the spiritual energy that is knowingly or unknowingly being invoked at both locations with potential ramifications for Petrus Romanus…and beyond.

The US capital has been called the "Mirror Vatican" due to the strikingly similar layout and design of its primary buildings and streets. This is no accident. In fact, America's forefathers first named the capital city "Rome." But the parallelism between Washington and the Vatican is most clearly illustrated by the Capitol building and dome facing the obelisk known as the Washington Monument, and at St. Peter's Basilica in the Vatican by a similar dome facing a familiar obelisk—both of which were, according to their own official records, fashioned after the Roman Pantheon, the circular-domed rotunda "dedicated to all pagan gods." This layout—a domed temple facing an obelisk—is an ancient, alchemical blueprint that holds significant esoteric meaning.

For those who may not know, the US Capitol building in Washington, DC, is historically based on a pagan Masonic temple theme. Thomas Jefferson, who shepherded the anti-Christian "Roman Pantheon" design, wrote to the Capitol's architect, Benjamin LaTrobe, defining it as "the first temple dedicated to…embellishing with Athenian taste the course of a nation looking far beyond the range of Athenian destinies"[565] (the "Athenian" empire was first known as "Osiria," the kingdom of Osiris). In 1833, Massachusetts Representative Rufus Choate agreed, writing, "We have built no national temples but the Capitol."[566] William Henry and Mark Gray, in their book, *Freedom's Gate: Lost Symbols in the U.S. Capitol*, add that, "The U.S. Capitol has numerous architectural and other features that unquestionably identify it with ancient temples."[567] After listing various features to make their case that the US Capitol building is a "religious temple"—including housing the image of a deified being, heavenly beings, gods, symbols, inscriptions, sacred geometry, columns, prayers, and orientation to the sun—they conclude:

> The designers of the city of Washington DC oriented it to the Sun—especially the rising Sun on June 21 and December 21 [the same day and month as the end of the Mayan calendar in 2012]. The measurements for this orientation were made from the location of the center of the Dome of the U.S. Capitol, rendering it a "solar temple." Its alignment and encoded numerol-

ogy point to the Sun as well as the stars. A golden circle on the Rotunda story and a white star in the Crypt marks this spot.... It is clear that the builders viewed the Capitol as America's sole temple: a solemn...Solar Temple to be exact.[568]

To understand what these statements may soon mean for the future of the world, one needs to comprehend how these [stargate] aparati—the dome and the obelisk facing it—facilitate important archaic and modern protocols for invigorating *prophetic* supernatural alchemy. In ancient times, the obelisk represented the god Osiris' "missing" male organ, which Isis was not able to find after her husband/brother was slain and chopped into fourteen pieces by his evil brother Seth (or Set). The story involves a detailed account of the envious brother and seventy-two conspirators [important numerology we will get to later in this chapter] tricking Osiris into climbing inside a box, which Seth quickly locked and threw into the Nile. Osiris drowned, and his body floated down the Nile River, where it snagged on the limbs of a tamarisk tree. In Byblos, Isis recovered his body from the river bank and took it into her care. In her absence, Seth stole the body again and chopped it into fourteen pieces, which he threw into the Nile. Isis searched the river bank until she recovered every piece, except for the genitals, which had been swallowed by a fish (Plutarch says a crocodile). Isis recombined the thirteen pieces of Osiris' corpse and replaced the missing organ with a magic facsimile (Obelisk), which she used to impregnate herself, thus giving rise to Osiris again in the person of his son, Horus. This legendary ritual for reincarnating Osiris formed the core of Egyptian cosmology (as well as the Rosicrucian/Masonic dying-and-rising myths) and was fantastically venerated on the most imposing scale throughout all of Egypt by towering Obelisks (representing the phallus of Osiris) and Domes (representing the pregnant belly of Isis) including at Karnak where the upright Obelisks were "vitalized" or "stimulated" from the energy of the masturbatory Sun god Ra shining down upon them.

There is historical evidence that this elaborate myth and its rituals may have been based originally on real characters and events. Regarding this, it is noteworthy that in 1998, former secretary general of Egypt's Supreme Council of Antiquities, Zahi Hawass, claimed to have found the burial tomb of the god Osiris (Apollo/Nimrod) at the Giza Plateau. In the article, "Sandpit of Royalty," from the newspaper *Extra Bladet* (Copenhagen), January 31, 1999, Hawass was quoted saying:

> I have found a shaft, going twenty-nine meters vertically down into the ground, exactly halfway between the Chefren Pyramid and the Sphinx. At the bottom, which was filled with water, we have found a burial chamber with four pillars. In the middle is a large granite sarcophagus, which I expect to be the grave of Osiris, the god.... I have been digging in Egypt's sand for more than thirty years, and up to date this is the most exciting discovery I have made.... We found the shaft in November and began pumping up the water recently. So several years will pass before we have finished investigating the find.[569]

As far as we know, this discovery did not ultimately provide the physical remains of the deified person. But what it did illustrate is that at least some very powerful Egyptologists believe Osiris was a historical figure, and that his body was stored somewhere at or near the Great Pyramid. Manly P. Hall, who knew that the Masonic legend of Hiram Abiff was a thinly veiled prophecy of the resurrection of Osiris, may have understood what Zahi Hawass (not to mention Roerich, Roosevelt, and Wallace with their sacred Osiris Casket was looking for, and why. Consider that he wrote in *The Secret Teachings of All Ages*: "The Dying God [Osiris] shall rise again! The secret room in the House of the Hidden Places shall be rediscovered. The Pyramid again shall stand as the ideal emblem of...resurrection, and regeneration."[570]

In Egypt, where rituals were performed to actually "raise" the spirit of Osiris into the reigning Pharaoh, political authority in the form of divine kingship or theocratic statesmanship was established (later reflected in the political and religious doctrine of royal and political legitimacy or "the divine right of kings," who supposedly derived their right to rule from the will of God, with the exception in some countries that the king is subject to the Church and the pope). This meant, among other things, the Egyptian pharaoh enjoyed extraordinary authority as the "son of the sun god" (Ra) and the incarnation of the falcon god Horus during his lifetime. At death, the pharaoh became the Osiris, the divine judge of the netherworld, and on earth, his son and predecessor took his place as the newly anointed manifestation of Horus. Thus each generation of pharaohs provided the gods with a spokesman for the present world and for the afterlife while also offering the nation divinely appointed leadership.

Yet the observant reader may wonder, "Was there something more to the pharaoh's deification than faith in ritual magic?" The cult center of Amun-Ra at Thebes may hold the answer, as it was the site of the largest religious structure ever built—the temple of Amun-Ra at Karnak—and the location of many extraordinary mysterious rites. The great temple with its one hundred miles of walls and gardens (the primary object of fascination and worship by the nemesis of Moses—the pharaoh of the Exodus, Ramses II) was the place where each pharaoh reconciled his divinity in the company of Amun-Ra during the festival of Opet. The festival was held at the temple of Luxor and included a procession of gods carried on barges up the Nile River from Karnak to the temple. The royal family accompanied the gods on boats while the Egyptian laity walked along the shore, calling aloud and making requests of the gods. Once at Luxor, the pharaoh and his entourage entered the holy of holies, where the ceremony to raise the spirit of Osiris into the king was performed and pharaoh was transmogrified into a living deity. Outside, large groups of dancers and musicians waited anxiously. When the king emerged as the "born again" Osiris, the crowd erupted in gaiety. From that day forward, the pharaoh was considered to be—just as the god ciphered in the Great Seal of the United States will be—the son and spiritual incarnation of the Supreme Deity. The all-seeing eye of Horus/Apollo/Osiris above the unfinished pyramid on the Great Seal represents this event.

Modern people, especially in America, may view the symbols used in this magic—the dome representing the habitually pregnant belly of Isis, and the obelisk, representing the erect phallus of Osiris—as profane or pornographic. But they were in fact ritualized fertility objects, which the ancients believed could produce tangible reactions, properties, or "manifestations" within the material world. The obelisk and dome as imitations of the deities' male and female reproductive organs could, through government representation, invoke into existence the being or beings symbolized by them. This is why inside the temple or dome, temple prostitutes representing the human manifestation of the goddess were also available for ritual sex as a form of imitative magic. These prostitutes usually began their services to the goddess as children, and were deflowered at a very young age by a priest or, as Isis was, by a modeled obelisk of Osiris' phallus. Sometimes these prostitutes were chosen, on the basis of their beauty, as the sexual mates of sacred temple bulls who were considered the incarnation of Osiris. In other places, such as at Mendes, temple prostitutes were offered in coitus to divine goats. Through such imitative sex, the dome and obelisk became "energy receivers," capable of assimilating Ra's essence from the rays of the sun, which in turn drew forth the "seed" of the underworld Osiris. The seed of the dead deity would, according to the supernaturalism, transmit upward [through the portal] from out of the underworld through the base (testes) of the obelisk and magically emit from the tower's head into the womb (dome) of Isis where incarnation into the sitting pharaoh/king/president would occur (during what Freemasons also call *the raising [of Osiris] ceremony*). In this way, Osiris could be habitually "born again" or reincarnated as Horus and constantly direct the spiritual destiny of the nation.

This metaphysical phenomenon, which originated with Nimrod/Semiramis and was central to numerous other ancient cultures, was especially developed in Egypt, where Nimrod/Semiramis were known as Osiris/Isis (and in Ezekiel chapter 8 the children of Israel set up the obelisk ["image of jealousy," verse 5] facing the entry of their temple—just as the dome faces the obelisk in Washington, DC, and in the Vatican City—and were condemned by God for worshipping the Sun [Ra] while weeping for Osiris [Tammuz]). The familiar Masonic figure of the point within a circle is the symbol of this union between Ra, Osiris, and Isis. The "point" represents Osiris' phallus in the center of the circle or womb of Isis, which in turn is enlivened by the sun rays from Ra, just as is represented today at the Vatican, where the Egyptian obelisk of Osiris sits within a circle, and in Washington, DC, where the obelisk does similarly, situated so as to be the first thing the sun (Ra) strikes as it rises over the capital city and which, when viewed from overhead, forms the magical point within a circle known as a *circumpunct*. The sorcery is further amplified, according to ancient occultic beliefs, by the presence of the Reflecting Pool in DC, which serves as a mirror to heaven and "transferring point" for [the immortals'] spirits and energies.

And just what is it the spirits see when they look downward on the Reflecting Pool in Washington? They find a city dedicated to and built in honor of the legendary deities Isis and Osiris complete with the thirteen gathered pieces of Osiris (America's original thirteen colonies); the required obelisk known as the Washington Monument; the Capitol dome (of Isis) for impregnation and incarnation of deity into each pharaoh (President); and last but not least, the official government buildings erected to face their respective counterparts and whose cornerstones—including the US. Capitol dome—were dedicated during astrological alignments related to the zodiacal constellation Virgo (Isis) as required for the magic to occur.

Where the Vitality of Osiris/Apollo (the Beast that Was, and Is Not, and Yet Is) Pulsates in Anticipation of His Final "Raising"

The 330-ton obelisk in St. Peter's Square in the Vatican City is not just any obelisk. It was cut from a single block of red granite during the fifth dynasty of Egypt to stand as Osiris' erect phallus at the Temple of the Sun in ancient Heliopolis, the city of "On" in the Bible, dedicated to Ra, Osiris, and Isis. The obelisk was moved from Heliopolis to the Julian Forum of Alexandria by Emperor Augustus and later from thence (approximately AD 37) by Caligula to Rome to stand at the spine of the circus. There, under Nero, its excited presence maintained a counter vigil over countless brutal Christian executions, including the martyrdom of the apostle Peter (according to some historians). Over fifteen hundred years following that, Pope Sixtus V ordered hundreds of workmen under celebrated engineer-architects Giovanni and Domenico Fontana (who also erected three other ancient obelisks in the old Roman city, including one dedicated to Osiris by Rameses III—at the Piazza del Popolo, Piazza di S. Maria Maggiore, and Piazza di S. Giovanni in Laterano) to move the phallic pillar to the center of St. Peter's Square in Rome. This proved a daunting task, which took over four months, nine hundred laborers, one hundred forty horses, and seventy winches. Though worshipped at its present location ever since by countless admirers, the proximity of the obelisk to the old Basilica was formerly "resented as something of a provocation, almost as a slight to the Christian religion. It had stood there like a false idol, as it were vaingloriously, on what was believed to be the center of the accursed circus where the early Christians and St. Peter had been put to death. Its sides, then as now, were graven with dedications to [the worst of ruthless pagans] Augustus and Tiberius."[571]

The fact that many traditional Catholics as well as Protestants perceived such idols of stone to be not only objects of heathen adoration but the worship of demons (see Acts 7:41–42; Psalms 96:5; and 1 Corinthians 10:20) makes what motivated Pope Sixtus to erect the phallus of Osiris in the heart of St. Peter's Square, located in Vatican City and bordering St. Peter's Basilica, very curious. To ancient Christians, the image of a cross and symbol of Jesus sitting atop (or emitting from) the head of a demonic god's erect manhood would have been at a minimum a very serious blasphemy. Yet Sixtus was not content with simply restoring and using such ancient pagan relics (which were believed in those days to actually house the pagan spirit they represented) but even destroyed Christian artifacts in the process. Michael W. Cole, associate professor in the department of the history of art at the University of Pennsylvania, and Professor Rebecca E. Zorach, associate professor of art history at the University of Chicago, raise critical questions about this in their scholarly book *The Idol in the Age of Art* when they state:

Whereas Gregory, to follow the chroniclers, had ritually dis-
membered the city's *imagines daemonem* [demonic images], Sixtus fixed what was in disrepair, added missing parts, and made
the "idols" into prominent urban features. Two of the four obelisks had to be reconstructed from found or excavated pieces....
The pope was even content to destroy *Christian* antiquities in
the process: as Jennifer Montagu has pointed out, the bronze
for the statues of Peter and Paul came from the medieval doors
of S. Agnese, from the Scala Santa at the Lateran, and from a
ciborium at St. Peter's.

[Sixtus] must have realized that, especially in their work
on the two [broken obelisks], they were not merely repairing
injured objects, but also restoring a *type*... In his classic book
The Gothic Idol, Michael Camille showed literally dozens of
medieval images in which the freestanding figure atop a column betokened the pagan idol. The sheer quantity of Camille's
examples makes it clear that the device, and what it stood for,
would have been immediately recognizable to medieval viewers,
and there is no reason to assume that, by Sixtus's time, this had
ceased to be true.[572]

The important point made by professors Cole and Zorach is that
at the time Sixtus was busy reintroducing to the Roman public square
restored images and statues on columns, the belief remained strong that
these idols housed their patron deity, and further that, if these were not
treated properly and even placed into service during proper constellations related to their myth, it could beckon evil omens. Leonardo da
Vinci had even written in his Codex Urbinas how those who would
adore and pray to the image were likely to believe the god represented
by it was alive in the stone and watching their behavior. There is strong
indication that Sixtus believed this too, and that he "worried about the
powers that might inhabit his new urban markers."[573] This was clearly
evident when the cross was placed on top of the obelisk in the midst of

St. Peter's Square and the pope marked the occasion by conducting the ancient rite of exorcism against the phallic symbol. First scheduled to occur on September 14 to coincide with the liturgical Feast of the Exaltation of the Cross and not coincidently under the zodiacal sign of Virgo (Isis), the event was delayed until later in the month and fell under the sign of Libra, representing a zenith event for the year. On that morning, a pontifical High Mass was held just before the cross was raised from a portable altar to the apex of Baal's Shaft (as such phallic towers were also known). While clergy prayed and a choir sang Psalms, Pope Sixtus stood facing the obelisk and, extending his hand toward it, announced: "Exorcizote, creaturalapidis, in nomine Dei" ("I exorcize you, creature of stone, in the name of God"). Sixtus then cast sanctified water upon the pillar's middle, then its right side, then left, then above, and finally below to form a cross, followed by, "In nomine Patris, et Filij, et Spiritussancti. Amen" ("In the Name of the Father and of the Son and of the Holy Ghost. Amen"). He then crossed himself three times and watched as the symbol of Christ was placed atop Osiris' erect phallus.

Washington dome facing obelisk

Vatican dome facing obelisk

Yet if what Sixtus established in the heart of Vatican City gives some readers pause (numerous other signature events by Sixtus aligned the Sistine city with constellations sacred to Osiris and Isis, which we are not taking time to discuss here but that caused Profs. Zorach and Cole to conclude that, in the end, Sixtus wanted to remain *in the good graces of the pagan gods*), in Washington, DC, near the west end of the National Mall, the obelisk built by Freemasons and dedicated to America's first president brings the fullest meaning to the Nephilim-originated and modern porn-industry impression that "size matters." This is no crude declaration, as adepts of ritual sex-magic know, and dates back to ancient women who wanted to give birth to the offspring of the gods and who judged the size of the male generative organ as indicative of the "giant" genetics or divine seed needed for such offspring. While such phallic symbols have been and still are found in cultures around the world, in ancient Egypt, devotion to this type "obscene divinity" began with Amun-Min and reached its crescendo in the obelisks of Osiris.

Throughout Greece and Rome, the god Priapus (son of Aphrodite) was invoked as a symbol of such divine fertility and later became directly linked to the cult of pornography reflected in the more modern sentiments about "size." This is important because, in addition to the Washington Monument being intentionally constructed to be the tallest obelisk of its kind in the world at 6,666 (some say 6,660) inches high and 666 inches wide along each side at the base, one of the original concepts for the Washington Monument included Apollo (the Greek version of Osiris) triumphantly returning in his heavenly chariot, and another illustrating a tower "like that of Babel" for its head. Any of these designs would have been equally appropriate to the 3,300-pound pyramidal capstone it now displays, as all three concepts carried the meaning necessary to accomplish what late researcher David Flynn described as "the same secret knowledge preserved by the mystery schools since the time of the Pelasgians [that] display modern Isis Osiris worship."[574] This is to say, the "seed" discharged from a Tower-of-Babel-shaped head would magically issue forth the same as would proceed from the existing Egyptian capstone—the offspring of Apollo/Osiris/Nimrod.

The greatest minds in Freemasonry, whose beliefs set the tone for the design of the capital city, its Great Seal, its dome, and its obelisk, understood and wrote about this intent. Albert Pike described it as Isis and Osiris' "Active and Passive Principles of the Universe...commonly symbolized by the generative parts of man and woman,"[575] and Freemason writer Albert Mackey described not only the obelisk, but added the importance of the circle around its base, saying, "The Phallus was an imitation of the male generative organ. It was represented...by a column [obelisk] that was surrounded by a circle at the base."[576]

In Egypt, where the parodies and rituals for raising Osiris to life through these magical constructs was perfected, pharaoh served as the "fit extension" for the reborn god to take residence in as the "sex act" was ritualized at the temple of Amun-Ra. The all-seeing eye of Horus/Osiris/Apollo above the unfinished pyramid on the Great Seal of the United States forecasts the culmination of this event—that is, the actual return of Osiris—for the United States closely following the year 2012, and the dome and obelisk stand ready for the metaphysical ritual to be performed in secret by the elite. We use the phrase "performed in secret" because what the vast majority of people throughout America do not know is that the "raising" ceremony is still conducted inside the head-quarters of the Scottish Rite Freemasonry in the House of the Temple by the Supreme Council 33rd Degree over Washington, DC, for at least two reasons. First, whenever a Mason reaches the Master level, the ritual includes a parody representing the death, burial, and future resurrection of Hiram Abiff (Osiris). The world at large finally caught a glimpse of this custom when Dan Brown, in his book *The Lost Symbol,* opened with a scene depicting the start of the tradition:

> The secret is how to die.
>
> Since the beginning of time, the secret had always been how to die.
>
> The thirty-four-year-old initiate gazed down at the human skull cradled in his palms. The skull was hollow, like a bowl, filled with bloodred wine.
>
> Drink it, he told himself. You have nothing to fear.
>
> As was tradition, he had begun his journey adorned in the ritualistic garb of a medieval heretic being led to the gallows, his loose-fitting shirt gaping open to reveal his pale chest, his left pant leg rolled up to the knee, and his right sleeve rolled up to the elbow. Around his neck hung a heavy rope noose—a "cable-tow" as the brethren called it. Tonight, however, like the brethren bearing witness, he was dressed as a master.
>
> The assembly of brothers encircling him all were adorned in their full regalia of lambskin aprons, sashes, and white gloves. Around their necks hung ceremonial jewels that glistened like ghostly eyes in the muted light. Many of these men held power-ful stations in life, and yet the initiate knew their worldly ranks meant nothing within these walls. Here all men were equals, sworn brothers sharing a mystical bond.
>
> As he surveyed the daunting assembly, the initiate wondered who on the outside would ever believe that this collection of men would assemble in one place…much less this place. The room looked like a holy sanctuary from the ancient world.

The truth, however, was stranger still.

I am just blocks away from the White House.

This colossal edifice, located at 1733 Sixteenth Street NW in Washington, D.C., was a replica of a pre-Christian temple—the temple of King Mausolus, the original mausoleum…a place to be taken after death. Outside the main entrance, two seventeen-ton sphinxes guarded the bronze doors. The interior was an ornate labyrinth of ritualistic chambers, halls, sealed vaults, libraries, and even a hallow wall that held the remains of two human bodies. The initiate had been told every room in the building held a secret, and yet he knew no room held deeper secrets than the gigantic chamber in which he was currently kneeling with a skull cradled in his palms.

The Temple Room.[577]

While such drama makes for excellent fiction, *The Lost Symbol* turns out to be at best a love fest and at worst a cover up between Dan Brown and the Freemasons. However, one thing Brown said is true—the Temple Room in the Heredom does hold an important *secret*. We've been there, stood inside and prayed for protection under our breath, because according to our sources (who provided facts that have not been denied when we were interviewed by a US congressman, US senator, and even a 33rd-Degree Freemason on his radio show), in addition to when a Mason reaches the Master level, the ancient raising ceremony is conducted following the election of an American president—just as their Egyptian forefathers did at the temple of Amun-Ra in Karnak—in keeping with the tradition of installing within him the representative spirit of Osiris until such time as the god himself shall fulfill the Great Seal prophecy and return in flesh.

In the prologue of 33rd-Degree Freemason Manly P. Hall's book, *The Lost Keys of Freemasonry*, detailed recounting of the underlying and familiar story of Hiram Abiff (Osiris) is told, who sets out to construct the temple of the Great Architect of the Universe, but is killed by three spectres. This story, impersonated every time an initiate reaches the level of Master Mason, is by admission of Freemasons a retelling of the death-epic of the god Osiris. In *Lost Keys*, Hall narrates how the Great Architect gives Hiram (Osiris) the trestleboard for the construction of the great temple, and when he is killed by three ruffians, the Great Architect bathes him in "a glory celestial," as in the glory surrounding the all-seeing eye of Osiris above the pyramid on the Great Seal. The Great Architect follows this by charging those who would finish the building with the task of finding the body of Hiram (Osiris) and raising him from the dead. When *this* has been accomplished, the great work will conclude and the god will inhabit the (third) temple:

> Seek ye where the broken twig lies and the dead stick molds away, where the clouds float together and the stones rest by the hillside, for all these mark the grave of Hiram [Osiris] who has carried my Will with him to the tomb. This eternal quest is yours until ye have found your Builder, until the cup giveth up its secret, until the grave giveth up its ghosts. No more shall I speak until ye have found and raised my beloved Son [Osiris], and have listened to the words of my Messenger and with Him as your guide have finished the temple which I shall then inhabit. Amen.[578]

Thus the appearance of the uncapped pyramid of Giza on the Great Seal of the United States echoes the ancient pagan as well as Masonic beliefs concerning the old mysteries and the prophecy of the return of Osiris/Apollo/Nimrod. In *Rosicrucian and Masonic Origins*, Hall, who had said in *The Secret Teachings of All Ages* that the Great Pyramid was "the tomb of Osiris,"[579] explains that Preston, Gould, Mackey, Oliver, Pike, and nearly every other great historian of Freemasonry were aware of this connection between Freemasonry and the ancient mysteries and primitive ceremonials based on Osiris. "These eminent Masonic scholars have all recognized in the legend of Hiram Abiff an adaptation of the Osiris myth; nor do they deny that the major part of the symbolism of the craft is derived from the pagan institutions of antiquity when the gods were venerated in secret places with strange figures and appropriate rituals."[580] In *Morals and Dogma*, Albert Pike even enumerated the esoteric significance of the Osiris epic at length, adding that lower-level Masons (Blue Masonry) are ignorant of its true meaning, which is only known to those who are "initiated into the Mysteries."[581] Pike also spoke of the star Sirius—connected to Isis and at length to Lucifer/Satan—as "still glittering" in the Masonic lodges as "the Blazing Star." Elsewhere in *Morals and Dogma*, Pike reiterated that the "All-Seeing Eye…was the emblem of Osiris"[582] and that the "Sun was termed by the Greeks the Eye of Jupiter, and the Eye of the World; and his is the All-Seeing Eye in our Lodges."[583]

Magic Squares, 666, and Human Sacrifice?

While finding the body of Osiris and resurrecting it—either figuratively or literally—is central to the prophetic beliefs of Freemasonry, until Apollo/Osiris return, formal procedures will continue in secret for installing within America's national leader the divine right of kingship through the raising of Osiris ceremony. It is very important to note how, when this ritual is carried out in the Temple Room of the Heredom, it unfolds below a vast thirty-six-paneled skylight that forms a stylized "magic 666 square." Around the four sides of the skylight can be seen the winged sun-disc. This positioning above the altar is in keeping with historical occultism. Egyptian magicians employed the same symbolism above the altar for invoking the sun deity. In the St. Martin's Press book *Practical Egyptian Magic* it is noted: "Emblematic of the element of air, this consists of a circle or solar-type disk enclosed by a pair of wings. In ritual magic it is suspended over the altar in an easterly direction and used when invoking the protection and co-operation of the sylphs." [584] The Renaissance occultist Paracelsus describes these sylphs as invisible beings of the air, entities that the New Testament book of Ephesians (2:2) describes as working beneath "the prince [Lucifer/Satan] of the power of the air, the spirit that now worketh in the children of disobedience."

In applied magic, the "magic square of the sun" itself was associated in antiquity with binding or loosing the sun god Apollo/Osiris and was the most famous of all magical utilities because the sum of any row, column, or diagonal is equal to the number 111, while the total of all the numbers in the square from 1 to 36 equals 666. In the magical Hebrew Kabbalah, each planet is associated with a number, intelligence, and spirit. The intelligence of the sun is Nakiel, which equals 111, while the spirit of the sun is Sorath and equals 666. It makes sense therefore that Freemasons built the Washington Monument obelisk to form a magic square at its base and to stand 555 feet above earth, so that when a line is drawn 111 feet directly below it toward the underworld of Osiris, it equals the total of 666 (555+111=666)—the exact values of the binding square of the Sun God Apollo/Osiris installed in the ceiling above where the Osiris raising ceremony is conducted in the House of the Temple.

6	32	3	34	35	1
7	11	27	28	8	30
19	14	16	15	23	24
18	20	22	21	17	13
25	29	10	9	26	12
36	5	33	4	2	31

Magic 666 square

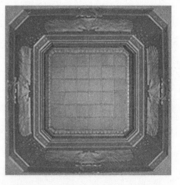

Thirty-six paneled magic-square skylight above the altar in the House of the Temple

Freemason and occultist Aleister Crowley practiced such Kabbalah and likewise connected the number 111 with the number 6, which he described as the greatest number of the sun or sun god. He employed the magic square in rituals to make contact with a spirit described in *The Book of the Sacred Magic of Abramelin the Mage*, a work from the 1600s or 1700s that involves evocation of demons. In Book Four of the magic text, a set of magical word-square talismans provides for the magician's

Holy Guardian Angel who appears and reveals occult secrets for calling forth and gaining control over the twelve underworld authorities, including Lucifer, Satan, Leviathan, and Belial. In addition to Crowley, the most influential founding father and Freemason, Benjamin Franklin, not only used such magic squares, but according to his own biography and numerous other authoritative sources even created magic squares and circles for use by himself and his brethren. Yet the gentle appearance and keen astuteness of America's most famous bespeckled Freemason might have hidden an even darker history than the story told by those magic squares, which his strong, deft hands once held. Award-winning filmmaker Christian J. Pinto explains:

> One of the most influential founding fathers, and the only one of them to have signed all of the original founding documents (the Declaration of Independence, the Treaty of Paris, and the U.S. Constitution) was Benjamin Franklin. Franklin was… without question, deeply involved in Freemasonry and in other secret societies. He belonged to secret groups in the three countries involved in the War of Independence: America, France, and England. He was master of the Masonic Lodge of Philadelphia; while over in France, he was master of the Nine Sisters Lodge, from which sprang the French Revolution. In England, he joined a rakish political group founded by Sir Francis Dashwood (member of Parliament, advisor to King George III) called the "Monks of Medmenham Abbey," otherwise known as the "Hellfire Club." This eighteenth-century group is described as follows:
>
> > The Hellfire Club was an exclusive, English club that met sporadically during the mid-eighteenth century. Its purpose, at best, was to mock traditional religion and conduct orgies. At worst, it involved the indulgence of satanic rites and sacrifices. The club to which Franklin belonged was established by Francis Dashwood, a member of Parliament and friend of Franklin. The club, which

consisted of "The Superior Order" of twelve members, allegedly took part in basic forms of satanic worship. In addition to taking part in the occult, orgies and parties with prostitutes were also said to be the norm.

Pinto continues this connection between Benjamin Franklin and dark occultism:

On February 11, 1998, the *Sunday Times* reported that ten bodies were dug up from beneath Benjamin Franklin's home at 36 Craven Street in London. The bodies were of four adults and six children. They were discovered during a costly renovation of Franklin's former home. The *Times* reported: "Initial estimates are that the bones are about two hundred years old and were buried at the time Franklin was living in the house, which was his home from 1757 to 1762 and from 1764 to 1775. Most of the bones show signs of having been dissected, sawn or cut. One skull has been drilled with several holes."

The original *Times* article reported that the bones were "deeply buried, probably to hide them because grave robbing was illegal." They said, "There could be more buried, and there probably are." But the story doesn't end there. Later reports from the Benjamin Franklin House reveal that not only were human remains found, but animal remains were discovered as well. This is where things get very interesting. From the published photographs, some of the bones appear to be blackened or charred, as if by fire…. It is well documented that Satanists perform ritual killings of both humans and animals alike.[585]

While many students of history are aware of the magic 666 square and its use by occultists down through time to control the spirit of Apollo/Osiris, what some will not know is how this magical binding and loosing of supernatural entities also extends to the testes of Washington's 6,666-inch-high phallic obelisk, dedicated by Freemasons seventy-two years following 1776 [note again the magic number 72], where a Bible (that Dan Brown identified as the "Lost Symbol" in his latest book) is encased within the cornerstone of its 666-inch-square base. One wonders what type of Bible this is. If a Masonic version, it is covered with occult symbols of the Brotherhood and Rosicrucianism and the purpose for having it so encased might be to energize the Mason's interpretation of Scripture in bringing forth the seed of Osiris/Apollo from the testes/ cornerstone. If it is a non-Masonic Bible, the purpose may be to "bind" its influence inside the 666 square and thus allow the seed of Osiris/ Apollo to prevail. The dedication of the cornerstone during the astrological alignment with Virgo/Isis as the sun was passing over Sirius indicates a high degree of magic was indeed intended by those in charge.[586]

Prophecy about the Coming of Apollo/Osiris

After documenting how Freemason US President Franklin D. Roosevelt and his Vice President Henry Wallace, also a Freemason, pushed to get the Great Seal of the United States placed on the one-dollar bill, and how both men believed the symbolism and mottoes of the seal were a Masonic-approved prophecy about a New World Order that would start at the second coming of Apollo/Osiris/Nimrod, Tom Horn continued in *Zenith 2016*:

Whatever the case for Wallace, like Manly Hall had, he and Roosevelt viewed the all-seeing eye above the unfinished pyramid as pointing to the return (or reincarnation) of this coming savior, whose arrival would cap the pyramid and launch the New World Order. The all-seeing eye on the Great Seal is fashioned after the Eye of Horus, the offspring of Osiris (or Osiris resurrected), as both men surely understood. Aliester Crowley, 33rd-Degree Freemason (the "wickedest man on earth") and a Roerich occult contemporary, often spoke of this as the "New Age of Horus" and the breaking dawn of the rebirth of Osiris. That [the United states president, vice president, and] such mystics and Freemasons simultaneously used such identical language is telling, given that the Great Seal's mottoes and symbolism relate to both Osiris and Apollo specifically, yet as one. Osiris is the dominant theme of the Egyptian symbols, his resurrection and return, while the *mottoes* of the seal point directly to Apollo, and the eagle, a pagan emblem of Jupiter, to Apollo's father. For instance, the motto *annuity coeptis* is from Virgil's *Aeneid*, in which Ascanius, the son of Aeneas from conquered Troy, prays to Apollo's father, Jupiter [Zeus]. Charles Thompson, designer of the Great Seal's final version, condensed line 625 of book IX of Virgil's *Aeneid*, which reads, *Juppiter omnipotes, audacibus annue coeptis* ("All-powerful Jupiter favors [the] daring under-takings"), to *Annuitcoeptis* ("He approves [our] undertakings"), while the phrase *novus ordo seclorum* ("a new order of the ages") was adapted in 1782 from inspiration Thompson found in a prophetic line in Virgil's Eclogue IV: *Magnus ab integro seclorum nascitur ordo* (Virgil's *Eclogue IV*, line 5), the interpretation of the original Latin being, "And the majestic roll of circling centuries begins anew." This phrase is from the Cumaean Sibyl (a pagan prophetess of Apollo, identified in the Bible as a demonic deceiver) and involves the future birth of a divine son, spawned of "a new breed of men sent down from heaven" (what Roosevelt, Wallace, and Roerich were looking for) when he receives "the life of gods, and sees Heroes with gods commingling." According to the prophecy, this is Apollo, son of Jupiter (Zeus), who returns to earth through mystical "life" given to him from the gods when the deity Saturn returns to reign over the earth in a new pagan golden age.

From the beginning of the prophecy we read:

> Now the last age by Cumae's Sibyl sung Has come and gone, and the majestic roll Of circling centuries begins anew: Justice returns, returns old Saturn's reign, With a new breed of men sent down from heaven. Only do thou, at the boy's birth in whom The iron shall cease, the golden race arise, Befriend him, chaste Lucina; 'tis thine own Apollo reigns.
>
> He shall receive the life of gods, and see Heroes with gods commingling, and himself Be seen of them, and with his father's worth Reign o'er a world....

> Assume thy greatness, for the time draws nigh, Dear child of gods, great progeny of Jove [Jupiter/Zeus]! See how it totters— the world's orbed might, Earth, and wide ocean, and the vault profound, All, see, enraptured of the coming time![587]

According to Virgil and the Cumaean Sibyl, whose prophecy formed the *novus ordo seclorum* of the Great Seal of the United States, the New World Order begins during a time of chaos when the earth and oceans are tottering—a time like today. This is when the "son" of promise arrives on earth—Apollo incarnate—a pagan savior born of "a new breed of men sent down from heaven" when "heroes" and "gods" are blended together. This sounds eerily similar to what the Watchers did during the creation of the Nephilim and to what scientists are doing this century through genetic engineering of human-animal chimeras. But to understand why such a fanciful prophecy about Apollo, son of Jupiter, returning to earth should be important to you: In ancient literature, Jupiter was the Roman replacement of Yahweh as the greatest of the gods—a "counter-Yahweh." His son Apollo is a replacement of Jesus, a "counter-Jesus." This Apollo comes to rule the final New World Order, when "Justice returns, returns old Saturn's [Satan's] reign." The ancient goddess Justice, who returns Satan's reign (*Saturnia regna*, the pagan golden age), was known to the Egyptians as Ma'at and to the Greeks as Themis, while to the Romans she was Lustitia. Statues and reliefs of her adorn thousands of government buildings and courts around the world, especially in Washington, DC, as familiar Lady Justice, blindfolded and holding scales and a sword. She represents the enforcement of secular law and is, according to the Sibyl's conjure, the authority that will require global compliance to the zenith of Satan's dominion concurrent with the coming of Apollo. What's more, the Bible's accuracy concerning this subject is alarming, including the idea that "pagan justice" will require surrender to a satanic system in a final world order under the rule of Jupiter's son.

In the New Testament, the identity of the god Apollo, repeat-coded in the Great Seal of the United States as the Masonic "messiah" who returns to rule the earth, is the same spirit—verified by the *same name*—that will inhabit the political leader of the end-times New World Order. According to key Bible prophecies, the Antichrist will be the progeny or incarnation of the ancient spirit, *Apollo*. Second Thessalonians 2:3 warns: "Let no man deceive you by any means: for that day shall not come, except there come a falling away first, and that man of sin be revealed, the son of *perdition* [*Apoleia*; Apollyon, Apollo]" (emphasis added). Numerous scholarly and classical works identify "Apollyon" as the god "Apollo"—the Greek deity "of death and pestilence," and *Webster's Dictionary* points out that "Apollyon" was a common variant of "Apollo" throughout history. An example of this is found in the classical play by the ancient Greek playwright Aeschylus, *The Agamemnon of Aeschylus*, in which Cassandra repeats more than once, "Apollo, thou destroyer, O Apollo, Lord of fair streets, Apollyon to me."[588] Accordingly, the name Apollo turns up in ancient literature with the verb *apollymi* or *apollyo* (destroy), and scholars including W. R. F. Browning believe apostle Paul may have identified the god Apollo as the "spirit of Antichrist" operating behind the persecuting Roman emperor, Domitian, who wanted to be recognized as "Apollo incarnate" in his day. Such identifying of Apollo with despots and "the spirit of Antichrist" is consistent even in modern history. For instance, note how Napoleon's name literally translates to "the true Apollo."

Revelation 17:8 likewise ties the coming of Antichrist with Apollo, revealing that the Beast shall ascend from the bottomless pit and enter him:

> The Beast that thou sawest was, and is not; and shall ascend out of the Bottomless Pit, and go into *perdition* [*Apolia*, Apollo]: and they that dwell on the Earth shall wonder, whose names were not written in the Book of Life from the foundation of the world, when they behold the Beast that was, and is not, and yet is. (emphasis added)

Among other things, this means the Great Seal of the United States is a prophecy, hidden in plain sight by the Founding Fathers and devotees of Bacon's New Atlantis for more than two hundred years, foretelling the return of a terrifying demonic god who seizes control of earth in the new order of the ages. This supernatural entity was known and feared in ancient times by different names: Apollo, Osiris, and even farther back as Nimrod, whom Masons consider to be the father of their institution.[589]

The Washington Stargate

Through Masonic alchemistry, presidential *apotheosis*—that is, the leader of the United States (America's pharaoh) being transformed into a god within the Capitol dome/womb of Isis in sight of the obelisk of Osiris (the Washington Monument to those whom Masons call "profane," the uninitiated)—actually began with America's first and most revered president, Master Freemason George Washington. In fact, Masons in attendance at Washington's funeral in 1799 cast sprigs of acacia "to symbolize both Osiris' resurrection and Washington's imminent resurrection in the realm where Osiris presides."[590] According to this Masonic enchantment, Osiris (Horus) was rising within a new president in DC as Washington took his role as Osiris of the underworld. This is further simulated and symbolized by the three-story design of the Capitol building. Freemasons point out how the Great Pyramid of Giza was made up of three main chambers to facilitate Pharaoh's transference to Osiris, just as the temple of Solomon was a three-sectioned tabernacle made up of the ground floor, middle chamber, and Holy of Holies. The US Capitol building was thus designed with three stories—Washington's Tomb, the Crypt, and the Rotunda—capped by a dome. Each floor has significant esoteric meaning regarding apotheosis, and the tomb of Washington is empty. The official narrative is that a legal issue kept the government from placing Washington's body there. However, just as the tomb of Jesus Christ was emptied before His ascension, Washington is not in his tomb because he has travelled to the home of Osiris, as depicted high overhead in the womb/dome of Isis.

When visitors to Washington, DC, tour the Capitol, one of the unquestionable highlights is to visit the womb of Isis—the Capitol Dome—where, when peering upward from inside Isis' continuously pregnant belly, tourists can see hidden in plain sight Brumidi's 4,664-square-foot fresco, *The Apotheosis of George Washington*. The word "apotheosis" means to "deify" or to "become a god," and explains part of the reason US presidents, military commanders, and members of Congress lay in state in the Capitol dome. The womb of Isis is where they go at death to magically reach apotheosis and transform into gods.

Those who believe the United States was founded on Christianity and visit the Capitol for the first time will be surprised by the stark contrast to historic Christian artwork of the ascension of Jesus Christ compared to the "heaven" George Washington rises into from within the energized Capitol dome/womb of Isis. It is not occupied by angels, but with devils and pagan deities important to Masonic belief. These include Hermes, Neptune, Venus (Isis), Ceres, Minerva, and Vulcan (Satan), of course, the son of Jupiter and Juno to which human sacrifices are made and about whom Manly Hall said brings "the seething energies of Lucifer" into the Mason's hands.[591]

For high-degree Masons and other illuminatus, the symbolism of Washington surrounded by pagan entities and transformed into a heathen god is entirely appropriate. Deeply rooted in the mysteries of ancient societies and at the core of Rosicrucianism and those rituals of the Brotherhood that founded the United States is the idea that chosen humans are selected by these supernatural forces and their earthly kingdoms are formed and guided by these gods. As a deist, George Washington believed that by following the enlightened path guided by principles of Freemasonry, he would achieve apotheosis and become deified. Affirming this widespread belief among America's founding fathers are numerous works of art throughout Washington, DC. On an 1865 card titled "Washington and Lincoln Apotheosis," Abraham Lincoln is depicted transcending death to meet Washington among the gods. What god did Lincoln become? Humanist and American poet Walt Whitman eulogized him as the "American Osiris." Horatio Greenough's

1840, government-commissioned statue of George Washington shows the first president enthroned as the god Jupiter/Zeus. On one side of Washington/Zeus is his son Hercules clutching two serpents, and on the other side is his son Apollo. Greenough admitted this vision was based on presenting Washington as a deified figure, the father of Apollo similar to what the Hebrew God is to Jesus. Another representation of Washington as Jupiter/Zeus is a painting by Rembrandt Peale that hangs in the Old Senate Chamber. Peale painted it in a "poetic frenzy" in a stone oval window atop a stone sill engraved "PATRIAE PATER" ("Father of His Country"). The window is decorated with a garland of oak leaves, which was sacred to Jupiter, and is surmounted by the "Phydian head of Jupiter" (Peale's description) on the keystone. The symbol of Jupitor/Zeus, the father of Apollo above Washington's head, reflects the same conviction scripted on America's Great Seal—that the divine being watching over Washington and the founding of the country was Jupiter/Zeus (Lucifer in the Bible), whose son is coming again to rule the *novus ordo seclorum*. Even the name "Capitol Hill" for the government center in Washington originated with this concept. Thomas Jefferson selected it to reflect Capitoline Hill from ancient Rome, where Jupiter (Jove) was the king of the gods. In more recent times, the Congressional Prayer Room was set up next to the Rotunda, where representatives and senators can go to meditate. The centerpiece in this room is a large, stained-glass window with George Washington between the two sides of the Great Seal of the United States. What is striking about this feature is that the order of the seal is inverted against protocol, with the reverse side of the seal, which should be at the bottom, above Washington's head, and the front of the seal, which should be at the top, under his feet. In this position, Washington is seen on his knees praying beneath the uncapped pyramid and the all-seeing eye of Horus/Osiris/Apollo. I leave the reader to interpret what this clearly is meant to signify.

Beside those pagan gods which accompany Washington inside the Capitol dome, the scene is rich with symbols analogous with ancient and modern magic, including the powerful trident—considered of the utmost importance for sorcery and indispensable to the efficacy

The Apotheosis of George Washington Above 72 Pentagrams

of infernal rites—and the caduceus, tied to Apollo and Freemasonic Gnosticism in which Jesus was a myth based on Apollo's son, Asclepius, the god of medicine and healing whose snake-entwined staff remains a symbol of medicine today. Occult numerology associated with the legend of Isis and Osiris is also encoded throughout the painting, such as the thirteen maidens, the six scenes of pagan gods around the perimeter forming a hexagram, and the entire scene bounded by the powerful Pythagorian/Freemasonic "binding" utility—seventy-two five-pointed stars within circles.

Seventy-Two (72) Pentagrams to Control the Immortals

Much has been written by historians within and without Masonry as to the relevance of the number seventy-two (72) and the alchemy related to it. In the Kabbalah, Freemasonry, and Jewish apocalyptic writings, the number equals the total of wings Enoch received when transformed into Metatron (3 Enoch 9:2). This plays an important role for the Brotherhood, as Metatron or "the angel in the whirlwind" was enabled as the guiding spirit over America during George W. Bush's administration for the purpose of directing the *future* and *fate* of the United States (as also prayed by Congressman Major R. Owens of New York before the House of Representatives on Wednesday, February 28, 2001).

But in the context of the Capitol dome and the seventy-two stars that circle Washington's apotheosis in the womb of Isis, the significance of this symbolism is far more important. In sacred literature, including the Bible, stars are symbolic of angels, and within Masonic Gnosticism, seventy-two is the number of fallen angels or "kosmokrators" (reflected in the seventy-two conspirators that controlled Osiris' life in Egyptian myth) that currently administer the affairs of earth. Experts in the study of the Divine Council believe that, beginning at the Tower of Babel, the world and its inhabitants were disinherited by the sovereign God of Israel and placed under the authority of seventy-two angels (the earliest records had the number of angels at seventy, but this was later changed to seventy-two), who became corrupt and disloyal to God in their administration of those nations (Psalm 82). These beings quickly became worshipped on earth as gods following Babel, led by Nimrod/Gilgamesh/Osiris/Apollo. Consistent with this tradition, the designers of the Capitol dome, the Great Seal of the United States, and the obelisk Washington Monument circled the *Apotheosis of Washington* with seventy-two pentagram stars, dedicated the obelisk seventy-two years after the signing of the Declaration of Independence, and placed seventy-two stones on the Great Seal's uncapped pyramid, above which the eye of Horus/Osiris/Apollo stares. These three sets of seventy-two (72), combined with the imagery and occult numerology of the Osiris/obelisk, the Isis/dome, and the oracular Great Seal, are richly symbolic of the influence of Satan and his angels over the world (see Luke 4:5–6, 2 Corinthians 4:4, and Ephesians 6:12) with a prophecy toward Satan's final earthly empire—the coming *novus ordo seclorum*, or new golden pagan age.

In order for the "inevitable" worship of Osiris to be "reestablished" on earth, the seventy-two demons that govern the nations must be controlled, thus they are set in magical constraints on the Great Seal, the Washington obelisk, and the pentagram circles around the *Apotheosis of Washington* to bind and force the desired effect.

In The Secret Destiny of America, Hall noted as well that the seventy-two stones of the pyramid on the Great Seal correspond to the seventy-two arrangements of the Tetragrammaton, or the four-lettered name of God in Hebrew. "These four letters can be combined in seventy-two combinations, resulting in what is called the Shemhamforesh, which represents, in turn, the laws, powers, and energies of Nature."[592] The idea that the mystical name of God could be invoked to bind or loose those supernatural agents (powers and energies of nature, as Hall called them) is meaningful creed within many occult tenets, including Kabbalah and Freemasonry. This is why the seventy-two stars are pentagram-shaped around the deified Freemason, George Washington. Medieval books of magic, or grimoires such as the Key of Solomon and the Lesser Key of Solomon not only identify the star systems Orion (Osiris) and Pleiades

(Apollo) as the "home" of these powers, but applies great importance to the pentagram shape of the stars for binding and loosing their influence. Adept Rosicrucians and Freemasons have long used these magical texts—the Key of Solomon and the Lesser Key of Solomon—to do just that. Peter Goodgame makes an important observation about this in "The Giza Discovery":

> One of the co-founders of the occult society known as the Golden Dawn[593] was a Rosicrucian Freemason named S. L. Mac-Gregor Mathers, who was the first to print and publish the Key of Solomon (in 1889) making it readily available to the public. Mathers describes it as a primary occult text: "The fountainhead and storehouse of Qabalistic Magic, and the origin of much of the Ceremonial Magic of mediaeval times, the 'Key' has been ever valued by occult writers as a work of the highest authority." Of the 519 esoteric titles included in the catalogue of the Golden Dawn library, the Key was listed as number one. As far as contents are concerned, the Key included instructions on how to prepare for the summoning of spirits including…demons.… One of the most well-known members of the Golden Dawn was the magician [and 33rd-degree freemason] Aleister Crowley. In 1904 Crowley published the first part of the five-part Lesser Key of Solomon known as the Ars Goetia,[594] which is Latin for "art of sorcery." The Goetia is a grimoire for summoning seventy-two different demons that were allegedly summoned, restrained, and put to work by King Solomon [according to Masonic mysticism] during the construction of the Temple of YHWH.[595]

Unlike other grimoires including the sixteenth-century *Pseudomonarchia Daemonum* and the seventeenth-century *Lemegeton*, the Key of Solomon does not contain the "Diabolical Signature" of the devil or demons, which the Ars Goetia describes as numbering seventy-two and who were, according to legend, constrained to assist King Solomon after he bound them in a bronze vessel sealed by magic symbols. Such books routinely contain invocations and curses for summoning, binding, and loosing these demons in order to force them to do the conjurers will. Even members of the church of Satan sign letters using the Shemhamforash, from the Hebrew name of God or Tetragrammaton, producing a blasphemous reinterpretation of the seventy-two entities. And then there is Michelangelo, who painted what we have called the "Sign of the Sixth Knuckle" inside the Sistine Chapel [mentioned elsewhere in *Zenith 2016*] that tied the prophecy on the Great Seal of the United States from the Cumaean Sibyl to the return of the Nephilim Apollo. But incredibly, Michelangelo also produced the Shemhamforash on the Vatican's famous ceiling, as his fresco has "an architectural design of 24 columns. On each of these columns are two cherubs, which are mirror imaged on the adjoining column totaling 48 cherubs figures. Then on the 12 triangular spandrels flanking the ceiling borders are an additional 24 nude figures (two bronze nude figures per triangular spandrel) also mirror imaging each other. This totals to 72 cherub figures or the 72 angels of God or names of God [or conversely, the 72 angels that fell and are now the demons or kosmokrators over the nations of the earth]."[596]

Once one understands the importance that these mystical keys hold in Kabbalah, Rosicrucianism, Freemasonic mysticism, and other mystery traditions, there can be (and is) but one reasonable interpretation for the connection in the Vatican and the seventy-two pentagrams at the base of the Apotheosis of Washington. These are there to bind and control the demons over the nations to honor the dedication made by early American Freemasons and certain Roman devotees for a New Atlantis and New World Order under the coming anti-Christ deity Osiris/Apollo.[597]

In other words, what may be the most powerful stargates in the world are in Washington DC and at the Vatican. And they are ready now to open, that the god of the immortals may come through to establish his new and final Golden Pagan Age.

Notes

1. Strongs # G0093, *Strong's Enhanced Lexicon,* BibleWorks for Windows 9.0 (Norfolk, VA: BibleWorks, 2013).
2. Ibid., # G1753.
3. Chuck Missler, "Bible Study: It's Time to Get Serious," KHouse (accessed February 11, 2015).
4. Francis Brown, Samuel Rolles Driver, and Charles Augustus Briggs, *Enhanced Brown-Driver-Briggs Hebrew and English Lexicon* (Oak Harbor, WA: Logos Research Systems, 2000), 521.
5. S. A. Meier, "Angel I," ed. Karel van der Toorn, Bob Becking, and Pieter W. van der Horst, *Dictionary of Deities and Demons in the Bible* (Leiden; Boston; Köln; Grand Rapids, MI; Cambridge: Brill; Eerdmans, 1999) 47.
6. Brown, Driver, and Briggs, *Enhanced Hebrew and English Lexicon,* 838.
7. Kenneth D. Boa, Robert M. Bowman Jr., *Sense and Nonsense about Angels and Demons* (Grand Rapids, MI: Zondervan, 2009) Kindle Location, 503.
8. Ibid., 507–514.
9. Meier, "Angel I," *Dictionary of Deities and Demons,* 47.
10. Robert L. Thomas, *New American Standard Hebrew-Aramaic and Greek Dictionaries: Updated Edition* (Anaheim: Foundation Publications, 1998).
11. T. N. D. Mettinger, "Seraphim," ed. Karel van der Toorn, Bob Becking, and Pieter W. van der Horst, *Dictionary of Deities and Demons in the Bible* (Leiden; Boston; Köln; Grand Rapids, MI; Cambridge: Brill; Eerdmans, 1999) 742.
12. "4Q Amram[b] (4Q544)," Geza Vermes, *The Dead Sea Scrolls in English,* revised and extended 4th ed. (Sheffield: Sheffield Academic Press, 1995) 312. (Previous ed.: London: Penguin, 1987.)
13. Mettinger, "Cherubim," *Dictionary of Deities and Demons,* 189–190.
14. "Putti" at arthistory.about.com.04-13.-2012, http://arthistory.about.com/cs/glossaries/g/p_putti.htm (accessed February 11, 2015).
15. Zohar Hadash, Ruth 95c in Bernard J. Bamberger, *Fallen Angels: Soldiers of Satan's Realm* (Philadelphia: Jewish Publication Society of America, 2006) 179.

16. James Strong, #H5175, *The Exhaustive Concordance of the Bible* (Ontario: Woodside Bible Fellowship, 1996).

17. Ibid., #H5172.

18. Ibid., #H5153, #H5702.

19. B. Waltke and M. O'Connor, *An Introduction to Biblical Hebrew Syntax* (Winona Lake, IN: Eisenbrauns, 1990) 261–262.

20. Michael S. Heiser, "The Nachash and His Seed: Some Explanatory Notes on Why the 'Serpent' in Genesis 3 Wasn't a Serpent," Dept. of Hebrew and Semitic Studies, UW-Madison, http://www.pidradio.com/wp-content/uploads/2007/02/nachashnotes.pdf.

21. Michael S. Heiser, *The Myth That Is True* (first draft, January 2, 2012, of what will be published as *The Unseen Realm* in 2015) 70.

22. MS Word 2013, *Bing Dictionary*.

23. Calvin B. Kendall, *The Allegory of the Church: Romanesque Portals and Their Verse Inscriptions* (Toronto: University of Toronto Press, 1998), xi.

24. James H. Holden, *A History of Horoscopic Astrology* (Tempe, AZ: American Federation of Astrologers, 1996) 1.

25. Prash Trivedi, *The 27 Celestial Portals: The Real Secret Behind the 12 Star Signs Revealed* (New Dehli: Sagar Publications, 2004) vii.

26. Carol Zaleski, Otherworld Journeys: Accounts of Near-death Experiences in Medieval and Modern Times (New York: Oxford, 1987), 24, cited in Hume, Portals, 10.

27. William Becker and Bethe Hagens, "The Planetary Grid: a New Synthesis," in *Anti-Gravity and the World Grid:* Lost Science Series, David Hatcher Childress ed., (Stelle, IL: Adventures Unlimited Press, 1987) 35.

28. Stephen Wagner, "Paranormal Hotspots," About.com, http://paranormal.about.com/cs/earthanomalies/a/aa110303_3.htm (accessed February 11, 2015).

29. John A. Keel, *Why UFOs: Operation Trojan Horse* (New York: Manor Books, 1970) 182.

30. John A. Keel, *Our Haunted Planet* (London: Futura Publications, 1975) 53.

31. Patrecia Gray, *The* Thing: *Mothman Devil, or Spirit* (CreateSpace Independent Publishing Platform, 2012) 1.

32. Keel, *Why UFOs*, 182.

33. Peter A. McCue, *Zones of Strangeness: An Examination of Paranormal and UFO Hot Spots* (Bloomington, IN: Authorhouse, 2012) 11.

34. Christopher O'Brien, *Secrets of the Mysterious Valley* (SCB Distributors, 2013) Kindle Locations 1101–1104.

35. Ibid., 53–56.

36. Zack Van Eyck, "Frequent Flyers," *Deseret News,* June 30 1996, http://www.deseretnews.com/article/498676/FREQUENT-FLIERS.html?pg=all (accessed February 11, 2015).

37. Van Eyck, "Frequent Flyers."

38. Brandon Griggs, *Utah Curiosities: Quirky Characters, Roadside Oddities and Other Offbeat Stuff,* Curiosities Series (Guilford, Conn.: Insiders, 2007) 102.

39. McCue, *Zones of Strangeness,* 418.

40. Ibid.,420.
41. Rob Riggs, *In the Big Thicket: On the Trail of the Wild Man, Exploring Nature's Mysterious Dimension* (New York: Paraview Press, 2001) 12, https://books.google. com/books?id=kGmLGWcnOLcC&lpg=PP1&dq=In%20the%20Big%20 Thicket%20%3A%20On%20the%20Trail%20of%20the%20Wild%20 Man&pg=PA12#v=onepage&q=howling%20like%20banshees&f=false.
42. Stephen Wagner, "Paranormal Hotspots," About.com, http://paranormal.about. com/cs/earthanomalies/a/aa110303_3.htm (accessed February 11, 2015).
43. Ross A. Muscato, "Tales from the Swamp: From Ape-like Creatures to Glowing Lights, Hockomock Has Kept Its Secrets for Centuries," *Boston Globe*, October 30, 2005 (accessed January 22, 2015), http://www.boston.com/news/local/ articles/2005/10/30/tales_from_the_swamp/.
44. Ibid.
45. "The Bennington Triangle," http://www.benningtontriangle.com/ (accessed February 11, 2015).
46. Carl Hughes(2000), "Vanishing Point," StrangeNation.com.au.
47. Geofferey Sea, "History Got it Wrong: Scientists Now Say Serpent Mound as Old as Aristotle," *Indian Country*, August 17, 2014, http:// indiancountrytodaymedianetwork.com/2014/08/07/rethinking-ohios-history-serpent-mound-older-some-its-dirt-156268 (accessed February 11, 2015).
48. Rene Chateaubriand, *Voyage to America*, Illinois Wesleyan University, http://titan. iwu.edu/~matthews/inwild.html (accessed February 12, 2015).
49. F.W. Putnam, *The Serpent Mound of Ohio*, https://books.google.com/ books?id=QFZbAAAAQAAJ&dq=FW%20Putnam%20Giant%20skeleton&pg=P A879#v=onepage&q&f=false, p. 879.
50. Alfred E. Lee, *History of the City of Columbus, Capital of Ohio* (Columbus OH: Franklin County Genealogical and Historical Society, 1892), 52,https://books. google.com/books?id=ZYQ_AQAAMAAJ&dq=editions%3AHr3Jjs-CPt8C&pg= PA52#v=onepage&q&f=false.
51. Ross Hamilton, "Giants of the Ancient Ohio Valley" (Serpent Mound Museum, Ohio: self-published monograph) 12.
52. Julius D W. Staal, *The New Patterns in the Sky: Myths and Legends of the Stars* (Blacksburg, Va.: McDonald and Woodward, 1988) 237.
53. Ernest L. Martin, *The Star that Astonished the World* (1996), as quoted here: "The Time of Jesus' Birth," *Associates for Scriptural Knowledge*(accessed January 11, 2013), http://askelm.com/star/star006.htm. Also, Dr. Michael Heiser made a short video about it here: http://youtu.be/KQt9pBSYY5Y.
54. Mary Annette Pember, "Crazy Theories Threaten Serpent Mound, Demean Native Heritage," *Indian Country* June 6, 2013, http://indiancountrytodaymedianetwork. com/2013/06/06/crazy-theories-threaten-serpent-mound-demean-native-heritage-149733 (accessed February 12, 2015).
55. Ibid.
56. C. S. Lewis, *Mere Christianity* (NY: Harper Collins, 2001) 122.
57. Robert L. Thomas, *Revelation 8–22: An Exegetical Commentary* (Chicago: Moody, 1995) 133.

58. Chuck Missler, "Hosea and Amos: Prophets to the Northern Kingdom," http://www.khouse.org/articles/2011/962/ (accessed September 2, 2011).

59. Arnold G. Fruchtenbaum, *The Footsteps of the Messiah: A Study of the Sequence of Prophetic Events*, (Tustin, CA: Ariel Ministries, 2003) 226.

60. Walter Martin, "A Christian View: UFO Encounters," audio recording, *Sermon Audio* http://www.sermonaudio.com/sermoninfo.asp?SID=2190615720 (accessed January 15, 2013).

61. Dr. Walter Martin, Jill Martin Rische, and Kurt Van Gorden, *The Kingdom of the Occult* (Nashville, TN: Thomas Nelson, 2008) 372–373.

62. Geza Vermes, *The Dead Sea Scrolls in English*, Revised and extended 4th ed. (Sheffield: Sheffield Academic Press, 1995), 141 [1 QM 15.2-3].

63. R. H. Charles and W. O. E. Oesterley, *The Book of Enoch* (London: Society for Promoting Christian Knowledge, 1917) Enoch 56:5–8.

64. Thomas Horn, Cris Putnam, *Exo-Vaticana* (Crane, MO: Defender, 2013) 59–60.

65. http://www.bbc.com/news/world-us-canada-29357103.

66. Leslie Kean, *UFOs: Generals, Pilots and Government Officials Go On the Record*, Kindle ed. (Random House, 2010) 262.

67. http://en.wikipedia.org/wiki/Sacrifice_in_Maya_culture.

68. Thomas Horn, *Zenith 2016* (Crane, MO: Defender, 2013) 194.

69. Wayne N. May, *This Land: America 2,000 B. C. to 500 A. D.* (Google eBook, Hayriver Press, June 18, 2012) 220.

70. Photograph by Chris Florio Photography http://www.floriopics.com.

71. https://www.sedonaaz.gov/Sedonacms/modules/ShowDocument.aspx?documentid=11551.

72. David Herzog, *Glory Invasion: Walking under an Open Heaven* (Shippensburg: Destiny Image, 2007) 68.

73. National UFO Reporting Center, http://www.nuforc.org/webreports/ndxloc.html (accessed January 23, 2015).

74. John A. Keel, *Why UFOs: Operation Trojan Horse* (New York: Manor Books, 1970) 145–146 (pdf).

75. http://pubs.usgs.gov/of/2002/0352/ofr02-352.txt; also see http://mrdata.usgs.gov/geophysics/surveys/geophysics2/AZ/AZ_3056A.jpg.

76. Walter Martin, Jill Martin Rische, Kevin Rische, *The Kingdom of the Occult* (Thomas Nelson, 2008) 222.

77. http://www.arizonaruins.com/sedona/sedona_geology.html.

78. M.A. Persinger, "Transient Geophysical Bases for Ostensible UFO-related Phenomena and Associated Verbal Behavior? *Perceptual and Motor Skills* (1976) 43, 215–221 on the "Sedona Effect," see http://sedonanomalies.weebly.com/research-papers.html for a number of scientific papers.

79. "From PSYOP to MindWar: The Psychology of Victory," https://flowofwisdom.files.wordpress.com/2013/07/mindwar-mindwar_co_authored_by_michael-aquino.pdf.

80. https://xeper.org//maquino/nm/AquinoVitae.pdf.

81. Michael A. Aquino, *Mindwar* (CreateSpace Independent Publishing Platform, 2013) 1.

82. Harvey J. Irwin,; Caroline A. Watt, *An Introduction to Parapsychology*, 5th ed.

(McFarland Publishing. Kindle Edition, 2007), Kindle Locations 5025–5026.Also see papers: V. Tandy, "Something in the Cellar," *Journal of the Society for Psychical Research*, 64 (2000), 129–140; V. Tandy and T. R. Lawrence, "The Ghost in the Machine," *Journal of the Society for Psychical Research*, 62 (1998) 360–364.

83. Lynne Hume, *Portals: Opening Doorways to Other Realities through the Senses* (Oxford, UK: Berg, 2007) 1.

84. http://www.lovesedona.com/history1.htm.

85. Adrian Ryan, "New Insights into the Links between ESP and Geomagnetic Activity," *Journal of Scientific Exploration*, Vol. 22, No. 3 (2008) 335–358.

86. Toraya Ayres, "The History of New Age Sedona,"http://www.lovesedona.com/history1.htm (accessed December 28, 2015).

87. "Etymology,"https://www.google.com/webhp?sourceid=chrome-instant&ion=1&espv=2&ie=UTF-8#q=Albion+etymology.

88. http://verdenews.com/main.asp?SectionID=239&SubSectionID=904&ArticleID=51841.

89. Pete A Sanders, *Scientific Vortex Information*, (Flagstaff, AZ, Graphtec: 2005) 21.

90. Tony Shearer, *Lord of the Dawn: Quetzalcoatl* (Healdsburg, CA: Naturegraph Publishing, 1971) 184.

91. Aztec tale "The Feathered Serpent"; the Mayan myth of "The Rain Goddess and the Egg Child"; the Incan story "How Manco-Capac Made the First People" in Diana Ferguson, *Tales of the Plumed Serpent: Aztec, Inca, and Mayan Myths* (New York, NY: Collins & Brown, 2000).

92. http://amozeshi.aliexirs.ir/The-Vortex-Energy-Mysteries-of-Sedona.html.

93. Elizabeth R. Rose, "Sedona Arizona Energy Vortexes—What is a Vortex, Vortices, or Vortexes? The Vortex Energy Mysteries of Sedona," About.com, http://gosw.about.com/od/sedonaarizona/a/sedonavortex.htm (accessed August 9, 2014).

94. Pete A. Sanders, *Scientific Vortex Information*, (Flagstaff, AZ: Graphtec, 2005) 13.

95. Richard Bullivant, *Beyond Time Travel—Exploring Our Parallel Worlds: Amazing Real Life Stories in the News* (Kindle Edition, 2014) Kindle Locations 721–725.

96. Norman Geisler, *Christianity under Attack* (Dallas: Quest, 1985) 43.

97. Dennis Andres, *What Is a Vortex: Sedona's Vortex Sites—A Practical Guide* (Sedona, AZ: Meta Adventures, 2000) 12.

98. *Exo-Vaticana*, 339.

99. http://en.wikipedia.org/wiki/Chapel_of_the_Holy_Cross_(Sedona,_Arizona)#mediaviewer/File:DenglerSW-CHC-Sedona-20050329-1050x800.jpg.

100. Sanders, 49.

101. Joseph McMoneagle, *TheStargate Chronicles: Memoirs of a Psychic Spy* (Charlottesville, VA: Hampton Roads, 2002) 73.

102. Scott Ventureyra, "Challenging the Rehabilitation of Pierre Teilhard de Chardin," *Crisis Magazine*, January 20, 2015, http://www.crisismagazine.com/2015/challenging-rehabilitation-pierre-teilhard-de-chardin (accessed January 21, 2015).

103. Ken Mandel, "Pope Francis: I Would Even Baptize Martians If Aliens Came, Asked," *Newsmax*, May 14, 2014, http://www.newsmax.com/TheWire/pope-francis-baptize-aliens/2014/05/13/id/571146/ (accessed January 21, 2015).

104. http://www.sciencedaily.com/releases/2015/01/150121083648.htm.

105. Larry Sprague "Earth Wisdom Tours," http://www.earthwisdomtours.com/our-guides/larry-sprague (accessed January 17, 2015).

106. David Garner, "In Search of the Vortex Vibe in Sedona," *The New York Times,* April 9, 2006, http://www.nytimes.com/2006/04/09/travel/09sedona.html?pagewanted=all&_r=0 (accessed January 17, 2015).

107. Transcribed from video clip by Cris Putnam.

108. Robert Ghost Wolf, http://www.wolflodge.org/CouldThisBeTrue/Stone%20People_2%20the%20Superstitions.htm.

109. http://en.wikipedia.org/wiki/Sipapu#mediaviewer/File:Image-sipapu.JPG.

110. Brian Stross, "The Mesoamerican Sacrum Bone: Doorway to the Otherworld," (University of Texas at Austin) 5; http://research.famsi.org/aztlan/uploads/papers/stross-sacrum.pdfgoogle books.

111. Pueblo Indian, Rina Swentzell, cited in Paul Devereux, *Places of Power: Measuring the Secret Energy of Ancient Sites,* 2nd ed. (London: Blandford, 1999) 13.

112. Ibid.

113. Toraya Ayres, "The History of New Age Sedona," http://lovesedona.com/history1.htm.

114. Richard Dannelley, *Sedona Vortex 2000* (Sedona, AZ: Light Technology, 2001) 100.

115. Joe Mcneill and Steven Korn, "Shhhh, It's Secret Sedona: 10 things You Won't Believe Happened in Sedona," *Sedona Monthly,* March 2003, http://www.sedonamonthly.com/2003/03/ssssh-secret-sedona/ (accessed January 18, 2015).

116. http://www.lawoftime.org/infobooth/hc24.html, Harmonic Convergence info.

117. Photo by Shelley Huisman Putnam, January 15, 2015.

118. Conversation transcribed by Putnam from audio recording.

119. Richard Dannelley, *Sedona Vortex 2000* (Sedona, AZ: Light Technology, 2001) 100.

120. Ibid, https://books.google.com/books?id=8_NvMBgBY7oC&lpg=PT12&dq=sedona%20vortex&pg=PT117#v=onepage&q=ufo&f=false.

121. Jerome Clark, "Jacques Vallée Discusses UFO Control System," *UFO Evidence,* original in FATE Magazine, 1978, http://www.ufoevidence.org/documents/doc608.htm (accessed February 5, 2013).

122. http://sedonaworldwisdomdays.com/.

123. Barbara Max Hubbard, *Happy Birth Day Planet Earth: The Instant of Co-Operation* (Ocean Tree Books, 1986) 17.

124. Barbara Marx Hubbard, *The Revelation: A Message of Hope for the New Millenium* (Novato, CA: Nataraj, 1995) 225.

125. Ibid., 294.

126. Barbara Max Hubbard, *The Book of Co-Creation* (self-published, 1980) 59.

127. Image of book cover http://ecx.images-amazon.com/images/I/51HXY1kDMsL._SX258_BO1,204,203,200_.jpg.

128. Tom Dongo, *Mysterious Sedona: Year 2000 Edition* (Light Technology, 2000), Kindle Location 831.

129. A Day in the West, "About Us," http://www.adayinthewest.com/about_us.php (accessed January 20, 2015).

130. Dongo, *Mysterious Sedona*, Kindle Locations 756–758.

131. Tim Cotroneo, "Sedona Rocks," *American Business Magazine*, August 03, 2010, http://www.americanbusinessmag.com/2010/08/sedona-rocks/(accessed January 20, 2015).

132. "The Land Preservation Task Force,"http://www.keepsedonabeautiful.org/interactive-map/land-preservation.html.

133. Steve Korn, http://www.sedonamonthly.com/2003/07/into-the-sunset/.

134. Hugh Ross, Kenneth Samples, and Mark Clark, *Lights in the Sky & Little Green Men: A Rational Christian Look at UFOs and Extraterrestrials* (Colorado Springs, CO: NavPress, 2002) 59.

135. Ibid., 119.

136. David K. Miller, *Teachings from the Sacred Triangle Volume 2* (Flagstaff, AZ: Light Technology, 2012), http://books.google.com/books?id=WCwwlHVqH28C&lpg=PT12&ots=sYjdjeVe8o&dq=Sacred%20Triangle%20of%20Sedona&pg=PT204#v=onepage&q&f=false.

137. Linda Bradshaw and Tom Dongo, *Merging Dimensions: The Opening Portals of Sedona* (Flagstaff, AZ:Light Technology: 1995, Kindle edition) Kindle location 166–169.

138. Ibid., 194–196.

139. Ibid., 223.

140. AJ, "In Search of Bradshaw Ranch" UFO Digest, August 2011, http://ufodigest.com/article/search-bradshaw-ranch%E2%80%A6 (accessed January 21, 2015).

141. A Day in the West, "Orb/Conspiracy Theory Tour," http://www.adayinthewest.com/toursDetail.php?Specialty-Tours-Conspiracy-Theory-Tour-28.

142. Bradshaw Hill, https://goo.gl/maps/eYm14.

143. http://www.timeanddate.com/weather/usa/sedona/historic.

144. http://www.mindreader.com/loyd/.

145. Loyd Auerbach, *Hauntings and Poltergeists: A Ghost Hunter's Guide* (Kindle Locations 886–887).

146. Auerbach, "They See Dead People," 10.

147. Philip J. Imbrogno, *Interdimensional Universe: The New Science of UFOs, Paranormal Phenomena and Otherdimensional Beings* (Kindle edition) Kindle locations 1315–1320.

148. Bradshaw and Dongo, *Merging Dimensions*.

149. Linda Ball, *Dimensional Journey: Encounters and Teachings* (Flagstaff, AZ: Light Technology, 2003).

150. Ball, *Dimensional Journey*, xvi.

151. Ibid., 79.

152. 1) "A Day in the West "Orb/Conspiracy Theory tour," http://www.adayinthewest.com/toursDetail.php?Specialty-Tours-Conspiracy-Theory-Tour-28. 2) Tom Dongo,"UFO Sky Watch,"http://tomdongo.com/tours/ufo-sky-watch.html. 3) Kim Carlsberg,"Sedona UFO Sky Tours," http://www.sedonaufoskytours.com/Tour_Instructions.html. 4) "Sedona UFO Sighting Tours," http://sedonanewagestore.com/sedona-visitors/ufo-tours/. "Inner Journeys Angel Medicine,"http://www.sedona-spiritualretreats.com/energy-healing.html "Encounter Sedona UFO Tours" http://www.encountersedona.com/.

153. Raquel Cepeda, "Abandoning Doubt in Sedona, Arizona," *NY Times*, January 1, 2015, http://www.nytimes.com/2015/01/04/travel/abandoning-doubt-in-sedona-arizona-.html (accessed January 26, 2015).

154. Tom Dongo, *Mysterious Sedona: Year 2000 Edition* (Flagstaff, AZ: Light Technology) Kindle locations 1030–1032.

155. Ibid.,1069-1071.

156. https://docs.google.com/file/d/0Bwei1VX3HNebWmpQelJSMG1UZjg/edit?usp=drive_web.

157. Dongo, *Mysterious Sedona*,1034–1037.

158. https://docs.google.com/file/d/0Bwei1VX3HNebbXk3U0VBd3lDazA/edit?usp=drive_web.

159. Personal email, L. A. Marzulli to author Cris Putnam, January 22, 2015.

160. "Supernatural Orbs," http://www.maxgreinerart.com/AngelOrbsSupernaturalPage6.htm (accessed January 26, 2015).

161. Marie Trevelyan, *Folk-Lore and Folk-Stories of Wales* (London: EP Publishing, 1909) 178.

162. "Spooklight" in Brad Steiger and Sherry Hansen Steiger, *The Gale Encyclopedia of the Unusual and Unexplained* vol. 3, (Detroit: Gale Group, 2003) 22.

163. Troy Taylor, "The Hornet Spooklight," *American Hauntings,* http://www.prairieghosts.com/devprom.html (accessed January 22, 2015).

164. "Project 10073 Record Card," November 8, 1957, United States Air Force, http://projectbluebook.theblackvault.com/documents/1950s/1957%2011%206781798%20Joplin%20Missouri/1957-11-6781798-Joplin-Missouri.pdf (accessed January 22, 2015).

165. Spar Giedeman, "The Yakima Ufo Enigma," http://psiapplications.com/spar11.html.

166. Greg Long, *Examining the Earthlight Theory: the Yakima Ufo Microcosm* (Chicago, IL: J Allen Hynek Center for UFO Studies, 1990) 36.

167. Vallée, *Dimensions*, xvi–96

168. http://en.wikipedia.org/wiki/1561_celestial_phenomenon_over_Nuremberg#mediaviewer/File:Aerial_conflict.jpg.

169. Richard Dannelley, *Sedona Vortex 2000* (Sedona, AZ: Light Technology, 2001) 92. here<link>

170. Personal email, Daniel Wright to author Cris Putnam, January 23, 2015.

171. Personal email, Stan Deyo to author Cris Putnam, January 25, 2015.

172. "TR-3B Anti-Gravity Spacecrafts," http://www.military.com/video/aircraft/military-aircraft/tr-3b-aurora-anti-gravity-spacecrafts/2860314511001/.

173. https://www.youtube.com/watch?x-yt-cl=84503534&v=av3yEUsie-Y&feature=player_embedded&x-yt-ts=1421914688.

174. Richard Dannelley, *Sedona UFO Connection* (Sedona AZ: Light Technology, 1993) 56.

175. Dannelly, *Sedona UFO*, 57.

176. A representative example from SedonaMystic at Above Top Secret.com, http://www.abovetopsecret.com/forum/thread705082/pg1#pid11510342.

177. Dannelley, *Sedona UFO*, 58.

178. "Early Inhabitants of the Verde Valley," Verde Valley Archeology Center, http://www.verdevalleyarchaeology.org/EarlyInhabitants (accessed January 30, 2015).

179. Robert S. McPherson, *New Directions in Native American Studies*, vol. 9, *Viewing the Ancestors: Perceptions of the Anaasázi , Mokwic, and Hisatsinom* (Norman: University of Oklahoma Press, 2014) 15.

180. Christy G. Turner and Jacqueline A. Turner, *Man Corn: Cannibalism and Violence in the Prehistoric American Southwest* (Salt Lake City: University of Utah Press, 2011) 463.

181. McPherson, *New Directions*, 56.

182. Lee Brown, *Native American Indian Prophecies* (Fairbanks, AL: Continental Indigenous Council, 1986) http://www.ausbcomp.com/redman/hopi_prophecy.htm.

183. http://www.history.com/shows/countdown-to-apocalypse/episodes; view here: http://www.amazon.com/Hopi-Blue-Star/dp/B00AGDXQDY.

184. Frank Waters, *Book of the Hopi* (Harmondsworth, England: Penguin, 1963) 334.

185. Armin W. Geertz, *The Invention of Prophecy: Continuity and Meaning in Hopi Indian Religion* (Berkeley: University of California Press, 1994) 275.

186. Bob Frissell, *Something in This Book Is True* (Berkeley, CA: Frog, 2003) 3334, link here.

187. Ibid., 34.

188. "Rainbow Prophecy" Ancient Origins, http://www.ancient-origins.net/myths-legends/warriors-rainbow-prophecy-001577#sthash.wFAlTu4G.dpuf (accessed January 30, 2015).

189. Armin W. Geertz, *The Invention of Prophecy: Continuity and Meaning in Hopi Indian Religion* (Berkeley: University of California Press, 1994), 420, link here.

190. "History of the Diocese of Gallup," Diocese of Gallup, http://www.dioceseofgallup.org/history.html (accessed January 31, 2015).

191. Alex Patterson, *A Field Guide to Rock Art Symbols of the Greater Southwest* (Boulder: Johnson Books, 1992) 211. Also see Garrick Mallery, "Picture-Writing of the American Indians," Annual Report of the Bureau of Ethnology (Washington DC U.S. Government Printing Office, 1893) 10:604-605; and Patterson, *Hopi Pottery Symbols* (Boulder: Johnson Books, 1994) 27, 250.

192. Mariko Namba Walter and Eva Jane Neumann Fridman, eds., *Shamanism: An Encyclopedia of World Beliefs, Practices, and Culture* (Santa Barbara, Calif.: ABC-CLIO, 2004) 221.

193. Edmund Nequatewa, *Truth of a Hopi: Stories Relating to the Origin, Myths and Clan Histories of the Hopi*, (Museum of Northern Arizona Bulletin No. 8., 1936) 24; Sacred texts link here.

194. Ibid, 24–25.

195. Keam's Canyon Giant Photo: http://en.wikipedia.org/wiki/Navajo_County,_Arizona#mediaviewer/File:Giants,_Petroglyphs_at_Rock_Art_Ranch.jpg.

196. "About Sedona, History," http://www.sedonaaz.gov/Sedonacms/index.aspx?page=249 (accessed December 28, 2014).

197. http://en.wikipedia.org/wiki/Montezuma_Castle_National_Monument#mediaviewer/File:Montezumas_castle_arizona.jpg.

198. "The Yavapai-Apache Nations," http://yavapai-apache.org/ (accessed January 27, 2015).

199. As recorded in *The Yavapai of Fort McDowell* by Sigrid Khera, cited in Richard Sutphen, *Dick Sutphen Presents Sedona: Psychic Energy Vortexes*, new updated and expanded ed. (Malibu, CA: Valley of the Sun, 1993) 23.

200. Frederick Webb Hodge, *Handbook of American Indians North of Mexico* (Washington, DC: Smithsonian Institution, Bureau of American Ethnology, 1910–1968),994.Link here.

201. "Yavapai Creation Story" River of Time Museum, http://www. riveroftimemuseum.org/content/docent_content/Yavapai%20Creation%20Story. pdf (accessed January 27, 2015).

202. Robert Quin, "Mystic Arizona: Discover the Mysterious Superstition Mountains Where Legends and Ghosts Come Alive," Strange Sounds, http://strangesounds. org/2013/09/mystic-arizona-discover-the-mysterious-supersition-mountains-where-legends-and-ghosts-come-alive.html (accessed January 27, 2015).

203. Stephen Quayle, *True Legends: Tales of Giants and the Plumed Serpents*, 307.

204. William R. Cooper, *The Serpent Myths of Ancient Egypt*, (London: Hardwicke, 1873) 5, https://archive.org/details/cu31924099385209.

205. Ibid., 12.

206. Ugaritic language texts.

207. William W. Hallo and K. Lawson Younger, *The Context of Scripture* (Leiden; New York: Brill, 1997) 265.

208. C. Uehlinger, "Leviathan," ed. Karel van der Toorn, Bob Becking, and Pieter W. van der Horst, *Dictionary of Deities and Demons in the Bible* (Leiden; Boston; Köln; Grand Rapids, MI; Cambridge: Brill; Eerdmans, 1999) 513.

209. Alexander Kulik (translator), *The Apocalypse of Abraham*, based on Alexander Kulik, *Retroverting Slavonic Pseudepigrapha* (Atlanta, GA: Society of Biblical Literature, 2004 and Leiden: Brill, 2005). http://www.marquette.edu/maqom/ kuliktranslation.html (accessed January 28, 2015).

210. B. F. Batto, "Behemoth," ed. Karel van der Toorn, Bob Becking, and Pieter W. van der Horst, *Dictionary of Deities and Demons in the Bible* (Leiden; Boston; Köln; Grand Rapids, MI; Cambridge: Brill; Eerdmans, 1999) 165.

211. As discussed in chapter 1 What Is This All About? – "4Q Amram^{b} (4Q544)," Geza Vermes, *The Dead Sea Scrolls in English*, revised and extended 4th ed. (Sheffield: Sheffield Academic Press, 1995) 312.(Previous ed.: London: Penguin, 1987).

212. "Teotihuacan—Temple of the Feathered Serpent-3035," by jschmeling, originally posted to Flickr as Teotihaucan-3035. Licensed under CC BY 2.0 via Wikimedia Commons: http://commons.wikimedia.org/wiki/File:Teotihuacan-Temple_of_ the_Feathered_Serpent-3035.jpg#mediaviewer/File:Teotihuacan-Temple_of_the_ Feathered_Serpent-3035.jpg.

213. William M. Ringle, Tomás Gallareta Negrón, and George J. Bey, "The Return of Quetzalcoatl," *Ancient Mesoamerica* (London: Cambridge University Press, 1998) 183–232.

214. Paul R. Steele and Catherine J. Allen, "Amaru Tupa," *Handbook of Inca Mythology, Handbooks of World Mythology* (Santa Barbara, CA: ABC-CLIO, 2004) 96.

215. S. Smith, "Generative Landscapes: The Step Mountain Motif in Tiwanaku Iconography," *Ancient America*, 12m (2011): 1–69.
216. Steele and Allen, 98.
217. Ibid., 96.
218. Steele and Allen, "Huauque," 193.
219. "The Death of Quetzalcöatl," *Anales de Cuauhtitlan* (Codex Chimalpopoca, sections 5 to 8) http://pages.ucsd.edu/~dkjordan/nahuatl/ReadingQuetzalcoatl.html (accessed January 28, 2015).
220. Bernardino de Sahagún, *Monographs of the School of American Research*, vol. 14, "General History of the Things of New Spain: Florentine Codex" (Santa Fe, N.M.: School of American Research, 1950–1982) 79.
221. Patrick Chouinard (09-28-2013), *Lost Race of the Giants: The Mystery of Their Culture, Influence, and Decline throughout the World* (Inner Traditions/Bear & Company) 129–130.
222. Steele and Allen, "Viracocha," 265.
223. Howard Schwartz, *Tree of Souls: The Mythology of Judaism* (Oxford: Oxford University, 2004) 461.
224. Joseph Barclay, *The Talmud* (London: John Murray, 1878): 23; Heinrich Ewald and Georg Heinrich August von Ewald, *The History of Israel* (London: Longmans, Green, and Company, 1883) 228.
225. John M. Ingham, "Human Sacrifice at Tenochtitln," *Society for Comparative Studies in Society and History* 26 (1984) 379–400.
226. Gabrielle Vail, Christine Hernández, "Human Sacrifice in Late Postclassic Maya Iconography and Texts" in Vera Tiesler and Andrea Cucina, *New Perspectives on Human Sacrifice and Ritual Body Treatment in Ancient Maya Society* (New York: Springer, 2007) 120–164.
227. Rebecca Morelle, "Inca Mummies: Child Sacrifice Victims Fed Drugs and Alcohol," BBC News, http://www.bbc.com/news/science-environment-23496345 (accessed January 30, 2015).
228. Louis Ginzberg, *The Legends of the Jews* (Baltimore: Johns Hopkins University Press, 1998) 125.
229. Jacques Soustelle, *La Vida Cotidiana de Los Aztecas En Vísperas de La Conquista*, 2. ed., Sección de Obras de Antropología (México: Fondo de Cultura Económica, 1970) 102.
230. George L. Cowgill, "Ritual Sacrifice and the Feathered Serpent Pyramid at Teotihuacán, México," Foundation for the Advancement of Mesoamerican Studies, 1997, http://www.famsi.org/reports/96036/index.html (accessed January 30. 2015).
231. Ardy Sixkiller Clarke, *Sky People: Untold Stories of Alien Encounters in Mesoamerica* (Pompton Plains, NJ: New Page, 2014) 172.
232. Quayle, *True Legends*, 294.
233. Thomas Horn, *Zenith 2016* (Crane, MO: Defender, 2013) 357–359.
234. Ken Hudnall, *The Occult Connection II: The Hidden Race* (Omega Press, 2004) 207.
235. *Pseudepigrapha of the Old Testament*, ed. Robert Henry Charles (Bellingham, WA: Logos Research Systems, 2004) 2:497.

236. Charles Gould, *Mythical Monsters*, http://www.gutenberg.org/files/40972/40972-
h/40972-h.htm#Page_22.

237. Howard Giskin and Bettye S. Walsh, eds., "Chinese Dragon Worship Began as
Early as the Fifth Millennium BC," ,*An Introduction to Chinese Culture through the
Family* (Albany: State University of New York Press, 2001) 126.

238. David E. Jones, *An Instinct for Dragons* (New York: Routledge, 2002) 19.

239. John Frame, "Forward," *On Global Wizardry: Techniques of Pagan Spirituality and a
Christian Response* (Kindle Locations 32–33).

240. Lynne Hume, *Portals: Opening Doorways to Other Realities through the Senses*
(Oxford, UK: Berg, 2007) 1.

241. Walter Martin, Jill Rische, Kevin Rische, *The Kingdom of the Occult* (Nashville:
Thomas Nelson. 2008) 222.

242. As cited in John Carter, *Sex and Rockets: The Occult World of Jack Parsons*, new ed.
(Los Angeles, CA: Feral House, 2004) 188.

243. John Greer, *The New Encyclopedia of the Occult*, 9781567183368.

244. "Babalon" in *Thelemapedia,* http://www.thelemapedia.org/index.php/
Babalon#Babalon_as_the_Gateway_to_the_City_of_Pyramids (accessed February
22, 2015).

245. "Babalon as the Gateway to the City of Pyramids," *Thelemapedia* http://www.
thelemapedia.org/index.php/Babalon#Babalon_as_the_Gateway_to_the_City_of_
Pyramids (accessed February 22, 2015).

246. "City of the Pyramids," Thelemapedia, http://www.thelemapedia.org/index.php/
City_of_the_Pyramids (accessed February 22, 2015).

247. "The Scarlet Woman Aspect" in Babalon, Thelemapedia http://www.
thelemapedia.org/index.php/Babalon#Individual_Scarlet_Women (accessed
February 22, 2015).

248. Hugh B. Urban, *Magia Sexualis: Sex, Magic, and Liberation in Modern Western
Esotericism* (Berkeley, CA: University of California Press, 2006) 135–37.

249. George Pendle, *Strange Angel: The Otherworldly Life of Rocket Scientist John
Whiteside Parsons*, 266.

250. Hillary Rodham Clinton (October 26, 1947), a potential 2016 presidential
candidate, https://www.readyforhillary.com/splash/hillary. —However, it seems
she was born a few months too late, according to Parsons, who thought she was
incarnate in the womb by March 1946 requiring a December 1946 or January
1947 birth date.

251. Paul Davies, *Are We Alone?* (New York: Basic Books, 1995) 133.

252. "Anger, Kenneth" at *GLBTQ: An Encyclopedia of Gay, Lesbian, Bi-sexual,
Transgender, and Queer Culture,* http://www.glbtq.com/arts/anger_k.html (accessed
February 28, 2015).

253. *Lucifer Rising* (1981), *366 Weird Movies,* http://366weirdmovies.com/102-lucifer-
rising-1981/ (accessed February 28, 2015).

254. Jack Hunter, *Moonchild: The Films of Kenneth Anger* (London: Creation Books,
2002) 8.

255. Hume, *Portals*, 117.

256. Rick Strassman, *DMT: The Spirit Molecule,* (Rochester, Vt.: Park Street Press,
2001) 8.

257. Ibid., 191.

258. Ibid., 314.

259. Graham Hancock, *Supernatural: Meetings with the Ancient Teachers of Mankind*, rev. ed. (New York: Disinformation Co., 2007) 270.

260. Strassman, *DMT*, 54.

261. http://www.rickstrassman.com/index.php?option=com_content&view=article&id=62&Itemid=68.

262. Strassman, DMT, xvii.

263. Strassman, DMT, 311.

264. David Deutsch, ""uantum Theory, the Church-Turing Principle and the Universal Quantum Computer," *Proceedings of the Royal Society* A 400, 1818 (July 1985) 97–117, http://web.archive.org/web/20030915061044/http:/www.qubit.org/oldsite/resource/deutsch85.pdf.

265. Graham Hancock, *Supernatural: Meetings with the Ancient Teachers of Mankind*, rev. ed. (New York: Disinformation Co., 2007) 101–2.

266. Strassman, *DMT,* 55.

267. Brad Steiger; Sherry Steiger, *Real Encounters, Different Dimensions and Otherworldly Beings* (Visible Ink Press, 2013) Kindle Edition, 139–141.

268. Orkneyjar, *The Odin Stone.*

269. They were built between 5,400 and 4,500 years ago; http://www.historic-scotland.gov.uk/propertyresults/propertydetail.htm?PropID=PL_280.

270. "Pagan Stone Circle Built at US Air Force Training Academy," *The Telegraph*, November 2011, http://www.telegraph.co.uk/news/newstopics/howaboutthat/8920124/Pagan-stone-circle-built-at-US-Air-Force-training-academy.html (accessed February 25, 2015).

271. "The 9,000-Year-Old Underground Megalithic Settlement of Atlit Yam," *Ancient Origins,* http://www.ancient-origins.net/ancient-places-asia/9000-year-old-underground-megalithic-settlement-atlit-yam-001579.

272. Yuval Ne'eman, "Astronomy in Israel: From Og's Circle to the Wise Observatory," *Cataclysmic Variables and Related Objects, Astrophysics and Space Science Library,* Volume 101, 1983, 323–329.

273. Michael Heiser, "The Nephilim," http://sitchiniswrong.com/nephilim/nephilim.htm (accessed December 31, 2014).

274. Howard Schwartz, *Tree of Souls: The Mythology of Judaism* (Oxford: Oxford University, 2004) 461. google books link here.

275. "Solving the Mystery of a Megalithic Monument in the Land of Giants," http://popular-archaeology.com/issue/september-2011/article/solving-the-mystery-of-a-megalithic-monument-in-the-land-of-giants.

276. Barry Chamish, "Did Biblical Giants Build the Circle of the Refaim?" http://www.ccg.org/Creation%20Articles/Circle%20of%20the%20Refaim.htm (accessed February 28, 2015).

277. Barry Chamish, "Did Biblical Giants Build the Circle of the Refaim?" http://www.ccg.org/Creation%20Articles/Circle%20of%20the%20Refaim.htm (accessed February 28, 2015).

278. "Solving the Mystery of a Megalithic Monument in the Land of Giants," *Popular Archaeology*, http://popular-archaeology.com/issue/september-2011/article/solving-

the-mystery-of-a-megalithic-monument-in-the-land-of-giants (accessed January 1, 2015).

279. David Rapp, "In the Wildcat's Pile of Stones: Rujm al-Hiri in the Golan Heights is not a burial ground around which a monumental site was erected, but rather a monumental site in which there is a burial ground," *Haaretz*, May 2, 2003, http://www.haaretz.com/life/arts-leisure/in-the-wildcat-s-pile-of-stones-1.11251 (accessed September 29, 2014 and February 19, 2015).

280. Ibid.

281. Wolfgang Rölling in "Eine neue phoenizische Inschrift aus Byblos" (Neue Ephemeris für Semitische Epigraphik, vol 2, 1–15 and plate 1) 1974, http://archiv.ub.uni-heidelberg.de/propylaeumdok/1101/.

282. 7496 rapha in *New American Standard Hebrew-Aramaic and Greek Dictionaries,* ed. Robert L. Thomas, (Anaheim: Foundation Publications, 1998).

283. "Necromancy" in *Encyclopedia of Occultism and Parapsychology,* 5th edition, editor J Gordon Melton (Detroit: Gale Group, 2001) 1096.

284. Francis Barrett, *The Magus or Celestial Intelligencer Book II, Part II, The Cabala; or The Secret Mysteries of Ceremonial Magic* (London: Lackington, Alley, and Co: 1801) 69. http://www.sacred-texts.com/grim/magus/ma231.htm.

285. Judd Burton, *Interview With the Giant,* http://www.lulu.com/us/en/shop/judd-burton/interview-with-the-giant/paperback/product-5943477.html, 80.

286. http://www.bibleistrue.com/qna/banias5.jpg.

287. James A. Swanson, Thomas J. Kollenborn, *Circlestone: A Superstition Mountain Mystery* (AZ: Goldfield Press, 1986) 67.

288. Martin Doutré, "Circlestone Observatory, Arizona," http://www.celticnz.org/images/Circlestone/Circlestone1.htm (accessed February 28, 2015).

289. "The Circlestone Ruin," Mesa Community College, http://www.mesacc.edu/~bruwn09481/circlestone/maps.htm (accessed February 28, 2015).

290. Doutré (accessed February 28, 2015).

291. Stephen Wagner, "Paranormal Hotspots," About.com, http://paranormal.about.com/cs/earthanomalies/a/aa110303_3.htm (accessed February 11, 2015).

292. Matt Williams, "A Universe of Ten Dimensions," published on December 10, 2014, at Universe Today, http://www.universetoday.com/48619/a-universe-of-10-dimensions/ (accessed January 24, 2015).

293. R. Laird Harris, Robert Laird Harris, Gleason Leonard Archer, and Bruce K. Waltke, *Theological Wordbook of the Old Testament,* electronic ed. (Chicago: Moody Press, 1999, c1980) 946.

294. English Translation of Septuagint, http://www.ecmarsh.com/lxx/Psalms/index.htm (accessed January 24, 2015).

295. "807 archōn," *Dictionary of Biblical Languages with Semantic Domains: Greek* (New Testament) ed. James Swanson (Oak Harbor: Logos Research Systems, 1997).

296. Johannes P. Louw and Eugene Albert Nida, vol. 1, *Greek-English Lexicon of the New Testament: Based on Semantic Domains,* electronic ed. of the 2nd ed. (New York: United Bible Societies, 1996) 146–47.

297. Jim Stinehart, "MLK vs. Abimelech vs. Abi-Molech," April 4, 2009, http://lists.ibiblio.org/pipermail/b-hebrew/2009-April/038024.html (accessed January 24, 2015).

298. The story of Abraham and Nimrod is taken from an article by Nissan Mindel, http://www.chabad.org/library/article_cdo/aid/112333/jewish/Nimrod-and-Abraham.htm (accessed January 24, 2015).

299. Avraham Negev, *The Archaeological Encyclopedia of the Holy Land* (New York: Prentice Hall Press, 1990).

300. http://www.bible-history.com/babylonia/BabyloniaThe_Ziggurat.htm.

301. Victor P. Hamilton, *The Book of Genesis. Chapters 18–50, The New International Commentary on the Old Testament* (Grand Rapids, MI: Eerdmans, 1995) 240.

302. Victor P. Hamilton, *The Book of Genesis. Chapters 18-50*, The New International Commentary on the Old Testament (Grand Rapids, MI: Wm. B. Eerdmans Publishing Co., 1995), 239.

303. C. Houtman, "What Did Jacob See in His Dream at Bethel?: Some Remarks on Genesis XXVIII 10-22'" *Vetus Testamentum*, Vol. 27, Fasc. 3 (Jul., 1977), 347.

304. Midrash Tanhuma, http://www.sacred-texts.com/jud/mhl/mhl04.htm (accessed December 11, 2014).

305. Ernst Jenni and Claus Westermann, *Theological Lexicon of the Old Testament* (Peabody, MA: Hendrickson Publishers, 1997) 649.

306. "3947 *laqach*," *The Exhaustive Concordance of the Bible: Showing Every Word of the Text of the Common English Version of the Canonical Books, and Every Occurrence of Each Word in Regular Order.* Ed. James Strong (Ontario: Woodside Bible Fellowship, 1996) H3947.

307. 5492a in *New American Standard Hebrew-Aramaic and Greek Dictionaries: Updated Edition*, ed. Robert L. Thomas (Anaheim: Foundation Publications, 1998).

308. "5486," *New American Standard Hebrew-Aramaic and Greek Dictionaries.*

309. Johannes P. Louw and Eugene Albert Nida, *Greek-English Lexicon of the New Testament: Based on Semantic Domains* (New York: United Bible Societies, 1996) 220.

310. Robert L. Thomas, *New American Standard Hebrew-Aramaic and Greek Dictionaries: Updated Edition* (Anaheim: Foundation Publications, 1998).

311. "A courteous distance," *The Economist* January 26, 2015, http://www.economist.com/blogs/erasmus/2015/01/church-and-state-greece.

312. SabbyMionis, "Greece's Jewish voters are faced with an impossible choice," Haaretz, June. 10, 2012, "http://www.haaretz.com/opinion/greece-s-jewish-voters-are-faced-with-an-impossible-choice-1.435484 (accessed February 13, 2015).

313. Jonathan A. Goldstein, *I Maccabees: A New Translation With Introduction and Commentary*, includes indexes (New Haven; London: Yale University Press, 2008) 206.

314. Walter A. Elwell and Barry J. Beitzel, *Baker Encyclopedia of the Bible* (Grand Rapids, MI: Baker Book House, 1988) 10.

315. Helena Smith, "Pope Francis the 'Pontiff of the Poor,' says Greece's Alexis Tsipras," *The Guardian*, September 8, 2014, http://www.theguardian.com/world/2014/sep/18/pope-francis-alexis-tsipras-vatican (accessed February 15, 2015).

316. "Pope Francis meets with Alexis Tsipras," http://www.alexistsipras.eu/index.php/9-press-releases/298-pope-francis-meets-with-alexis-tsipras (accessed February 17, 2015).

317. Horn, *Zenith 2016,* 29–35.
318. Leland Ryken, et al., *Dictionary of Biblical Imagery* (Downers Grove, IL: InterVarsity Press, 2000) 68.
319. A. C. Myers (1987), *The Eerdmans Bible Dictionary.* rev., augm. translation of: Bijbelseencyclopedie, rev. ed. 1975 (117) (Grand Rapids, MI: Eerdmans).
320. "1101a, balal," Robert L. Thomas, *New American Standard Hebrew-Aramaic and Greek Dictionaries: Updated Edition* (Anaheim: Foundation, 1998).
321. http://www.bible-history.com/babylonia/BabyloniaThe_Ziggurat.htm.
322. Paul J. Achtemeier, *Harper's Bible Dictionary* (San Francisco: Harper & Row, 1985) 1164.
323. Norriss S. Hetherington, ed., *Garland Reference Library of the Humanities,* vol.1634, "Cosmology: Historical, Literary, Philosophical, Religious, and Scientific Perspectives" (New York: Garland, 1993) 44.
324. Verse 117, "Inana's Descent to the Nether World," The Electronic Text Corpus of Sumerian Literature, http://etcsl.orinst.ox.ac.uk/section1/tr141.htm (accessed December 30, 2014).
325. *The Epic of Gilgamesh,* translated by Maureen Gallery Kovacs, electronic Ed., by Wolf Carnahan, 1998, http://www.sjsu.edu/people/cynthia.rostankowski/courses/119a/s4/The%20Epic%20of%20Gilgamesh.pdf (accessed December 30, 2014).
326. Rivkah Schärf Kluger and Yehezkel Kluger, *The Archetypal Significance of Gilgamesh: A Modern Ancient Hero,* ed. Yehezkel Kluger (Einsiedeln, Switzerland: Daimon, 1991) 163.
327. The Manumission of Umanigar (3.134A) [Reading [K]Á.GAL-mah-ki-a[n-na] / ᵈNin-urta-k[a]. Cf. Steinkeller 1989:73 n. 209.] In William W. Hallo and K. Lawson Younger, *Context of Scripture* (Leiden; Boston: Brill, 2003) 301.
328. *Zondervan NIV Study Bible: Loose-Leaf Edition* (Grand Rapids, MI: Hendrickson, 2005) 22.
329. http://en.wikipedia.org/wiki/Ziggurat_of_Ur#mediaviewer/File:Ancient_ziggurat_at_Ali_Air_Base_Iraq_2005.jpg.
330. Gary Stearman, *Prophecy in the News Magazine* (October 2013) 11.
331. http://www.raidersnewsupdate.com/labyrinth8.htm.
332. Samuel Noah Kramer, *The Sumerians,* (Chicago: University of Chicago Press, 1963) 291, as cited in Joseph P. Farrell, *The Grid of the Gods* (2013) Kindle Locations 5012–5016.
333. Joseph P. Farrell (11-21-2013), *The Grid of the Gods* (SCB Distributors, Kindle edition) 5125–5131.
334. Asger Aaboe, "The Culture of Babylonia: Babylonian Mathematics, Astrology, and Astronomy," *The Assyrian and Babylonian Empires and other States of the Near East, from the Eighth to the Sixth Centuries B.C.E,* Eds. John Boardman, I. E. S. Edwards, N. G. L. Hammond, E. Sollberger and C. B. F. Walker (Cambridge University Press, 1991).
335. "Jewish Concepts: Angels & Angelology," Jewish Virtual Library, http://www.jewishvirtuallibrary.org/jsource/Judaism/angels.html.

336. *Pseudepigrapha of the Old Testament,* R. H. Charles, ed. (2:363) (Bellingham, WA: Logos Research Systems, 2004).

337. *Lemegeton Clavicula Salomonis: The Lesser Key of Solomon, Detailing the Ceremonial Art of Commanding Spirits Both Good and Evil;* ed. Joseph H. Peterson (Maine: Weiser Books, 2001).

338. S. L. M. Mathers, ed., *Goetia: The Lesser Key of Solomon. The Book of Evil Spirits,* with an introduction by Aleister Crowley [1904] (Chicago: De Laurence, Scott & Co., 1916) 45 (reissued by Weiser, Boston, 1995).

339. Iain M. Duguid, Zechariah 1:10–11 note in *The ESV Study Bible* (Wheaton, IL: Crossway Bibles, 2008) 1753–1754.

340. Thomas Horn, *Nephilim Stargates* (Crane, MO: Defender, 2007) 34–35.

341. Allen C. Myers, *Eerdmans Bible Dictionary* (Grand Rapids, MI: Eerdmans, 1987) 117.

342. David Noel Freedman, *The Anchor Bible Dictionary* (New York: Doubleday, 1996, c1992) 1:563.

343. J I. Packer, Merrill C. Tenney, and William White, eds., *The World of the Old Testament,* Nelson Handbook Series (Nashville: T. Nelson, 1982) 154.

344. http://www.schoyencollection.com/historyBabylonian.html.

345. MS 2063, "The Tower of Babel Stele," http://www.schoyencollection.com/history-collection-introduction/babylonian-history-collection/tower-babel-stele-ms-2063 (accessed December 30, 2014).

346. "Levels of a Ziggurat," http://faculty.evansville.edu/rl29/art105/img/ziggurat_diagram.gif.

347. Private email to Putnam.

348. http://www.thehistoryblog.com/archives/14185.

349. William W. Hallo and K. Lawson Younger, *Context of Scripture* (Leiden; Boston: Brill, 2000) 315.

350. Herodotus, *Histories,* 1.181.

351. "Alexander the Great Enters Babylon," http://www.livius.org/aj-al/alexander/alexander_t44.html.

352. Avraham Negev, *The Archaeological Encyclopedia of the Holy Land* (New York: Prentice Hall, 1990).

353. http://whc.unesco.org/en/tentativelists/1837/.

354. Chuck Missler, "The Most Important City in Iraq: The World Capital?" *Personal Update News Journal* (June 2004), KHouse, http://www.khouse.org/articles/2004/523/ (accessed December 31, 2014).

355. Ibid.

356. Charles H. Dyer, *The Rise of Babylon: Is Iraq at the Center of the Final Drama?,* updated ed. (Chicago: Moody, 2003).

357. Mark Hitchcock, *The Second Coming of Babylon* (Sisters, OR: Multnomah, 2003).

358. "The Sacred Complex of Babylon," http://whc.unesco.org/en/tentativelists/1837/.

359. Tim F. LaHaye and Bob Phillips, *Babylon Rising: The Europa Conspiracy* (New York: Bantam, 2005) 167.

360. Chuck Missler, "The Most Important City in Iraq: The World Capital?" *Personal Update News Journal* (June 2004), KHouse, http://www.khouse.org/articles/2004/523/ (accessed December 31, 2014).

361. "A Room of Quiet" The Meditation Room, United Nations Headquarters, http://www.un.org/Depts/dhl/dag/meditationroom.htm (accessed December 31, 2014).

362. Crossway Bibles, *ESV Study Bible* (Wheaton, IL: Crossway Bibles, 2008) 1233.

363. Chuck Missler, "The Most Important City in Iraq: The World Capital?" *Personal Update News Journal* (June 2004), KHouse, http://www.khouse.org/articles/2004/523/ (accessed December 31, 2014).

364. Joel Kalvesmaki, Septuagint Online, http://mysite.verizon.net/rgjones3/Septuagint/spexecsum.htm.

365. *The Septuagint*, transl. Sir Lancelot C. L. Brenton, 1851.

366. Johan Lust, Erik Eynikel, and Katrin Hauspie, *A Greek-English Lexicon of the Septuagint: Revised Edition* (Deutsche Bibelgesellschaft: Stuttgart, 2003).

367. Cris Putnam and Thomas R. Horn, *Exo-Vaticana: Petrus Romanus, Project L.u.c.i.f.e.r. and the Vatican's Astonishing Plan for the Arrival of an Alien Savior* (Crane, MO: Defender, 2013) 31–32.

368. *Pseudepigrapha of the Old Testament*, ed. Robert Henry Charles (Bellingham, WA: Logos Research Systems, 2004) 2:198.

369. George W. E. Nickelsburg and Klaus Baltzer, *1 Enoch: A Commentary on the Book of 1 Enoch, Includes the Text of the Ethiopic Book of Enoch in English Translation* (Minneapolis, MN: Fortress, 2001) 274.

370. James H. Charlesworth, *The Old Testament Pseudepigrapha and the New Testament*, Volume 2, 2:76.

371. Maśṭēmâ originates from the Hebrew root śṭm, a by-form of śṭn (Wanke 1976: 821–822; [Satan], in *Dictionary of Deities and Demons in the Bible DDD*, 2nd extensively rev. ed. K. van der Toorn, Bob Becking and Pieter Willem van der Horst (Leiden; Boston; Grand Rapids, MI.: Brill; Eerdmans, 1999) 553.

372. Michael L. Galaty and Charles Watkinson, eds., *Archaeology under Dictatorship* (New York: Kluwer Academic/Plenum, 2004) 203.

373. *Encyclopedia of the Developing World*, ed., Thomas M. Leonard, 793.

374. William Henry, "Saddam Hussein, The Stairway to Heaven and the Return of Planet X," http://www.bibliotecapleyades.net/exopolitica/esp_exopolitica_k_1.htm (accessed December 30, 2014).

375. http://exopolitics.org/Study-Paper2.htm.

376. J. M. Eisenberg, "The Looting of Iraq's Cultural Heritage: An Up-Date," in *Minerva* (UK), September-October 2003.

377. http://www.exopolitics.org/Study-Paper2.htm.

378. G. H. Pember, *Earth's Earliest Ages*, Defender Publishing, 5th ed. (July 15, 2012), 172–175.

379. *Antiquities*, "Chapter 2.Concerning the Posterity of Adam, and the Ten Generations from Him to the Deluge.Online," ebook http://www.gutenberg.org/files/2848/2848-h/2848-h.htm (accessed January 27, 2015).

380. *The Researchers Library of Ancient Texts: Volume One—The Apocrypha* (Includes the Books of Enoch, Jasher, and Jubilees). (Crane, MO: Defender), 291.

381. Carl Sagan, *Carl Sagan's Cosmic Connection: An Extraterrestrial Perspective* (Cambridge: Cambridge University Press, 2000), 248. Follow link here.

382. Kip Throne, "The Science of Interstellar," http://video.wired.com/watch/exclusive-the-science-of-interstellar-wired (00:50).

383. Paul Franklin, "The Science of Interstellar," http://video.wired.com/watch/exclusive-the-science-of-interstellar-wired (01:54–02:09).

384. From *Interstellar,* http://news.discovery.com/space/interstellar-black-hole-is-best-black-hole-in-sci-fi-141029.htm.

385. Farook Rahaman, Paolo Salucci, et al., "Possible Existence of Wormholes in the Central Regions of Halos," *Annals of Physics*, Vol. 350, November 2014, 561–567, (http://arxiv.org/pdf/1501.00490v1.pdf).

386. Milky Way Could Be a "Galactic Transport System," http://scitechdaily.com/milky-way-galactic-transport-system/.

387. Ibid.

388. Russell McCormmach, "Archimedes, New Studies in the History and Philosophy of Science and Technology," vol. v.28, *Weighing the World: The Reverend John Michell of Thornhill* (Dordrecht: Springer, 2012), 177, http://public.eblib.com/eblpublic/publicview.do?ptiid=885997 (accessed August 6, 2014).

389. Alasdair Wilkins, i09, December 23, 2012, The forgotten genius who discovered black holes. over 200 years ago (accessed August 6, 2014).

390. "This Month in Physics History: November 27, 1783: John Michell Anticipates Black Holes," http://www.aps.org/publications/apsnews/200911/physicshistory.cfm (accessed August 6, 2014).

391. Video, "How Are Black Holes Detected?" Space.com, http://www.space.com/10257-black-holes-detected.html (accessed November 21, 2014).

392. http://en.wikipedia.org/wiki/Accretion_disc#mediaviewer/File:NGC_4261_Black_hole.jpg.

393. See explanation at http://www.nasa.gov/mission_pages/hubble/science/hercules-a.html. For image alone: http://www.nasa.gov/images/content/709514main_hs-2012-47-a-print.jpg.

394. http://www.space.com/24936-supermassive-black-hole-spin-quasar.html.

395. Michio Kaku, *Parallel Worlds: A Journey through Creation, Higher Dimensions, and the Future of the Cosmos,* reprint ed. (Anchor, 2006) 121.

396. S. L. Shapiro and S. A. Teukolsky, "Kerr Black Holes," §12.7 in *Black Holes, White Dwarfs, and Neutron Stars: The Physics of Compact Objects* (New York: Wiley 1983) 338.

397. Sissa Medialab, "In Theory, the Milky Way Could Be a 'Galactic Transport System,'" *Science Daily,* January 21, 2015, http://www.sciencedaily.com/releases/2015/01/150121083648.htm (accessed January 23, 2015).

398. Ibid.

399. Rebecca Boyle, "Lucifer Instrument Helps Astronomers See through Darkness to Most Distant Observable Objects," *Popular Science,* April 23, 2010, http://www.popsci.com/science/article/2010-04/devil-named-telescope-helps-astronomers-see-through-darkness.

400. Image NGC 4736, Large Binocular Telescope observers: N. Bouche, P. Buschkamp, P. Smith and O. Kuhn, http://www.lbto.org/images/Astronomical_Images/zaritsky_m94_lbt1.jpg (accessed January 23, 2015).

401. David Shiga, "Could Black Holes Be Portals to Other Universes?" *New Scientist,* April 2007, http://www.newscientist.com/article/dn11745-could-black-holes-be-portal#.VIItFzHF-xU (accessed December 5, 2014).

402. Lewis Page, "Something May Come through Dimensional 'Doors' at LHC," *The Register*, November 11, 2009, http://www.theregister.co.uk/2009/11/06/lhc_dimensional_portals/ (accessed September 5, 2014).

403. Ibid.

404. Richard Bullivant, *Beyond Time Travel—Exploring Our Parallel Worlds: Amazing Real Life Stories in the News* (Time Travel Books, 2014) Kindle Edition, 781–785.

405. "Girl Suicide 'Over Big Bang Fear,'" http://news.bbc.co.uk/2/hi/south_asia/7609631.stm (accessed September 20, 2014).

406. See "What Is a Wormhole?" Space.com, http://www.space.com/20881-wormholes.html, explained in video here: https://www.youtube.com/watch?v=HbwvTBaLLqo.

407. Jim Al-Khalili, *Black Holes, Wormholes and Time Machines* (Bristol, UK: Institute of Physics, 1999), 206.

408. Philip Gibbs, "What Is the Cashmir Effect?" University of California Riverside, http://math.ucr.edu/home/baez/physics/Quantum/casimir.html (accessed December 4, 2014).

409. "Space and Time Warps," Hawking.org.uk.

410. Michael Morris, Kip Thorne, Ulvi Yurtsever (1988), "Wormholes, Time Machines, and the Weak Energy Condition," *Physical Review Letters,* 61 (13): 1446–1449.

411. Ford Sopova (2002), "The Energy Density in the Casimir Effect," Physical Review D, 66 (4): 045026. Roman Ford, (1995),"Averaged Energy Conditions and Quantum Inequalities," *Physical Review D* 51(8): 4277–4286.Olum (1998),"Superluminal Travel Requires Negative Energies,". *Physical Review Letters*, 81 (17): 3567–3570.

412. Matt Visser, "Traversable Wormholes: Some Simple Examples," *Physical Review,* D 39, no. 10 (1989): 3182.

413. John G Cramer, "Squeezing the Vacuum," *Analog: Science Fiction and Fact* (12-2-1991), http://www.npl.washington.edu/AV/altvw53.html (accessed December 5, 2014).

414. Matt Visser, *Lorentzian Wormholes: From Einstein to Hawking*, Aip Series in Computational and Applied Mathematical Physics (Woodbury, N.Y.: American Institute of Physics, 1995) 143. Also see Elias Gravanis; Steven Willison (2007). "'Mass without Mass' from Thin Shells in Gauss-Bonnet Gravity," Phys. Rev. D 75 (8), http://journals.aps.org/prd/abstract/10.1103/PhysRevD.75.084025.

415. http://en.wikipedia.org/wiki/Einstein-Rosen_Bridge#mediaviewer/File:Wurmloch.jpg.

416. http://www.cfa.harvard.edu/news/2014–05.

417. http://www.skyandtelescope.com/astronomy-news/direct-evidence-of-big-bang-inflation/.

418. "Big Bang Inflation Evidence Inconclusive."

419. Max Tegmark, "Parallel Universes," http://space.mit.edu/home/tegmark/multiverse.pdf (accessed 12-03-2014).

420. Jeffrey A. Zweerink., *Who's Afraid of the Multiverse* (Pasadena CA: Reasons to Believe, 2008) 9.

421. "Astronomers Find First Evidence of Other Universes," Xb, December 13, 2010 http://www.technologyreview.com/view/421999/astronomers-find-first-evidence-of-other-universes/ (accessed December 3, 2014).

422. Paul Steinhardt (March 9, 2014), "Theories of Anything, *edge.org*, 2014. What Scientific Idea Is Ready for Retirement? (Archived from the original on March 9, 2014; retrieved March 9, 2014).

423. Ibid.

424. Steinhardt, transcribed from: *Through the Wormhole*, season 2, episode 10, "Are There Parallel Universes?" (original air date: 8-3-2011), Discovery Channel.

425. Ibid.

426. Alejandro Rojas, "Lockheed Skunk Works Director Says ESP Is the Key to Interstellar Travel" (video). Open Minds, July 26, 2013, http://www.openminds.tv/lockheed-skunk-works-director-says-esp-is-the-key-to-interstellar-travel-video-1092/23042 (accessed December 4, 2014).

427. Curtis Fuller, Proceedings of the First International UFO Congress (New York, NY: Warner Books, 1980), 164–165.

428. "Dr Quantum—Double Slit Experiment," https://www.youtube.com/watch?v=DfPeprQ7oGc.

429. http://www.ascsi.org/pubs/SM_holding_bay/lanza_soul.html.

430. B. Alan Wallace, *Hidden Dimensions: The Unification of Physics and Consciousness*, pbk. ed., The Columbia Series in Science and Religion (New York: Columbia University Press, 2010) 1.

431. Cris Putnam, *Supernatural Worldview*, 438–446.

432. Lynne Hume, *Portals: Opening Doorways to Other Realities through the Senses* (Oxford, UK: Berg, 2007) 149.

433. Hume, *Portals*, 1.

434. Chris Savia, "Gill Padilla: Ghosts: Do They Exist?", *Who Forted?*http://whofortedblog.com/2014/09/03/gill-padilla-ghosts-exist/ (accessed September 19, 2014).

435. Owen Gingerich, cited in Dinesh D'Souza, *What's so Great About Christianity* (Carol Stream, Ill.: Tyndale House., 2007) 87.

436. CERN's official names and founding information come from the Wikipedia entry, available at http://en.wikipedia.org/wiki/CERN (accessed January 12, 2015).

437. "The Nataraja Dance of Shiva," Wikipedia, http://en.wikipedia.org/wiki/Nataraja (accessed January 20, 2015).

438. Wendy Doniger O'Flaherty, *History of Religions* Vol. 20, No. 1/2, Twentieth Anniversary Issue (Aug.–Nov., 1980), 81–111, (University of Chicago Press) available online via JSTOR, http://www.jstor.org/discover/10.2307/1062337?sid=21105662919083&uid=4&uid=3739640&uid=2&uid=3739256 (accessed January 20, 2015).

439. D. Lewis-Williams (2002), *A Cosmos in Stone: Interpreting Religion and Society through Rock Art* (Walnut Creek, CA: Altamira Press) 39.

440. "Restarting the LHC: Why 13 TeV?" CERN website: http://home.web.cern.ch/about/engineering/restarting-lhc-why-13-tev (accessed January 20, 2015).

441. Thomas Horn, *Zenith 2016* (Crane, MO: Defender, 2013) 138.

442. Peter Goodgame, "The Mighty One" (Red Moon Rising), available online via http://www.redmoonrising.com/Giza/Asshur9.htm (accessed January 20, 2015).

443. Horn, *Zenith 2016*, 139–140.

444. A. S. Belyaev, I. L. Shapiro, et al, "Torsion Phenomenology at the LHC" (December 2006), Cornell Library, http://arxiv.org/abs/hep-ph/0701002 (accessed January 20, 2015).

445. Barry Chamish, "Strange UFO Sightings in Israel," published online at http://www.mt.net/~watcher/chamishgiants.html (accessed January 23, 2015).

446. Dr. Michael S. Heiser, "Ezekiel's Vision, Part 2," Paleobabble, http://michaelsheiser.com/PaleoBabble/2008/08/ezekiels-vision-part-2/ (accessed January 23, 2015).

447. David Bay, "Masonic Symbols of Power in Their Seat of Power—Washington D.C.," Cutting Edge Ministries, http://www.cuttingedge.org/n1040.html (accessed January 23, 2015).

448. Eliezer Posner, "What is the Significance of the Number 8?",http://www.chabad.org/library/article_cdo/aid/606168/jewish/Whats-the-Significance-of-the-Number-Eight.htm (accessed January 23, 2015).

449. Worldwide LHC Computing Grid information from CERN's website: http://home.web.cern.ch/about/computing/worldwide-lhc-computing-grid (accessed January 20, 2015).

450. From LHC Computing Grid's "Public Site," http://wlcg-public.web.cern.ch/ (accessed January 20, 2015).

451. John Dryden, trans., Georgetown University Online.

452. Sarah Lacy, , TechCrunch, February 27, 2011, http://techcrunch.com/2011/02/27/the-haves-and-have-nots-the-true-story-of-a-reader-suddenly-de-invited-from-ted/ (accessed February 3, 2015).

453. Marco Rodin, "Vortex Based Mathematics, Basis for the Extraordinary Rodin Coil," http://www.rexresearch.com/rodin/2-vbm.pdf (accessed February 3, 2015).

454. Ibid.

455. YouTube video presentation of '3, 6, and 9' https://www.youtube.com/watch?v=inWnhZp_A-M.

456. Dr. Michael K. Lake, "The Shinar Directive," (Crane, MO: Defender) 257.

457. Christopher Columbus log quoted from http://www.bermuda-triangle.org/html/columbus.html (accessed February 3, 2015).

458. Bermuda Triangle Famous Incidents and Disappearances, http://www.bermuda-attractions.com/bermuda2_000051.htm (accessed February 3, 2015).

459. Author unknown, "Malaysia Airlines flight MH370 disappearance mystery," March 10, 2014, http://www.liveleak.com/view?i=23f_1394458001 (accessed February 3, 2015).

460. Mt. Shasta Spirit website: http://mtshastaspirit.org/msspirit/gen/mysteries-of-mount-shasta/ (accessed February 3, 2015).

461. Author's pseudonym: Appalachian Lady, "The Mothman, the Thunderbird, and the Curse of Chief Cornstalk," http://appalachianlady.com/2013/10/14/mothman/ (accessed February 3, 2015).

462. "Terror as Ghostly Slender Man Figure Spotted in Same Area as Black-eyed Ghost Child," *Daily Star*, January 25, 2015, http://www.dailystar.co.uk/news/weird-

news/422007/Slender-Man-spotted-Cannock-area-Black-Eyed-Ghost-child-seen (accessed February 3, 2015).

463. Wikipedia entry for Lake Angikuni, http://en.wikipedia.org/wiki/Angikuni_Lake (accessed February 3, 2015).

464. Legend of Lacus Curtius, found at http://www.livius.org/place/rome/rome-forum-romanum/lacus-curtius/ (accessed February 3, 2015).

465. "Cumaean Sibyl,: Wikipedia, http://en.wikipedia.org/wiki/Cumaean_Sibyl (accessed February 3, 2015).

466. "Scientists May Have Identified Echoes of Ancient Earth," Phys Org, June 09, 2014, http://phys.org/news/2014-06-scientists-echoes-ancient-earth.html.

467. Andy Coghlan, Massive 'Ocean' Discovered towards Earth's Core" *New Scientists,* June 12, 2014, http://www.newscientist.com/article/dn25723-massive-ocean-discovered-towards-earths-core.html#.VNfrCvnF98E.

468. Richard Lefors Clark, "The Earth Grid, Human Levitation, and Magnetic Anomalies," http://www.bibliotecapleyades.net/ciencia/antigravityworldgrid/ciencia_antigravityworldgrid03.htm (accessed February 4, 2015).

469. "Tromso, Norway," Wikipedia, http://en.wikipedia.org/wiki/Troms%C3%B8 (accessed February 4, 2015).

470. Dr. Richard C. Hoagland, "A Nobel Torsion Message over Norway?" http://www.enterprisemission.com/Norway-Message.htm (accessed February 4, 2015).

471. Jimmy Orr, "Norway Spiral: Space Aliens Welcoming Obama?" *Christian Science Monitor,* http://www.csmonitor.com/USA/Politics/The-Vote/2009/1210/norway-spiral-space-aliens-welcoming-obama (accessed February 4, 2015).

472. Fatima resource: "The Secret in Three Parts, The Second Part," http://www.fatima.org/essentials/message/tspart2.asp (accessed February 4, 2015).

473. YouTube video covering "strange sounds," https://www.youtube.com/watch?v=oLIyh_L0_M8 (accessed February 4, 2015).

474. "Hidden Portals in Earth's Magnetic Field,"NASA's missions site, http://www.nasa.gov/mission_pages/sunearth/news/mag-portals.html#.VNJd6GjF-Sp (February 4, 2015).

475. Video blogger known as "halfasheep" can be found at YouTube via https://www.youtube.com/user/halfasheep/about (accessed February 4, 2015).

476. "Ingress," Wikipedia, http://en.wikipedia.org/wiki/Ingress_%28game%29 (accessed February 5, 2015).

477. David Hatcher Childress, ed., *Anti-Gravity and the World Grid*, Lost Science Series (Stelle, IL: Adventures Unlimited, 1987) 6.

478. Mircea Eliade, *Images and Symbols: Studies in Religious Symbolism*, Mythos (Princeton, N.J.: Princeton University Press, 1991) 47.

479. Joseph P. Farrell, *The Grid of the Gods*, (SCB Distributors, 2013) Kindle Locations 2476–2479.

480. Ivan T. Sanderson, *Invisible Residents: The Reality of Underwater Ufos* Kindle edition (Kempton, Ill.: Adventures Unlimited, 1970, 2005) Kindle Locations 2045–2046.

481. Ivan T. Sanderson, *Invisible Residents: The Reality of Underwater Ufos,* Kindle Locations 2119–2121

482. Chris Bird, "Planetary Grid," Mission-Ignition, http://missionignition.net/bethe/planetgrid_chrisbird1975.php (accessed February 28, 2015).

483. William Becker and Bethe Hagens, "The World Grid: A New Synthesis," in *Anti-Gravity and the World Grid*, Lost Science Series editor David Hatcher Childress (Stelle, IL: Adventures Unlimited Press, 1987), available at Mission-Ignition, http://missionignition.net/bethe/planetary_grid.php (accessed February 28, 2015).

484. See US patent 2682235, https://www.google.com/patents/US2682235?dq=268 2235&hl=en&sa=X&ei=Qwf2VISoAc3jsASHxYDoBg&ved=0CB4Q6AEwAA (accessed February 28, 2015).

485. William Becker and Bethe Hagens, "The World Grid: A New Synthesis," in *Anti-Gravity and the World Grid*, Lost Science Series editor David Hatcher Childress, (Stelle, IL: Adventures Unlimited Press, 1987), 31.

486. Bethe Hagens, "Basic Instructions for Exploring the UVG Grid with Google Earth," http://www.vortexmaps.com/hagens-grid-google.php (accessed February 28, 2015).

487. Aime Michel, *Flying Saucers and the Straight-Line Mystery* (Albany, NY: S G Phillips, 1958) 54.

488. Bruce L. Cathie, *The Energy Grid*, (Kempton, Ill.: Adventures Unlimited Press, 1997), http://www.bibliotecapleyades.net/ciencia/energygrid_harmonic695/energygrig01.htm#1.- THE BRANCHING AREAS FOR INVESTIGATION (accessed February 28, 2015).

489. See Bruce Cathie, http://www.antigravitymovie.com/cathie.htm. He also developed world grid software: http://www.worldgrid.net/order/ (accessed February 28, 2015).

490. John Michael Greer, *Earth Divination, Earth Magic: A Practical Guide to Geomancy* (St. Paul, MN: Llewellyn Publications, 1999) 5.

491. Greer, *Earth Divination*, 3.

492. Ernest J Eitel as cited in Paul Devereux, *Places of Power: Measuring the Secret Energy of Ancient Sites Paul Devereux*, 2nd ed. (London: Blandford, 1999) 14.

493. "Feng Shui" in *Encyclopedia of Occultism and Parapsychology Volume 1*, 4th ed. 2 vols., J. Gordon, Melton, ed. (Detroit: Gale Research, 1996) 554.

494. Devereux, *Places of Power*, 18.

495. Alfred Watkins, *The Old Straight Track* (London: Abacus, 1974) 221.

496. Mircea Eliade, *Images and Symbols: Studies in Religious Symbolism*, Mythos (Princeton, N.J.: Princeton University Press, 1991) 47.

497. Cort Lindahl, "The Geomancy of St. Peter's Square and the Vatican," http://survivalcell.blogspot.com/p/geomancy-of-st-peters-square-and.html (accessed February 28, 2015).

498. Table VII in Malthe Conrad Bruun, *Universal geography, or A description of all the parts of the world* (London: Adam Black and Longman, 1822) 629. Find the link here.

499. http://survivalcell.blogspot.com/p/geomancy-of-st-peters-square-and.html; also see video *StargateVatican: The Axis and Templum of Rome* (7:56) http://youtu.be/w_isGhysLWc?t=7m56s.

500. Oleg Grabar, *The Dome of the Rock* (Cambridge, MA: Belknap Press of Harvard University Press, 2006) 64.

501. Giulio Meotti, "Expose: The Vatican Wants to Lay its Hands on Jerusalem," *Israel National News*, December 15, 2011, http://www.israelnationalnews.com/News/News.aspx/150757#.TzV9aORnDmd.

502. Cheryl K. Chumley, "Vatican Makes History: Pope Allows Islamic Prayers, Koran Readings, " *The Washington Times*, June 9, 2014, http://www.washingtontimes.com/news/2014/jun/9/vatican-makes-history-pope-allows-islamic-prayers-/ (accessed February 28, 2015).

503. Peter Tompkins, *The Magic of Obelisks* (New York: Harper & Row, 1981) 99.

504. Christopher Lehrich, *The Occult Mind: Magic in Theory and Practice* (Cornell University Press, 2012) link.

505. Rome Piazza San Pietro, http://www.hotelmilazzo.com/Rome%20piazza%20san%20pietro.html (accessed February 28, 2015).

506. "AL-MI'RAJ: The Alleged Ascent to Heaven," *Answering Islam*, http://answering-islam.org/Gilchrist/Vol1/3d.html (accessed February 28, 2015).

507. Karin Laub, "Scroll Said Resembles Sea Scrolls," *Washington Post* (September 27, 1999), http://www.washingtonpost.com/wp-srv/aponline/19990927/aponline195514_000.htm (accessed January 28, 2013).

508. Barry Chamish, "New 'Angel' Dead Sea Scroll Contains Astral Implications," *Rense*, October 5, 1999, http://rense.com/politics5/astral.htm (accessed January 28, 2013).

509. Michael S. Heiser, *The Façade* (SuperiorBooks.com Inc., 2001) 211. Also verified in personal email to Cris Putnam.

510. Joseph P. Farrell, *The Grid of the Gods* (SCB Distributors), Kindle Locations 2632–2637.

511. Image: Public domain, Wikipedia's Creative Commons Attribution-ShareAlike 3.0 License. Photo taken and uploaded by Jerry Wills: "File: Doorway-lg.jpg," *Wikipedia Commons*, http://en.wikipedia.org/wiki/File:Doorway-lg.jpg (last accessed February 5, 2015).

512. Image taken and uploaded to *DeviantArt* by Allison Lotterhos, user name "asalott," February 2011: "Amaru Muru—The Inner-Dimensional [Inter-Dimensional] Doorway" http://asalott.deviantart.com/art/Amaru-Muru-The-Inner-Dimensional-Doorway-267695889 (last accessed February 5, 2015). Photo free to share, copy, or redistribute in any medium or format under the Creative Commons Attribution-NonCommercial-NoDerivs 3.0 License (CC BY-NC-ND 3.0), http://creativecommons.org/licenses/by-nc-nd/3.0/. No changes were made to original photo.

513. "The Ancient Astronaut Theory," http://imaginealiens.weebly.com/gate-of-the-gods.html (last accessed February 5, 2015).

514. John Black, "Lake Titicaca—Gate of the Gods," *Ancient Origins*, January 28, 2013, http://www.ancient-origins.net/ancient-places-americas/lake-titicaca-gate-gods-003 (last accessed February 5, 2015).

515. New documentary release announcement, "The Mysterious Stone Monuments of Markawasi, Peru," as seen on "The Documentary Channel," *BBC Video*, http://www.bcvideo.com/markawasi.html (last accessed February 5, 2015).

516. "10 Ancient Settlements that Were Abandoned for Mysterious Reasons," *Urban Ghosts Media*, September 29, 2014, http://www.urbanghostsmedia. com/2014/09/10-ancient-settlements-abandoned-mysterious-reasons/4/. (last accessed February 5, 2015).

517. "Puerta de HayuMarka, Doorway of the AmaruMeru (AmaruMuru)," *Labyrinthina*, http://www.labyrinthina.com/amaru.htm (last accessed February 5, 2015).

518. Referenced as "14,000 years old" as well as "14000 BP" regularly. As examples: Dan Eden, "The Amazing Engineering Designs of Tiahuanaco: Gateway to the Gods," *ViewZone*, http://www.viewzone.com/tiax.html (last accessed February 5, 2015). (See the breakdown of the site-dating and its controversy under the heading "How old is this site?"; Rebecca Stone-Miller, *Art of the Andes: From Chavin to Inca* (Thames & Hudson, New York: 1996); Brian M. Fagan, *The Seventy Great Mysteries of the Ancient World: Unlocking the Secrets of Past Civilizations* (Thames & Hudson, New York: 2001).

519. Dan Eden, "Amazing Engineering Designs," http://www.viewzone.com/tiax.html.

520. Ibid.

521. Ibid., under the heading "How old is this site?"

522. Ibid.

523. "Tiwanaku," *Wikipedia: The Free Encyclopedia*, under the heading "Structures," last modified January 27, 2015, http://en.wikipedia.org/wiki/ Tiwanaku#Structures (last accessed February 5, 2015).

524. Image released freely into the public domain for unrestrained use by its owner: "File:Zonnepoort tiwanaku.jpg," uploaded by user "Mhwater," *Wikipedia: The Free Encyclopedia*, http://commons.wikimedia.org/wiki/File:Zonnepoort_ tiwanaku.jpg (last accessed February 5, 2015).

525. This image is in the public domain in the United States because it was published (or registered with the US Copyright Office) before January 1, 1923. Retrieved: "File:Puerta monolitica (Puertadel Sol.) 1903–1904.jpg," uploaded by user "Jduranboger," *Wikipedia: The Free Encyclopedia*, http://commons.wikimedia. org/wiki/File:Puerta_monolitica_(Puerta_del_Sol.)_1903-1904.jpg (last accessed February 5, 2015).

526. This image is in the public domain in the United States because it was published (or registered with the US Copyright Office) before January 1, 1923. Retrieved: "File:Centro de la puerta 1903–1904.jpg," uploaded by user "Jduranboger," *Wikipedia: The Free Encyclopedia*, http://commons.wikimedia.org/wiki/ File:Centro_de_la_puerta_1903-1904.jpg, (last accessed February 5, 2015).

527. "Viracocha," *Wikipedia: The Free Encyclopedia*, under the heading "Cosmogony according to Spanish accounts," last modified January 8, 2015, http:// en.wikipedia.org/wiki/Viracocha (last accessed February 5, 2015).

528. This image is in the public domain in the United States because it was published (or registered with the US Copyright Office) before January 1, 1923. Retrieved: "File:Viracocha.jpg," uploaded by user "Le K@l!," *Wikipedia: The Free Encyclopedia*, http://commons.wikimedia.org/wiki/File:Viracocha.jpg (last accessed February 5, 2015).

529. "Viracocha," *Wikipedia*, http://en.wikipedia.org/wiki/Viracocha.

530. For more information on these historic periods, see: "Pre-Pottery Neolithic A," *Wikipedia: The Free Encyclopedia*, last modified November 26, 2014, http://en.wikipedia.org/wiki/Pre-Pottery_Neolithic_A (last accessed February 4, 2015).

531. Andrew Curry, "Göbekli Tepe: The World's First Temple?: Predating Stonehenge by 6,000 Years, Turkey's Stunning Göbekli Tepe Upends the Conventional View of the Rise of Civilization," *Smithsonian.com*, November 2008, http://www.smithsonianmag.com/history/gobekli-tepe-the-worlds-first-temple-83613665/?no-ist (last accessed February 3, 2015).

532. Ibid.

533. Ibid., emphasis added.

534. Ibid.

535. Ibid., emphasis added.

536. Image captured in 2008, released freely into the public domain for unrestrained use by its owner: "File:GobeklitepeHeykel.jpg," uploaded by user "Erkcan," *Wikipedia: The Free Encyclopedia* http://commons.wikimedia.org/wiki/File:GobeklitepeHeykel.jpg, (last accessed February 5, 2015).

537. "Göbekli Tepe," *Wikipedia: The Free Encyclopedia*, last modified February 1, 2015, http://en.wikipedia.org/wiki/G%C3%B6bekli_Tepe#cite_ref-23 (accessed February 4, 2015).

538. Charles C. Mann, "The Birth of Religion," *National Geographic Magazine*, June 11, 2011, http://ngm.nationalgeographic.com/print/2011/06/gobekli-tepe/mann-text (last accessed February 4, 2015).

539. This theory appears in many places throughout research. For further reading, consider: "Which Came First, Monumental Building Projects Or Farming?" *Archaeo News*, December 18, 2008, last accessed February 4, 2015, http://www.stonepages.com/news/archives/003061.html.

540. "Göbekli Tepe," *Wikipedia*, under the heading "Interpretation," http://en.wikipedia.org/wiki/G%C3%B6bekli_Tepe#cite_ref-23. Original text German, as cited from: Klaus-Dieter Linsmeier, *Eine Revolution imgroßenStil*, "Interview mit Klaus Schmidt," *AbenteuerArchäologie. Kulturen, Menschen, Monumente* (Spektrum der Wissenschaft, Heidelberg 2006) 2.

541. Manfred Heun et al., "Site of Einkorn Wheat Domestication Identified by DNA Fingerprinting," *Science Magazine*, vol. 278, November 1997, 1312–1314; viewable here: http://www.ndsu.edu/pubweb/~mcclean/plsc731/homework/papers/huen%20et%20al%20-%20site%20of%20einkorn%20wheat%20domestication%20identified%20by%20DNA%20fingerprinting.pdf.

542. Sandra Scham, "The World's First Temple," *Archaeology Magazine*, vol. 61, November/December 2008; viewable here: http://archive.archaeology.org/0811/abstracts/turkey.html.

543. "History," *The Baalbeck International Festival Official Website*, http://www.baalbeck.org.lb/index.php/en/the-festival/lang-enhistorylanglang-frhistoirelang (last accessed January 19, 2015).

544. Ibid.

545. Paolo Matthiae, *Proceedings of the 6ᵗʰ International Congress of the Archaeology of the Ancient Near East* (Harrassowitz, 2010), 210. For more information on these

historic periods, see: "Pre-Pottery Neolithic B," *Wikipedia: The Free Encyclopedia*, last modified December 23, 2014, last accessed January 26, 2015, http://en.wikipedia.org/wiki/Pre-Pottery_Neolithic_B; "Iron Age," *Wikipedia: The Free Encyclopedia*m last modified January 21, 2015, last accessed January 26, 2015, http://en.wikipedia.org/wiki/Iron_Age.

546. Nina Jidejian, *Baalbek: Heliopolis, "City of the Sun"* (Dar el-Machreq Publishers, 1975) 15.

547. Tara MacIsaac, "Largest Known Ancient Megalith Discovered—Who Really Made It?" *Epoch Times*, December 20, 2014, last accessed January 27, 2015, http://www.theepochtimes.com/n3/1154047-largest-known-ancient-megalith-block-discovered-who-really-made-it/.

548. Erwin M. Ruprechtsberger, *VomSteinbruchzumJupitertempel von Heliopolis/Baalbek (Libanon)* [*From the Quarry to the Jupiter Temple of Heliopolis/Baalbek (Lebanon)*] (Linzer ArchäologischeForschungen: 1990) 30: 7–56. Quoted frequently online, and sourced at: "Stone of the Pregnant Woman," *Wikipedia: The Free Encyclopedia*, last modified January 18, 2015, last accessed January 27, 2015, http://en.wikipedia.org/wiki/Stone_of_the_Pregnant_Woman#CITEREFRuprechtsberger1999.

549. James Edward Hanauer, *Folk-lore of the Holy Land: Moslem, Christian and Jewish* (Duckworth & Company: 1907), 74. Viewable online through Google Books here: http://books.google.com/books?id=r4cTAAAAYAAJ&pg=PA74#v=onepage&q&f=false (last accessed January 27, 2015).

550. Paul Doyle, *Lebanon* (Bradt Travel Guides: 2012), 213. Viewable online through Google Books here: http://books.google.com/books?id=tzsRk0hvb_MC&pg=PA213#v=onepage&q&f=false.

551. Ibid., among other sources with the same claim.

552. Daniel B. Shepp, *The Holy Land Photographed* (Chicago, IL: Globe Bible Publishing, 1894) 109. This image, as well as the quoted caption, is in the public domain in the United States because it was published (or registered with the US Copyright Office) before January 1, 1923. This book can be downloaded and viewed here: "The Holy Land Photographed (1894)," *Internet Archive*, last accessed January 29, 2015, https://archive.org/details/Holy_Land_Photographed_D.Shepp.

553. J. J. Coulton, "Lifting in Early Greek Architecture," *The Journal of Hellenic Studies, Volume 94* (1994) 16.

554. Dienel, Hans-Liudger; Meighörner, Wolfgang, "Der Tretradkran," *Publication of the Deutsches Museum* (*Technikgeschichte* series) 2nd ed. (München: 1997) 13.

555. Lynne Lancaster, "Building Trajan's Column," *American Journal of Archaeology 103 (3)*(Archaeological Institute of America: 1999) 419–439.

556. Shepp, *Holy Land Photographed*, 110. This image, as well as the quoted caption, is in the public domain in the United States because it was published (or registered with the US Copyright Office) before January 1, 1923.

557. Original article appeared in: *Syria* 54:1–2 (1977): 31–63.

558. Michael Heiser, "Transporting the Trilithon Stones of Baalbek: It's About Applied Physics, Not Ancient Aliens," *MichaelSHeiser.com*, August 23, 2012,

last accessed January 29, 2015, http://michaelsheiser.com/PaleoBabble/2012/08/transporting-trilithon-stones-baalbek-applied-physics-ancient-aliens/.

559. This image is in the public domain in the United States because it was published (or registered with the US Copyright Office) before January 1, 1923. Retrieved: "File:Thunder Stone.jpg," uploaded by user "RedAndr," *Wikipedia: The Free Encyclopedia*, last accessed February 5, 2015, http://commons.wikimedia.org/wiki/File:Thunder_Stone.jpg.

560. This image is in the public domain, bound by the Creative Commons Deed, contributed by user juliacasado1 via *Pixabay.com* on August 4, 2013. Last accessed February 2, 2015, http://pixabay.com/en/st-petersburg-russia-petersburg-512450/.

561. David Urquhart, *The Lebanon: Mount Souria. A History and a Diary, Volume 2* (Thomas Cautley Newby, London: 1860), 374-377. Viewable online through Google Books here: https://books.google.com/books?id=25oBAAAAQAAJ&pg=PA376&lpg=PA376&dq=The+builders+of+Baalbeck+must+have+been+a+people+who+had+attained+to+the+highest+pinnacle+of+power+and+science&source=bl&ots=WuzoRqCrw8&sig=ILhTUw-l67l4nv9ZmEY8tiusTC4&hl=en&sa=X&ei=uSe4VKzdEYSwyQTfyoKwDw&ved=0CCMQ6AEwAQ#v=onepage&q=The%20builders%20of%20Baalbeck%20must%20have%20been%20a%20people%20who%20had%20attained%20to%20the%20highest%20pinnacle%20of%20power%20and%20science&f=false, last accessed January 26, 2015.

562. Michael Snyder, "Newly Found Megalithic Ruins in Russia Contain the Largest Blocks of Stone Ever Discovered," *InfoWars*, March 11, 2014, last accessed February 6, 2015, http://www.infowars.com/newly-found-megalithic-ruins-in-russia-contain-the-largest-blocks-of-stone-ever-discovered/.

563. Daniel and Isabela Mastral, *Rastros do Oculto Da História À Teologia Do Princípio das TrevasaosSelados de Deus* (São Paulo, Brazil: Deyver, 2008), 255. Available in Portuguese: https://www.scribd.com/doc/4555474/Isabela-e-Eduardo-Daniel-Mastral-Rastros-do-Oculto

564. Marcos, "Ex-Satanist Details Illuminati Spiritual Plan," Henrymakow.com, http://www.henrymakow.com/ex-satanist-details-illuminati-spiritual-plan.html, accessed February 28, 2015.

565. "Growth of a Young Nation," *U.S. House of Representatives: Office of the Clerk*, last accessed January 30, 2012, http://artandhistory.house.gov/art_artifacts/virtual_tours/splendid_hall/young_nation.aspx.

566. "1964–Present: September 11, 2001, The Capitol Building as a Target," *United States Senate*, last accessed January 30, 2012, http://www.senate.gov/artandhistory/history/minute/Attack.htm.

567. William Henry and Mark Gray, *Freedom's Gate: Lost Symbols in the U.S.* (Hendersonville, TN: Scala Dei, 2009) 3.

568. Ibid., 4.

569. "Sandpit of Royalty,"*Extra Bladet* (Copenhagen, January 31, 1999).

570. Manly P Hall, *Secret Teachings*, 104.

571. James Lees-Milne, *Saint Peter's: The Story of Saint Peter's Basilica in Rome* (Little, Brown, 1967), 221.

572. Rebecca Zorach and Michael W. Cole, *The Idol in the Age of Art* (Ashgate, 2009) 61.

573. Rebecca Zorach and Michael W. Cole, *The Idol in the Age of Art*, 63.

574. David Flynn, *Cydonia: The Secret Chronicles of Mars* (Bozwman, MT: End Time Thunder, 2002) 156.

575. Albert Pike, *Morals and Dogma: Of the Ancient and Accepted Scottish Rite of Freemasonry* (Forgotten Books) 401.

576. Albert Mackey, *A Manual of the Lodge* (1870) 56.

577. Dan Brown, *The Lost Symbol* (Anchor; Reprint edition, 2010) 3–4.

578. Manly P. Hall, *Lost Keys of Freemasonry*, Prologue.

579. Manly P. Hall, *Secret Teachings*, 116–120.

580. Manly P. Hall, "Rosicrucianism and Masonic Origins," from *Lectures on Ancient Philosophy—An Introduction to the Study and Application of Rational Procedure* (Los Angeles: Hall, 1929) 397–417.

581. Albert Pike, *Morals and Dogma*, 335.

582. Ibid., 16.

583. Ibid., 472.

584. Hope, Murry, Practical Egyptian Magic (New York: St. Martin's Press, 1984) 107. Quoted by Fritz Springmeier, *The Watchtower & the Masons* (1990, 1992) 113, 114.

585. Thomas Horn, *Apollyon Rising 2012*, 7–10.

586. Thomas Horn, *Zenith 2016* (Crane, MO: Defender, 2013) 324–348.

587. John Dryden, trans., as published by Georgetown University Online; also appears in: Thomas Horn, *Apollyon Rising 2012*.

588. Peter Goodgame, *The Giza Discovery, Part Nine: The Mighty One*, http://www.redmoonrising.com/Giza/Asshur9.htm (last accessed January 23, 2012).

589. Horn, *Zenith 2016*, 136–140.

590. Martin Short, *Inside the Brotherhood: Explosive Secrets of the Freemasons* (UK: HarperCollins, 1995) 122.

591. Manly P. Hall, *The Lost Keys*, 48.

592. Manly P. Hall, *Secret Destiny of America* (Penguin Group, 2008), chapter 18.

593. See: http://en.wikipedia.org/wiki/Hermetic_Order_of_the_Golden_Dawn.

594. See: http://en.wikipedia.org/wiki/Ars_Goetia#Ars_Goetia.

595. See: http://www.redmoonrising.com/Giza/DomDec6.htm.

596. "Shemhamphorasch," *Wikipedia*, last modified December 6, 2011, http://en.wikipedia.org/wiki/Shemhamphorasch.

597. Horn, *Zenith 2016*.